Emerging-Economy State and International Policy Studies

Series editors

Tetsushi Sonobe, National Graduate Institute for Policy Studies, Tokyo, Japan
Takashi Shiraishi, Prefectural University of Kumamoto, Kumamoto, Japan
Akihiko Tanaka, National Graduate Institute for Policy Studies, Tokyo, Japan
Keiichi Tsunekawa, National Graduate Institute for Policy Studies, Tokyo, Japan
Akio Takahara, Graduate School of Public Policy, The University of Tokyo, Tokyo, Japan

This is the first series to highlight research into the processes and impacts of the state building and economic development of developing countries in the non-Western World that have recently come to influence global economy and governance. It offers a broad and interactive forum for discussions about the challenges of these countries and the responses of other countries to their rise. The term 'emerging-economy state,' a part of the series title, or its shorthand 'emerging states,' is intended to promote dialogues between economists who have discussed policy problems faced by 'emerging-market economies' and scholars in political science and international relations who have discussed 'modern state formation.' Many emerging states are still in the middle-income status and not immune from the risk of falling into the middle-income trap. The manner of their external engagement is different from that of the high-income countries. Their rise has increased the uncertainty surrounding the world. To reduce the uncertainty, good understanding of their purpose of politics and state capacity as well as their economies and societies would be required. Although the emerging states are far from homogenous, viewing them as a type of countries would force us into understand better the similarity and differences among the emerging states and those between them and the high-income countries, which would in turn to help countries to ensure peace and prosperity. The series welcomes policy studies of empirical, historical, or theoretical nature from a micro, macro, or global point of view. It accepts, but does not call for, interdisciplinary studies. Instead, it aims to promote transdisciplinary dialogues among a variety of disciplines, including but not limited to area studies, economics, history, international relations, and political science. Relevant topics include emerging states' economic policies, social policies, and politics, their external engagement, ensuing policy reactions of other countries, ensuing social changes in different parts of the world, and cooperation between the emerging states and other countries to achieve the Sustainable Development Goals (SDGs). The series welcomes both monographs and edited volumes that are accessible to academics and interested general readers.

More information about this series at http://www.springer.com/series/16114

Keijiro Otsuka · Kaoru Sugihara
Editors

Paths to the Emerging State in Asia and Africa

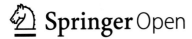

Editors
Keijiro Otsuka
Graduate School of Economics
Kobe University
Kobe, Hyogo, Japan

Kaoru Sugihara
Research Institute for Humanity and Nature
Kyoto, Japan

ISSN 2524-5023 ISSN 2524-5031 (electronic)
Emerging-Economy State and International Policy Studies
ISBN 978-981-13-3130-5 ISBN 978-981-13-3131-2 (eBook)
https://doi.org/10.1007/978-981-13-3131-2

Library of Congress Control Number: 2018961696

© The Editor(s) (if applicable) and The Author(s) 2019, corrected publication 2022. This book is an open access publication.
Open Access This book is licensed under the terms of the Creative Commons Attribution-NonCommercial-NoDerivatives 4.0 International License (http://creativecommons.org/licenses/by-nc-nd/4.0/), which permits any noncommercial use, sharing, distribution and reproduction in any medium or format, as long as you give appropriate credit to the original author(s) and the source, provide a link to the Creative Commons licence and indicate if you modified the licensed material. You do not have permission under this licence to share adapted material derived from this book or parts of it.

The images or other third party material in this book are included in the book's Creative Commons licence, unless indicated otherwise in a credit line to the material. If material is not included in the book's Creative Commons licence and your intended use is not permitted by statutory regulation or exceeds the permitted use, you will need to obtain permission directly from the copyright holder.

This work is subject to copyright. All commercial rights are reserved by the author(s), whether the whole or part of the material is concerned, specifically the rights of translation, reprinting, reuse of illustrations, recitation, broadcasting, reproduction on microfilms or in any other physical way, and transmission or information storage and retrieval, electronic adaptation, computer software, or by similar or dissimilar methodology now known or hereafter developed. Regarding these commercial rights a non-exclusive license has been granted to the publisher.

The use of general descriptive names, registered names, trademarks, service marks, etc. in this publication does not imply, even in the absence of a specific statement, that such names are exempt from the relevant protective laws and regulations and therefore free for general use.

The publisher, the authors, and the editors are safe to assume that the advice and information in this book are believed to be true and accurate at the date of publication. Neither the publisher nor the authors or the editors give a warranty, express or implied, with respect to the material contained herein or for any errors or omissions that may have been made. The publisher remains neutral with regard to jurisdictional claims in published maps and institutional affiliations.

This Springer imprint is published by the registered company Springer Nature Singapore Pte Ltd.
The registered company address is: 152 Beach Road, #21-01/04 Gateway East, Singapore 189721, Singapore

Preface

Economic history and development economics are both interested in the development of economy from poor agrarian society to emerging state through agricultural development and industrialization. While historical studies are concerned with the long-term development of specific countries, regions, and the world, development studies are mainly interested in the short-term development of low-income and middle-income economies across the world. The former generally adopt descriptive and interpretative approach because detailed statistical data suitable for econometric analyses are usually unavailable, whereas the latter often use econometric techniques based on survey data which are available only for a short period of time in certain locations. Yet, it is clear that the issues addressed by these two strands of economics discipline are no different and that the two types of analyses are highly complementary. Nonetheless, economic historians and development economists have seldom collaborated in the past. This study is a unique attempt to synthesize studies of economic histories and development economics.

Authors of this volume strongly believe that in order to grasp the evolutionary process of economic development towards the emerging state, which is the main theme of the entire project leading to four volumes including this one, a synthesis of historical and development studies is indispensable. Why did Meiji Japan succeed in economic development through fairly rapid industrialization to become an emerging state, while India and China followed different paths of economic development and took longer to emerge as powerful emerging states? What was the role of agriculture in the development of prewar Japanese economy as well as high-performing Asian countries in the postwar period? Why has sub-Saharan Africa (SSA) largely failed in both agricultural development and industrialization so far? What are the lessons to be learned from the Asian experiences for the future development path of SSA towards the emerging state? Considering that international trade was surprisingly active in the economic history of East, Southeast, and South Asia, it is highly relevant for this volume to inquire exactly how and why local, regional, and long-distance trade played such crucial roles in the historical development of Asian economies, while it did much less in the recent development of the economies of SSA. These are the questions that authors of this book collectively address. Some chapters were written by economic historians while others by development economists. All of them collaborated through repeated workshops in the course of preparing this volume for the last 5 years. We believe that the questions raised above are pertinent for proper understanding of the issue of emerging economy and state.

A large number of people have contributed to the preparation of this book. In particular, we would like to thank Gareth Austin, Chris Baker, Linda Grove, Tetsuji Okazaki, Tirthankar Roy, Osamu Saito, Takashi Shiraishi, Tetsushi Sonobe, Keiichi Tsunekawa, and Bin Wong for useful comments during the workshops and on the earlier versions of various chapters. We are also grateful to GRIPS staff, Yu Ito, Eriko Kimura, and Yasuko Takano for their dedicated assistance for organizing the seminars and workshops, and to Fumiyo Aburatani, Yumiko Iwasaki, and Aya Yamamoto for editorial assistance.

Funding for our project leading to this book publication was provided by Japan Society for Promotion of Science (JSPS) KAKENHI Grant numbers 25101001, 25101002, 25101003, and 15K2178. We highly appreciate the financial support of JSPS.

Kobe, Japan	Keijiro Otsuka
Kyoto, Japan	Kaoru Sugihara

The original version of the book was revised: The print ISSN has been updated in copyright page. The correction to the book is available at https://doi.org/10.1007/ 978-981-13-3131-2_13

Contents

1. **Multiple Paths to Industrialization: A Global Context of the Rise of Emerging States** 1
   Kaoru Sugihara

2. **Technology Transfer and Agricultural Development: A Comparative Study of Asia and Africa** 35
   Keijiro Otsuka

3. **Southeast Asia and International Trade: Continuity and Change in Historical Perspective** 55
   Ryuto Shimada

4. **Role of State and Non-state Networks in Early-Modern Southeast Asian Trade** 73
   Atsushi Ota

5. **Growth of Regional Trade in Modern Southeast Asia: The Rise of Singapore, 1819–1913** 95
   Atsushi Kobayashi

6. **Labour-Intensive Industrialization and the Emerging State in Pre-war Japan** 115
   Masayuki Tanimoto

7. **Changing Patterns of Industrialization and Emerging States in Twentieth Century China** 141
   Toru Kubo

8. **Historical Roots of Industrialisation and the Emerging State in Colonial India** 169
   Chikayoshi Nomura

9	**Industrial Policy, Industrial Development, and Structural Transformation in Asia and Africa** Yuki Higuchi and Go Shimada	195
10	**Transformation of Rural Economies in Asia and Africa** Jonna P. Estudillo, Elyzabeth F. Cureg and Keijiro Otsuka	219
11	**Agricultural Market Intervention and Emerging States in Africa** Masayoshi Honma	253
12	**Role of Community and Government in Irrigation Management in Emerging States: Lessons from Japan, China, and India** Kei Kajisa	273

Correction to: Paths to the Emerging State in Asia and Africa C1
Keijiro Otsuka and Kaoru Sugihara

Contributors

Elyzabeth F. Cureg Center for Local and Regional Governance (CLRG-NCPAG), University of the Philippines, Quezon City, Philippines

Jonna P. Estudillo National Graduate Institute for Policy Studies, Minato-ku, Tokyo, Japan

Yuki Higuchi Graduate School of Economics, Nagoya City University, Nagoya, Japan

Masayoshi Honma Department of Economics, Division of International Economics, Seinan Gakuin University, Fukuoka, Japan

Kei Kajisa Aoyama Gakuin University, Tokyo, Japan

Atsushi Kobayashi Osaka Sangyo University, Osaka, Japan

Toru Kubo Shinshu University, Matsumoto, Japan

Chikayoshi Nomura Graduate School of Literature and Human Science, Osaka City University, Osaka, Japan

Atsushi Ota Keio University, Tokyo, Japan

Keijiro Otsuka Graduate School of Economics, Kobe University, Nada, Kobe, Hyogo, Japan

Go Shimada Meiji University, Tokyo, Japan

Ryuto Shimada Graduate School of Humanities and Sociology, The University of Tokyo, Tokyo, Japan

Kaoru Sugihara Research Institute for Humanity and Nature, Kyoto, Japan

Masayuki Tanimoto Graduate School of Economics, Faculty of Economics, The University of Tokyo, Tokyo, Japan

List of Figures

Fig. 1.1	Geographical composition of world industrial production, 1750–1913. *Source and Note* Bairoch (1982: 292). In Bairoch's overall data Japan is included in 'developed countries', but I reclassified her under 'developing countries', as this Figure refers to the period up to 1913..............	6
Fig. 1.2	Structure of world trade, 1840. *Sources and Notes* Sugihara (2015c, 29). Trade data include original estimates. Figures for each region are intra-regional trade. Those in brackets are very rough estimates. The size of the circle expresses the relative proportion of each region in world GDP (Maddison 2009).....	10
Fig. 1.3	Structure of world trade, 1910. *Sources and Notes* Sugihara (2015c, 33). Trade data are original estimates. Figures for each region are intra-regional trade. Those in brackets are very rough estimates. The size of the circle expresses the relative proportion of each region in world GDP (Maddison 2009).....	10
Fig. 1.4	Rail- and river-borne trade in India, 1888. *Source and Notes* Rail- and River-borne Trade, 1888/89–1892/93. Figures are sums of exports and imports. Thin arrows represent a million rupees and above, while thick arrow 10 million and above	12
Fig. 1.5	Trade of Calcutta and its environs, 1877/78. *Source* Report on the Administration of Bengal (1877/78)	13
Fig. 1.6	Long distance trade and regional trade, 1910. *Sources and Notes* Sugihara (2013). Circles show major trading countries and regions. Figures indicated within the circle shows the value of exports to Asian and African regions over that of total exports. Figures for the Presidencies and the Provinces of India and Aden are derived from the references originally used in Sugihara (1996) (186) and Sugihara (2002) (28). Figures refer to sea-borne trade only. As coastal trade in British India is included here, the ratio of intra-regional trade is greater than	

	the usual calculation made from the geographical composition of foreign trade. Figures for Hong Kong was estimated from those in 1913. See Sugihara (1996) (107).	15
Fig. 1.7	Import tariff rates in India, China and Japan, 1864–1940. *Notes and Sources* India: Sugihara (2002, 30–31), China: Hsiao (1974, 22–24, 132–33), Japan: Okurasho (1948). Rates refer to the share of total import revenue divided by total value of imports. The Japanese data exclude colonial imports after 1919	21
Fig. 1.8	Commodity composition of exports from 4 ASEAN countries and Singapore, 1950–1997. *Source* Takanaka (2000)	25
Fig. 1.9	Commodity composition of imports to 4 ASEAN countries and Singapore, 1950–1997. *Source* As per Fig. 1.8	25
Fig. 1.10	Geographical composition of exports from Sub-Saharan Africa, 1990–2017. *Source* As per Table 1.2	29
Fig. 1.11	Geographical composition of imports from Sub-Saharan Africa, 1990-2017. *Source* As per Table 1.2.	30
Fig. 2.1	Changes in grain production, cultivation area, population, and grain yield in Prewar Japan (Index: 1880 = 100). *Source* Umemura et al. (1966)	37
Fig. 2.2	Changes in rice yield per hectare in Prewar Japan, Taiwan, and Korea, and Postwar Philippines, Five-Year Moving averages (reproduced from Hayami and Godo 2005, p. 101)	38
Fig. 2.3	Changes in grain production, harvested area, population, and grain yield in tropical Asia (Index: 1961 = 100). *Source* FAOSTAT (2016).	40
Fig. 2.4	Changes in rice yield in Northeast, Southeast, and South Asia. *Source* FAOSTAT (2016).	41
Fig. 2.5	World production and real prices for rice and maize, 1961–2016. *Source* United States Department of Agriculture database	42
Fig. 2.6	Arable land per rural population in tropical Asia and SSA, 1961–2013. *Source* FAOSTAT (2016)	44
Fig. 2.7	Changes in grain production, harvested area, population, and grain yield in SSA (Index: 1961 = 100). *Source* FAOSTAT (2016).	44
Fig. 2.8	Changes in aggregate harvested area in SSA by major crop. *Source* FAOSTAT (2016)	45
Fig. 2.9	Changes in average rice yield in SSA, top 10 and bottom 10 countries, and India. *Source* FAOSTAT (2016)	46
Fig. 2.10	Changes in average maize yields in SSA, top 10 and bottom 10 countries, and India. *Source* FAOSTAT (2015)	48
Fig. 2.11	Linkages between agricultural development and industrialization	50

List of Figures

Fig. 3.1	International trade and socio-economic changes in Southeast Asia	56
Fig. 4.1	Export from the Dutch ports in the Outer Islands, 1846–69 (Dutch guilders). *Sources* Direkteur der Middelen en Domeinen 1851–70	87
Fig. 4.2	Imports into the Dutch Outer-Islands Ports, 1846–1869 (1,000 Dutch guilders). *Sources* Direkteur der Middelen en Domeinen 1851–70	88
Fig. 4.3	Destinations of items exported from the Dutch ports in the Outer Island, 1846–69 (Dutch guilders). *Sources* Direkteur der Middelen en Domeinen 1851–70	89
Fig. 5.1	Singapore's regional export index, 1831–1913. *Source Tabular Statements*, 1839–1865; *Blue Book*, 1868–1913. *Note* The export index is expressed in real terms and estimated by deflating the nominal export value by the export price index. The price index is adopted from Kobayashi (2017)	97
Fig. 5.2	Singapore's regional import index, 1831–1913. *Source Tabular Statements*, 1839–1865; *Blue Book*, 1868–1913. *Note* The import index is estimated using the same mean as that in Fig. 5.1	98
Fig. 5.3	Foreign trade and coasting trade in Kuching, 1860–1917. *Source Sarawak Gazette*, Sarawak Trade Returns; *Sarawak Government Gazette*, Sarawak Trade Returns. *Note* The units are expressed in Straits dollars	107
Fig. 5.4	Coastal rice exports and imports in Kuching, 1881–1930. *Source Sarawak Gazette*, Sarawak Trade Returns; *Sarawak Government Gazette*, Sarawak Trade Returns; *Sarawak Annual Report*. *Notes* The values are measured in piculs	109
Fig. 6.1	GDP per capita in comparison with Japan	117
Fig. 6.2	Japan's export, import and trade balance against GNP. *Source* Ohkawa et al. (1974)	118
Fig. 6.3	Export of miscellaneous goods. *Source* Toyokeizai Shinposha (1935)	126
Fig. 6.4	Production organization of the toy manufacturing industry in Tokyo	129
Fig. 6.5	Japan's export trades after World War II. *Source* Tsushosangyoseisakushi Hensaniinkai (1992)	136
Fig. 7.1	Industrial production index, 1912–1949. *Source* Table 7.5	148
Fig. 7.2	Ratio of paid-in capital of governmental and private companies in free China, 1936–1944. *Source* Kubo (2004: 183)	149
Fig. 7.3	**a** Proportion of spindles in Chinese and foreign cotton mills, 1894–1936, **b** proportion of weaving machines in Chinese and foreign cotton mills, 1894–1936 *Source* Kubo et al. (2016 :25)	152

Fig. 7.4	Profit rates of Chinese cotton mills and Japanese cotton mills in China, 1922–36. *Source* Kubo et al. (2016: 28)	154
Fig. 8.1	Sector shares in NDP in India. *Source* Sivasubramonian (2000)	173
Fig. 8.2	Sector shares in GDP in Japan. *Source* Okawa et al. (1974)	174
Fig. 8.3	Nominal short term interest rates (%). *Sources* Nomura (2018). *Note 1* India's bank rates from Jan. to June were generally higher than those from July to Dec. *Note 2* India's *hundi* rates in June were generally equivalent to the average annual rates.	177
Fig. 8.4	Nominal daily wages for manufacturing labours (in Indian rupee). *Sources* Nomura (2018) *Note 1* The sharp drop in wages in Japan during the 1930s was due to a marked decline in yen-based nominal wages and a sudden depreciation of the yen against the rupee after 1931 (Rs./Yen decreased from 1.47 in 1931 to 1.05 in 1932 and 0.79 in 1933).	179
Fig. 8.5	India's share of government revenue against NDP. *Source* Data of NDP from Sivasubramonian (2000). Data of British India's government revenue from Reserve Bank of India (1954). Data of population size of British India and princely states from Government of India. *Statistical Abstract of British India*. New Delhi: Department of Commercial Intelligence and Statistics. *Note 1* The government revenue includes revenues of both British India's central and local government of, which was separated from the central government after an enactment of the Government of India Act 1919. *Note 2* Original data of the government revenue in *Banking and Monetary Statistics* includes only central and local government revenue of British India, while excluding data on revenue of princely states. We estimate the government revenue of the princely state based on their relative size of population. According to *Statistical Abstract of British India*, total population in British India and princely states are as follows. 231 million and 63 million in 1901, 244 million and 70 million in 1911, 247 million and 71 million in 1921, and 271 million and 81 million in 1931. Based on these figures, we assume that the government revenue of the princely states were 22% of the government revenue of British India throughout the period of the figure. On the assumption, we firstly estimated total government revenue of India. And then, to figure out the India's revenue share in NDP, the estimated government revenue of India was divided by Sivasubramonian's total India's NDP, which includes NDP data of both British India and princely states	182

List of Figures

Fig. 8.6　Japan and the UK's share of government revenue against GDP. *Source* Data of Japan's government revenue from Emi and Shionoya (1966). Data of Japan's GDP from Okawa et al. (1974). Data of the UK from Mitchell (1988). *Note 1* The government revenues include revenues of both central and local government in the respective countries................ 183

Fig. 8.7　Government revenue (absolute figure in million rupee). *Source* Data of exchange rate from same source with Fig. 8.4. Other data are from same sources with Figs. 8.5 and 8.6........... 183

Fig. 8.8　Shares of central government's public debt against GDP/NDP. *Source* Data of India's NDP from Sivasubramonian (2000). Data of British India's central government debt from Reserve Bank of India (1954). Data of Japan's GDP from Okawa et al. (1974). Data of Japan's central government debt from Emi et al. (1988); Toyo Keizai Shinposha, *The Oriental economist* (Toyo Keizai Shinposha), Tokyo: Toyo Keizai Shinposha. Data of the UK from Mitchell (1988). *Note 1* As was the case of Fig. 8.5, original data of the government revenue in *Banking and Monetary Statistics* includes only central government debt of British India, excluding data on princely states' debt. Again, using the population size, we assume that the princely states' government debt were 22% of the government debt of British India. On the assumption, we estimated total central government debt of India. And then, to figure out the India's central government debt share in NDP, the estimated central government debt of India was divided by Sivasubramonian's total India's NDP, which includes NDP data of both British India and princely states.............................. 185

Fig. 8.9　Exchange rate of Indian rupee and Japanese yen against Sterling pound. *Source* Indian rupee data before 1918/19 from Shirras (1920). Indian rupee data after 1919/20 from Government of India. *Statistical Abstract of British India*. New Delhi: Department of Commercial Intelligence and Statistics. Japanese yen data from Government of Japan (1949)......... 186

Fig. 8.10　Import tariff rate and custom revenue share among total government revenue in India (%). *Source* Tariff rate data from Mitchell (1995). Custom revenue and total revenue data from same sources with Fig. 8.5. *Note 1* Tariff rate is estimated by custom revenue. *divided by* total imports................. 187

Fig. 8.11　Percentage of rings and mules: India. *Source* Otsuka et al. (1988, p. 9).. 189

Fig. 8.12　Percentage of rings and mules: Japan. *Source* Otsuka et al. (1988, p. 10)....................................... 190

Fig. 9.1	Changes in sectoral GDP per capita in Asia and Sub-Saharan Africa. *Source* Penn World Table, World Development Indicators. *Note* GDP per capita is in USD (in PPP-adjusted 2011 constant price) and is presented in log scale. Panel A presents weighted averages (weight by population) of BGD, CHN, IDN, IND, KOR, LKA, MYS, NPL, PAK, PHL, and THA and Panel B presents numbers in JPN. Similarly, Panel C presents weighted averages of BDI, BEN, BFA, CAF, CIV, CMR, COG, GHA, GNB, KEN, LSO, MDG, MLI, MRT, MWI, NER, RWA, SDN, SLE, SWZ, TCD, TGO, UGA, ZMB, and ZWE and Panel D presents numbers in ZAF.	200
Fig. 9.2	Changes in GDP per capita in all Sub-Saharan African countries. *Source* Penn World Table, World Development Indicators. GDP per capita is in USD (in PPP-adjusted 2011 constant price) and is presented in log scale. All Sub-Saharan countries, whose GDP data is available are included	212
Fig. 10.1	Sectoral composition of gross domestic product in selected countries in Asia and Africa, 1985–2015. Drawn using data from World Development Indicators database.	222
Fig. 10.2	Arable land per rural population in tropical Asia and sub-Saharan Africa, 1961–2013. Figure was drawn using data from FAOStat and World Population Prospects (United Nations, Department of Economic and Social Affairs, Population Division 2015); "Tropical Asia" refers to Southeast Asia and South Asia.	225
Fig. 10.3	Total area equipped for irrigation in selected countries in Asia and Africa, 1961–2013. Drawn using data from FAOStat; "Tropical Asia" refers to Southeast Asia and South Asia	228
Fig. 10.4	Area planted with modern rice varieties in selected countries in Asia, 1966–2012. Drawn using data from World Rice Statistics	229
Fig. 10.5	Average crop yield in tropical Asia and sub-Saharan Africa, 1961–2014	230
Fig. 10.6	Gross primary enrolment ratio (%) in selected countries in Asia and Africa, 1970–2014	231
Fig. 10.7	Gross secondary enrolment ratio (%) in selected countries in Asia and Africa, 1970–2014	232
Fig. 10.8	Interrelationship between population pressure, Green Revolution, and the development of nonfarm sector	233
Fig. 10.9	Location of Central Luzon, the Philippines.	244
Fig. 11.1	Nominal rates of assistance to agriculture, by regions, 1980–84 and 2000–04 (percent). *Source* Anderson (ed.) (2009). *Note* LAC is Latin America and Caribbean, ECA is Europe and	

	Central Asia, ANZ is Australia and New Zealand, and WE is Western Europe	255
Fig. 11.2	Nominal rate of assistance (NRA) in Africa and Asia, 1955–2010. *Source* World Bank, National and Global Estimates of Distortions to Agricultural Incentives 1955–2011	256
Fig. 11.3	Rerationship between GDP per capita and NRA in Africa, 1961–2010. *Source* World Bank, National and Global Estimates of Distortions to Agricultural Incentives 1955–2011	257
Fig. 11.4	Relationship between rural population share and NRA in Africa, 1961–2010. *Source* World Bank, National and Global Estimates of Distortions to Agricultural Incentives 1955–2011	258
Fig. 11.5	Political determination of agricultural protection level	262
Fig. 12.1	Population and employment by sector in Japan, China, and India from 1950 to 2015. *Source* FAOSTAT	275
Fig. 12.2	Proportion of financial support for land improvement investment by the central and local government in Japan from 1910 to 2004. *Sources* National Research Institute of Agricultural Economics (1967) and Ministry of Agriculture, Forestry and Fisheries (various years)	279
Fig. 12.3	Japan's land improvement investment, rice production value, and rice income from 1960 to 2015. *Source* Data are from the home page of Ministry of Agriculture, Forestry, and Fisheries (Accessed November 2017). The sources of each series are as follows. Land improvement investment: *Nougyou shokuryou kanren no keizai keisan*. Rice production value: *Seisannnougyou syotoku toukei*. Rice income: *Nousanbutu seisanhi toukei*. Note Rice income is computed as rice income per 10 are times rice cultivated area in 10 acre. Rice cultivated area was taken form *Skumotu toukei* at the homepage above. The definition of rice income per 10 are is as follows. Income = revenue − (total production cost − (imputed family labor cost + imputed capital payment + imputed land rent)). Subsidies are not included in the revenue	281
Fig. 12.4	The proportion of sample farmers in the four types of irrigation institutions by the volumetric price of reservoir water, Zhanghe Irrigation System, Hubei, China in 2008. *Source* Kajisa and Dong (2017)	284
Fig. 12.5	Percentage share of well-irrigated and tank-irrigated area in total irrigated area in Tamil Nadu from 1960 to 2005. *Source* Kajisa et al. (2007)	287

List of Tables

Table 1.1	Growth of intra-Asian trade, 1950–2014 (in billion US dollars)	20
Table 1.2	The growth of intra-regional trade in Sub-Saharan Africa, 1950–2015 (in billion US dollars)	28
Table 3.1	Four spheres of the trade of Batavia	60
Table 3.2	Merchandise Exports at Current Price, 1870–1998 (million dollars at current exchange rates)	65
Table 3.3	Trading Partners of International Trade in Southeast Asia, 1883–1938 (million pounds sterling)	65
Table 5.1	Imports and exports in Singapore's trade, 1822–1913	99
Table 5.2	Imports and exports in Singapore's regional trade, 1828–1913	103
Table 5.3	Commodities of foreign exports and coasting imports in Kuching, 1870–1904	108
Table 6.1	Distribution of working population of manufacturing industries in 1909	117
Table 6.2	Trade and production of cotton goods in the late 19th century Japan (unit: 10,000 kin)	120
Table 6.3	Distribution of businesses and workers by production forms of weaving industry in 1905	121
Table 6.4	Japan's export trade in 1937	127
Table 6.5	Content of workshops classified by the size of capital in Tokyo 1932	133
Table 6.6	Proportion of commodities in export to US	137
Table 7.1	General trends of foreign trade, 1871–2013 (100 million US$)	142
Table 7.2	General trends of foreign investment, 1902–2014. Million US$	143
Table 7.3	Sectoral composition of foreign investment, 1914 and 1931 (%)	143
Table 7.4	Railway construction, 1890–2014 (km)	144

Table 7.5	Industrial development, 1912–1949	145
Table 7.6	Ratio of domestic supply of Chinese industrial production, 1890–1936 (%)	148
Table 7.7	Composition of production, 1933–2014 (value added) (%)	149
Table 7.8	Composition of industrial production, 1933–1993 (%)	150
Table 7.9	Production and trade of machine-made cotton yarn and cotton pieces, 1880–1990	152
Table 7.10	Geographical distribution of spindles of Chinese and Japanese cotton mills in China, 1922–36. Unit: 1,000 spindles; () index (1930 = 100)	153
Table 7.11	Production of iron foundries, 1919–37 (1,000 tons)	157
Table 7.12	Sales of Anshan and Benxihu foundries (1,000 tons (%))	158
Table 8.1	Top seven cotton spindle holding countries (1,000)	170
Table 8.2	Top nine pig iron producers (1,000 metric tons)	171
Table 8.3	Manufacturing production 1926–28	172
Table 9.1	GDP per capita and contribution of each sector in the selected years	203
Table 9.2	Sectoral share of labor in selected years	205
Table 9.3	Sectoral GDP per capita and share of labor in selected years	207
Table 9.4	Decomposition of GDP per capita growth	210
Table 9.5	Data availability	213
Table 10.1	Growth rate of per capita gross domestic product (GDPPc) in selected countries in Asia and Africa, 1980–2015	222
Table 10.2	Sectoral composition of total employment in selected countries in Asia and Africa, 1980–2014	223
Table 10.3	Poverty and inequality in selected countries in Asia and Africa, 1983–2012	224
Table 10.4	Growth rates of arable land and population in selected countries in Asia and Africa, 1961–2013	226
Table 10.5	Sources of rural household income in selected countries in Asia, 1985–2010	238
Table 10.6	Technology adoption, demographic characteristics, and income sources of sample households in Central Luzon, the Philippines, 1966–2011	245
Table 11.1	NRA and GDP per capita in 20 African countries	259
Table 11.2	Results of regressions of nominal protection coefficient (NPC) in Africa	267

Table 12.1	Water price and water use by water institution of sample farmers, Zhanghe Irrigation System, Hubei, China in 2008	285
Table 12.2	Comparison of rice yield, income, poverty ratio, and rice profit by irrigation status of sample farmers, Tamil Nadu, India, in 1999.	288

Chapter 1
Multiple Paths to Industrialization: A Global Context of the Rise of Emerging States

Kaoru Sugihara

1.1 Introduction

This volume addresses the issue of how a country, which was incorporated into the world economy as a periphery, could create a path of economic development and industrialization as the 'emerging state' in Asia and Africa. We offer historical and contemporary case studies of development paths, as well as the international background under which a transition to the emerging state was successfully made, delayed or failed.

In this chapter I describe how diverse paths of economic development emerged in various regions of the world, and show that interactions of such 'multiple paths', rather than the diffusion of modern technology and institutions from Western Europe to the rest of the world, determined the timing and pace of global industrialization over the last two centuries. The industrial revolution in England, which began in the late eighteenth century, was first transmitted to Continental Europe, the United States and Japan in the 'long' nineteenth century. During the period of interwar instability and after World War II, a variety of state-led industrialization programs, including socialist models, were implemented, which had varying degrees of success. The diffusion of industrialization has been often interpreted along the Gerschenkronean framework of 'advantage of backwardness' and late development (Gerschenkron 1962; Austin 2013, 288–90). In a broad sense, any state engaged in 'catching-up' industrialization qualifies the emerging state. Thus the first type of the emerging state exploits its respective factor endowment advantages in relation to the more advanced countries. If an Asian country such as Japan is labour abundant and capital scarce, she might focus on the development of labour-intensive industries, in addition to fostering capital-intensive ones for political and military reasons.

K. Sugihara (✉)
Research Institute for Humanity and Nature, Kyoto, Japan
e-mail: sugihara@chikyu.ac.jp

© The Author(s) 2019
K. Otsuka and K. Sugihara (eds.), *Paths to the Emerging State in Asia and Africa*,
Emerging-Economy State and International Policy Studies,
https://doi.org/10.1007/978-981-13-3131-2_1

Meanwhile, as early development economists such as W. A. Lewis pointed out, many countries of Asia and Africa under colonial rule or domination were not given the chance to industrialize, either because industrialized West sought an international division of labour where the latter specialized in manufactured goods while the former was encouraged to specialize in primary products, or, perhaps more fundamentally, because resource and environmental constraints in Asia and Africa, especially their tropical parts, made it difficult for their people to raise agricultural productivity, thus depressing the chance to increase the real wage and the opportunity to train labour (Lewis 1954, 1970).

Another, somewhat related line of development was the state-led, import-substitution industrialization strategy, pursued in India and China among others, which aimed at political and economic independence at the cost of seeking gains from international trade and technological transfer from advanced countries, especially the United States. The idea of 'import-substitution' was widely shared among the leaders of newly independent states, crossing over the political division between non-allied and socialist countries, which reflected their experiences as a 'periphery' and the impact of 'forced' free trade. In general, this form of 'third world industrialization' and 'state-led development' did not successfully close the gap between the 'North' and the 'South' in terms of per capita GDP or living standards. Nor was it often associated with democracy. But in all cases the state played a powerful role in determining the type of industrialization with varied implications for economic growth and living standards. Industrialization of China in the Mao period, in spite of its stormy politics, left a particularly lasting impression for the study of the role of the state in economic development, not least because it contributed to the improvement of health and education of a very large number of people. Thus the second type of the emerging state as a driver of industrialization came out of the ideology of politico-economic independence and import-substitution, rather than as a result of the exploitation of factor endowment advantages.

A major change came from the western rim of the Pacific in the post-war period. In contrast to Japan's late development since the Meiji period, which we term labour-intensive industrialization and categorize as the first type of the emerging state, the Japanese high economic growth in the 1950s and the 1960s resulted in a rapid convergence of per capita GDP to advanced western countries. This could be seen as an extension of pre-war labour-intensive industrialization to a large extent in that its comparative advantage remained firmly in relatively cheap, competitive labour. Newly Industrializing Economies (NIEs) and some Southeast Asian countries adopted the strategy of export-oriented industrialization also by taking advantage of cheap, competitive labour and by meeting the demand from the mass-consumer markets of advanced countries (Sugihara 2013). Then, some states, such as Japan, South Korea and Taiwan, also began to take on the task of creating competitive capital- and resource-intensive industries, and successfully pursued them. This is 'developmentalism', which relies the legitimacy of its existence on growth, willing to go beyond the simple pursuit for exploiting its factor endowment advantages. The state could exercise power to promote industrial technology, build infrastructure and mobilize human and natural resources by prioritizing growth over democracy, equality and environmental concerns.[1] The 'developmental state' with commitment to international trade and growth ideology thus constitutes the third type of the emerging state. It is worth noting that this regional development occurred when mainland China and India were largely outside the orbit of the international economy.

Set against the high economic growth at the western rim of the Pacific, China and India made policy changes around 1979 and 1991 respectively, to re-enter the international economy. There too a fusion between capital-intensive and labour-intensive paths took place, that is, emphasis on capital-intensive, heavy industries (represented by steel and machinery sectors) was eventually replaced by or absorbed into the industrialization strategy with attention to a greater range of industries, including those which were more employment-generating and human-capital-intensive. Thus the growth of the Asia-Pacific economy and regional integration accelerated, and led global industrialization. By the end of the twentieth century the majority of world population lived in industrialized or rapidly industrializing countries, especially in Asia. It is now spreading to the rest of the world. Some emerging economies have built their economy on resource exports and trade, while some states lack the experience of centralized administration. But global industrialization emerged as a formidable force, both as an economic competition and as an ideology, regardless of the preparedness of each developing country. It is this global process of transition that provides the economic context of the rise of emerging states today.

Is there any theory that can explain the timing, pace and underlying causes of this process? This chapter suggests that the key to answering this question lies in the examination of the ways in which regional trade, long distance trade and technology transfer successively released local and regional resource constraints in various parts of the world. Local and regional resource constraints, such as shortage of land, scarcity of water and the lack of access to biomass energy, would reduce the chance for securing food and other necessities, hence a sustainable path of economic development. Intercontinental trade may provide export outlets, while advanced countries could provide technology, capital and human resources, to build an infrastructure and offer advice on policy. From the point of view of a developing country, however, imported resources had to find matching local ones to make economic sense. Earnings from primary exports had to be translated into securing livelihood goods, which normally meant securing supplies locally or through regional trade. Intra-regional trade could mitigate local resource constraints at a critical moment (think of famines). Likewise, modern technology and institutions had to be adapted to the local context of production and consumption. Machinery and means of transport had to adapt to local factor endowment conditions and the effective use of traditional technology and resources (When necessary, the material for the frame of the power-loom, made by steel, temporarily went back to wood, while modern factories and railways resorted to the use of timber, instead of coal, for fuel). Above all, the industrialization drive had to be supported by (thus 'embedded' in) the agricultural economy and population; There technology and institutions would change only very slowly. It is the nature and

---

[1] For discussion on the effects of developmentalism and the developmental state on the environment, see Sugihara (2017).

mechanism of these 'multiple paths' to industrialization and the role various kinds of emerging states played in them that need to be understood.

In the next section we describe the emergence of a three-tier international division of labour where capital-intensive industrialization, labour-intensive industrialization and exports of primary products characterized each region, mainly referring to the period up to World War II. In the third section we focus on the growth of intra-Asian trade, to show local and regional agencies for the growth of world economy and trade. It contributed to labour-intensive industrialization, as well as the growth of the export economy of primary products. The fourth section extends the discussion from the pre-war to the post-war period, and comments on the industrialization experiences of East Asia, and Southeast Asia, from the perspective of the region's respective position in the world economy. The final section discusses the role of the emerging state in relation to industrialization and economic development of Sub-Saharan Africa.

1.2 Emergence of a Three-Tier International Division of Labour

1.2.1 The Beginning

Before 1800, most local agricultural societies in Asia and Europe developed a system of production and reproduction by accepting local resource constraints, imposed by nature. Reflecting a large 'population-carrying capacity' of monsoon Asia (see Sugihara 2017), 66% of world population is thought to have lived in Asia, and 22% in Europe in 1820 (Maddison 2009). The fate of many societies was only partially altered or complemented by regional or intercontinental trade, although some societies were affected by the more drastic interventions such as epidemics and violence. In Asia the arrival of knowledge from outside was often not taken advantage of, unless enlightened rulers made it compatible with the technologies and institutions governing local and regional systems. Thus the Malthusian logic prevailed, even in the early modern period when a gradual but sustained expansion of the market occurred in several core regions of the world (Richards 2003). The balance between population and food had to be retained in the long run.

In what ways was this Malthusian trap overcome? In the "European miracle" narrative, technological breakthroughs during the period from the scientific revolution to the industrial revolution have been highlighted, and accompanying institutional developments, especially emergence of the nation state and the regime of private property rights, have been identified as essential conditions for industrialization and economic growth (Jones 1981). Once agricultural productivity rose and coal became available in some places, major resource constraints such as shortage of land and danger of deforestation began to be significantly eased. Cheap coal helped the diffusion of steam engines in modern factories and transport sectors. Overseas expansion aided by the development of navigation and military technologies also helped ease regional resource constraints, through the imports of raw materials and food. Pomeranz called such a resource bonanza 'coal and North America' (Pomeranz 2000). By the early nineteenth century the environmental conditions of Western Europe largely ceased to constrain economic growth. By the second half of the nineteenth century intercontinental trade centering on the Atlantic but also involving Asia grew, and formed an international division of labour where Western Europe exported manufactured goods to, and imported primary products from, the rest of the world.

However, this was a solution specific to Western Europe. The ways in which resource constraints were eased in the subsequent process of global industrialization differed region by region (Sugihara 2015a). The level of constraints in the United States and other regions of recent European settlement (such as Canada, Australia and New Zealand) was much lower than that in Western Europe in some crucial measures (such as land and biomass stock), making room for them, especially the United States, to pursue an even more capital- and resource-intensive path than countries in Western Europe. In East Asia, meanwhile, land was much more scarce relative to population, and people were fed, clothed and organized quite differently, mainly through rice farming and associated proto-industry and social institutions. It created the more labour-intensive and eventually resource-saving path (for the socio-ecological foundations for this path, see Oshima 1987). In other words, neither the United States nor East Asia followed the path Western Europe had created. The critical importance of the availability of water, and the frequency of epidemics and natural disasters, especially in the tropical parts of Asia, Africa and Latin America, further signaled the difference of resource endowments of various regions of the world, hence the impossibility of conceptualizing the relationship between industrialization and the environment on the basis of the experience of Western Europe.

1.2.2 The Western Supremacy and Reorganization of Asian Industries

Between 1750 and 1840 an overwhelming proportion of world industrial production, mostly un-mechanized, was located in Asia, especially in China and India (see Fig. 1.1). Even in 1840 the impact of mechanized industries was limited. In industrializing Europe a half of textile production was still un-mechanized. By 1910 the world market of textiles was dominated by the modern English cotton textile industry. The decline of traditional industries, especially cotton textile industry in India (and to a lesser extent China), was a serious global event that involved a loss of employment on an unprecedented scale (Bagchi 1976; Roy 2005: 106–15). Asia's share in world GDP declined from 60% in 1820 to 25% in 1913, while that of Western Europe rose from 20 to 31%, and North America from 2 to 20% in these years (Maddison 2009). This mainly reflected the widening gap in real wages between Asia and the West, although the growth of GDP in North America reflected the rapid growth of migrant population as well. Asia became an importer of English textiles and an exporter

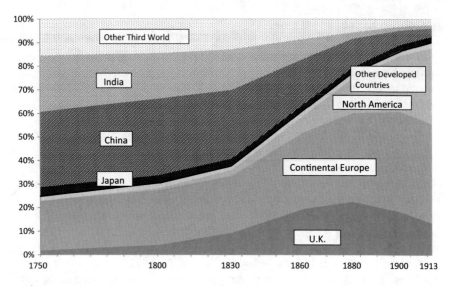

Fig. 1.1 Geographical composition of world industrial production, 1750–1913. *Source and Note* Bairoch (1982: 292). In Bairoch's overall data Japan is included in 'developed countries', but I reclassified her under 'developing countries', as this Figure refers to the period up to 1913

of tea, rice, sugar, tin, rubber, raw cotton, raw silk, raw jute and wheat. Thus an international division of labour emerged between industrialized West as exporters of manufactured goods, and Asia as exporters of primary products. The environmental implication of this division of labour was the transfer of (mainly land-derived) natural resources from the latter to the former, in exchange for the improvement of transport, urbanization and mass-produced consumer goods. Industrialization in this context has typically been portrayed as an agent of both resource exploitation and the diffusion of modern science and technology.

However, Asia's response to Western impact also contained another feature, namely labour-intensive industrialization. Asia was not just de-industrialized but was reorganized into a new form of industrialization. Thus there were two different routes of diffusion of industrialization, the capital-intensive route originating in the West, and the labour-intensive one originating in the East. In addition, the latter tended to be less resource-intensive than the former. I describe below the emergence of a three-tier international division of labour between capital-intensive manufactured goods, labour-intensive manufactured goods and primary products, and an increasingly uneven global resource allocation in favour of Europe and regions of recent European settlement, in the period from the nineteenth century to the 1930s. I also suggest that this three-tier structure was developed into the main pattern of the international division of labour by the end of the twentieth century.

First, the growth of the Atlantic economy represents the main global route to industrialization in terms of leading technological and institutional developments. Countries in Continental Europe and the regions of recent European settlement achieved industrialization by learning new technology and/or by importing capital, labour and machinery with their export earnings. In the New World, the integration of vast natural resources into the international economy served as the engine of economic growth. Labour was scarce and land and other resources were abundant, and the difference in factor endowments between the old and the new worlds induced a growth of trade, migration and investment. In the nineteenth and early twentieth centuries, the growth of the Atlantic economy was prominent in intercontinental trade. An implication of this development was that the regions of recent European settlement had a better incentive than Britain to raise labour productivity, using abundant natural resources and employing imported capital. The movement towards the development of labour-saving, capital-intensive and resource-intensive technology was most clearly observed in the United States (for the significance of different factor endowments behind different institutions within the Americas, see Engerman and Sokoloff 2011). The need to save skilled labour led to standardization of industrial production such as the use of transferable parts, which in turn facilitated the transfer of technology across industries and the development of mass production, as well as 'deskilling' of labour. Industrialization became associated with the exploitation of economies of scale.

The American frontier was exhausted around 1890, and by the early 1920s migration from Europe ceased to be encouraged. But American technology continued to lead the world, by raising labour productivity through automation, the introduction of more systematic labour management and mass marketing. Looking back from the twenty-first century, the British industrial revolution only began to show the explosive power of labour-saving technology through the use of coal and steam engines, and merely paved the way for a fuller replacement of skilled labour by capital and technology. Therefore, although the conditions for the industrial revolution may have been laid in Europe, the 'Western path', with emphasis on capital-intensive and resource-intensive technology, arguably only became fully established as a result of the growth of the Atlantic economy.

As far as the direction of technology and institutions is concerned, the Soviet model of 'big push' resembled the American one, in so far as it was capital- and resource-intensive. In this model emphasis on heavy and chemical industries, and on high-technology sectors backed by the state, was quite explicit. Although some aspects of these industrialization strategies were successful (see Allen 2005), many socialist economies eventually failed to foster internationally competitive industries.

Second, a different model developed in Asia. Although earlier efforts tended to attempt at a direct transfer of Western technology and institutions, the Japanese government by the 1880s had developed an industrialisation strategy quite distinct from such attempts. Recognizing that both land and capital were scarce, while labour was abundant and of relatively good quality, the new strategy was to encourage active use of the tradition of labour-intensive technology, modernisation of traditional industry, and conscious adaptation of Western technology to different conditions of factor endowment. The path Japan developed can be termed 'labour-intensive industrialisation', as it absorbed and utilised labour more fully and depended less on the replacement of labour by machinery and capital than the Western path. Some traditional industries not only survived but developed. For example, hand-weaving industry sustained a large employment with the use of machine-made yarn, contributing to the development of a market for mass consumer goods by combining the efficiency of machine made intermediate goods with traditional clothing patterns.

The comparative advantage of labour-intensive industries in Asia was reinforced by the divergence through the growth of real wage gap between the Atlantic high-wage economy and the non-European low-wage economies. The persistence of this gap was partly helped by migration laws in the United States and other regions of recent European settlement. A largely unintended consequence of this was that it progressively became easier for Japan, the first industrial nation in Asia, to compete with Western manufacturers in the international market of labour-intensive manufactured goods where wage differences mattered. The difference between the structure of consumption in Asia and the West was another important factor that made it possible for Asia to industrialise itself. Thus industries of Asia and Europe developed, each with separate niches.

Under the imposition of the free trade regime, labour-intensive industrialization constituted the core of Asia's development path, and the expansion of its trade served as an engine of regional industrialization. The rate of growth of intra-Asian trade between 1880 and 1938 was faster than that of Asia's trade with the West or world trade, as the division of labour between agriculture and industry grew at local and regional levels, and merchant networks exploited slight differences in price and quality of commodities, including manufactured goods. Thus, like the Japanese hand-weavers mentioned above, Chinese hand-weavers used Indian, and later Japanese, machine-made yarn before the modern Chinese spinning industry provided it to them. A substantial proportion of Japanese yarn by this time was made from Indian raw cotton. Thus there developed a competitive international commodity chain within Asia (Sugihara 1996, 2005a). Since most of Asia were labour abundant, successful industrializers needed to possess a pool of competitive labour, that is, cheap labour relative to efficiency. The effort to improve the quality of labour was an important feature of Japan's industrialization, while intra-Asian trade, led by Chinese and Indian merchant networks, was a main mechanism through which massive employment was maintained and the quality of labour was tested at each point of labour absorption.

An important consequence of the emergence of the three-tier international division of labour was that both capital-intensive industrialization and labour-intensive industrialization needed the supplier of primary products. There was a transfer of natural resources from primary producers to industrial countries, especially to those pursuing capital- and resource-intensive industrialization. But those pursuing labour-intensive industrialization also exploited natural resources from other parts of Asia and beyond. As we will see in Sect. 1.5, the rapid development of economic relationships between growth Asia and Sub-Saharan Africa suggests that Asia, along with the West, acts as a major importer of natural resources, while retaining a competitive position in the international market of labour-intensive manufactures at the same time.

1.3 Intra-regional Trade as an Agent of Economic Development

1.3.1 Integration of Asia and Africa into the World Economy

Figure 1.2 shows that intercontinental trade in 1840 was centred on Western Europe, while there were very large regional trading zones both in Europe and Asia. One of the reasons why my figures on intra-Asian trade (especially rough figures) are so large is that I have included all intra-Asian trade, regardless of whether they are indigenous commodities, imported foreign goods or commercial crops for export. Thus, if English textiles were brought to Bombay or Singapore, and then were redistributed by Indian or Chinese merchants within India or Southeast Asia, we would count the latter transaction as intra-Asian trade. Unless English textiles were consumed within Bombay or Singapore, therefore, most imported goods would be counted as regional trade as well. This is appropriate in my view, as most of the time English or European traders were unable to penetrate into the interior or smaller markets of Asia, and were dependent on the initiatives of Asian merchants for the maintenance of their intercontinental trade. The same points can be made with regard to much of Asia's exports to the West. Peasant producers in the hinterland were most likely to deal with local or regional Asian merchants, who would in turn sell their produce to Western merchants at large ports. Behind the strength of Asian merchants were their extensive local and regional networks, which were developed with the use of their languages and under the influence of their cultures and social institutions. A large difference in the two figures for intra-Asian trade in Figs. 1.2, mainly comes from the inclusion of local trade relating to long-distance trade, and definition of territorial units. The units in Asia at this point was larger than anywhere else in the world.

By 1910 the structure of world trade became much more multilateral (Fig. 1.3). The United States became an important participant, while many primary producers in Latin America, parts of Asia (such as Middle East) and Africa were integrated into the trade structure as a satellite of the metropolitan economy. But this well-known multilateral pattern of trade settlement, illustrated by S. B. Saul referring to the centrality of the U.K. (Saul 1960), also grossly underrepresents the depth of intra-Asian trade, hence the importance of intra-regional trade for world trade. Intra-Asian trade is shown to have been 432 million pounds in Fig. 1.3, which corresponds to the smaller figure of 42 million in 1840 in Fig. 1.2. If the growth of intra-Asian trade at the unrecorded level was roughly at the same pace as that of the recorded one, the real amount of intra-Asian trade in 1910 must have been much larger. We will show some evidence to support this statement below.

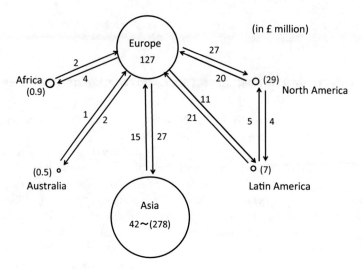

Fig. 1.2 Structure of world trade, 1840. *Sources and Notes* Sugihara (2015c, 29). Trade data include original estimates. Figures for each region are intra-regional trade. Those in brackets are very rough estimates. The size of the circle expresses the relative proportion of each region in world GDP (Maddison 2009)

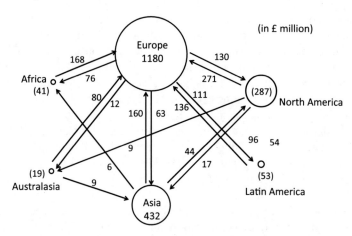

Fig. 1.3 Structure of world trade, 1910. *Sources and Notes* Sugihara (2015c, 33). Trade data are original estimates. Figures for each region are intra-regional trade. Those in brackets are very rough estimates. The size of the circle expresses the relative proportion of each region in world GDP (Maddison 2009)

1.3.2 Local and Regional Trade in British India[2]

In order to show the magnitude of local and regional trade, it is useful to look at British India, a region with a massive amount of trade-related statistics. Here we show some examples of different types of statistics such as coasting trade, rail- and river-borne and road-borne trade, in addition to foreign trade. Figure 1.4 shows the magnitude of rail- and river-borne trade of India (largely British India except Burma, but includes many princely states) in 1888. By then large port cities such as Calcutta, Bombay and Madras (and its surrounding ports) became regional hubs of Bengal, Bombay and Madras Presidencies respectively, and rail- and river-borne, coasting and road networks were developed to link them to hinterlands, often beyond each presidency. Manufactured goods such as British cotton textiles were carried inland, and in turn primary products were brought to port cities (for details, see Sugihara 2015b). According to the traditional interpretation, this was an attempt to build a transport infrastructure through a combination of British investment in Indian railways and promotion of long-distance trade. The British government of India discouraged the development of Indian industries through tariff and exchange rate policies and preferential imports of British textile machinery and railway-related goods.

While such an account highlights an important aspect of development under colonial rule, a closer look at regional statistics indicates a more complex picture. Figure 1.5 compares foreign trade, coasting trade, rail-borne trade, river-borne trade and road-borne trade of Calcutta and its environs around 1877. According to *Report on the Administration of Bengal*, the source of Fig. 1.5, foreign trade amounted to 500 million rupees, while 330 million rupees of commodities were carried by rail, 40 million by steam boats, 20 million by road (captured at a small number of 'cordons'), and 190 million by 'country boats'. The traditional understanding of the role of the large port cities such as Calcutta was to import manufactured goods from abroad and distribute them to districts of Bengal and other parts of North India, and to export primary products collected from inland areas. Indeed cotton textiles, liquors and wines, and iron imported from Britain were transported by rail to other districts, while indigo, rice, linseed, wheat and raw jute were carried, mainly by rail, from Bengal, North Western Provinces and Oudh, Bihar and Punjab to Calcutta, and parts or most of them were exported. Tea was carried by steam boats from Assam to Calcutta, most of which were exported to Europe and the United States.

At the same time, those who operated in the central markets of the economy of Calcutta and its environs were mainly Indian and India-based merchants. For them Calcutta was also a place of exchange of domestic goods, with the combined use of four vastly different types of transport, railways and steam boats on the one hand, and traditional road transport and country boats on the other. From this perspective, the combined statistics reveal that the greater part of imports of rice, raw jute, linseed and grams and pulse were actually imported by country boats rather than by rail. The greater part of both salt and rice trade (imports and exports) was conducted by

---
[2]The contents of this and next section are based on Sugihara (2019b).

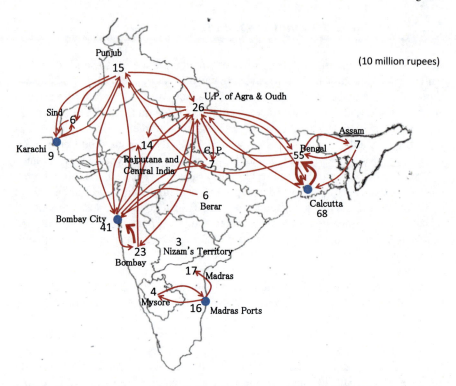

Fig. 1.4 Rail- and river-borne trade in India, 1888. *Source and Notes* Rail- and River-borne Trade, 1888/89–1892/93. Figures are sums of exports and imports. Thin arrows represent a million rupees and above, while thick arrow 10 million and above

country boats and road transport. In this particular year a large amount of rice and other commodities were sent to Madras under the famine. In normal years, however, a very large proportion of grains and salt that came into the city must have consumed there. Given the recording of road-borne trade was limited and a large proportion of imports to the city was consumed within, it is reasonable to assume that about a half of the commodity flows in the city economy were unrelated to foreign trade.

By the end of World War I it became the norm that the majority of rail-borne trade was more closely related to the domestic market than to foreign trade. A large part of this change came from the expansion of commodity chains driven by the growth of modern industries, such as the Bombay-driven flows of raw cotton to cotton piece goods and the Bengal-driven flows for raw jute to jute bags. At the same time, domestic markets of major grains such as rice and wheat emerged, and they were accompanied by a wide circulation of traditional spices and daily necessities. Materials for the construction and maintenance of railways, roads and urban infrastructure were also among the major items of domestic trade (Sugihara 2002, 2015b). An important feature is that railways and steam boats did not simply replace the more traditional road- and river-borne trade, but the former often activated the latter.

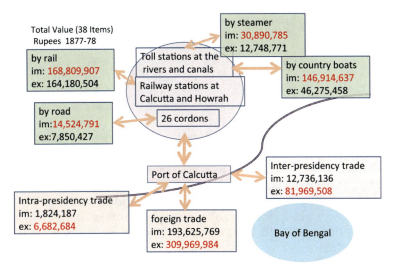

Fig. 1.5 Trade of Calcutta and its environs, 1877/78. *Source* Report on the Administration of Bengal (1877/78)

The growth of the domestic market was not confined to the urban centers such as Calcutta, as shown above. Construction of a railway station in the relatively remote part of inland areas, for example, often led to the construction of feeder roads from the station, and they were then often linked to traditional road networks (for Bombay presidency see Sugihara 2015b). The transport infrastructure of British India thus served, albeit in a largely unintended fashion, for the growth of the domestic market and labour-intensive industrialization.

After independence, the British-driven development of modern infrastructure was eventually transferred to serve for the domestic market, consisting of diverse local and regional merchant networks and new nation-wide networks, largely unrelated to imports and exports. Although replacement investment in railways was insufficient towards the end of the colonial period, and the independent government had to bear rather heavy costs from the beginning, the railway networks nevertheless acted as a backbone of capital-intensive industrialization. At the same time, it acted as a vehicle of the distribution of food and clothing and other necessities, which were increasingly standardized and modernized. The admittedly slow development of mass consumer culture emerged, largely as a result of activities of domestic merchants rather than with the aid of the state.

1.3.3 Indian Ocean Trade

The scale of local and regional trade in India was already quite large by the time of the development of the territorial rule by the English East India Company. Even in Bengal where long-distance trade grew fast from the end of the eighteenth century, the sum of Calcutta's intra-Asian trade, trade with other parts of India, and trade within the Bengal Presidency in 1811 was still greater than Calcutta's long-distance trade. Local and regional trade was much greater than long-distance trade in Bombay and Madras for that year (Sugihara 2009).

This picture changes dramatically by 1840. These three port cities greatly strengthened links with Britain. A large part of traditional Indian Ocean trade declined, while European manufactures penetrated into the domestic market. Even so, the distribution of European goods and the transport of primary products to port cities were largely conducted by Indian and India-based merchants. For example, sea-borne trade statistics of the city of Bombay records a large increase of both foreign trade and coasting trade. Most of raw cotton was imported to the city of Bombay from other ports of Bombay Presidency before being exported mostly to Britain (Bombay Presidency Report of the Commerce of Bombay; Bombay Trade and Navigation Annual Statements). This means that even the most typical 'long-distance trade' was not under the full control of Britain, but was dependent on the traditional trade networks. For local merchants this was a new business. Available statistics alone does not tell us a clear overall decline of local and regional networks.

Did regional trade really decline in the mid-nineteenth century onwards? It is clear that there was a strong and sustained surge of long-distance trade of British India after the 1860s, led by the sudden increase of raw cotton from Bombay in the 1860s (against the 'cotton famine') and the opening of the Suez Canal. On the other hand, a sharp decline of coasting trade only reflects the change of the recording methods of trade statistics (intra-Presidency trade statistics largely disappear from the Bombay Presidency data, for example). In reality, the establishment of the Suez Canal route led to the reorganization of both India's domestic trade and the Indian Ocean trade, involving Southeast Asia, East Asia, the Middle East, East Africa and South Africa. The rate of growth differed region by region and was not as rapid as long-distance trade, but an increase of the absolute amount of regional trade seems clear.

Figure 1.6 shows the composition of geographical distribution of trade of each country or region of the Indian Ocean and East Asia in 1910. The numbers refer to the proportion of exports to Asia and Sub-Saharan Africa to the total amount of exports. The statistics come from the presidency data of British India and the British parliamentary papers. I have included the amount of coasting trade for British India trade statistics in this calculation, on the ground that they are trades between different regional economies, and are closer to other components of intra-Asian trade (such as the trade between the Straits Settlements and Siam). The Figure however excludes all land trade (and, for that matter, all domestic trade in China), so it grossly underestimates the magnitude of local and regional trade. Nevertheless, it is clear that many major ports were oriented towards regional trade rather than long-distance

1 Multiple Paths to Industrialization: A Global Context …

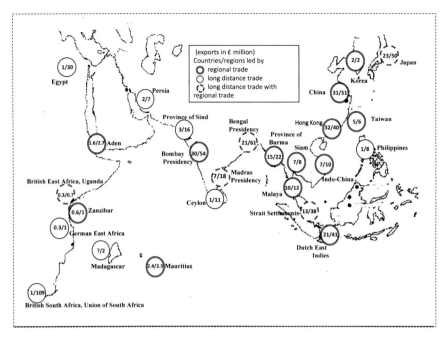

Fig. 1.6 Long distance trade and regional trade, 1910. *Sources and Notes* Sugihara (2013). Circles show major trading countries and regions. Figures indicated within the circle shows the value of exports to Asian and African regions over that of total exports. Figures for the Presidencies and the Provinces of India and Aden are derived from the references originally used in Sugihara (1996) (186) and Sugihara (2002) (28). Figures refer to sea-borne trade only. As coastal trade in British India is included here, the ratio of intra-regional trade is greater than the usual calculation made from the geographical composition of foreign trade. Figures for Hong Kong was estimated from those in 1913. See Sugihara (1996) (107)

trade, and that intra-Asian trade constituted an essential part of Asian trade, together with Asia's trade with the West (for other periods, see Sugihara 1996, 2005a). The regional trade was primarily conducted by merchant networks based in Asia and Africa (including some non-Asian traders based in the region).

Let us first briefly describe the nature of trade of the Indian Ocean. First, it changed from traditional commodity flows to the more 'industrialization-driven trade', that is, it increasingly included the exports of Bombay cotton cloth and other manufactured goods to other parts of Asia and imports of primary products such as rice and sugar from there for urban and rural consumption, arising from a marginal rise in the purchasing power of local population (Sugihara 1996, Chap. 6).

Second, over 30 million people migrated from India from 1834 to 1930, mainly to Ceylon, Burma and Malaya to seek employment in plantations and mines and in commercial agriculture. There was also a long-distance migration within India to work for plantations and mines. Most of these people stayed in host locations from a few months to three years, and returned home. Their income benefitted the home village, sometimes resulting in the improvement of the farmers' status through the purchase of cattle or land (Yanagisawa 1996). A large amount of intra-Asian trade in this period is related to such temporary migration, consisting of food and other necessities the migrants used. Indian merchant networks (and sometimes moneylenders as well) followed the migration. Indian migrants were also seen in East Africa, South Africa and the Caribbean, but an overwhelming proportion of them moved within the British Empire. Migration to regions of recent settlement (such as Canada, Australia and New Zealand) where high wages were on offer was extremely limited (Sugihara 1996, Chap. 9, 1999).

Third, activities of merchant networks based in India expanded to Southeast and East Asia. With the opening of ports to foreign trade in East Asia, Sassoons, for example, extended their networks to China and Japan, to deal with opium and other Asian produce. Given the significance of India's cotton yarn in the 1870s to the 1890s, India clearly acted as an exporter of manufactured goods to East Asia at this stage. However, Indian merchant networks soon faced a competition from Chinese networks. Also, with the more successful industrialization of Japan, India-based merchants increasingly handled imports of Japanese manufactured goods and exports of primary products. Japan's labour-intensive industries were competitive in the relatively cheap range of cotton textiles and sundries, and penetrated into diverse consumer markets of the Indian Ocean. Japanese goods were often interpreted in local cultural contexts (for example, Japanese matches were sold in Chinese or Indian labels), and in some areas import substitution of Japanese manufactured goods took place (Sugihara 1996, Chaps. 1 and 2; Oishi 2015).

The Indian Ocean trade as an arena possessed a high level of merchant abilities of organizing trade and production. Merchant networks did not necessarily bring major innovation in production, but were capable of organizing production networks and easing local resource constraints. Thus they connected cotton producing areas to modern spinning to hand-weaving, and created commodity chains. They also created networks of grain trade, easing local food shortages and enabling peasants to specialize in commercial production. In addition to Hindu and Muslim people, Parsis, a Zoroastrian community, and Jewish merchants originally from Baghdad were among those who exploited cultural and ecological diversities in their own ways. Their presence reinforced the diverse nature of Indian Ocean trade, and helped make changes in commodity production and consumption compatible with religious and linguistic characteristics.

To put this into the longer term perspective, early modern South Asia was at the center of a large regional trading world (Chaudhuri 1985). The South Asian path of economic development was capable of coexisting with long-distance trade, a quality absent in the European path of economic development which pursued its own long-distance trade and territorial expansion, and in the East Asian path which severely restricted it. The Indian Ocean was the only large trading area that embraced regional and global commodity flows in this period. The British rulers took advantage of this quality for the economic integration of both the subcontinent and the Indian Ocean.

1.3.4 The Wider Contexts

Figure 1.6 also charts East Asian countries and ports to show the relative significance of Intra-Asian trade in 1910. As indicated above, the numbers refer to the proportion of exports to Asia and Sub-Saharan Africa to the total amount of exports. At this point the bulk of trade for East Asian ports was with East Asian and Southeast Asian ports, with some crucial links with Indian ports.

We have already referred to intra-Asian cotton trade in relation to labour-intensive industrialization in Sect. 1.2. In addition, Japan imported rice and sugar from Southeast Asia before Korea and Taiwan under Japanese rule became providers of these items. By the interwar period the Chinese position shifted from an importer of cotton yarn from India and Japan to exporters of a small amount of cotton cloth to Southeast Asia, reflecting import-substitution industrialization. Perhaps more important was a large amount of remittances of overseas Chinese from Southeast Asia. Between 1891 and 1938 at least 14 million people migrated to Southeast Asia, mostly for a short period. Unlike Indian counterparts, it was relatively easy to move from labourers to merchants, and within merchant communities from small shop keepers to wholesalers to foreign traders. Dialect-based groups constituted powerful migration networks across Southern China and Southeast Asia, to freely move labourers around, often via Hong Kong and Singapore (Sugihara 2005b).

Hong Kong and Singapore also played as a hub of intra-Asian trade, linking it to both long-distance trade and intra-Southeast-Asian trade. Three chapters of this volume discuss aspects of the path dependency of Southeast Asia as a pivotal region of Asia's trade. It not only acted as a region of active trading at all levels, but played a vital role in linking economies surrounding the Indian Ocean and countries under the tributary trade system in East Asia. In early modern Asia, China and India fed the bulk of population, while first serious European contacts with East Asia were likely to be made in or through Southeast Asia. In Chap. 3 Shimada outlines Southeast Asia's long-term path of economic development, and argues for the fundamental importance of intra-Asian trade in shaping it. In Chap. 4 Ota captures the persistence and development of 'China-oriented trade' from the eighteenth to the nineteenth century, and describes the changing relationships between trade and the state. Commerce was often as important as production for state formation. At one point, part of the state functions was performed by commercial groups and their military wings. Examination of the distinct trajectory of trade-sensitive regional governance goes a long way towards explaining how it was possible for agriculturally fragile and environmentally and politically unstable parts of maritime Asia to handle an intra-regional trade of this magnitude. In Chap. 5 Kobayashi describes the growth of Singapore by examining the period from the early nineteenth to the early twentieth century, and locates it in the context of the region's path of economic development. The Western impact, colonialism and globalization did not destroy the long-term path. Development of Singapore as a trading and information hub shows that an originally colonial port city exhibited an extraordinary capacity to embrace environmental, technological and institutional diversities within the region.

By the end of the nineteenth century Southeast Asia's imports of Indian textiles became small, and gradually shifted towards a higher value added range. By contrast exports of lower value added range of Indian cloth to East Africa remained important, and competed with European textiles to some extent. In other words, intra-regional trade sought complementarity with long-distance trade, and expanded its geographical scope by connecting to new markets on the one hand, and by upgrading the range of manufactured goods on the other.

Finally, intra-East-Asian trade grew very fast after World War I, mainly as a result of the growth of trade of Korea and Taiwan with Japan. By the late 1930s intra-yen-bloc trade numerically dominated intra-Asian trade. The composition of this trade also changed to include exports of machinery, reflecting industrialization in Korea (Hori 2009). While these developments are important for the economic development of Korea and Taiwan under colonial rule, their trade was severely confined to trade with Japan. The Japanese strategy for trade expansion in Asia increasingly sought autarchy, ignoring the position of Asia in world trade. For example, the bulk of rubber exports from Malaya to the United States and Europe could not possibly have been absorbed within the imagined Japanese 'co-prosperity sphere'. Neither would Japan have survived without the imports of oil and minerals, as well as raw cotton, from outside the Japanese sphere of influence. In these respects the mechanism of pre-war intra-Asian trade was destroyed as a result of Japanese aggression. A post-war order was built on the new trend of decolonization and the Cold War divide, as well as the experiences of the war-time controlled economy.

1.4 Paths to Industrialization

1.4.1 Regional Industrialization

The previous section addressed the question of why the growth of intra-Asian trade was important for the emergence of the international division of labour, including labour-intensive industrialization. To recapture, the world economy in the long nineteenth century was not entirely generated by the dynamics of Atlantic economy, nor was it 'bipolarised' by the development of the 'enclave economies'. Looking at the period from 1820 to 1950 as a whole, the intra-regional trading sphere of Asia showed a common tendency to expand by commercializing its agriculture and reorganizing its traditional industries, and by linking modern manufacturing to this expansion, which resulted in the evolution of the system comprising the division of labour between agriculture and industry within the region. The period saw that Western powers (and regions of recent settlement) and Asia (and the tropical regions to which Asian workers emigrated) simultaneously developed high-wage and low-wage economies (see Lewis 1978: especially 194–224 for a similar formulation; for criticism see Sugihara 2013: 21, 22, 27). The former used more resources, while the latter fed more people. Uneven allocation of resources underpinned two different paths to industrialization. Together, they fuelled and sustained the expansion of the world economy.

During the interwar period labour-intensive industrialization was more systematically extended from Japan to China and Korea, with state and colonial reinforcement, and the 'flying geese pattern of economic development' (Akamatsu 1962) emerged between Japan and China (see Abe 2005). By 1938 intra-Asian trade, by then dominated by the Yen bloc, was the second largest area of intra-regional trade, next to intra-European trade, consisting of 9% of world trade at the level of recorded statistics.

After a heavy intervention of the emergence, development and abrupt collapse of the Yen bloc in the 1930s and the first half of the 1940s, intra-Asian trade recovered fast among a smaller number of countries. By 1950, India, China, many Southeast Asian countries, and North Korea withdrew from the regime of free trade, while the countries along the western Pacific coast (Japan, South Korea, Taiwan, Hong Kong and Malaya-Singapore among others) were integrated into the U.S.-led world economy.

Table 1.1 summarizes the growth of Asia's trade and intra-Asian trade in relation to world trade. In the early post-war period, the share of the U.S. (and other Western countries) in Asia's trade was large, and its influence was dominant. However, the U.S. share rapidly declined, and was replaced by the growth of regionally-driven trade. In 1965 the share of ten major Asian countries in world exports was 14%, but this share increased to 23% in 2000, and to 31% in 2015. More important, the share of intra-Asian trade in Asia ten's exports increased from 35% in 1965 to 51% in 2000, and to 70% in 2015, a figure comparable to intra-E.U. trade.

The post-war diffusion of industrialization, beginning in Japan and spreading to other Asian countries, followed the same interactive path between intra-regional trade and industrialization as in the prewar years, first among a small number of countries under the regime of free trade, and gradually embracing others. For example, think of the 'Asian textile complex' in the 1970s, in which Japan produced rayon yarn, Taiwan wove rayon cloth, and Hong Kong made the cloth into an apparel and exported the apparel to the United States (Arpan et al. 1984: 112–7, 136–49, 159). New intermediate goods included cheap plastics, man-made fibres, machine parts, and eventually IC chips. As in the pre-war period, we do not see such a dynamic relationship between regions in Africa, Middle East or Latin America. South Africa and Brazil proceeded with industrialization without accompanying regional integration. It is only in Asia that economic nationalism has embraced regional integration.

Generally speaking, therefore, the labour-intensive path of economic development was suited to Asia's factor endowment in relation to the rest of the world. In practice, each industrialization was country-specific (or rather the modern nation state was often created to realize industrialization and modernization). This volume offers three chapters on industrialization experiences of Japan, China and India.

The most obvious country that benefitted from both transfer of Western technology and institutions, and availability of a very large market for cheap manufactured goods in Asia was Japan. In Chap. 6 Tanimoto discusses the nature of Japan's pre-war industrialization, in which to locate labour-intensive industrialization, with special

Table 1.1 Growth of intra-Asian trade, 1950–2014 (in billion US dollars)

	(1) World exports total	(2) Asia exports total	(3) Intra-Asian trade total	(3)/(2)%
1950	58.0 (100.0)	10.7 (18.4)	2.9 (5.0)	27.1
1955	93.9 (100.0)	13.4 (14.3)	4.0 (4.3)	29.9
1960	128.9 (100.0)	18.3 (14.2)	5.9 (4.6)	32.2
1965	188.2 (100.0)	25.7 (13.7)	9.1 (4.8)	35.4
1970	320.7 (100.0)	44.4 (13.8)	15.6 (4.9)	35.1
1975	887.4 (100.0)	143.4 (16.2)	49.8 (5.6)	34.7
1980	2018.1 (100.0)	332.6 (16.5)	135.9 (6.7)	40.9
1985	1987.0 (100.0)	424.2 (21.3)	167.7 (8.4)	39.5
1990	3601.2 (100.0)	805.4 (22.4)	357.3 (9.9)	44.4
1995	5325.1 (100.0)	1460.6 (27.4)	764.8 (14.4)	52.4
2000	6385.6 (100.0)	1456.8 (22.8)	738.9 (11.6)	50.7
2005	10369.0 (100.0)	2285.5 (22.0)	1330.0 (12.8)	58.2
2010	14937.3 (100.0)	4495.3 (30.1)	3073.9 (20.6)	68.4
2014	18442.9 (100.0)	5603.2 (30.4)	3905.9 (21.2)	69.7

Sources and Notes Takanaka (2000). For figure from 2000 onwards, IMF, Direction of Trade Statistics Yearbook. The former work is based on UN commodity trade statistics, which is slightly wider in the scope of coverage than the IMF data, but the differences are small. Intra-Asian trade total refers to the value of exports from ten Asian countries (Japan, four NIEs, four ASEAN countries and China) and their imports from the smaller Asian countries (adjusted by FOB-CIF conversion)

reference to urban small-scale manufacturing industry. While the bulk of cotton textiles and sundries were indeed exported to Asia, the examples Tanimoto offers here include the growth of production of 'new' commodities, such as toys, that were mainly exported to Europe and the United States. He further links this development to the emergence of yet another generation of small-scale manufacturing in the post-war period. Tanimoto's account is an important reminder of the potential of labour-intensive industries and their contributions to global industrialization.

Figure 1.7 shows that Japan adopted a policy of selective protectionism, that is, setting up tariff barriers only against imports directly competing with the domestic industry attempting import-substitution but pursuing the benefit of free trade, as a result of which her overall tariff rate stayed relatively low, while China and India raised tariff rates during the interwar period, partly for revenue purposes but also to more comprehensively protect domestic industries. Japan's dependence for the imports of raw materials was much greater than that of the other two countries.

In Chap. 7 Kubo discusses the historical processes of China's industrialization with reference to different types of states and economic policies in the twentieth century. Originally integrated into the international economy from the 1840s, mainly as exporters of tea, raw silk and other primary products, China eventually established a modern state in the 1920s and the 1930s, capable of demanding tariff autonomy

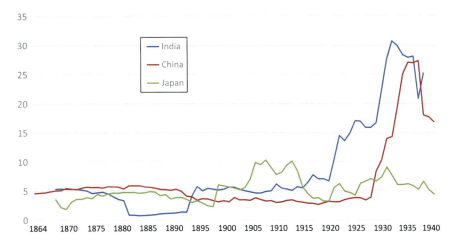

Fig. 1.7 Import tariff rates in India, China and Japan, 1864–1940. *Notes and Sources* India: Sugihara (2002, 30–31), China: Hsiao (1974, 22–24, 132–33), Japan: Okurasho (1948). Rates refer to the share of total import revenue divided by total value of imports. The Japanese data exclude colonial imports after 1919

and negotiating the currency reform under the Nationalist government. The selective tariff protection adopted in this period can be interpreted as an import-substitution industrialization strategy under the regime of free trade (Kubo 2005). However, Kubo then turns to the various regimes emerging under the war-time conditions, in which he skillfully describes the economic policies of Manchuria, the Nationalist government, the communist regime etc., and their changing relationships. He emphasizes that elements of 'planned economy' were variously experimented in this period, which formed the basis for the economic policy of communist China during the Mao period. For Kubo, industrialization of China was best characterized as a parallel development of capital-intensive and labour-intensive industries. The nature of the state in the planning economy period is distinct in the sense that it aimed at the strengthening of political and economic power of the country rather than following the signals of comparative advantage of each industry in international market place. Even so, after the policy reform China was able to take advantage of its comparative advantage to export labour-intensive products in massive quantities. There are similarities and a degree of continuities between the pre-war path and post-reform path (see Pomeranz 2013).

Although the first modern cotton industry in Asia took root in Bombay in the 1850s, labour-intensive industrialization was less successful in colonial India than in Japan and perhaps China. In Chap. 8 Nomura compares factor endowments of labour and capital between India and Japan, to show that labour abundant and capital scarce conditions, which prompted Japan to proceed with labour-intensive industrialization, were not present in India as clearly as in Japan. The laissez-faire economic policy, including free trade, is not in themselves a sufficient condition for stagnant industrialization, although it may have affected the potentiality of industrialization through the fiscal stringency of the British government of India, leading to the lack of encouragement of education, for example. It also argues that other factors such as the slow technological transfer arising from the nature of Indian organization and management must be taken into account.

In independent India, import-substitution industrialization strategy made it difficult to pursue labour-intensive industrialization, in spite of the fact that it had long historical roots (Roy 2005, Chap. 6). There was the heritage of the nationalist movement, which advocated the protection and development of traditional cottage industries, including economically inefficient sectors like khadi and handloom segments. Partly inheriting the Gandhian tradition and partly in a more explicit effort to create employment, these sectors had been isolated from international competition. Meanwhile, the government protected the large-scale modern cotton textile industry, which in turn provided the traditional weaving industries with cheap machine-made yarn. Labour in the organized sector was legally protected, which made it difficult for any factory to lay off its workers. Furthermore, because of the virtual prohibition of the imports of textile machinery and the installation of new machinery in the factory, there was little chance of raising productivity or improving the quality of yarn. As a result, the Indian cotton textile industry went through a long period of isolation from the rapid technological advance in Asian countries, led by Japan. More generally, the ideology for the political and economic autonomy remained powerful in India.

In India several attempts were made to liberalize the economy after 1965 without much success. The policy shift of 1991 realized a degree of liberalization of trade and capital flows, and was a step towards deregulation, but it did not represent a major ideological change in economic policy among the Indian elites. In particular, the rate of increase in the expenditure on education and welfare for the ordinary people, relative to that for elites, has been slow. Yet a high level of capability based on primary and secondary education (the literacy rate remains a major problem) and hygiene (especially low infant mortality) is clearly a necessary, though not sufficient, condition for economic development. In this respect the Chinese achievement during the pre-reform period (1949–1979) was far more impressive (Dreze and Sen 1995, 1997).

Nevertheless, the economic reforms of 1991 sharply corrected India's bias towards strong economic ties with the Soviet Union and other socialist countries. Export growth in the 1990s mainly came from labour-intensive industrial goods, including woven cloth, knitwear, garments, leather, machine components and software. Primarily through exports of textiles and apparel, India became progressively integrated into the international economy during the 1990s (Sugihara 2001). By 2000 India was trading more with the Asia-Pacific countries than with Western Europe, the Middle East, the former socialist countries and Africa combined.

1.4.2 The Resource Nexus

From the perspective of spatial resource allocation, particularly important was the expansion of the scope of competitive modern industries in Japan: Prewar industrialization was largely based on light industries (for textiles and sundries) and was labour-intensive, while the post-war path included heavy and chemical industries (for steel, machinery and petrochemical products), which were usually more capital- and resource-intensive. Imports of fossil fuels, including oil, and raw materials from all over the world became essential to the economic growth of Asia. Thus, during the period of high-speed growth, geography, human habitat and resource use were redefined and relocated to accommodate them. A number of industrial complex were created, typically along the Pacific coast, with transport connections to major urban centers. The spatial allocation of human and natural resources was now driven by the need to secure access to industrial imports, as well as by the availability of land, capital and labour. A large proportion of population moved to cities, or a large part of rural areas became administratively 'urban', to develop the mass domestic consumer market. In prewar Japan rural industrialization remained important, especially in labour-intensive industries, while agriculture provided industry with labour force, purchasing power and food and raw materials. Traditional considerations for industrial locations included local employment with relatively low wages (e.g. female by employment in the peasant household economy), and supply of water, food and energy (both biomass and electricity). All of these functions had to be retained under the industrial-complex-driven national land development policy, and the value of natural resources (e.g. land, forest, water) reassessed under the new light, not least because sections of new industries needed to use lots of water, while others needed clean air. In fact most heavy and chemical industries, which depended on the imports of raw materials and energy for their production, simultaneously needed some non-tradable resources (e.g. land and water), competing for their procurement with traditional users.

Urbanization also changed the traditional resource endowment regime, which dominated the pre-fossil-fuel economy. This first happened in Japan (In 1945 the rate of urbanization in Japan and other parts of Asia was significantly lower than in industrial countries in the West. See Sugihara 2003, 111–2). Urban space not only combined basic livelihood needs such as water, food and electricity with employment in manufacturing, distribution and services, but added new demands such as education, health and leisure, as well as the urban transportation system. The 'civil' living space, that is, free from air pollution and congestion, became a target for local government and citizens movement. Capital- and resource-intensive industries began to be pushed out from urban and suburban landscapes, and were increasingly relocated to rural areas (Kobori 2017). Tokyo grew into the first mega-city, while Osaka and other major cities followed. The rate of growth of cities was very rapid. The critical aspects of this development lay in the perceived combination of industrial development and the securement of civil and environmentally acceptable living space through the negotiation between national land development plans, local government initiatives and the citizens movement. The general direction of the political process was to enable heavy and chemical industrialization to take root, without entirely losing rural landscapes and civil living spaces in urban settings.

Overall, however, the driving force behind the reorganization of economy and ecology was 'developmentalism' behind the central government policy. The concurrent growth of cities and the industrial complex created an 'urban-industrial nexus' where various tradable and non-tradable resources were identified as a set of 'factor endowments' necessary for creating an international 'comparative advantage' of manufacturing industry. Labour-intensive manufacturing in urban areas was embedded in the newly created 'resource nexus', with intensive use of space, and retained its strength, along with capital- and resource-intensive industries in the industrial complex (see Sugihara 2019a).

1.4.3 Structural Transformation in Southeast Asia

Southeast Asia as a region experienced perhaps the fastest structural transformation in global history from the export economies of primary products to industrialized countries. In 1950 four countries of Southeast Asia (Indonesia, Philippines, Malaysia and Thailand; hereafter ASEAN 4) and Singapore (territorial changes were adjusted wherever possible) were all exporters of primary products *par excellence*. By the end of the twentieth century they became exporters of labour-intensive manufactured goods and importers of capital-intensive manufactured goods. Following the lead of South Korea and Taiwan, a rapid shift took place in the 1970s and the 1980s. Figures 1.8 and 1.9 suggest a fundamental change in the five countries' position in the international economy.

There are at least three reasons why Southeast Asia managed to transform itself so quickly. First, the region successively found the market for their products in the postwar period, first by exporting primary products to the expanding American market, then by participating in the commodity chain of labour-intensive manufactured goods initiated by Japanese, American and other foreign companies, and finally exporting competitive labour-intensive manufactured goods by themselves or in corporation with multinational companies. After the second half of the 1960s, it was able to benefit from foreign investment and, through it, the transfer of technological and managerial knowledge for industrial development. Although the region suffered many wars and conflicts, and many other Southeast Asian countries were left out from this dynamics for a long time, ASEAN slowly expanded its membership and steadily increased its economic influences.

Second, against the background of population growth, there was a growth of labour-intensive industries, which absorbed labour. In 1974 Indonesia, for example, had manufacturing employment of around four million, mostly in very small establishments in rural areas engaging in food processing and other traditional industries (van der Eng 2013). This was too big a sector for the capital-intensive manufacturing sector to absorb. In 1970 Harry Oshima argued for a systematic effort to make these

1 Multiple Paths to Industrialization: A Global Context …

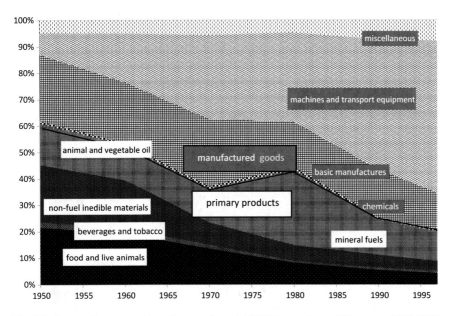

Fig. 1.8 Commodity composition of exports from 4 ASEAN countries and Singapore, 1950–1997. *Source* Takanaka (2000)

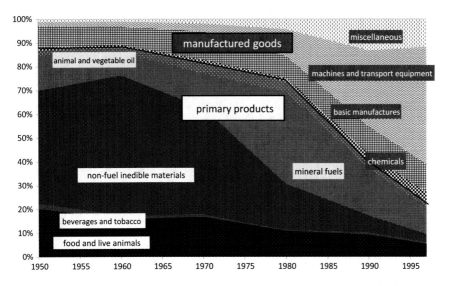

Fig. 1.9 Commodity composition of imports to 4 ASEAN countries and Singapore, 1950–1997. *Source* As per Fig. 1.8

small industries internationally competitive, with a fuller and the more efficient use of labour, training of skilled labour, better marketing and the more detailed government support for information gathering and export promotion (Oshima 1970). This was a strategy close to the East Asian (especially Japanese) path, signalling a clear departure from the heavy industry orientation the earlier orthodoxy had advocated. On the one hand, labour, both rural and urban, was absorbed into sweat shops and modern factories as unskilled labour, with low wages and harsh working conditions. The society became unequal in many ways. At the same time, ethnic and institutional barriers to social mobility became less serious, and increasingly large numbers of primary and secondary school graduates with better health became available. And the quality of workforce gradually improved. This was a major reason why the pace of industrialization of ASEAN 4 accelerated by the 1980s, overtaking early industrializers such as India.

Third, it was on this basis that export-oriented industrialization strategy diffused rapidly. In many respects the strategy looked 'shallow'; It was externally induced (often with export processing zones and other government measures to promote investment of multinational companies); The sequential upgrading of an industrial structure, typically seen in earlier industrializations from light industry to heavy industry with all 'basic' industries and complicated linkages, was missing; The land reform was incomplete, and rural inequality remained a macroeconomic issue. But it was not a shallow kind of industrialization, in the sense that it was supported by competitive labour (cheap labour able to produce goods in a competitive market). It was natural that countries of NIEs and ASEAN 4 with smaller population were keener on export-orientation than the United States or Japan (both with a low ratio of trade to GDP). The growth of a relatively homogenous market for cheap, labour-intensive manufactured goods across East and Southeast Asia, as well as the lower end of the American market, made a regional industrialization possible.

The core ideology behind this process was 'developmentalism' which was created to pool all the resources for economic development (Suehiro 1998). It advocated both regional and international economic cooperation through trade, capital flows and technological transfer in strongest terms. Part of this idea came from Japan and diffused to NIEs to ASEAN countries, and, helped by Australians, took the form of 'open nationalism' (Garnout and Drysdale 1994). It argued for a free trade within the region, but without discriminating against outsiders. Southeast Asia played a key role in the diffusion of this principle. And its economic success, linking intra-Asian dynamism to world trade, was eventually to help China and India to change course. Developmentalism was distinct from both the principle of unfettered free trade without national and regional considerations, and socialism with emphasis on planning and autonomy. Although its practice suffered from authoritarian rule and the Cold War divide, it was committed to raising living standards for the ordinary people, and survived the criticisms of liberal democracy and 'market fundamentalism'. Developmentalism was not only the guiding principle of the developmental state. It largely created a regional order.

1.5 Paths to the Emerging State

1.5.1 A Summary

The notions of multiple development paths and the emerging state in the periphery do not come directly from the Eurocentric perspective of the diffusion of industrialization or civilizing missions of imperialism. The terms adopted here do not assume a country-based linear stage theory, in which a nation such as England and Japan would make a transition from feudalism to capitalism or from pre-industrial to an industrial nation. In Asia and Africa the development path of each country was often non-linear, with plenty of disturbances from colonialism, famines and epidemics and environmental degradations, and its pace was largely determined by their own socio-cultural preferences (or reservations) for economic development. While all countries have been affected by the forces of global industrialization and economic development in one way or another, we note that the path each country followed was diverse, non-linear and more locally and regionally rooted than standard economic history and development economics had allowed for.

This chapter mainly discussed the trade and industrialization components of this view, largely leaving the issues relating to agriculture to Chap. 2. Its aim was to identify relevant historical contexts, that is, the 'initial conditions' and internal and external forces which governed the path, and to understand what current developing countries with low-income economies require for their transition to the emerging state. We suggested that local and regional trade fed employment in agriculture and industry, hence population-carrying capacity, by mitigating local resource constraints. Given the nature of constraints, long-distance trade is not always a solution. We end our discussion with a brief observation on Sub-Saharan Africa, to suggest that the emerging state should implement a development plan to promote local and intra-regional trade, to more systematically link resource exports to an increase of agricultural and industrial production and employment.

1.5.2 Intra-regional Trade of Sub-Saharan Africa

Historically, Sub-Saharan Africa actively engaged with local, regional and long distance (intercontinental) trade. After the decline of slave trade and the rise of 'legitimate commerce' in the nineteenth century, the region began to export primary products to Europe and other places. With the integration of local and regional economies into world trade, the former responded to the trade opportunities created within the region.

However, at the level recorded as foreign trade statistics, intra-regional trade declined sharply after the First World War, never to be recovered till the end of the twentieth century.

Table 1.2 shows the growth of trade and the proportion of intra-regional trade in Sub-Saharan Africa for a period similar to Table 1.1.[3] The proportion of Sub-Saharan Africa in world trade has always been small, and most of exports went outside the region, especially to advanced industrial countries. Europe remained the major trading partner throughout the second half of the twentieth century. More important, Sub-Saharan Africa as a whole has always acted as a primary producer exchanging the regional natural resources for manufactured goods and services, in spite of industrialization of some countries such as South Africa. Main export commodities changed over time, but the tendency for each country to rely on a single commodity such as oil persisted. The export diversification index has not improved much. Each economy remained a satellite linked to the metropolis.

A closer look at the Table suggests that the proportion of intra-regional trade began with 11% in 1950, and then went down because Rhodesia's trade statistics became unavailable (trade actually collapsed too), but the statistical collection was restored since around 1965, and the coverage of countries were more or less stabilized since. The Table clearly shows a surge of the amount of intra-regional trade, but the more important comparative observation is that the level of intra-regional trade had

Table 1.2 The growth of intra-regional trade in Sub-Saharan Africa, 1950–2015 (in billion US dollars)

	(1) World trade total	Number of countries	(2) Sub-Saharan Africa's (SSA) exports to the world	(3) SSA exports to SSA	(3)/(2)
1950	47.63 (100.00)	13	2.16 (4.53)	0.24 (0.50)	11.12
1955	82.41 (100.00)	13	2.69 (3.27)	0.10 (0.12)	3.75
1960	105.98 (100.00)	24	3.14 (2.97)	0.12 (0.11)	3.75
1965	159.92 (100.00)	36	6.86 (4.29)	0.64 (0.40)	9.38
1970	281.56 (100.00)	43	10.24 (3.64)	0.97 (0.34)	9.44
1975	771.15 (100.00)	42	26.15 (3.39)	1.56 (0.20)	5.98
1980	1,830.87 (100.00)	43	43.73 (2.39)	2.83 (0.15)	6.47
1985	1,872.67 (100.00)	44	47.94 (2.56)	2.60 (0.14)	5.42
1990	3,375.34 (100.00)	44	61.68 (1.83)	4.82 (0.14)	7.82
1995	5,070.79 (100.00)	44	68.56 (1.35)	8.11 (0.16)	11.83
2000	6,412.83 (100.00)	45	92.09 (1.44)	12.07 (0.19)	13.10
2005	10,398.42 (100.00)	45	184.15 (1.77)	23.68 (0.23)	12.86
2010	15,133.15 (100.00)	45	331.45 (2.19)	60.19 (0.40)	18.16
2015	16,386.42 (100.00)	46	295.29 (1.80)	63.60 (0.39)	21.54

Source IMF, IMF Data, Access to Macroeconomic and Financial Data, Direction of Trade Statistics http://data.imf.org/?sk=9D6028D4-F14A-464C-A2F2-59B2CD424B85&sId=1409151240976

---

[3]The sources of the two tables, both originally from IMF, slightly differ, and so does the amount of world trade, but they do not affect main observations here.

remained low. The crucial issue is not so much import-substitution of a single country as its lack on a regional scale.

Figures 1.10 and 1.11 show the geographical distribution of Sub-Saharan Africa's exports and imports respectively from 1990 to 2017. Between 2000 and 2105 the main trading partners changed from Europe and the United State to emerging and developing countries, including China and India. But there was little change in the components of exports, which were concentrated on a few commodities, especially oil and mineral resources, without much processing before exports. Imports, on the other hand, consisted of goods for infrastructure building and consumer goods. There was little progress on the exports of labour-intensive manufactured goods and processed food-stuffs from the region.

In fact, *African Economic Outlook* argues, there is a huge potential for the development of labour-intensive manufacturing exports within the region. 'Trade between African countries has the greatest potential for building sustainable economic development' (AfDB/OECD/UNDP 2017, 82). At the moment, however, most of the labour-intensive manufactured goods and processed food-stuffs which could be provided within the region are imported from emerging economies, especially from China and other Asian countries. In fact, amongst the surge of the proportion of intra-African trade in total African exports between 2005 and 2015, the proportion of intra-African trade in manufactured goods in total African manufacturing exports declined from 18 to 15% (ibid, 83–84. Figures refer to Africa rather than Sub-Saharan Africa). 'Transportation and communication infrastructure for intra-African trade is less developed than those that connect Africa to the rest of the world. This under-

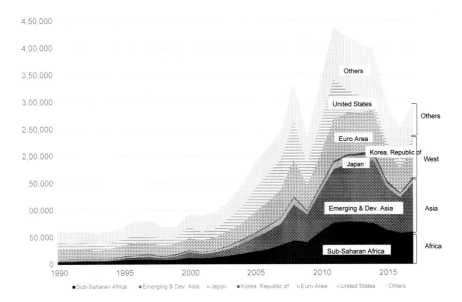

Fig. 1.10 Geographical composition of exports from Sub-Saharan Africa, 1990–2017. *Source* As per Table 1.2

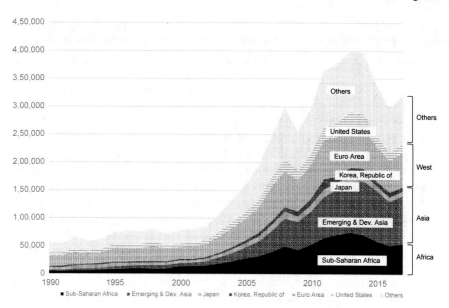

Fig. 1.11 Geographical composition of imports from Sub-Saharan Africa, 1990-2017. *Source* As per Table 1.2

mines the impacts of regional integration and development' (ibid. 89). In any case, 'Africa's imports of heavy machinery and transport equipment are among the lowest in the world' (ibid. 80). 'Light manufacturing could help Africa reduce its imports from outside the continent and increase intra-African trade with countries that have agricultural production and processing capacity' (ibid, 78).

Chapter 9 endorses the view that much of Africa's growth of GDP and employment in the recent period came from the service sector and improved agricultural productivity (reflecting the declining share of agricultural employment), and argues the need for the development of the labour-intensive sector and industrial policy to effect it. Perhaps we should go back to the pre-war intra-Asian trade to find a parallel situation in Southeast Asia, where a combination of merchant networks, trading and information hubs and trade-sensitive regional governance offered critical 'initial conditions' for structural transformation.

References

Abe, T. (2005). The Chinese market for Japanese cotton textile goods, 1914–30. In K. Sugihara (Ed.), *Japan, China and the growth of the Asian International Economy, 1850–1949* (pp. 49–100). Oxford: Oxford University Press.

AfDB/OECD/UNDP. (2017). Trade policies and regional integration in Africa. In *African Economic Outlook 2017: Entrepreneurship and Industrialisation*. Paris: OECD Publishing.

Akamatsu, K. (1962). A historical pattern of economic growth in developing countries. *Developing Economies*, Preliminary Issue, 3–25.
Allen, R. C. (2005). *Farm to factory: A reinterpretation of the Soviet Industrial Revolution*. Princeton: Princeton University Press.
Arpan, J. S., Barry, M., & Van Tho, T. (1984). The textile complex in the Asia-Pacific region: The patterns and textures of competition and the shape of things to come. *Research in International Business and Finance, 4-B,* 101–164.
Austin, G. (2013). Labour-intensive industrialization and global economic development: Reflections. In G. Austin & K. Sugihara (Eds.), *Labour-intensive industrialization in global history* (pp. 280–302). London: Routledge.
Bagchi, A. K. (1976). Deindustrialization in India in the nineteenth century: Some theoretical implications. *Journal of Development Studies, 12*(2), 135–164.
Bairoch, P. (1982). International industrialization levels from 1750 to 1980. *Journal of Economic History, 11*(2), 269–333.
Bombay Presidency Report of the Commerce of Bombay, Bombay.
Bombay Trade and Navigation Annual Statements, Bombay.
Chaudhuri, K. N. (1985). *Trade and civilisation in the Indian Ocean: An economic history from the rise of Islam to 1750*. Cambridge: Cambridge University Press.
Dreze, J., & Sen, A. (1995). *India: Economic development and social opportunity*. Delhi: Oxford University Press.
Dreze, J., & Sen, A. (1997). *Indian development: Selected regional perspectives*. Delhi: Oxford University Press.
Engerman, S. L., & Sokoloff, K. L. (2011). *Economic development in the Americas since 1500: Endowments and institutions*. Cambridge: Cambridge University Press.
Garnout, R., & Drysdale, P. (1994). Asia Pacific regionalism: The issues. In R. Garnout & P. Drysdale (Eds.), *Asia Pacific regionalism: Readings in international economic relations* (pp. 1–7). Pymble, Australia: Harper Educational.
Gerschenkron, A. (1962). *Economic backwardness in historical perspective: A book of essays*. Cambridge, MA: Belknap Press of Harvard University Press.
Hori, K. (2009). *Higashi-Ajia Shihonshugishi-ron 1* (Treatise on the history of East Asian Capitalism, Part 1). Kyoto: Mienruva Shobo.
Hsiao, L. (1974). *China's foreign trade statistics, 1864–1949*. Cambridge, MA: Harvard University Press.
India Annual Rail- and River-borne Trade Returns, 1888/89–1892/93, Calcutta.
International Monetary Fund (IMF) (various years), *Direction of Trade Statistics Yearbook*.
International Monetary Fund (IMF), Direction of Trade Statistics. http://data.imf.org/?sk=9D6028D4-F14A-464C-A2F2-59B2CD424B85&sId=1409151240976. Accessed August 24, 2018.
Jones, E. L. (1981). *The European miracle: Environments, economies and geopolitics in the history of Europe and Asia*. Cambridge: Cambridge University Press.
Kobori, S. (2017). Rinkai kaihatsu, kogai taisaku, shizen hogo: Kodo seicho-ki Yokohama no kankyoshi (Seafront development, anti-pollution policy and nature conservation: An environmental history of Yokohama in the period of high-speed growth). In S. Shoji (Ed.), *Sengo Nihon no Kaihatsu to Minshushugi: Chiiki ni Miru Sokoku* (Development and democracy of Japan in the post war era: The conflicts seen from the region) (pp. 71–104). Kyoto: Showado.
Kubo, T. (2005). The tariff policy of the nationalist government, 1926–36: A historical assessment. In K. Sugihara (Ed.), *Japan, China and the growth of the Asian International Economy, 1850–1949* (pp. 145–176). Oxford: Oxford University Press.
Lewis, W. A. (1954). The economic development with unlimited supplies of labour. *Manchester School of Economic and Social Studies, 22*(2), 139–191.
Lewis, W. A. (Ed.). (1970). *Tropical development, 1880–1913: Studies in economic progress*. Evanston: Northwestern University Press.
Lewis, W. A. (1978). *Growth and fluctuations, 1870–1913*. London: George Allen and Unwin.

Maddison, A. (2009). Statistics on world population, GDP and per capita GDP, 1-2008 AD. http://www.ggdc.net/maddison/.

Oishi, T. (2015). Kan-indoyo sekai to indojin shonin, kigyoka no nettowaku: Shokuminchi-ki ni okeru fukugosei, tayosei (The world of Indian Ocean Rim and Indian merchant-entrepreneur networks: Plurality and diversity in the colonial period). In A. Tanabe, K. Sugihara, & K. Wakimura (Eds.), *Shirizu Gendai Indo 1: Tayosei Shakai no Chosen* (Challenges for a diversity-driven society: Contemporary India Series 1) (pp. 169–196). Tokyo: Tokyo Daigaku Shuppankai.

Okurasho Shuzeikyoku [Japanese Ministry of Finance Government Bureau of Taxation]. (1948). *Dai-15-kai Kokkai Kanzei Sankosho* (Reference material on customs tariff for the 15th Parliament). Tokyo: Okurasho.

Oshima, H. (1970). The role of small industries in the acceleration of Asian growth. In Economic Commission for Asia and the Far East (ECAFE), *Small industry bulletin for Asia and the Far East* (Vol. 7, pp. 134–136). New York: U. N.

Oshima, H. (1987). *Economic development in Monsoon Asia: A comparative study*. Tokyo: University of Tokyo Press.

Pomeranz, K. (2000). *The great divergence: China, Europe, and the making of the modern world economy*. Princeton: Princeton University Press.

Pomeranz, K. (2013). Labour-intensive industrialization in the rural Yangzi Delta: Late imperial patterns and their modern fates. In G. Austin & K. Sugihara (Eds.), *Labour-intensive industrialization in global history* (pp. 122–143). London: Routledge.

Report on the Administration of Bengal, 1877/78, Calcutta.

Richards, J. (2003). *The unending frontier: An environmental history of the early modern world*. Berkeley: University of California Press.

Roy, T. (2005). *Rethinking economic change in India: Labour and livelihood*. London: Routledge.

Saul, S. B. (1960). *Studies in British overseas trade, 1870–1914*. Liverpool: Liverpool University Press.

Suehiro, K. (1998). Hatten tojokoku no kaihatsu-shugi (Developmentalism in developing countries). In Tokyo Daigaku Shakai Kagaku Kenkyusho (Ed.), *20-seiki Sekai Shisutemu 4: Kaihatsu-shugi* (The World System of the twentieth century 4: Developmentalism) (pp. 13–46). Tokyo: Tokyo Daigaku Shuppankai.

Sugihara, K. (1996). *Ajia-kan Boeki no Keisei to Kozo* (Patterns and development of intra-Asian trade). Kyoto: Mineruva Shobo.

Sugihara, K. (1999). Kindai sekai shisutemu to ningen no ido (The modern world system and human migration). In *Iwanami Koza Sekai Rekishi 19: Chiiki o Musubu Dainamizumu* (Iwanami lectures of the World History 19: Dynamic forces that connect regions) (pp. 3–64). Tokyo: Iwanamai Shoten.

Sugihara, K. (2001). India and the rise of the Asia-Pacific economy, c. 1947–1997. In N. Kondo (Ed.), *The 'Nation-State' and Transnational Forces in South Asia*. Research project 'Institutions, Networks and Forces of Change in Contemporary South Asia' (pp. 43–67), Tokyo, March 2001, Conference Proceedings.

Sugihara, K. (2002). Indo kindaishi ni okeru enkakuchi boeki to chiiki koeki, 1868-1938-nen (The long-distance trade and regional trade in modern Indian history, 1868–1938). *Toyo Bunka, 82*, 1–46.

Sugihara, K. (2003). The East Asian path of economic development: A long-term perspective. In G. Arrighi, T. Hamashita, & M. Selden (Eds.), *The resurgence of East Asia: 500, 150 and 50 year perspectives* (pp. 78–123). London: Routledge.

Sugihara, K. (2005a). An introduction. In K. Sugihara (Ed.), *Japan, China and the growth of the Asian International Economy, 1850–1949* (pp. 1–19). Oxford: Oxford University Press.

Sugihara, K. (2005b). Patterns of Chinese emigration to Southeast Asia, 1869–1939. In K. Sugihara (Ed.), *Japan, China and the growth of the Asian International Economy, 1850–1949* (pp. 244–274). Oxford: Oxford University Press.

Sugihara, K. (2009). The resurgence of intra-Asian trade, 1800–1850. In G. Riello & T. Roy (Eds.), *How India clothed the world: The world of South Asian textiles* (pp. 1500–1850). Leiden: Brill.

Sugihara, K. (2013). Labour-intensive industrialization in global history: An interpretation of East Asian experiences. In G. Austin & K. Sugihara (Eds.), *Labour-intensive industrialization in global history* (pp. 20–64). London: Routledge.

Sugihara, K. (2015a). Global industrialization: A multipolar perspective. In J. R. McNeill & K. Pomeranz (Eds.), *Cambridge world history. Volume 8: Production, connection and destruction, 1750-Present* (1, pp. 106–35). Cambridge: Cambridge University Press.

Sugihara, K. (2015b). Shokuminchiki ni okeru kokunai shijo no keisei (Formation of a domestic market in the colonial period). In A. Tanabe, K. Sugihara & K. Wakimura (Eds.), *Shirizu Gendai Indo 1: Tayosei Shakai no Chosen* (Challenges for a diversity-driven society: Contemporary India Series 1) (pp. 197–221). Tokyo: Tokyo Daigaku Shuppankai.

Sugihara, K. (2015c). Asia in the growth of world trade: A re-interpretation of the 'long nineteenth century'. In U. Bosma & A. Webster (Eds.), *Commodities, ports and Asian maritime trade c. 1750–1950* (pp. 17–58). Basingstoke: Palgrave Macmillan.

Sugihara, K. (2017). Monsoon Asia, intra-regional trade and fossil-fuel-driven industrialization. In G. Austin (Ed.), *Economic development and environmental history in the anthropocene: Perspectives on Asia and Africa* (pp. 119–144). London: Bloomsbury Academic.

Sugihara. K. (2019a). Varieties of industrialization: An Asian regional perspective. In G. Riello & T. Roy (Eds.), *Global economic history* (pp. 195–214). London: Bloomsbury Academic.

Sugihara, K. (2019b). Guro-baru hisutori no nakano minami ajia (South Asia in global history). In N. Nagasaki (Ed.), *Taikei Minami Ajia-shi 4: Kingendai* (Outline of South Asian history 4: The modern and contemporary period). Tokyo: Yamakawa Shuppansha.

Takanaka, K. (2000). *Higashi-ajia Choki Keizai Tokei 9: Gaikoku Boeki to Keizai Hatten* (Long-term economic statistics of East Asia. Volume 9: Foreign trade and economic development). Tokyo: Keiso Shobo.

van der Eng, P. (2013). Government promotion of labour-intensive industrialization in Indonesia, 1930–1975. In G. Austin & K. Sugihara (Eds.), *Labour-intensive industrialization in global history* (pp. 176–200). London: Routledge.

Yanagisawa, H. (1996). *A century of change: Caste and irrigated lands in Tamilnadu, 1860s–1970s*. New Delhi: Manohar.

Open Access This chapter is licensed under the terms of the Creative Commons Attribution-NonCommercial-NoDerivatives 4.0 International License (http://creativecommons.org/licenses/by-nc-nd/4.0/), which permits any noncommercial use, sharing, distribution and reproduction in any medium or format, as long as you give appropriate credit to the original author(s) and the source, provide a link to the Creative Commons licence and indicate if you modified the licensed material. You do not have permission under this licence to share adapted material derived from this chapter or parts of it.

The images or other third party material in this chapter are included in the chapter's Creative Commons licence, unless indicated otherwise in a credit line to the material. If material is not included in the chapter's Creative Commons licence and your intended use is not permitted by statutory regulation or exceeds the permitted use, you will need to obtain permission directly from the copyright holder.

Chapter 2
Technology Transfer and Agricultural Development: A Comparative Study of Asia and Africa

Keijiro Otsuka

2.1 Introduction

A few centuries ago, Malthus predicted that famine will inevitably take place because, while the population grows exponentially, food production increases only arithmetically. Following the Malthusian argument, the Club of Rome predicted in the early 1970s that famine cannot be avoided in tropical Asia (Meadows et al. 1972).[1] However, serious famine has never taken place in this region for the past half century and, hence, Malthus' prediction may appear questionable. However, by reviewing the history of growth of population and food production, his prediction turns out to be almost correct (Otsuka 2013). What he failed to predict was the technological change induced by population pressure (Hayami and Ruttan 1985), which resulted in the rapid growth of food production, thereby restoring or more than restoring the balance between population and food production. In other words, the fear of Malthusian hardship, or severe food insecurity, begot efforts to overcome it by means of technological changes based on international technology transfer.

Indeed, the Green Revolution for rice as well as wheat, defined as the development and diffusion of high-yielding varieties, took place in tropical Asia in the 1970s and 1980s, when the population pressure on the limited land became severe enough (David and Otsuka 1994). However, the Green Revolution for major grains has failed to hitherto take place in sub-Saharan Africa (SSA), although current population pressure is as severe as in tropical Asia in the 1960s (Otsuka and Larson 2013, 2016). Unless a sufficient food supply is secured, the economy can unlikely evolve from a poor agrarian state to an emerging state with decent development of manufacturing industries and service sectors. Indeed, as agriculture is a dominant industry at the early

---

[1] Tropical Asia refers to Southeast and South Asia.

K. Otsuka (✉)
Graduate School of Economics, Kobe University, Kobe, Hyogo, Japan
e-mail: otsuka@econ.kobe-u.ac.jp

© The Author(s) 2019
K. Otsuka and K. Sugihara (eds.), *Paths to the Emerging State in Asia and Africa*,
Emerging-Economy State and International Policy Studies,
https://doi.org/10.1007/978-981-13-3131-2_2

stages of economic development, its progress is a prerequisite for overall economic development.

The first major issue to be addressed in this chapter is identifying the conditions under which the Green Revolution successfully took place in Asia. For this purpose, I review the historical experiences of the prototype Green Revolutions in rice production in prewar Japan, Taiwan, and Korea, and tropical Asia in the 1970s and 1980s. I find that a major determinant of the Green Revolution was technology transfer. Indeed, Hayami and Godo (2005) argue, among others,[2] that the essence of the Asian Green Revolution in rice was the transfer of intensive rice farming systems from Japan to tropical Asia, which is characterized by the adoption of fertilizer-responsive high-yielding varieties, intensive use of commercial fertilizer, and application of improved management practices. While it is understandable that the transfer of technologies from a temperate zone, such as Japan, to tropical Asia would have been difficult because of the substantial climate differences, it is not easily understandable why it is so difficult to transfer technology from one tropical zone to another (i.e., from tropical Asia to SSA). An exploration into the causes for the failure of the Green Revolution in SSA is the second major issue to be addressed in this chapter.

However, agricultural development alone is not sufficient for the economy to evolve from an agrarian to an emerging state, as there are strong relationships between agricultural development and that of nonfarm sectors (e.g., supply of food and processing materials and labor from agriculture and demand for products and services provided by nonfarm sectors in rural areas). Therefore, to identify the significance of agricultural development, this chapter identified paths to the emerging state based on the analysis in this chapter and the companion studies on agricultural development and policies reported in Chaps. 10–12, as well as the industrial development policies in SSA discussed in Chap. 9.

The organization of this chapter is as follows. While Sect. 2.2 reviews the prototype Green Revolutions in rice farming in prewar Japan, Taiwan, and Korea, Sect. 2.3 assesses the Green Revolution in rice farming in Southeast and South Asia in the 1970s and 1980s. Section 2.4 examines the possibility of a Green Revolution in SSA, focusing on its constraints on this continent. Finally, Sect. 2.5 discusses the role of agricultural development in steering the economy towards an emerging state.

2.2 Prototype Green Revolutions in Prewar Japan, Taiwan, and Korea

There was a race between population growth and expansion of food production during the Meiji era (1868–1912) in Japan, principally because the country is characterized by meagre endowments of cultivable land relative to its population. In fact, the average farm size was merely one hectare. However, as shown in Fig. 2.1, grain

---

[2] Both agricultural economists (e.g., Dalrymple (1986) and Hsieh and Ruttan (1967)) and agricultural scientists (e.g., Tanaka (2012) and Tanaka and Imai (2006)) express similar views.

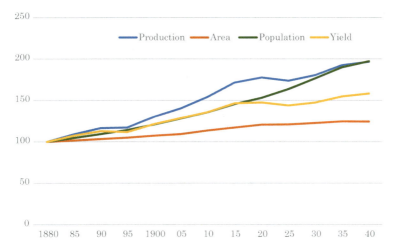

Fig. 2.1 Changes in grain production, cultivation area, population, and grain yield in Prewar Japan (Index: 1880 = 100). *Source* Umemura et al. (1966)

production increased rapidly from 1880 to roughly 1915 due to the sustained increase in grain yield per hectare, although cultivation area increased slowly throughout the prewar period due to the limited availability of unused land. Suddenly, grain production and yield stopped increasing around 1915 and grain production per capita continued to decline thereafter, as population growth surpassed that of food production. Nonetheless, this increasing "food deficiency" did not induce grain yield growth in the subsequent prewar period in Japan. As a result, rice price increased, and the rice riot occurred in 1918, in which people violently attacked rice dealers who were suspected to control rice markets and increase rice prices. Since rice is a so-called wage good or the good on which urban households spend large proportions of their income, increases in its price tend to trigger not only social instability but also increase in wage cost, which is in turn detrimental to the development of industries and other nonfarm sectors.

Grain production and yield increased rapidly in the Meiji era primarily because of the rapidly increasing rice yield (see Fig. 2.2).[3] According to Hayami and Godo (2005, p. 99), "[c]rop varieties similar to those of modern varieties were selected through trial and error by experienced farmers" before and during the Meiji era. While modern varieties (MVs) developed for tropical Asia since the late 1960s are semi-dwarf, possessing short stems, the improved varieties developed in Japan during

---

[3]Note that rice yield is measured as tons of brown rice per hectare in Fig. 2.1. On the other hand, in developing countries, it is measured in terms of tons of paddy rice. Since paddy is roughly 20% heavier than brown rice, rice yield in Japan at the beginning of Meiji era was estimated to be roughly 2.4 tons per hectare in terms of paddy.

Fig. 2.2 Changes in rice yield per hectare in Prewar Japan, Taiwan, and Korea, and Postwar Philippines, Five-Year Moving averages (reproduced from Hayami and Godo 2005, p. 101)

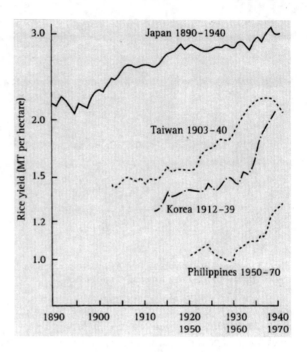

the Meiji period were not necessarily semi-dwarf.[4] Similar to MVs, those improved rice varieties in Japan were resistant against lodging, so that a heavier application of fertilizers leads to higher yield. Such fertilizer-responsive varieties were initially selected in the western region and their diffusion boosted registered yield growth from 1895 to 1910. Such superior varieties in the western region served as parental varieties to developing improved varieties suitable for the ecologies of the eastern region by leading farmers and experiment-station workers. Consequently, yield growth took place five to ten years later in this region. However, once new varieties were completely diffused, yield became stagnant throughout Japan by the mid-1910s.

Facing the risk of high rice prices and drain on scarce foreign exchange by large-scale rice imports, the Japanese government decided to increase rice production and imports from the overseas territories of Korea and Taiwan. Further, the government actively invested in irrigation and water control and in research and extension to develop and diffuse high-yielding Japanese varieties adapted to the local ecologies of Korea and Taiwan and transfer improved agronomic practices (Hayami and Ruttan 1985). As a result, fertilizer-responsive, high-yielding *ponlai* varieties were developed in Taiwan, which were cross-bred between Japonica and Indica rice varieties and also between improved Japonica varieties. Tanaka and Imai state (2006) that the expansion of rice production in Taiwan was made possible by the transfer of

---

[4]However, Dalrymple (1986) points out that the first efforts to develop semi-dwarf rice varieties occurred in Japan in the late 19th century, leading to the development of an improved variety called *Shinriki*.

the Japanese farming system, based on improved seeds, application of fertilizer, and irrigation. Hayami and Ruttan (1985) conclude that "the economic implication of the *ponlai* varieties for Taiwan in the 1920s were essentially equivalent to those of the modern rice varieties in the tropics today."[5] Similarly, Hsieh and Ruttan (1967) argue that new rice varieties now being developed in tropical Asia in the 1960s resemble, in terms of fertilizer responsiveness and yield potential, the *ponlai* varieties introduced to Taiwan in the mid-1920s.

As per Fig. 2.2, rice yield increased slowly during the 1910s and dramatically in the 1920s in Taiwan. This coincides with the development of *ponlai* varieties, the first one being Taiching 65, developed in 1924 from a cross of two Japanese varieties (Tanaka 2012). Rice production in Korea was less successful than in Taiwan because of the lower levels of irrigation and water control, but rice yield in this country nonetheless accelerated in the 1930s.[6] The yield growth in both Taiwan and Korea was obviously the result of technology transfer from Japan, where adaptive agricultural research, irrigation investment, and technological extension played critical roles. A stable supply of rice to Japan from Taiwan and Korea undoubtedly contributed to rice price stability and increased its availability in Japan, thereby contributing to the sustainable growth of nonfarm sectors in prewar Japan.

2.3 Green Revolution in Tropical Asia

Not only the Club of Rome (Meadows et al. 1972) but also the majority of those interested in the development of agriculture in tropical Asia were worried about the future balance between rice supply and demand in the 1960s and early 1970s in this region, because population was increasing, rice yield had stagnated, and uncultivated land had been largely exhausted (Barker and Herdt 1985). As is shown in Fig. 2.3, population grew in parallel with grain production in the 1960s in Tropical Asia. However, grain production fluctuated widely, which means that food shortages took place occasionally during poor crop years (e.g., in 1965–1966 in West Bengal). Without exaggeration, it can be argued that tropical Asia was on the verge of famine due to increasing population pressure, as predicted by Malthus.

As per Fig. 2.3, grain production began increasing since the mid-1960s and its growth rate accelerated in the 1970s and 1980s, thereby surpassing the population growth by a wide margin. Grain production increased not because of the expansion of land area, but largely because of yield growth. This is a result of the Green Revolution, primarily for rice but also for wheat in tropical Asia.

For rice, the first semi-dwarf, fertilizer-responsive, high-yielding MV, IR8, was released in 1966 by the International Rice Research Institute (IRRI) in the Philippines, which was established in 1960 by support of the Rockefeller and Ford Founda-

---

[5]Dalrymple (1986) points out that early *ponlai* varieties were not semi-dwarfs.
[6]It is also worth noting that rice yield in Japan began increasing in the 1930s due to the lagged effect of establishing modern agricultural research and extension systems during the Meiji era.

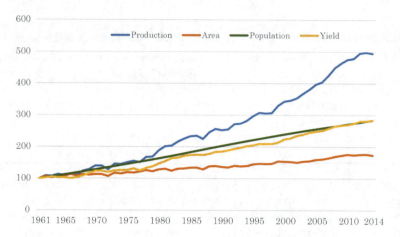

Fig. 2.3 Changes in grain production, harvested area, population, and grain yield in tropical Asia (Index: 1961 = 100). *Source* FAOSTAT (2016)

tions.[7] IR8 was the result of a cross between Peta, a tall variety from Indonesia, and Dee-Geowoo-Gen, a semi-dwarf variety from Taiwan. Although the contribution of Japanese scientists to the development of Dee-Geowoo-Gen in Taiwan is not clear, the basic idea of Green Revolution is obviously the same as the growth of rice yield based on the development of high-yielding varieties in Japan during the Meiji era. Indeed, Hayami and Godo (2005, p. 97) point out that "IR8 was modeled after the high-yielding Japanese varieties."[8]

The rice yield in Southeast Asia began increasing since 1966 and accelerated since the mid-1970s (Fig. 2.4). This is because IR8 and other early IRRI varieties were potentially high-yielding under favorable production environments but susceptible to pests and diseases, with major yield gains being achieved only after pest- and disease-resistant varieties were developed in the mid-1970s (David and Otsuka 1994). As a result, paddy yields in Southeast Asia were only half of those in Northeast Asia in the 1960s but increased to about two-thirds by the 2010s.[9]

It is remarkable that rice yield in South Asia began growing with a time lag of five to ten years compared with Southeast Asia. This is important because rice MVs were highly transferable from Southeast Asia to South Asia, not to mention from one

---

[7] For rice plant to be fertilizer responsive, it is desirable to be short and their stem thick. If the plant is fertilizer responsive, it is also high-yielding. Improved varieties used to be called "high-yielding varieties," but since they are not high-yielding in areas subject to drought and floods, they are now more commonly called "modern varieties".

[8] Japanese agricultural scientists made significant contributions to the development of IR8. IRRI also learned rice science from Japan by translating articles and books about rice from Japanese into English.

[9] Northeast Asia refers to Taiwan, South Korea, and Japan.

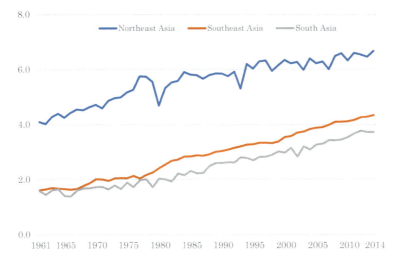

Fig. 2.4 Changes in rice yield in Northeast, Southeast, and South Asia. *Source* FAOSTAT (2016)

country to another within Southeast Asia.[10] In fact, IR8 and related varieties were widely grown in India and Bangladesh, although these varieties were later replaced by newer ones, generated by cross-breeding between IRRI and local traditional varieties (Janaiah et al. 2005). Rice yield in South Asia has been lower than in Southeast Asia, primarily because of lower availability of irrigation in the former, which indicates the decisive importance of irrigation for high rice yields (see Chap. 12).

In this way, rice production technology in tropical Asia improved, which led to sustainable growth in rice production. The upper panel of Fig. 2.5 shows that global rice production continued to increase over the past several decades. Since more than 90 percent of rice is produced in Asia, the rice Green Revolution significantly contributed to increasing rice production globally. In other words, technology transfer from Japan to Taiwan and further from Taiwan to tropical Asia resulted in a significant growth in rice production (Tanaka 2012). As a result, real rice prices continued to decline due to increasing rice production, coupled with price- and income-inelastic demand for rice, until the "food crisis" in 2008. The real rice price around 2000 was merely one-third of the level around 1970. This sharp reduction in real rice prices indicated that the major beneficiaries of the Green Revolution were rice consumers, including urban workers, whereas rice farmers who failed to adopt improved technology due to unfavorable production environments lost because of lower rice prices (David and Otsuka 1994). On the other hand, rice farmers who adopted improved rice technologies received benefit from enhanced production efficiency but still suffered

---

[10]For example, IRRI varieties were widely diffused not only in the Philippines, but also in Indonesia and rice yield was higher in the latter than the former.

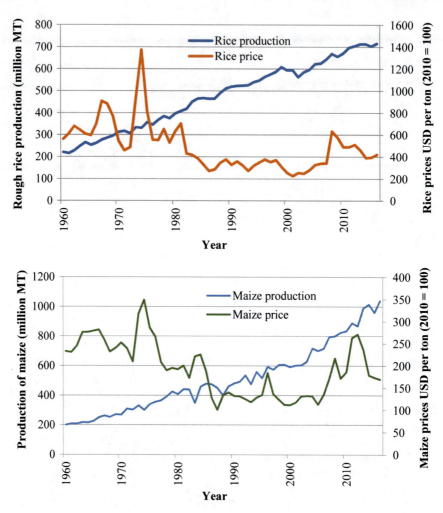

Fig. 2.5 World production and real prices for rice and maize, 1961–2016. *Source* United States Department of Agriculture database

from price reductions,[11] with the net effect more likely to be rather negative because of the sharp rice price reduction. The lower panel of Fig. 2.5 indicates that not only the real price of rice but also that of maize had been declining from the 1960s to the middle of the first decade of this century, because of the increasing maize yield and production.[12]

---

[11] Although there are no official statistics on the adoption rates of MVs in tropical Asia, they are likely to be between 75 and 80% as of now.

[12] Grain prices fluctuated widely around 1974 and 2008, partly because of the slight shortfall in production, but more importantly because of excessive speculation.

Although there is no direct evidence that the Green Revolution in tropical Asia contributed to building emerging states in this region, it would not be unrealistic to argue that a sufficient supply of such an important staple crop as rice contributed significantly to the stability of Asian societies by improving the well-being of rice consumers without excessively sacrificing the welfare of most rice farmers. Since rice is a wage good, the reduction in rice prices must have stimulated the development of industries and other nonfarm sectors by reducing the cost of living for urban workers. If there had been no Green Revolution, people in tropical Asia would have been adversely affected by the high rice prices, persistent food insecurity, and occasional famines in the worst-case scenario and the import of expensive grains from elsewhere in the world in the best-case scenario.

2.4 Possibility of a Green Revolution in SSA

Boserup (1965) argues that population pressure on limited land areas stimulates the spontaneous adoption of land-saving and labor-using production methods by farmers, which leads to an increase in crop yield. However, this view is not necessarily consistent with the reviewed historical experience. Even when population pressure increased in prewar Japan, rice yield did not increase without technological changes. Similarly, rice yield increased significantly in tropical Asia only after MVs were developed. Hayami and Ruttan (1985) argue that population pressure induces not only technological innovations but also institutional innovations, which supports the development and diffusion of innovations. As such, the Asian experience seems more consistent with this latter view than the Boserupian one.

Although there are a few land abundant countries in SSA, the ratio of arable land to rural population, on average, has been steadily declining (see Fig. 2.6). As a result, the land-population ratio in SSA now is similar to that in tropical Asia on the eve of the Green Revolution. However, since rainfall is lower in SSA, the quality-adjusted land-population ratio could be much lower than face value in SSA. Therefore, if the Hayami-Ruttan (1985) posited innovation hypothesis is relevant, it might be opportune for SSA to launch the Green Revolution.

From the trends of grain production,[13] cultivation area, population, and grain yield in SSA, it is clear that while population has been growing continuously, the growth of grain production was much slower from 1961 to around 2000 (Fig. 2.7). This is similar to or worse than the situation in tropical Asia in the 1960s (see Fig. 2.3). The imbalance between the growth of population and grain production contributes to the food insecurity in SSA, particularly around the turn of the century, when the gap between the trends of population and grain production growth was maximum. However, it is remarkable that grain production growth became faster than population growth over the past one and a half decades. Grain production increased not only

---

[13] Grain includes maize, sorghum millet, rice, and wheat, and production is the total quantity of the grain production. Note that yams, cassava, and plantain are also important staple foods in SSA.

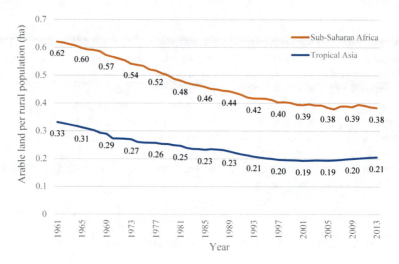

Fig. 2.6 Arable land per rural population in tropical Asia and SSA, 1961–2013. *Source* FAOSTAT (2016)

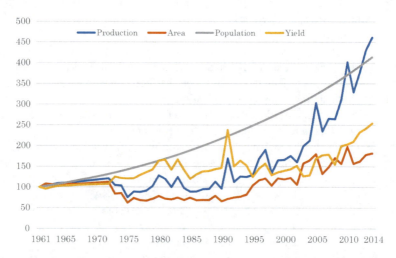

Fig. 2.7 Changes in grain production, harvested area, population, and grain yield in SSA (Index: 1961 = 100). *Source* FAOSTAT (2016)

because of the increase in cultivated area, but more importantly because of the rapid yield growth.

Such yield growth seems consistent with the arguments of Boserup (1965) and Hayami and Ruttan (1985). The question is whether it can be interpreted as an indicator of a nascent African Green Revolution. For this purpose, it is instructive to compare the yields of individual crops in SSA with those in India, a beneficiary of

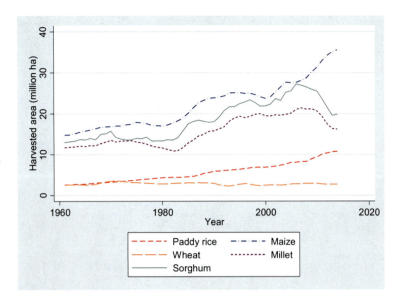

Fig. 2.8 Changes in aggregate harvested area in SSA by major crop. *Source* FAOSTAT (2016)

the Green Revolution in rice and wheat, whose agro-climate is relatively similar to that in SSA among the Asian countries.[14]

Before comparing the trends of individual grain yields, it would be useful to examine the relative importance of different grains in terms of harvested area (Fig. 2.8). Maize is by far the most important grain in SSA, whose harvested area has been expanding rapidly. Sorghum and millet are less and roughly equally important compared to maize, but their harvested areas have been declining in tandem during the past decade. Since their yields are comparatively low and stagnant,[15] harvested areas would have been replaced by maize areas. Rice harvested area has been much smaller, but it is steadily increasing primarily due to the conversion of uncultivated marshy land to lowland paddy fields. The importance of wheat is much lower, and its area has been largely constant because it can be grown only in cool climates, found primarily in South Africa and the highlands of eastern Africa. In the following, I focus on the analysis of rice and maize yields in SSA compared to those in India because these crops are more promising than other grains.

There are several important observations derived from the comparison of average rice yields in SSA with the yields of top and bottom 10 countries within SSA plus

---

[14] The major conclusions remain the same qualitatively, even if average yield in tropical Asia was used.

[15] Although not shown here, the yields of sorghum and millet are not only low and stagnant in both SSA and Asia but also similar between the two, indicating the Green Revolution of these crops did not take place in tropical Asia or SSA so far (Otsuka and Muraoka 2017).

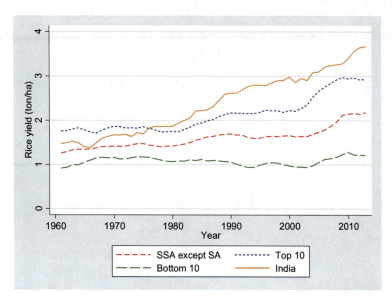

Fig. 2.9 Changes in average rice yield in SSA, top 10 and bottom 10 countries, and India. *Source* FAOSTAT (2016)

India (Fig. 2.9).[16] First, the average yield gap between SSA and India was small in the 1960s, refuting the often-held view that crop yield is higher in Asia due to more favorable climates. According to Nakano and Otsuka (2011), paddy yield was 3 tons per hectare in the Doho Irrigation Scheme in Uganda, even though no chemical fertilizers were applied, and double cropping had been practiced for more than two decades. Nakano et al. (2018a) report that rice yield is as high as 5 tons per hectare even in rainfed conditions in Kilombero Valley in Tanzania if proper cultivation practices are applied. These findings indicate that both agro-climate and soil conditions are favorable for lowland rice production, at least in some areas of Uganda and Tanzania. Although I cannot generalize these findings to the entire SSA, the literature review by Balasubramanian et al. (2007) concludes that rice yield potential in SSA is high. Furthermore, according to my own field observations, many rainfed paddy fields are located in valley bottoms in SSA, which are moist and fertile and, hence, favorable for rice production.

Second, rice yield began increasing in India by the late 1960s, although the improved rice varieties adopted in India at that time had been developed in the Philippines, such as IR8. Therefore, the early takeoff of rice yields in India suggests a high transferability of improved modern rice varieties from Southeast Asia to South Asia. Additionally, irrigation investments were induced in Asia, as the rate of return on such investments increased with the introduction of MVs (Hayami and

---

[16] Rice includes both lowland and upland rice, the latter accounting for nearly 40% of the total rice area. While the yield of upland rice is generally low, new upland varieties, called NERICA, are high yielding in some areas in SSA (e.g., Uganda; Kijima et al. 2011).

Kikuchi 1978). Chapter 10 reports that the irrigation ratio in Asia increased from 20% in 1965 to 45% in 2015 (see Fig. 10.3). According to my own observations, IRRI varieties and their offspring are widely grown in irrigation schemes across the continent, which also indicates the high transferability of Asian MVs to SSA. Third, the difference in yield between average and top 10 countries is large,[17] which implies paddy yield is considerably higher in the advanced regions in SSA. Indeed, the yield gap between the top 10 countries and India was relatively small, which strongly suggests that improved rice production systems have been successfully adopted at least in advanced areas in SSA. In fact, rice yields are higher than 5 tons per hectare in several irrigated areas in SSA, where MVs and improved management practices were adopted (Otsuka and Larson 2016), and also far higher than average rice yields in tropical Asia (see Fig. 2.4).

Rice yield is significantly higher under irrigated than rainfed conditions in Asia (e.g., David and Otsuka 1994; Otsuka and Hayami 1994) because of the decisive impact of irrigation on rice yield (see Chap. 12). Njeru et al. (2016) point out, based on case-study evidence, that as far as irrigated areas are concerned, there is no significant difference in the relationship between fertilizer application and yield per hectare between tropical Asia and SSA. This suggests that the properties of yield functions are similar between tropical Asia and SSA. However, the fertilizer application per hectare tends to be lower in SSA because real fertilizer priced tend to be higher. Although the irrigated area accounts for only 15% of the paddy area in SSA (Balasubramanian et al. 2007), Asian rice Green Revolution technologies function well in irrigated rice areas in SSA. Indeed, roughly 50% of paddy areas in the top 10 countries in SSA are irrigated.

Finally, average rice yield began increasing around 2005, which may indicate that the rice sector in SSA is currently transitioning to the Green Revolution. Indeed, adaptive crop breeding research developed a large number of improved rice varieties in SSA (Yamano et al. 2016).

For comparative purposes, Fig. 2.10 shows the yield trend of maize in SSA and India. First, similar to the case of rice, the yield gap between SSA and India was negligible in the 1960s and 1970s, which indicates either the difference in agroclimate between SSA and India is not a decisive determinant of maize yield or agroclimatic differences are small. Second, the maize yield in India began increasing in the mid-1980s due to the Green Revolution, resulting in a yield gap of roughly 1 ton per hectare between SSA and India in recent years. However, this gap is much smaller than for rice, where the yield gap amounts to two tons per hectare. Since improved maize varieties are highly location specific (Smale et al. 2013), improving the maize yield in SSA seems more difficult than for rice. Third, the difference in yield between the average and top 10 countries in SSA is relatively small,[18] which indicates the maize yield is low even in the most advanced regions in SSA. Therefore,

---

[17] Note that, although yield in the bottom 10 countries is very low, their harvested areas are relatively small, so that average yield is not significantly affected by the overly low yield.

[18] Note that, although yield in the bottom 10 countries is very low, harvested areas are small so that the average is not significantly affected by the low yield.

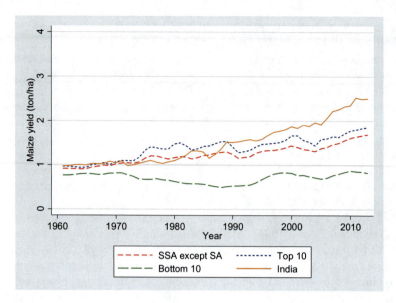

Fig. 2.10 Changes in average maize yields in SSA, top 10 and bottom 10 countries, and India. *Source* FAOSTAT (2015)

it seems safe to conclude that the maize Green Revolution did not take place on a large scale anywhere in SSA. The lack of adaptive research is likely to be one of the causes for the delay of an African maize Green Revolution. Fourth, similar to the case of rice, the maize yield in SSA began increasing around 2005, which may reflect the increasing adoption of new technologies, possibly leading to a maize Green Revolution in SSA. According to the review of literature on maize production in SSA by Otsuka and Muraoka (2017), the adoption of high-yielding hybrid seeds, use of chemical fertilizer as well as manure and compost, and application of inter-cropping with leguminous crops which have the capacity to fix nitrogen have been gradually increasing in SSA. Furthermore, responding to population pressure, markets have been developing and improved soil management technologies adopted in East Africa (Yamano et al. 2011).

The critical question is whether a full-fledged Green Revolution can take place in SSA and a related question is what its constraints are on this continent. According to Otsuka and Larson (2013, 2016), rice is the most promising crop in SSA, primarily because of the high transferability of the Asian Green Revolution technology. This view is consistent with the transfer history of rice technology from Japan to Taiwan, and further to the Philippines and South Asia. A major constraint of the Green Revolution in SSA is low grain prices (see Fig. 2.5), which would discourage farmers' incentives to adopt new technologies and those of researchers to develop them. Declining and small farm size in SSA is not a major concern, because an inverse relationship between farm size and productivity is widely observed in SSA (Larson et al. 2014), indicating that small farms relying on family labor are more productive than large farms relying on hired labor. Therefore, the Green Revolution is compatible with smallholder agriculture in SSA (Larson et al. 2016), as was the case in tropical Asia.

In my view, another and more serious constraint is the lack of recognition that the Green Revolution technology is "management intensive." The Green Revolution is alternatively called the "seed-fertilize" revolution in the literature (Johnston and Cownie 1969), which indicates that if improved fertilizer-responsive seeds and chemical fertilizers are adopted, it will take place. However, I believe this is incorrect as not only improved seeds and fertilizers, but also improved management practices, such as seed selection, bunding, leveling, transplanting in row, and weeding are critically important to improving rice yields. This has been proven by assessing the impact of improved management training on rice yield, income, and profit per hectare under both irrigated and rainfed conditions in SSA (deGraft-Johnson et al. 2014; Kijima et al. 2012; Nakano et al. 2018b; Otsuka and Larson 2016; Takahashi et al. 2018). Rice yield seems to increase by 25–50% if proper management practices are adopted, even if improved seeds and chemical fertilizers are not used. The importance of these improved management practices would not have been emphasized in tropical Asia in the 1960s and 1970s partly because it was considered "trivially" true and also because basic management practices had been adopted in Asia due primarily to its long tradition of rice farming.[19] The lack of recognition that that Green Revolution is management intensive leads to a lack of effective extension systems.[20] Consequently, the Green Revolution will not take place widely in SSA, unless and until proper extension systems are built. The failure to accomplish the Green Revolution will delay the evolution of African countries towards an emerging state, as discussed in the next section.

2.5 Agricultural Development and Paths to an Emerging State

Following de Janvry and Sadoulet (2002), Otsuka et al. (2009), and Estudillo and Otsuka (2016), Fig. 2.11 illustrates how technological innovations in agriculture and irrigation investment, which lead to the Green Revolution, affect rural household income directly by increasing the efficiency and profitability of farming and indirectly through the growth linkage effects on nonfarm sectors and changes in the prices of agricultural products.[21] The growth linkage effects of the Green Revolution

---

[19] I obtained this information from the former assistant of IRRI, Violy Cordova, who had worked for IRRI since 1970, Dr. Chukichi Kaneda who worked for IRRI in the early 1970s, and Professor Koji Tanaka of Kyoto University who has researched the history of the development of rice faming in Asia.

[20] This is true not only for rice but also for maize (Otsuka and Muraoka 2017).

[21] For simplicity, Fig. 2.11 does not consider the consumption linkage effect of agricultural innovations on nonfarm sectors, which arises from increases in farm household income. Additionally, the possible effect of human capital on the introduction of new technologies is ignored.

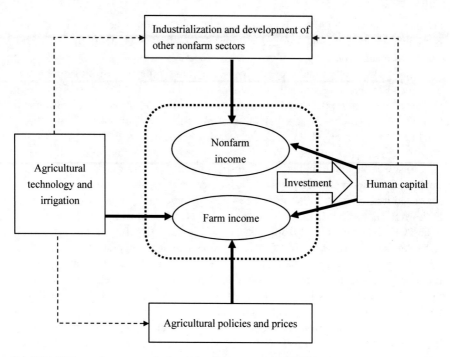

Fig. 2.11 Linkages between agricultural development and industrialization

on the development of nonfarm sectors arise from increased demand for chemical fertilizers and other purchased inputs and from an increased supply of farm products for processing activities. While rigorous estimations of the growth linkage effect are scant, Christiaensen et al. (2011) demonstrate that agricultural growth leads to the growth of the nonfarm economy by employing cross-country regressions. Because of the weak evidence, a dotted line is used for connecting agricultural technology and irrigation with industrial development. The reduction in food prices due to the Green Revolution has negative effects on farm household incomes and also provides negative incentives to generate new agricultural technologies and invest in irrigation. At the same time, lower food price will stimulate industrial development and the development of other nonfarm sectors by reducing the cost of living for urban workers. Another major factor that affects the income of rural households and development of nonfarm sectors is human capital. Schooling, a major component of human capital along with health, is known to affect farming efficiency (e.g., Foster and Rosenzweig 1996) and have a positive effect on the choice of nonfarm jobs and income (e.g., Jolliffe 2004; Matsumoto et al. 2006; Nakajima et al. 2018). An important point is that educational investment is strongly affected by the income of rural households (Estudillo and Otsuka 2016; Otsuka et al. 2009). An educated rural labor force tends to choose nonfarm jobs and thereby further contributes to its development.

In short, the Green Revolution aids the development of industries and other nonfarm sectors by supplying wage goods and an educated labor force to the extent that the Green Revolution increases the income of rural households and, consequently, stimulates educational investment. The failure of the Green Revolution in SSA may well be one of the major causes for the failure of industrial development and the weak effects of labor allocation from agriculture to other sectors on the labor productivity of African economies, as reported in Chap. 9.

Here, a critical question is the role of the state in promoting the Green Revolution. Since improved varieties are public goods, particularly when they can be reproduced by farmers, the government must play a major role in agricultural research.[22] Knowledge of improved agronomic practices can thus be shared among farmers in the locality and, hence, it is a local public good. Therefore, the government must take responsibility for agricultural extension. Furthermore, irrigation water is a common pool resource and, thus, the market fails to build irrigation facilities and allocate water efficiently (see Chap. 12 for details). Here too, the state must play a leading role. Therefore, whether the agrarian economy successfully evolves towards an emerging state critically hinges on the government's agricultural policy.

It is noteworthy that the income of a rural household is the major determinant of its investment in human capital (Otsuka et al. 2009). If a Green Revolution takes place, thereby improving farm income and stimulating the development of nonfarm sectors, there can be a virtuous circle of income growth, increased investment in human capital, and the subsequent development of farm and nonfarm sectors. The effects of the Green Revolution and human capital, as well as those of nonfarm sector development on farm household income in Asia and Africa are analyzed in depth in Chap. 10, using primary data.

Chapters 6–8 focus on industrialization in Asia, whereas Chap. 9 examines how industrialization can be promoted by policy means in SSA. A common finding is the importance of labor-intensive industrialization, particularly during the early stages of economic development. Although agricultural development can contribute to industrialization by supplying an educated labor force and cheap foods, its contribution is often curtailed by insufficient and inefficient extension systems, as pointed out in this chapter, and inappropriate irrigation policies, which will be discussed in Chap. 12. Particularly, the efficient management of ground water is extremely difficult because of the free access to this source of irrigation water. Practically, the most effective system is community irrigation because people know each other very well within a community and punishment on deviating behavior from the communal agreement is feasible and possibly severe. Chapter 12, which concerns irrigation management, demonstrates that insufficient or improper recognition of the importance of community irrigation systems by the government leads to mismanagement of irrigation water, which in turn, deters agricultural development.

---

[22]To the extent that improved varieties can be diffused across country borders, they are "global" or "regional" public goods. That is why international organizations, such as IRRI, undertake agricultural research.

The Green Revolution in Asia contributed to a reduction in grain prices, which must have reduced farm household income directly. Indirectly, lower food prices stimulate the development of nonfarm sectors, which creates nonfarm job opportunities for rural households. Furthermore, the governments of developing countries tend to "exploit" agriculture by intentionally reducing product prices and increasing input prices (e.g., by imposing export tax on agricultural products and import tariffs on imported agricultural inputs). Such policies reduce the incentives to realize a Green Revolution. On the other hand, to reduce the income gap between farm and nonfarm sectors, the governments of developed countries tend to "protect" agriculture by price support, input subsidies, and import restrictions. Such policies stimulate domestic production in developed countries excessively and reduce agricultural product prices internationally, thereby discouraging the agricultural development in developing countries. Chapter 11 examines whether the "development paradox" of exploiting agriculture in developing countries applies to Africa.

To sum up, based on the analysis of the evolutionary process of the Green Revolution in this chapter, Chaps. 10–12 attempt to identify the determinants of agricultural development, which will eventually contribute to guiding developing economies towards an emerging state.

References

Balasubramanian, V., Sie, M., Hijmans, R. J., & Otsuka, K. (2007). Increasing rice production in sub-Saharan Africa: Challenges and opportunities. *Advancement in Agronomy, 94*(6), 55–133.

Barker, R., & Herdt, R. (1985). *The Asian rice economy.* Baltimore: Johns Hopkins University Press.

Boserup, E. (1965). *The conditions of agricultural growth: The economics of agrarian change under population pressure.* London: George Allen and Unwin.

Christiaensen, L., Demery, L., & Kuhl, J. (2011). The (evolving) role of agriculture in poverty reduction: An empirical perspective. *Journal of Development Economics, 96*(2), 239–254.

David, C. C., & Otsuka, K. (1994). *Modern rice technology and income distribution in Asia.* Boulder: Lynne Rienner.

Dalrymple, D. G. (1986). *Development and spread of high-yielding rice varieties in developing countries.* Washington, DC: Agency for International Development.

deGraft-Johnson, M., Suzuki, A., Sakurai, T., & Otsuka, K. (2014). On the transferability of the Asian rice green revolution to rainfed areas in sub-Saharan Africa: An assessment of technology intervention in Northern Ghana. *Agricultural Economics, 45*(5), 555–570.

de Janvry, A., & Sadoulet, E. (2002). World poverty and role of agricultural technology: Direct and indirect effects. *Journal of Development Studies, 38*(4), 1–26.

Estudillo, J. P., & Otsuka, K. (2016). *Moving out of poverty: An inquiry into inclusive growth in Asia.* London, UK: Routledge.

Foster, A., & Rosenzweig, M. R. (1996). Technical change and human capital returns and investment: Evidence from the Green Revolution. *American Economic Review, 86*(4), 931–953.

Hayami, Y., & Godo, Y. (2005). *Development economics: From the poverty to the wealth of nations.* New York: Oxford University Press.

Hayami, Y., & Kikuchi, M. (1978). Investment inducements to public infrastructure: Irrigation in the Philippines. *Review of Economics and Statistics, 60*(1), 70–77.

Hayami, Y., & Ruttan, V. W. (1985). *Agricultural development: An international perspective*. Baltimore: Johns Hopkins University Press.

Hsieh, S. C., & Ruttan, V. W. (1967). Environmental, technological, and institutional factors in the growth of rice production: Philippines, Thailand, and Taiwan. *Food Research Institute Studies, 7,* 307–341.

Janaiah, A., Hossain, M., & Otsuka, K. (2005). Is the productivity impact of the Green Revolution in rice vanishing? *Economic and Political Weekly, 40*(53), 5596–5600.

Jolliffe, D. (2004). The impact of education in rural Ghana: Examining household labor allocation and returns on and off farm. *Journal of Development Economics, 73*(1), 287–314.

Johnston, B. F., & Cownie, J. (1969). The seed-fertilizer revolution and labor force absorption. *American Economic Review, 59*(4), 569–582.

Kijima, Y., Ito, N., & Otsuka, K. (2012). Assessing the impact of training on lowland rice productivity in an African setting: Evidence from Uganda. *World Development, 40*(8), 1619–1633.

Kijima, Y., Otsuka, K., & Sserunkuuma, D. (2011). An inquiry into constraints on a green revolution in sub-Saharan Africa: The case of NERICA rice in Uganda. *World Development, 39*(1), 77–86.

Larson, D., Otsuka, K., Matsumoto, T., & Kilic, T. (2014). Should African rural development strategies depend on small farms? An exploration of the inverse productivity Hypothesis. *Agricultural Economics, 45*(3), 355–367.

Larson, D., Muraoka, R., & Otsuka, K. (2016). Why African rural development strategies must depend on small farms. *Global Food Security, 10,* 39–51.

Matsumoto, T., Kijima, Y., & Yamano, T. (2006). The role of local nonfarm activities and migration in reducing poverty: Evidence from Ethiopia, Kenya, and Uganda. *Agricultural Economics, 35*(S3), 449–458.

Meadows, D. H., Meadows, D. L., Randes, J., & Behrens, W. W. (1972). *The limits to growth*. New York: Universe Books.

Nakajima, M., Yamano, T., & Otsuka, K. (2018). Jobs off the farm: Wealth, human capital, and social groups in rural eastern India. *Journal of Development Studies, 54*(1), 111–132.

Nakano, Y., & Otsuka, K. (2011). Determinants of household contributions to collective irrigation management: A case of the Doho rice scheme in Uganda. *Environment and Development Economics, 16*(5), 521–551.

Nakano, Y., Tanaka, Y., & Otsuka, K. (2018a). Impact of training on the intensification of rice farming: Evidence from rain-fed areas in Tanzania. *Agricultural Economics, 49*(2), 193–202.

Nakano, Y., Tsusaka, T. W., Aida, T., & Pede, V. O. (2018b, forthcoming). Is farmer-to-farmer extension effective? The impact of training on technology adoption and rice farming productivity in Tanzania. *World Development, 105,* 336–351.

Njeru, T., Mano, Y., & Otsuka, K. (2016). Role of access to credit in rice production in sub-Saharan Africa: The case of Mwea irrigation scheme in Kenya. *Journal of African Economies, 25*(2), 300–321.

Otsuka, K. (2013). Food insecurity, income inequality, and the changing comparative advantage in world agriculture. *Agricultural Economics, 44*(S1), 7–18.

Otsuka, K., Estudillo, J. P., & Sawada, Y. (Eds.). (2009). *Rural poverty and income dynamics in Asia and Africa*. London, UK: Routledge.

Otsuka, K., & Hayami, Y. (1994). Beyond the green revolution: agricultural development strategy into the new century. In J. Anderson (Ed.), *Agricultural technology: Policy issues for the international community* (pp. 15–42). Wallingford: CAB International.

Otsuka, K., & Larson, D. (Eds.). (2013). *An African Green Revolution: Finding ways to boost productivity on small farms*. Dordrecht: Springer.

Otsuka, K., & Larson, D. (Eds.). (2016). *In pursuit of an African Green Revolution: Views from rice and maize farmers' fields*. Dordrecht: Springer.

Otsuka, K., & Muraoka, R. (2017). A green revolution for sub-Saharan Africa: Past failures and future prospects. *Journal of African Economies, 26*(S1), i73–i98.

Smale, M., Byerlee, D., & Jayne, T. (2013). Maize revolution in sub-Saharan Africa. In K. Otsuka & D. Larson (Eds.), *An African Green Revolution: Finding ways to boost productivity on small farms* (pp. 165–195). Dordrecht: Springer.

Tanaka, K. (2012). Seizon kiban jizokugara hatten keiro o motomete: Ajia inasakuken no keiken kara (In search of sustainable livelihood system: a view from the experience of rice growing areas in Asia). In K. Sugihara, K. Wakimura, K. Fujita, & A. Tanabe A (Eds.), *Rekishi no nakano nettai seizon ken* (Livelihood space in history of tropics) (pp. 185–210). Kyoto: Kyoto University Press.

Tanaka, K., & Imai, R. (2006). Shokuminchi keiei to nogyo gujutu: Taiwan, Nanpo, Manshu (Management of colonies and agricultural technology: Taiwan, Tropics, and Manchuria). In K. Tanaka (Ed.), *Teikoku Nihon no Gakuchi* (Wisdom of the Empire Japan) (pp. 100–137). Tokyo: Iwanami Shoten.

Takahashi, K., Mano, Y., & Otsuka, K. (2018). Beyond the SUTVA: The dynamic impact of management training and subsequent information spillover on agricultural performance in Cote d'Ivoire. Mimeographed.

Umemura, M., Yamada, S., Hayami, Y., Takamatsu, M., & Kumazki, M. (1966). *Estimates of long-term statistics of Japan since 1868: Agriculture and forestry*. Tokyo, Japan: Toyo Keizai Shinposha.

Yamano, T., Arouna, A., Labarta, R. A., Huelgas, Z. M., & Mohanty, S. (2016). Adoption and impacts of international rice research technologies. *Global Food Security, 8,* 1–8.

Yamano, T., Otsuka, K., & Place, F. (Eds.). (2011). *Emerging development of agriculture in East Africa: Markets, soil, and innovations*. Amsterdam: Springer.

Open Access This chapter is licensed under the terms of the Creative Commons Attribution-NonCommercial-NoDerivatives 4.0 International License (http://creativecommons.org/licenses/by-nc-nd/4.0/), which permits any noncommercial use, sharing, distribution and reproduction in any medium or format, as long as you give appropriate credit to the original author(s) and the source, provide a link to the Creative Commons licence and indicate if you modified the licensed material. You do not have permission under this licence to share adapted material derived from this chapter or parts of it.

The images or other third party material in this chapter are included in the chapter's Creative Commons licence, unless indicated otherwise in a credit line to the material. If material is not included in the chapter's Creative Commons licence and your intended use is not permitted by statutory regulation or exceeds the permitted use, you will need to obtain permission directly from the copyright holder.

Chapter 3
Southeast Asia and International Trade: Continuity and Change in Historical Perspective

Ryuto Shimada

3.1 Introduction

International trade has been an essential element of the long-term economic development of Southeast Asia. Involvement in international trade has laid crucial foundations for the present-day economic growth of this region since the fourth quarter of the twentieth century.

This chapter aims to provide a general overview of the relations between international trade and the economy of Southeast Asia from a long-term perspective. First, a short description is supplied about the relationships between natural endowments and international trade of Southeast Asia before the European arrival. The second section is devoted to an analysis of international trade of Southeast Asia from the beginning of the sixteenth century to the middle of the second half of the nineteenth century. This is then followed by a case study of Batavia's trade. The third section focuses on the economic influences of international trade on the Southeast Asian economy and society, including the change in the patterns of production, during the same period. The forth section returns to a survey of trade, to extend it to the high colonial period and its aftermath roughly to 1975, identifying several characteristics of the modern Southeast Asian economy along the way. Finally, the last section touches on the most recent period of industrialization, to show that the historically specific path laid by international trade has been critically important for the understanding of the long-term economic development of Southeast Asia.

Figure 3.1 is an illustration of the structure of this chapter. It was drawn to suggest that, if we take a few centuries together, there was normally an intermediate level of trade, which might be called intra-Asian trade, that often linked and organized other levels of trade. Intra-Asian trade is distinguished from both global long-distance trade, usually with Europe and the Americas, and local trade, including

---

R. Shimada (✉)
Graduate School of Humanities and Sociology, The University of Tokyo, Tokyo, Japan
e-mail: r_shimada@nifty.com

© The Author(s) 2019
K. Otsuka and K. Sugihara (eds.), *Paths to the Emerging State in Asia and Africa*,
Emerging-Economy State and International Policy Studies,
https://doi.org/10.1007/978-981-13-3131-2_3

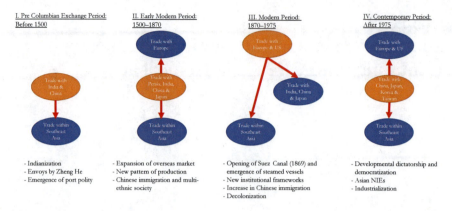

Fig. 3.1 International trade and socio-economic changes in Southeast Asia

intra-Southeast Asian trade. The implication of this formulation is that economy and society of the region have been developed by constant absorption of both Western and Asian civilizations through international trade and migration. Intra-Asian trade was the most significant driver of change of the Southeast Asian economy, although long-distance trade was the most important in the high colonial period. This chapter aims to examine the relationships of international trade and socio-economic changes of Southeast Asia, especially until the mid-twentieth century, along the line suggested by this figure.

In this chapter the 'early modern period' is defined in accordance with the periodization made from a perspective of global history rather than that of Southeast Asian history. It runs from the late fifteenth century, when Christopher Columbus "discovered" the Americas and the global economy became truly connected, to the middle of the second half of the nineteenth century, when steam vessels became dominant in place of sailing ships and global network of telegrams was created. Readers are reminded that this periodization does not follow the usual periodization in the historiography of Southeast Asia, where, for example, the early modern period is defined as from 1400 to 1830 by Barbara Watson Andaya and Leonard Y. Andaya (Andaya and Andaya 2015).

3.2 Southeast Asia Before the European Arrival

Reflecting the natural conditions of the tropics, the Southeast Asian economy experienced a path of economic development that is different from those in the temperate zone. Due to the high temperature and humidity in Southeast Asia, people were initially inclined to live in mountainous areas rather than in delta areas. In general, delta areas were an unfavorable place for people to live, because of the humidity and the high possibility of floods and the outbreak of infectious diseases such as malaria and dysentery. The difficulty of controlling large volumes of water was another reason for people's unwillingness to live in the delta. Thus most people lived in the cool and dry mountainous areas, and therefore did not utilize the delta areas by the seaside, an environment potentially richly endowed. For these reasons, Southeast Asia was comparatively sparsely populated during the pre-early modern period.

A major motivation for developing delta areas was to respond to the rise of profitable international maritime trade. High overseas demands for products supplied from the hinterland as well as large profits from transit trade inspired people to move and settle in lower areas from their mountainous dwellings. In this way, port cities such as Gresik in Java, Palembang in Sumatra and Ayutthaya in Thailand were established to facilitate maritime trade. These port cities were transport hubs where products from inland were gathered for export and overseas commodities were imported for distribution into the hinterland. Moreover, strong political regimes were often formed in such port cities. These political regimes are now called port-polity (Kathirithamby-Wells and Villiers 1990). In fact, Palembang and Ayutthaya are good examples of this, even though these ports were located far from the sea. These two cities were established at the point just between the plateau and the delta areas, which indicates that it was difficult to develop the delta areas at this time.

Historically, Southeast Asia engaged in two types of maritime trade. The first was intra-Asian trade. This type of trade has a very long history, spanning more than two thousand years. Geographically, it was of a very large scale. Since Southeast Asia is located between China and India, both of which had been powerful economic forces, Southeast Asia's trade developed along with the development of maritime trade of these Asian economic powers. Contacts with the Indian subcontinent had been significant over a longer period of time, as is reflected in India's strong cultural influence over Southeast Asia, which continues to this day. In addition, present-day Southeast Asia has Persian and Arabian imprints through the presence of the West Asian merchants who came to the region via maritime routes (Hall 2011). The kingdom of Champa is a good example to reveal the strong economic and cultural connections with China, India, and even West Asia. This kingdom, located in what is now mid-Vietnam, first had strong links with China around the third century, and sent tributary missions there. However, Champa began to be influenced by India and accepted Hindu culture, before the spread of Islamic influence began in the fourteenth century (Hardy et al. 2009).

Needless to say, Chinese influence has been as strong as Indian influence in Southeast Asia. The naval expeditions of Ming China between 1405 and 1433 directed by Zheng He, who was a Muslim Chinese admiral, and the tributary trade between Ming China and Southeast Asian states marked a climax of the intra-Asian trade before the European entry into Southeast Asia. The Ming imperial court sent large fleets seven times. The fleets visited Southeast Asia as well as Sri Lanka, the Indian subcontinent, the Arabian Peninsula, and East Africa. Due to the arrival of powerful fleets directed by Zheng He, Southeast Asian states in particular came under the strong political influence of Ming China. They sent to tributary missions to China and conducted maritime trade under the control of the Ming dynasty within the framework of the tributary system (Liu et al. 2014).

The second type of maritime trade was a regional trade within Southeast Asia. Along with the development of intra-Asian trade, intra-regional maritime trade also began to grow. Not only coastal trade such as that in Java and Vietnam, but also a fairly long-distance trade was developed within Southeast Asia. The combination of intra-Asian trade with India and China and regional trade created a path of economic development based on international maritime trade. The proto-type of this path is evidenced through the records of Srivijaya from the seventh to the tenth century. Srivijaya was a federation of Malay cities among the Malay Peninsula, Sumatra Island, and Java Island. Each port city reaped profits and benefits from maritime trade and, in return, the unified kingdom was a recipient of Buddhism from the Indian subcontinent (Munoz 2006).

While Southeast Asia enjoyed the proto-type of trade-based economic development comprising intra-Asian and intra-regional trade by the fifteenth century (Fig. 3.1), its economy stepped into a new age of modernization at the beginning of the sixteenth century, when European traders began participating in economic activities. It was the beginning of the age of economic globalization when the Europeans began to connect Eurasia, Africa, and the Americas.

3.3 Maritime Trade in the Early Modern Period

The global economy entered a new stage at the beginning of the so-called Columbian exchange in the late fifteenth century (Crosby 1972), when the Americas were connected by Christopher Columbus and his followers. International connections truly developed on a global scale. As part of this global economic evolution, the Southeast Asian economy witnessed several changes.

Goa was conquered by the Portuguese in 1510 and became a center for the Portuguese maritime empire in Asia. In the next year, the Portuguese attacked the kingdom of Malacca (Melaka) gaining control of this key port in Southeast Asia. Soon the Portuguese also acquired the maritime lines to the Moluccas (Maluku Islands) and to Macau from Malacca. It is generally believed that gaining control of the Moluccas was highly important for Portuguese global trade, as the islands were the only place in the world where the valuable spices of clove, nutmeg, and mace were produced. These spices were key commodities in the Euro-Asian trade by the Portuguese in the sixteenth century.

The spice trade was one of the main sources of profits for the Portuguese empire. Indeed, the Portuguese were also engaged in intra-Asian trade, which also brought impressive profits. They had several trading bases in maritime Asia, some of which were Portuguese colonial cities such as Goa, Hormuz, Colombo, Malacca, and Macau. On the other hand, they also had trading posts in port cities under the control of Asian indigenous political regimes, such as Cambay (Khambhat) in Gujarat, Ayutthaya in Thailand and Nagasaki in Japan. Through their trading networks in maritime Asia, the Portuguese obtained large profits (Souza 1986).

The history of the Portuguese provides us with a unique insight. It is true that the European arrival was a symbolic event in Southeast Asia during the early modern period. However, from the point of view of the region, the Portuguese were simply a new participant in Asia's maritime trade. The Portuguese were engaged in both intra-Asian trade and Euro-Asian trade, and these trading activities contributed to economic development of the region.

What the combination of Euro-Asian trade and intra-Asian trade could ultimately achieve were made much clearer by the Dutch East India Company (*Verenigde Oostindische Compagnie*, hereafter VOC), which existed from 1602 to 1799. The initial aim of the VOC was to directly procure Asian products for the European market. Spices such as pepper, nutmeg, mace, clove, and cinnamon in maritime Asia were the most desirable products for the VOC, although sugar, coffee, and tea emerged in the seventeenth and eighteenth centuries as other important Asian products. In order to acquire these products, the VOC brought American silver to Asia through Europe as a means of payment.

Besides Euro-Asian trade, the VOC attempted to participate in intra-Asian trade. Before the arrival of European traders to maritime Asia in the sixteenth century, intra-Asian trade was conducted by several indigenous traders such as Arabs, Persians and Chinese. Through commercial negotiations and military actions, European traders came to join this branch of trade. In the sixteenth century, local Portuguese traders were one of the most powerful groups of traders, while in the seventeenth century, the VOC began engaging in intra-Asian trade on a much larger scale. The VOC was a unique participant, as it was a single organization, which conducted both long distance trade and intra-regional trade on a large scale. Other European companies such as English and French East India Companies were engaged in Euro-Asian trade without such a commitment in intra-regional trade (Shimada 2006).

It is impossible to disregard the magnitude of maritime trade conducted by indigenous Asian merchants. Asian traders were clearly more important than European traders in the early modern period. The most remarkable among them were Chinese merchants. Before the arrival of Europeans, Chinese merchants were actively engaged in intra-Asian trade. Not only Chinese traders, but also overseas Chinese traders conducted trade between Southeast Asia and China, while also participating in regional trade within Southeast Asia.

Set against this background, we see the emergence of the Chinese maritime network in the eighteenth century as a natural course of development. When political peace was realized in the late seventeenth century after the confusion caused by the Ming-Qing transition, the Chinese economy expanded, which caused greater demand for Southeast Asian products such as rice and tin. Some scholars refer to this period as "the Chinese century" (Reid 1997; Blussé 1999), indicating the influence of the Chinese economy, which grew in Southeast Asia through international trade with China by Chinese traders (see Chap. 4 of this volume).

Muslim traders were also important in Southeast Asia. Bugis and Malay traders were active in regional maritime trade in insular Southeast Asia from the second half of the eighteenth century (Barnard 2003). Their trading networks were also highly important in the context of the expansion of Islam. Through these networks, Arabian religious influence kept expanding, which enabled the immigration of Arabs from Hadhramaut into Insular Southeast Asia in the mid-eighteenth century (Abushouk and Ibrahim 2009).

3.3.1 The Case of Batavia

To examine the international economic links of Southeast Asia, the case of Batavia provides a helpful example. In general, the trade of Batavia had four spheres: long distance trade, intra-Asian trade, regional trade with the Indonesian archipelago, and coastal and inland trade (Table 3.1).

The long-distance trade of Batavia was first conducted by the VOC, which established the city in 1619. The office of Governor-General, who occupied the top position in business and military administration of the VOC governing the entire Asian waters was located in Batavia. The VOC was engaged in two types of maritime trade, as mentioned above. The first type of trade was Euro-Asian trade. The VOC supplied silver to Batavia from the Netherlands, and of course most silver was brought to Europe from Latin America. On the other hand, the VOC sent Asian products for the European market. Spices such as pepper, clove, nutmeg, mace, and cinnamon were major Asian products with great demand in Europe in the latter half of the seventeenth century, while Indian cotton textiles, Javanese sugar, Javanese coffee and Chinese tea became important in the course of time. Batavia played a key role of serving as the entrepôt to collect Asian products and ship them to the Netherlands. It acted as Asia's center of the Euro-Asian trade of the VOC.

In the nineteenth century, several Western private traders took the role of connecting Batavia with Europe and Americas. When the VOC perished at the end of the eighteenth century, the administration of Batavia and colonies in Java fell to the Dutch colonial authorities under the government of the Netherlands except for a short period from 1811 to 1816, when the British occupied Java. Compared to the seventeenth and eighteenth centuries, the trade became open and its scale grew. In particular, with the freedom of participation, Western traders entered into the maritime trade of Java. Not only the Dutch, but also British, French, German, North European, and

Table 3.1 Four spheres of the trade of Batavia

Sphere	Type of trade	Major trading partners
1	Long-distance trade	The Netherlands, Europe, USA
2	Intra-Asian trade	Japan, China, Siam, India, Persia
3	Regional trade within the Indonesian archipelago	Ambon, Bali, Bima, Banjarmasin, Palembang
4	Coastal and inland trade	Semarang, Surabaya, *Ommelanden*, Priangan

American traders called Javanese ports such as Batavia and Surabaya, and engaged in the business of Euro-Asian or American-Asian trade (Shimada 2013).

The sphere of intra-Asian trade in Batavia were also controlled mainly by the VOC. The VOC had several trading posts in maritime Asia from Japan to Arabia. By connecting these trading posts, it succeeded in developing several patterns of intra-Asian trade. One representative pattern is the triangular trade that emerged between Japan, India and Southeast Asia. Japan exported silver, gold and copper to India. India then exported cotton textiles to Southeast Asia, where primary products such as sugar, sappanwood (a dye source), and deer hides were produced for the Japanese market. The VOC entered into this triangular trade with fierce force, and earned large profits. The profits from intra-Asian trade contributed to the success of the VOC, because the company was able to reduce the export of silver from the Netherlands to Asia and saved costs. For this intra-Asian trade Batavia was an important transit port in the VOC's shipping network, which linked up maritime Asian countries such as Japan, China, Siam, Mughal India, and Persia. This contributed to Asian economic development by establishing a system of international division of labor in maritime Asia, in which Batavia played a pivotal role in the VOC's trading network.

In these two spheres of trade, the Javanese economy played the role of exporting primary products. Sugar, coffee and later indigo were good examples. The huge demand for Javanese primary products was a stimulus for the economic development of Java and contributed to the growth of the port of Batavia.

The third sphere of trade was concerned with regional trade within the Indonesian archipelago. This trade was conducted mainly by Asian traders such as Chinese and Muslim traders, although it also involved the participation of the VOC in the seventeenth and eighteenth centuries and by private Western traders in the nineteenth century. The port of Batavia was not designed only for the Dutch vessels even in the seventeenth and eighteenth centuries. Indigenous Asian traders also utilized this port. Overseas Chinese traders in Batavia were the most significant customers of the port. While they accepted junk ships from mainland China and Chinese immigrants, they conducted their own shipping business. They sent their ships not only to other ports in Java such as Semarang and Surabaya but also to ports in the Indonesian archipelago like Bali and Banjarmasin (Shimada 2013). Their trading network formed a basis for the development of overseas Chinese power in the Indonesian archipelago. In this regional trading world, Batavia was one of the trading centers accustomed to importing and exporting regional products.

The fourth sphere was coastal trade and inland trade. Batavia was supplied with essential items like food products and timber through coastal trade. These products were necessary for the urban people of Batavia. This trade was conducted by Asian traders, the VOC and, later, Western private traders. In addition, the port of Batavia was an important port to which primary products could be sent from the hinterland. Already in the early eighteenth century, Batavia exported sugar produced in its suburban areas (*Ommelanden*) and coffee produced in Priangan. In this way, it was a significant trading port for the economic development of East Java (Jacobs 2006).

3.4 Social Changes in the Early Modern Period

During the early modern period from the fifteenth century to the mid-nineteenth century, Southeast Asia experienced a change towards the formation of the modern economy and society (Fig. 3.1).

3.4.1 Expansion of the Overseas Market

European entry into Southeast Asia's international trade expanded the market for primary products from Southeast Asia. Simultaneously, tropical agricultural production was developed due to the large demand in the overseas market. In the sixteenth and seventeenth centuries, large volumes of spices were exported to Europe. Pepper was exported from Sumatra and Java, while nutmeg, mace, and clove were exported from the Moluccas. Besides spices, cane sugar and coffee bean were exported from Java since the seventeenth and eighteenth centuries, respectively. Apart from these agricultural products, tin was also an important Southeast Asian product for the European market. It was produced in southern Thailand, the Malay states of the peninsula and, since the eighteenth century, Bangka Island.

In addition to the European market, Asian demand for Southeast Asian products increased as well. Highly connected links within maritime Asia were spurred by the competition among Asian as well as European traders. Southeast Asia maintained and expanded their trade links with East Asia and South Asia. For example, Japan imported cane sugar from Java and sappanwood, rayskin, and animal hide from Thailand. China imported rice, tin and dried marine products such as sea cucumber from Southeast Asia. India imported cane sugar, spices and tin. In exchange for these products Southeast Asia obtained silver from East Asia and cotton textiles from South Asia (Shimada 2018).

Rice was the most important product for both intra-Asian trade and intra-Southeast Asian trade. Even before the European entry, Thai rice was exported to many areas in Southeast Asia. In addition to Thai rice, Javanese rice was traded in both intra-Southeast Asian and coastal and inland trade. It was exported to other parts of the Indonesian archipelago, and through coastal trade within the island of Java. As the surrounding zone of Batavia became specialized in the production of sugar cane, rice had to be imported into Batavia from northeast coastal area of the island. In the middle of the first half of the eighteenth century, Thailand began to export rice to China. This was because China was facing a shortage of rice due to the rapid population increase during the eighteenth century. This Thai rice trade with China became the key trade for the Thai economy until the twentieth century.

Intra-Asian trade was conducted not only by Asian traders but also by European traders. The latter, such as the VOC and English and Portuguese private merchants, as well as Chinese and Indo-Persian traders engaged in comparatively long-distance trade. On the other hand, Asian traders such as overseas Chinese, overseas Arab, and Bugis specialized in coastal trade and regional trade in Southeast Asia. Rice trade, interestingly, was not conducted by European traders but was left to Asian traders.

3.4.2 A New Pattern of Production

Due to the growth of international trade, the mode of production changed over the course of time. One remarkable change was the introduction of the plantation system. Early European powers in Southeast Asia introduced the plantation system for sugar cane production. In the middle of the seventeenth century, the VOC attempted it in Taiwan. Although it was unsuccessful because of the abandoning of the Dutch colony in Taiwan in 1662, the VOC again attempted the introduction in Java on a large scale (Yao 2003). The Company sold the lands around Batavia to private European citizens, who in turn leased the land to Chinese entrepreneurs. These entrepreneurs managed the sugar cane cultivation and the cane sugar production for export (Blussé 1986). Laborers in this sugar industry were not only local Asians but also Chinese immigrants. In fact, overseas Chinese laborers outnumbered local Asians.

The mining sector too witnessed a change. Formerly, tin mining operated as a small-scale industry in southern Thailand and the Malay Peninsula. Tin was mined there by indigenous people as side work, and they contributed their products to the states as a sort of head tax. However, a new mode of production was introduced in the first half of the eighteenth century in Bangka and in the late eighteenth century in the Malay Peninsula. It involved a group of Chinese immigrant miners. Around fifty miners formed a group with a Chinese head, who was in charge of all the processes of mining and refinery (Shimada 2015). In addition to the tin mining sector, gold mining was also developing in West Borneo during the eighteenth century. The so-called Lanfang Republic (1777–1884) was a sort of state founded by prominent overseas merchants, who accumulated profits from gold mining in Borneo (Somers Heidhues 2003).

Without a doubt, the most predominant sector in Southeast Asia was the agricultural sector. It was traditional but was in transition. Recent research claims that in the early modern period small-scale, family-based patterns of agricultural production became widespread in the northern part of the mainland of Southeast Asia such as northern Vietnam and Burma (Lieberman 2003). This change in the unit of agricultural production was a similar phenomenon to that seen in East Asia, and resulted in an increase in living standards among small-scaled agricultural producers.

With regard to other parts of Southeast Asia, traditional patterns of small-scale agricultural production seem to have continued in the greater part of the agricultural sector. However, the fact that the traditional pattern evolved in response to the overseas demand cannot be ignored. Under the framework of the traditional small-scale family farming system, peasants had to work for a fixed number of days, for example a hundred days per year, to be submitted to the head of local community as tax. This compulsory labor system was authorized and exploited by European colonial authorities or local states, which could collect agricultural products for export through the heads of local community as efficiently as possible. The Dutch cultivation system of the nineteenth century is the best example (Elson 1994).

3.4.3 Immigration and Multi-ethnic Society

The establishment of colonial cities in Southeast Asia was driven largely by the European merchants desire to increase their efficiency in international trade. Malacca, which was originally the capital of the state of Malacca, is a good example of a European colonial city. Yet, it was occupied by the Portuguese, followed by the Dutch and the British. Spanish Manila and Dutch Batavia are also typical examples of European colonial cities established in the early modern period. These two cities were the centers of trading business for the Spanish and Dutch merchants in the initial stage; they served as capitals of the Spanish/US Philippines and the Dutch East Indies in the nineteenth century and are currently two megacities in Southeast Asia.

Even in European colonial cities, Europeans did not comprise the majority of the population. It was made up of huge varieties of Asian ethnic groups. The population of Batavia, for example, included a large number of Chinese immigrants with some Malay, Bugis, Balinese, Indo-Persians, and so on. These Asian populaces were mostly immigrants to the colonial city. Batavia in 1699 had a population of 21,911. Among them, European citizens accounted for only 8%, the Chinese 17%, Asian Portuguese freed-slaves (*mardijker*) 11%, South Asians 2%, Malay and Javanese 1%, and the Balinese and Makassarese 1%, although Asian slaves, who were immigrants or their descendants, accounted for more than the half of the total population (Raben 1996).

Being composed of several ethnic immigrants, these colonial cities were literally multi-ethnic societies. Through the long history of multi-ethnicity since the early modern period, the Southeast Asian society has accumulated the experiences of and benefits from multi-ethnic culture. This provided a powerful socio-cultural basis for the economy and society, which would willingly attract and accept immigrants, foreign products, overseas technology, and international trade.

3.5 The High Colonial Period and After

Throughout the nineteenth century, international trade rapidly increased in Southeast Asia. Although Table 3.2 shows the steady rise of merchandise exports from Southeast Asia from the first half of the nineteenth century to the end of the twentieth century, the whole structure of international trade and the economy of Southeast Asia changed drastically around 1870.

First, in terms of international trade, long-distance trade with Europe and USA expanded, as seen in Table 3.3. It was because of the increase in exports of primary products and imports of cotton textiles. Southeast Asia exported rubber, sugar, coffee, and tea while it imported manufactured goods from Europe and USA where industrialization was in progress. Moreover, the opening of the Suez Canal was a turning point not only in terms of shipping but also in terms of the impact on the whole economy. The canal was opened in 1869 and a huge number of Western steam

Table 3.2 Merchandise Exports at Current Price, 1870–1998 (million dollars at current exchange rates)

Year	1820	1870	1913	1950	1973	1990	1998
Burma	–	–	–	303	358	1,671	3,831
Indonesia	31	270	582	800	3,211	25,675	48,847
Philippines	29	48	163	331	1,885	8,068	27,783
Thailand	7	43	94	304	1,564	23,071	54,455
Total	67	361	839	1,738	7,018	58,485	134,916

Source Maddison 2001: 360

Table 3.3 Trading Partners of International Trade in Southeast Asia, 1883–1938 (million pounds sterling)

	1883		1898		1913		1928		1938	
	The west	Asia	The west	Asia	The west	Asia	The west	Asia	The west	Asia
Export	15.0	6.7	15.2	14.7	56.8	42.2	142.4	90.9	94.2	46.4
Import	13.5	8.4	16.0	14.2	48.0	31.7	96.8	59.1	63.9	35.7

Note Asia includes China, Japan and India only
Sources Sugihara 1996: 14, 96–97

vessels annually called on Southeast Asian ports. The shipping services were run by Western companies, which brought the Southeast Asian economy closer to the global market.

In addition to the global spread of steam vessels, the British policy of free trade spurred international trade in Southeast Asia. It is true that Southeast Asia comprised formal colonies under the British, Dutch, French, Spanish, and American empires, except for Thailand. Yet, basically, the order of international trade was fixed by the British policy of free trade, which was followed by other Western countries, and the policies of the Netherlands in particular. Singapore was established as the most important center in Southeast Asia for global and regional trade (see Chap. 5 of this volume). The trading network became well-equipped, as the facilities of the key ports improved and commercial institutions such as banking in sub key ports such as Batavia and Manila were modernized (Sugihara 2001).

Second, thanks to the emergence of long-distance trade with the West, intra-Asian trade expanded. Table 3.3 shows the values of intra-Asian trade, which comprised trade between Southeast Asia and other parts of Asia (exactly speaking, it means trade with China, Japan, and India). Although intra-Asian trade never exceeded trade with the West, it also rapidly expanded from 1883 to 1928. This growth was realized by Asian factors as well. Alongside the economic development of Japan, India, and China over the course of time, Southeast Asia expanded the market for its primary products in these countries. Furthermore, Southeast Asia imported manufactured goods such as cotton textiles and miscellaneous products like matches, tooth brushes, and medicine especially from Japan in the first half of the twentieth century (Kagotani 1995).

Third, intra-Southeast Asian trade also expanded. Rice trade was especially important. Rice cultivation expanded in the delta areas in Mainland Southeast Asia as well as Java. This rice was exported to countries outside Southeast Asia but also to insular Southeast Asia except for Java, where imported rice was a crucial commodity for the laborers engaged in plantation agriculture.

International trade in this high colonial period, however, was a sort of exceptional case in the history of Southeast Asia. In general, the engine of international trade was intra-Asian trade with India and East Asia. Yet, in this period, trade with the West became the engine that drove the entire international trade of Southeast Asia. Nevertheless, similar to other periods, Southeast Asia played the role of supplying primary products, while it imported manufactured goods from outside the region. This equation continued even after World War II, until the mid-1970s.

To sum up, Southeast Asia stepped into the high colonial period in the fourth quarter of the nineteenth century, causing an increase in international trade, which was led by long-distance trade with the West. This development in international trade influenced Southeast Asia's economy and society. In the process of responding to rising overseas demand for Southeast Asian products, the economy experienced the development of the agricultural sector, which resulted in economic growth, as well as the growth of population.[1]

In addition to economic and population growth, what were the other features of this period that have influenced the direction of economic development which remained after independence? The following two points stand out.

3.5.1 The New Institutional Framework

The colonial authorities and the Thai government attempted to introduce the modern landholding system, but in vain. However, in terms of commercial and financial affairs, the authorities succeeded in introducing modern institutions for economic growth. An example of this is the banking system for the supply of capital.

In the late nineteenth century, Southeast Asia received an influx of European capital. Before this, foreign capital was invested first in agricultural, then in mining and shipping sectors: this was done directly by individual private entrepreneurs. However, over the course of time of this high colonial period, the colonial banking system became well-formed, and operated to facilitate the investment of European capital (Lindblad 1998). Through Western colonial banks, there was an influx of capital from home countries into the colonial economy. Western private banks as

---

[1] Population growth is estimated as follows: In Burma from 4,245,000 in 1870 to 19,488,000 in 1950; in Indonesia, from 28,922,000 in 1870 to 79,043,000 in 1950; in the Philippines, from 5,063,000 in 1870 to 21,131,000 in 1950; in Thailand, from 5,775,000 in 1870 to 20,042,000 in 1950; and in Vietnam, from 10,146,000 in 1870 to 25,348,000 in 1950 (Maddison 2001: 213).

well as colonial central banks were suppliers of capital for projects in Southeast Asia.

Banking became a key business for wealthy Chinese merchants and replaced tax farming developed in the nineteenth century. These merchants were engaged in the international transfer of money from Southeast Asia to mainland China. In addition, there were family bankers with their own capital, who lent money to small-scale overseas Chinese and indigenous Asian customers. Besides their own capital, some Chinese merchants were provided with capital by Western colonial banks, and they lent Western capital as brokers to local merchants and entrepreneurs.

3.5.2 Increase of Chinese Immigrants

The second key characteristic concerns Chinese immigrants. Not only Western impacts but also other Asian impacts were significant for the economic development of Southeast Asia. Among several Asians, the influence of overseas Chinese stands out (Skinner 1957; Claver 2014).

Continuing from the pre-early modern period, a vast number of Chinese people immigrated to Southeast Asia. While their geographical origins in mainland China were mostly in Fujian in the early modern period, the Chinese origins expanded to the provinces of Guangdong and Hainan after the mid-nineteenth century. When they arrived in Southeast Asia they began to work as manual laborers in several sectors such as plantation and mining or as dockworkers. Chinese immigrants were mostly male and although they eventually returned to China after several decades, some of them remained in Southeast Asia. Because Southeast Asia's population was scarce at the initial stage, Chinese immigrants were a very important source of labor.

Besides manual laborers, Chinese merchants were also key contributors to the Southeast Asian economy. They took on the role of entrepreneurs in several sectors. Mostly they were engaged in the commercial business. Since the early modern period overseas Chinese merchants managed retail shops in port cities and organized peddlers in the hinterland. Moreover, some of them were engaged in maritime trade by making use of their network comprising Southeast Asia and the Chinese coastal area. From the late nineteenth century onwards, exports to Asian countries increased in general, which would not have been realized without the Chinese network especially regarding exports to East Asia. When Western steam shipping companies emerged in Asian waters in the late nineteenth century, overseas Chinese merchants became key shippers. By and large, they functioned as maritime traders as well as mediators to connect international maritime trade with inland producers and consumers.

In addition to the commercial business, wealthy Chinese merchants extended their business interests to other sectors. Some of them invested in and managed a few industrial ventures such as plantation, food processing and mining. Before the beginning of large-scale European immigration in the twentieth century, overseas Chinese were almost the only ethnicity that ran the industrial sectors in Southeast Asia. On the other hand, tax farming was also a key business of wealthy overseas

Chinese merchants. Several sorts of taxes such as market tax, gambling tax, and opium excises were collected mostly by these merchants, although tax farming was abolished from the late nineteenth century to the early twentieth century.

In this way, while Western and Chinese influences flourished at the height of colonialism, Southeast Asia made efforts to decrease the influence of Western and Chinese ethnic elements from the Great Depression of the 1930s and continued these efforts during the period of decolonization after the region's independence from colonial rule. The imaginary of the concept of nation-state building was useful for this purpose, although the characteristic of multi-ethnicity, historically accumulated in Southeast Asia remain in essence even today. In addition, in the context of international trade, the Southeast Asian economy was still a typical supplier of primary products to the West even after the region's independence, until the mid-1970s.

3.6 The Contemporary Period and Conclusions

This chapter traced the role of international trade in Southeast Asia's long-term path to socio-economic development, by dividing the region's history in accordance with changing relationships between trade and the economy and society. The relationships have been strong, and the economic development of Southeast Asia has been influenced by the changing trend of international trade. The region is located between China and India, both of which had been powerful economic forces, and has been economically and culturally influenced by the two civilizations. When Europeans participated in the trade of Southeast Asia in the early sixteenth century, the Southeast Asian economy was faced with greater demand for primary products. The high demand from outside Southeast Asia served as a strong motivation for socio-economic changes in the region.

From the arrival of the Europeans to the mid-nineteenth century, Southeast Asia experienced the following changes: The development of international trade and the large demand for Southeast Asian products from outside the region resulted in the development of agricultural and mining sectors. With regard to agriculture, the plantation system was introduced, while small-scale peasant agriculture also developed. In both cases, these changes were reflections of the high demand for Southeast Asia's primary products in international trade. In addition, the mining sector and the plantation system needed immigrants and technology from outside. Both of them were managed by wealthy overseas Chinese merchants. On the other hand, European colonial cities gathered immigrants from Asia and Europe, which resulted in the general acceptance of multi-ethnic societies in port cities.

During the high colonial period, the development of international trade brought about economic changes in Southeast Asia. With the introduction of modern institutions, foreign merchants received benefits when conducting their business in Southeast Asia. These foreign merchants were not only European and American but also Chinese. In particular, overseas Chinese merchants were successful in banking and tax farming as well as in trade and commerce. These changes brought about by the development of international trade became distinctive characteristics of the Southeast Asian economy. They remain so today.

Large influences of international trade on the Southeast Asian economy continues to this day as well. Throughout the process of decolonization after World War II, the Southeast Asian economy acted as a supplier of primary products to Europe and USA. Rubber, rice, timber and sugar were the main items exported from Southeast Asia. However, in the mid-1970s, the economic links with East Asia became more significant. While the Japan's high-speed economic growth was put to an end in the early 1970s due to the Nixon Shock in 1971 and the oil crisis in 1973, South Korea, Taiwan, Hong Kong and even Singapore began to enjoy economic growth as Asian Newly Industrializing Economies (Asian NIEs). This gave a momentum to many Southeast Asian countries to treat economic links with Asian countries more seriously rather than sticking to traditional links with Europe and USA. Thus the Southeast Asian economy began to direct its path of economic development, with intra-Asian trade and the international division of labor in maritime Asia in mind. This meant that the region partly served as a supplier of resources (oil and natural gas, as well as agricultural, forestry and marine products) but also acted as a producer of manufactured goods, or at least of manufacturing parts as part of supply chains of manufactured goods, thus promoting industrialization. Of course, it is well-known that the process of the economic growth in the fourth quarter of the twentieth century was often accompanied by the developmental directorship, at least in the initial period.

To conclude, as seen in Fig. 3.1, the Southeast Asian economy has strong historical roots and has obtained considerable benefits from international trade. Since the entry of the Europeans in the beginning of the sixteenth century in particular, Southeast Asia has been in touch with a wide range of overseas markets in Asia and Europe. Large demands for Southeast Asian products have stimulated the economic development of the region. The economy was largely developed for the mass production of primary products. Development of the delta areas, introduction of the plantation system, and the acceptance of Chinese immigrants are good examples of the region's capacity to respond to changes, before the production of manufactured goods became more important in the late twentieth century.

References

Abushouk, A. I., & Ibrahim, H. A. (Eds.). (2009). *The Hadhrami diaspora in Southeast Asia: Identity maintenance or assimilation?*. Leiden and Boston: Brill Academic Publishers.

Andaya, B. W., & Andaya, L. Y. (2015). *A history of early modern Southeast Asia, 1400–1830*. Cambridge: Cambridge University Press.

Barnard, T. P. (2003). *Multiple centres of authority: Society and environment in Siak and eastern Sumatra, 1674–1827*. Leiden: KITLV Press.

Blussé, L. (1986). *Strange company: Chinese settlers, mestizo women, and the Dutch in VOC Batavia*. Dordrecht: Foris Publications.

Blussé, L. (1999). Chinese century: The eighteenth century in the China Sea region. *Archipel, 58*(3), 107–129.
Claver, A. (2014). *Dutch commerce and Chinese merchants in Java: Colonial relationships in trade and finance, 1800–1942*. Leiden and Boston: Brill Academic Publishers.
Crosby, A. W., Jr. (1972). *The Columbian exchange: Biological and cultural consequences of 1492*. Westport: Greenwood Press.
Elson, R. E. (1994). *Village Java under the cultivation system, 1830–1870*. St Leonards: Allen and Unwin.
Hall, K. R. (2011). *A history of early Southeast Asia: Maritime trade and societal development, 100–1500*. Lanham: Rowman & Littlefield.
Hardy, A., Cucarzi, M., & Zolese, P. (Eds.). (2009). *Champa and the archaeology of Mỹ Sơn (Vietnam)*. Singapore: NUS Press.
Jacobs, E. M. (2006). *Merchants in Asia: The trade of the Dutch East India Company during the eighteenth century*. Leiden: CNWS Publications.
Kagotani, N. (1995). The role of Chinese merchants in the development of the Japanese cotton industry, 1880–1934. *Zinbun: Annals of the institute for research in humanities, Kyoto University, 30*, 149–183.
Kathirithamby-Wells, J., & Villiers, J. (Eds.). (1990). *The Southeast Asian port and polity: Rise and demise*. Singapore: Singapore University Press.
Lieberman, V. (2003). *Strange parallels: Southeast Asia in global context, c. 800–1830*, Vol. 1: *Integration on the mainland*. Cambridge: Cambridge University Press.
Lindblad, J. T. (1998). *Foreign investment in Southeast Asia in the twentieth century*. Basingstoke: Macmillan Press.
Liu, Y., Chen, Z., & Blue, G. (Eds.). (2014). *Zheng He's maritime Voyages (1405–1433) and China's relations with the Indian Ocean world: A multilingual bibliography*. Leiden and Boston: Brill Academic Publishers.
Maddison, A. (2001). *The world economy: A millennial perspective*. Paris: OECD.
Munoz, P. M. (2006). *Early kingdoms of the Indonesian Archipelago and the Malay Peninsula*. Singapore: Editions Didier Millet.
Raben, R. (1996). Batavia and Colombo: The ethnic and spatial order of two colonial cities, 1600–1800. Unpublished PhD thesis, Leiden University.
Reid, A. (1997). Introduction. In A. Reid (Ed.), *The last stand of Asian autonomies: Responses to modernity in the diverse states of Southeast Asia and Korea, 1750–1900* (pp. 1–25). London: Macmillan Press.
Shimada, R. (2006). *The intra-Asian Trade in Japanese copper by the Dutch East India Company during the eighteenth century*. Leiden and Boston: Brill Academic Publishers.
Shimada, R. (2013). The long-term pattern of maritime trade in Java from the late eighteenth century to the mid-nineteenth century. *Southeast Asian Studies, 2*(3), 475–497.
Shimada, R. (2015). Hinterlands and port cities in Southeast Asia's economic development in the eighteenth century: The case of tin production and its export trade. In T. Mizushima, G. B. Souza, & D. O. Flynn (Eds.), *Hinterlands and commodities: Place, space, time and the political economic development of Asia over the long eighteenth century* (pp. 197–214). Leiden and Boston: Brill Academic Publishers.
Shimada, R. (2018). Invisible links: Maritime trade between Japan and South Asia in the early modern period. In A. J. H. Latham & H. Kawakatsu (Eds.), *Asia and the history of the international economy: Essays in memory of Peter Mathias* (pp. 57–71). London and New York: Routledge.
Skinner, G. W. (1957). *Chinese society in Thailand: An analytical history*. Ithaca: Cornell University Press.
Somers Heidhues, M. (2003). *Golddiggers, farmers, and traders in the "Chinese districts" of West Kalimantan, Indonesia*. Ithaca: Southeast Asia Program Publications, Cornell University.
Souza, G. B. (1986). *The survival of empire: Portuguese trade and society in China and the South China Sea, 1630–1754*. Cambridge: Cambridge University Press.

Sugihara K. (1996). *Ajia kan boeki no keisei to kozo* (The Formation and structure of intra-Asian trade). Kyoto: Minerva Shobo: 1996.

Sugihara, K. (2001.) Kokusai bungyo to tonan ajia shokuminchi keizai (The international division of labor and the Southeast Asian colonial economy). In H. Kano (Ed.), *Shokuminchi keizai no hanei to choraku* (Prosperity and decline of the colonial economy), Tonan ajiashi (Southeast Asian history) (Vol. 6, pp. 249–272). Tokyo: Iwanami Shoten.

Yao, K. (2003). Two rivals on an island of sugar: The sugar trade of the VOC and overseasChinese in Formosa in the seventeenth century. In L. Blussé (Ed.), *Around and about Formosa: Essays in honor of Professor Ts'ao Yung-ho* (pp. 129–140). Taipei: Ts'ao Yung-ho Foundation for Culture and Education.

Open Access This chapter is licensed under the terms of the Creative Commons Attribution-NonCommercial-NoDerivatives 4.0 International License (http://creativecommons.org/licenses/by-nc-nd/4.0/), which permits any noncommercial use, sharing, distribution and reproduction in any medium or format, as long as you give appropriate credit to the original author(s) and the source, provide a link to the Creative Commons licence and indicate if you modified the licensed material. You do not have permission under this licence to share adapted material derived from this chapter or parts of it.

The images or other third party material in this chapter are included in the chapter's Creative Commons licence, unless indicated otherwise in a credit line to the material. If material is not included in the chapter's Creative Commons licence and your intended use is not permitted by statutory regulation or exceeds the permitted use, you will need to obtain permission directly from the copyright holder.

Chapter 4
Role of State and Non-state Networks in Early-Modern Southeast Asian Trade

Atsushi Ota

4.1 Introduction

An important characteristic in the history of economic growth of Southeast Asia is that the region had developed brisk trade networks well before the launch of the modern colonial rule during the nineteenth century. The precolonial trade development is a common phenomenon in parts of Europe and West, South, and East Asia, but it is not always the case in other regions including many parts of Africa and South America. Its historical uniqueness therefore deserves scholarly attention, as this can be considered one of the elements related to the recent economic growth of the region.

The precolonial trade in Southeast Asia had a long history, and its patterns were changing throughout different phases of history. Among them "the Age of Commerce" is a famous concept which highlights the trade boom in Southeast Asia from c. 1450 to 1680 (Reid 1993a). After a period of the VOC trade domination (c. 1680–1750), the late eighteenth century had been long considered as the period of decline and fragmentation in Southeast Asia. More recently, however, scholars proposed a concept of the "Chinese century," indicating the trade recovery in a reorganized form in the eighteenth century (Reid 1997; Blussé 1999). The Age of Commerce and Chinese century can be labelled as the early-modern period in Southeast Asia. In spite of the new understanding of the Chinese century, the trade patterns and systems in the early-modern period are still assumed to be very different from those in the following modern colonial period. We tend to consider that modern technology, capital, and political systems dramatically changed Southeast Asian economy and trading patterns during the colonial period, and they were finally subjugated to the West-dominated world economy. As a result, we tend to assume that the

---

A. Ota (✉)
Keio University, Minato-Ku, Tokyo, Japan
e-mail: ota@econ.keio.ac.jp

© The Author(s) 2019
K. Otsuka and K. Sugihara (eds.), *Paths to the Emerging State in Asia and Africa*, Emerging-Economy State and International Policy Studies, https://doi.org/10.1007/978-981-13-3131-2_4

modern colonial economic systems formed large parts of the basis of Southeast Asian economy today, disconnected from its early-modern past.

Against these assumptions, I argue in this chapter that the elements that characterizes in Southeast Asian trade were created and developed in the early-modern period, especially after the Age of Commerce. I rename the Chinese century as the Age of China-oriented trade, because what characterizes this period was not only Chinese trade and migration, as was often assumed, but the fundamental change in the state-commerce relationship, in which Southeast Asian actors played a crucial role, as a result of the shift in the nature of trade. I also argue that the China-oriented trade remained important until around 1870, buttressing the growing long-distance trade with Europe during the so-called early colonial period (c. 1820–1870), and beyond. Special focus is given not only to state politics on trade, but also to the role of non-state networks, in which crucial actors were traders as well as commercial-military groups, which are sometimes also called pirates. Because of my specialty, the discussion of this chapter concentrates on insular Southeast Asia.

In this chapter state refers to any autonomous political body that claims to exercise supreme authority over a certain territory and more strongly over people living there. This vague definition covers a wide range of political bodies from an early-modern petit statelet to a colonial state with rigid legal and taxation structure. Nevertheless such a wide coverage will enable us to explore various elements in politico-commerce relationship in a single framework, and to discuss their diversity and development effectively.

4.2 Age of Commerce

4.2.1 The Rise of the Trade and Its Basic Pattern

"The Age of Commerce" is a concept raised by the historian Anthony Reid, to refer to the trade boom from c. 1450 to 1680. In search of precious Southeast Asian products such as spices (e.g. nutmeg, mace, and clove), wood (sandalwood and aloeswood etc.), pepper, and various kinds of forest products, traders from West, South, and East Asia, and later those from Europe visited a number of trading ports in Southeast Asia.[1] These foreign traders brought their items either from their places of origin or from the transit ports that they passed by on the way. The most significant among them in Southeast Asian trade were Indian textiles, Japanese silver, and Chinese manufactured products such as porcelain and metal works.

According to Reid, the important elements to trigger the boom are (1) the incorporation of Southeast Asian states into the China-centered tributary system, (2) the arrival of Muslim traders from West Asia and Northwest India, and (3) the inflow of American and Japanese silver. First, in 1402 Yongle Emperor of the Ming dynasty

---

[1] For more information of the external elements that affected Southeast Asian trade, such as Chinese, Indian, and European traders, see Chap. 3 of this volume.

called for Asian rulers of independent states to participate in the Chinese tributary system, to expand his influence throughout maritime Asia. Under this system, southern "barbarian" rulers were requested to send their tributary missions to Nanjing, the Ming capital at that time, thereby accepting the authority of the Ming Emperor. In return they were granted the official permission to conduct trade with China, a lucrative commercial opportunity amidst the strict trade ban of the Ming dynasty. In addition, as the Ming Emperor strictly forbade the rulers under the tributary system from fighting with each other, the system also guaranteed peace among them.

Second, under the rule of the powerful empires such as the Abbasid Caliphate (750–1258, 1261–1517) and the Safavid dynasty (1501–1736), the activities of Muslim traders like the Arabs, Persians, and Gujaratis expanded to Southeast Asia, in search of precious tropical products. Third, the Japanese and American silver, the production of which expanded in the sixteenth century, was brought into Southeast Asia in large quantities, which facilitated the transactions of Southeast Asian products.

Southeast Asia was attractive for foreign traders, first of all because the region produced precious products available only in very limited areas, such as nutmeg and mace grown only in Banda Islands and clove in Ternate and Tidore islands. On the other hand, the demand for these Southeast Asian products were very strong in Asia and Europe because they were not only used for flavoring but also for medical purposes.

The basic pattern of trade in the Age of Commerce was the exchange between precious natural products from Southeast Asia (spices and woods etc.) and foreign manufactured products (especially Indian textiles and Chinese porcelain). In terms of traders, Southeast Asians were most prominent in the local trade (trade between producing areas and transit ports in Southeast Asia), while the regional trade (trade between transit ports in Southeast Asia) was conducted by Chinese, Indian and Southeast Asian traders. In long-distance trade (trade between Southeast Asia and other parts of the world) Chinese, Indian, and European traders were most prominent in the respective routes from their places of origin. Main consumers of Southeast Asian products in this period were a small number of rich and powerful people, such as members of the royal families, nobles, and privileged merchants, and items that they demanded were small-volume, high-value products (Reid 1993a). This basic trade pattern significantly changed in the mid-eighteenth century, as I discuss later.

4.2.2 Southeast Asian Characteristics

Considering the fact that a similar trade boom did not take place in many other parts of the world, such as Africa and South America, it is worth asking why the trade boom happened particularly in Southeast Asia. The existence of the products available only in this region, and its location between the great civilizations of India and China are frequently mentioned reasons, but they do not fully explain the trade boom. Outside traders would not have found these products, if there were not for local knowledge of the usefulness of the products, and for the local trade, which brought the products to the attention of outside traders. Local people created the network to bring the valuable products from the producing areas to nearby markets and transit ports. It was the existence of active local trade that gave foreign traders access to the precious products in Southeast Asia.

Why were the locals able to develop local trade in Southeast Asia? In fact, Southeast Asians had a very long history of maritime activities. Austronesians migrated from Taiwan to most areas of maritime Southeast Asia before 1500 B.C., fully making use of their excellent knowledge of shipbuilding and maritime navigation. Local trade in Southeast Asia must have been active before the first century B.C., as is known in Chinese sources, perhaps with the knowledge of monsoon winds. Indian traders were regularly dealing in spices grown only in small islands in East Indonesia in the first century A.D., according to a Greek text, perhaps because Southeast Asian traders brought them to transit ports. In addition, environmental elements were also favorable for trade. The seas among numerous islands are relatively calm, and a number of rivers were navigable. Deep forests provided ample wood materials for shipbuilding. The combination of these trade-friendly environments and the ancient knowledge of shipbuilding, long-distance navigation, and monsoon winds was unique in Southeast Asia, and this became the basis for the region to enjoy a trade boom in the early-modern era, in addition to the precious natural products grown or collected only in this region.

4.2.3 State Politics and Its Impact on Society

In order for foreign traders to obtain popular Southeast Asian products, it was necessary to find convenient transit ports, as the producing regions of these products were often very far from the main routes of maritime trade between China and India. They emerged in nodal points of traffic, such as the coast of the Gulf of Thailand, both sides of the Straits of Malacca, and the north coast of Java, and provided opportunities for foreign traders to exchange their goods they brought with them with the products from remote areas of Southeast Asia (Reid 1993a).

The growth of the transit ports soon led to the emergence of a particular type of state in Southeast Asia in the Age of Commerce—port state.[2] Different from the older agriculture-oriented states such as Angkor and Majapahit,[3] the rulers of the port states relied their wealth and power on maritime trade. Not only did they obtain large parts of income from the customs and trade-related taxes from local and foreign traders, but also they organized trade fleets by themselves. The typical examples

---

[2]This type of state has often been called port polity, probably in order to include small statelets typical in Southeast Asia in discussion. However, for the purpose of simplifying discussion, I use the term port state to mean any scale of political body, which relies its economic, political, and ideological base on ports under its influence.

[3]The Srivijaya Kingdom was also a sort of alliance of port states. See Chap. 3, Sect. 3.2.

of port states include Ayutthaya, Pasai, Aceh, Perak, Palembang, Banten, Demak, Gresik, Makassar, and Brunei, although they rose and fell in different periods during the Age of Commerce.

The politics of port states focused on the promotion of trade. In order to protect the ships laden with precious cargos from the attacks of pirates and gangsters, the rulers built walls and bulwarks, and organized naval fleets. As traders naturally preferred well protected ports, effective protection promised rulers more income from trading ships.

In order to effectively promote trade, however, military power was not enough. First, rulers attempted to make use of the knowledge and skills of foreigners, to attract their compatriot traders. The rulers often created special quarters for particular ethnic groups to reside in or immediately outside their capitals. These foreign communities actively conducted trade within and beyond the host state, and the rulers often appointed the representatives of each community in an important position such as the harbor master (*shahbandar*). As a result, the multi-ethnic formation of major port cities became the tradition in Southeast Asia, far before the colonial rule. Second, rulers attempted to establish peace and order in their ports and nearby waters, by issuing rules and regulations in their state. The Malay law codes, a corpus of rules and regulations first promulgated by the sultan of Malacca, was such an example. Many of the rules and regulations were concerned with smooth operation of trade and commercial transactions. Third, some rulers attempted to attract Muslim traders, by creating places for worship, such as mosques. In insular Southeast Asia, some rulers also chose to convert themselves to Islam.

The conversion to Islam and the promulgation of law codes were also elaborated strategies on the part of rulers for their legitimacy. For example, in the north coast of Java, rulers of the newly emerging port states like Demak adopted Islam as a new source of legitimacy, in order to counter the land-based Hindu Kingdom of Majapahit. Being the propagator of Islam in their states also meant that the ruler became a mediator between the local secular world and the (imagined) holy outside world. This must have attracted the awe and admiration from local people. Likewise, the rulers who established law codes were respected as the protector of peace and order. The wide application of Malay law codes and the popular use of the Malay language in commerce enhanced the position of the sultan of Malacca as the center of the Malay World.

The state was also involved in trade. The rulers monopolized not only the trade of important export items such as nutmeg and pepper, but also their production. For example, the rulers of Banda and Banten placed strict state control on the production of nutmeg and pepper respectively, and forced the cultivators to sell the products only to the rulers.

Through these sorts of politics, states played a prominent role in the promotion of trade. This is a most important characteristic in the Age of Commerce. State rulers protected their ports militarily, and they organized the systems for smooth transactions by creating amicable environments for traders. As these features were not necessarily the case after the eighteenth century, it is worth considering why it took place in the Age of Commerce. First, it should be noted that important export items in the Age of Commerce, such as nutmeg, mace, clove, pepper, and sandalwood were produced only in very limited areas, and therefore state control of the production and trade of these items was relatively easy. The ships laden with these high-value items must have tended to anchor in ports under the powerful ruler, in the expectation of effective protection. As ships tended to concentrate on a small number of influential ports, powerful port states had a chance for further prosperity. Second, these powerful states tended to monopolize the import of weapons. When state rulers were powerful enough to dominate trade, other influential members, either within or outside the royal family, had less chances of obtaining weapons from foreign traders. From these reasons, states were in a position to take an initiative in local and regional trade during the Age of Commerce.

What sort of impact did the trade boom during the Age of Commerce have on society in the history of Southeast Asia? First, the development of regional trade strengthened common material culture in Southeast Asia, such as the custom of betel chewing, flavoring with fermented fish, and the use of cotton for clothing. Second, as local trade developed, some port cities and cash-crop producing areas abandoned food production, relying on the supply from food-producing areas. The division of labor was considered to be a condition of economic development, and this took place particularly in the Age of Commerce in Southeast Asia. Seen from a different angle, however, the intensified division of labor also meant that some areas lost economic self-sustenance. Some port cities and cash-crop producing areas had to depend on trade to obtain food and other necessities. Food-producing regions also increased the production of food such as rice, by importing necessities such as textiles. This is how certain areas of Southeast Asia became a trade-dependent society during the Age of Commerce. This would explain the continuation of local trade in the following centuries.

Although influential merchant elites emerged in several trade-oriented states, capital did not accumulate among them. As Reid explained, this can be attributed to the strong interests of state rulers in commerce. Because they enthusiastically attempted to benefit from trade and production control, they were equally enthusiastic to prevent powerful merchants from becoming so rich and influential as to threaten their wealth and power (Reid 1993a). Capital accumulation did not take place, in the way that it did to prepare the birth of capitalism in Europe around the same time.

Reid explained that the Age of Commerce ended around 1680, when the Dutch East India Company (*Verenigde Oostindisch Compagnie* or VOC) had created their trade network centered on its Asian headquarters in Batavia. In return for military supports in internal conflicts in local states, the VOC forced the rulers to conclude treaties, which allowed monopoly rights for the VOC to trade their major export items. These items were first sent to Batavia, from which they were re-exported to many places in Asia and Europe. Finally, defeating its major rivals, Macassar and Banten by the 1680s, the VOC reorganized the trade pattern from the decentralized open system in the Age of Commerce to their centralized monopolistic system. In the states under their influence, the Dutch often placed the production of important cash crops under control. This usually resulted in production decline in many places because cultivators disliked the enforcement and unfavorable prices that the VOC had set. Some influential states such as Mataram and Aceh, losing their interest in external trade, concentrated more on the agricultural production in the inland. According to Reid, regional and local trade in Southeast Asia thus fell into decline in the late seventeenth century (Reid 1993a).

4.3 Age of China-Oriented Trade

4.3.1 Rise of a New Trade Pattern

Several years later after the publication of *The Age of Commerce in Southeast Asia*, however, Reid revised his argument of the trade decline after the late seventeenth century. Now he has emphasized the trade recovery in the mid-eighteenth century, which he has called the "Chinese century." He argues that Sino-Southeast Asian trade and the Chinese migration to Southeast Asia developed from the mid eighteenth century, because of the new Chinese interest in Southeast Asian products (Reid 1997). My own research largely agrees with Reid's view, while there are some differences in the following points. First, the term "Chinese century" gives an impression that the Chinese played a far more important role than others in the story of trade recovery. In fact Southeast Asians such as Bugis, Iranun, and Malays also took a crucial role. Second, the increase of trade in this period did not only mean the participation of new players and new trade items. It should be emphasized that it brought a total reorganization of trade patterns and state formation in Southeast Asia. Third, the "Chinese century" did not end with the fall of independent states during the nineteenth century, as Reid seems to imply, but it survived the colonial trade pattern. I call the new trade pattern that emerged in mid-eighteenth century Southeast Asia the China-oriented trade, and I identify the period of this trade pattern as roughly from c. 1750 to c. 1870. In this section I will explain the development and characteristics of this trade pattern, and the typical local politics towards the trade.

It was the economic growth in China that triggered the boom of Sino-Southeast Asian trade, as Reid has explained. First, in order to meet the food demand caused by the rapid population growth, the Qing government started to import rice from Saigon and Ayutthaya by loosening its maritime ban. Second, the expanding middle strata of the society in economically advanced areas, such as the South China coast, Beijing, and the middle- and downstream Yangzi basin, witnessed growing demand on exotic tropical products from Southeast Asia, such as marine products like sea cucumber and shark's fin, forest products like rattan and resin, and others such as birds' nests, pepper, and tin. Southeast Asian traders collected these products in numerous places in insular Southeast Asia, and brought them to regional trade hubs, from which Chinese traders brought them back to South China coast. This is how a new trade pattern, dealing with China-bound Southeast Asian natural products, emerged in the mid eighteenth century.

The demands on the abovementioned types of Southeast Asian products in China seem to be related to the "middle-class luxury" (Pomerantz 2000) among those who enjoyed growing purchasing power under the strong economy during the long reign of Qianlong Emperor (1735–99). It was around this period that dining places increased in large cities, and the royal cuisine spread to the wider circle of society. Those who newly obtained economic power wanted to have higher self-esteem and social recognition through the consumption of items that were consumed in the upper circle of society, among them imported items. Exotic edible items from Southeast Asia, such as sea cucumber, shark's fin, and birds' nests, were typical items for this type of consumption. These items were indeed rare and expensive, but they were still much more easily available than clove and sandalwood during the Age of Commerce. Other Southeast Asian items were also related to mass consumption. Tin was used for tea container and also for fake paper notes burnt in rituals, while rattan was processed into various kinds of furniture. These were new types of mass consumption items, which were still considered luxurious but widely used today across the wide spectrum of society.

4.3.2 *Shifting Trade Hegemony*

The Chinese traders headed for Southeast Asia in large numbers, especially after the lifting of maritime ban in 1727, and they tended to call at transit ports outside the Dutch sphere of influence. This is partly because they disliked the regulations imposed in Dutch ports such as Batavia and Malacca, and also because the Dutch were not interested in the China-bound items. Riau (South of Singapore), Saigon, Jolo (Sulu islands in the Southwest Philippines), and Spanish Manila were typical ports from which China-bound Southeast Asian items could be obtained.

Stimulated by the growing Chinese demand in Southeast Asian products, British traders joined this new pattern of trade. After the opening of Canton (Guangzhou) to Western traders in 1757, British, Dutch, and other European traders imported large amounts of tea from China to Northwestern Europe such as Britain, France, and the Netherlands. Tea party became an important opportunity for socialization among upper-class ladies in these states, and the custom of tea party expanded from the Netherlands to other countries, and also to wider strata of society. This is how this growing demand on China tea was also related to the emerging mass consumption culture in Northwest Europe. Europeans, however, did not have attractive items from home for the China market. In order to save precious silver drained in the purchase of tea, the English East India Company (EIC) and British country traders (those who conducted trade in Asia with the official permission from the government of British India) attempted to bring Asian products demanded in China. Large parts of their items brought to Guangzhou were Indian cotton and opium, but not small amounts of Southeast Asian tin, pepper, and other items were also imported (Ota 2006). In order to obtain these Southeast Asian items, British country traders also visited independent ports outside the Dutch sphere of influence, for the same reasons as those of Chinese traders. To Southeast Asia, British country traders mostly brought Indian textiles and opium, and Western weapons. Because these items had strong demand among local rulers, country traders soon became a main player in Southeast Asian trade. Because the state-chartered EIC had difficulties to deal with these clandestine items, it was mainly private country traders who dealt in them.

The visit of an increasing number of Chinese junks and British country traders to non-Dutch ports transformed the trade pattern in maritime Southeast Asia. Not only Chinese and British but also local traders gathered in these ports for the business with foreign traders after the mid-eighteenth century. Receiving these traders, independent ports such as Riau and Jolo, the capitals respectively of the Johor and the Sulu Kingdoms, emerged as important trade hubs. This development inevitably undermined the position of the VOC.

Although the abovementioned China-bound items were out of Dutch interest, the rise of these ports was a crucial threat for the VOC. For example, Jambi and Palembang started to export their tin and pepper to Riau, not to Batavia, in spite of the fact that these items were supposed to be placed under the VOC monopoly. Local traders preferred Riau because of the better conditions offered by Chinese and other traders. The rise of independent ports and their growing trade seriously undermined the VOC trade control.

From the 1780s Johor Sultanate and the VOC fiercely competed over the trade hegemony in Malay waters. The tension culminated in the military clash in 1784, and it resulted in the VOC conquest of Riau. Scholars had considered that the fall of Riau brought confusion and trade decline in Malay waters because it resulted in the absence of a strong state power to control trade before the British establishment of Singapore in 1819. However, I have discussed elsewhere that the Dutch conquest of Riau in the 1780s did not mean the end of active trading in the surrounding waters. First, although Riau indeed lost the function of a trade hub after the Dutch conquest, several other ports, such as Sukadana and Pontianak, soon emerged as alternatives. Chinese, Southeast Asian, and British traders visited these ports, in order to obtain China-bound Southeast Asian products (Ota 2010).

Second, although there were a number of records of "pirate" attacks in the Straits of Malacca after the fall of Riau, this did not necessarily mean trade decline. For example, after the end of the 1780s Dutch pepper trade was indeed heavily disturbed by so-called pirates, consisting of Bugis, Malay, Iranun, and other Southeast Asians. They frequently made assaults on passing cargo ships and on the inland pepper-producing areas in Lampung in South Sumatra, the largest pepper provider in Southeast Asia at that time. As Lampung pepper was supposed to be sold exclusively to the VOC on the basis of a treaty with the sultan, the "pirate" attacks were a serious problem for the VOC. For VOC officials, these Asian attackers were no doubt pirates. However, the pepper deprived by these groups was in fact circulated on a commercial domain. The attackers usually sold their pepper, a part of which they sometimes purchased in the producing regions, to Chinese and British traders waiting in meeting points outside Lampung. In a VOC record, the pepper deprived by non-Dutch actors around Lampung amounted to 3,400 picols or about 36% of the VOC pepper trade in Batavia in a year (Ota 2006). Considering the usual activities of

Chinese and British traders at this time, it is very likely that the deprived Lampung pepper was finally brought to China. In this way, so-called pirates played a role to bring the pepper placed under the Dutch monopoly to the China market, to meet the strong demand there. It therefore seems reasonable to call them armed traders or commercial-military groups. Because of their contribution trade actively continued in the Malay waters after the fall of Riau.

4.3.3 New Migration Patterns

In addition to the growth of the trade of China-bound products, another remarkable feature in the Age of China-oriented trade was active migration of various groups of people. As Reid and other scholars have discussed, Chinese migration was most prominent among them. Local rulers of thinly populated tin-mining regions in Malay Peninsula and Bangka Island agreed with Chinese traders to introduce Chinese labor and skills, in order to increase the production. Gold mines in West Kalimantan attracted waves of Chinese laborers. Chinese migrants also opened pepper and gambir gardens in Terengganu, Brunei, and Riau, to meet the demand in China. The products of these mines and gardens were almost exclusively exported to China by Chinese traders. These migrants were mostly from Fujian and Guangdong Provinces in South China. Under the population pressure during the eighteenth century, a number of Hokkien, Cantonese, Hakka, and Teochew, many of whom had experiences in commercial agriculture and mining in their hometown, headed for Southeast Asia (Reid 1997).

The Chinese migrants in this period often created their communities in inland areas around mines and gardens, different from those in the previous centuries, when Chinese communities usually concentrated in the coastal areas. The transit ports in the coastal areas, such as Malacca, Riau, and Pontianak, and later Singapore and Kuala Lumpur, played an important role in the trade with upstream migrant communities, to export the products from Chinese gardens or mines, and to import necessities for the Chinese migrant communities. Although it is generally understood that the emergence of this type of Chinese migration was a phenomenon in the high colonial period, in fact it started in the late eighteenth century, though on a smaller scale and without any colonial settings.

It should be also noted that not only Chinese but also Southeast Asians actively migrated in the Indonesian and Philippine Archipelagos, and they played a significant role in the transformation of the trade pattern. One of the prominent migrant groups was the Bugis, originally from around Makassar in South Sulawesi, known for their excellent knowledge and skills in maritime navigation, commerce, and battle. During and after the Makassar War in 1660–66, with which the VOC finally conquered Makassar, the Bugis took refuge to various parts of the Indonesian Archipelago, and they created their communities in the coastal areas. As the China-oriented trade developed, the Bugis played an important role in bringing marine and forest products to transit ports, utilizing their extensive network throughout insular Southeast Asia.

Another prominent migrant group, the Iranun, was originally from Magindanao in South Philippines, and formed an influential group in the Sulu Kingdom. As its capital Jolo grew with the expanding China-oriented trade, the activities of the Iranun also expanded. They collected marine products, and more notoriously abducted people to use them as marine-product collectors, rowers of their ships, and slaves in their communities. Malays and some other groups also actively migrated within the Indonesian Archipelago, conducting the trade of marine and forest products. It was also very common that different ethnic groups acted together under an outstanding leader (Ota 2014).

These Southeast Asian migrants were routinely involved in local and regional trade in a heavy-handed way, using their networks and violence, to obtain particular items. It was this type of migrant groups that formed the abovementioned commercial-military groups.

4.3.4 Basic Trade Pattern

Although Asian traders regained the leading role in the trade in this period, the new trade pattern was different in many respects from that in the Age of Commerce. The composition of major Southeast Asian exports changed from high-value small-volume natural products to the bulkier mass-consumption items, such as marine and forest products, tin, pepper, and birds' nests.

In return, Southeast Asia imported Indian textiles via Indian traders, opium and Western weapons via British traders, and Chinese sundry items such as paper and pottery from Chinese traders. Although Indian textile trade had shrunk towards the end of the Age of Commerce, Southeast Asians seem to have restarted its import. Opium consumption in the eighteenth century seems to have mostly concentrated on Chinese migrant workers. This type of opium consumption was well known in the high colonial period, but it surely started in some Chinese communities such as sugar gardens outside Batavia in the Age of the China-oriented trade (Ota 2006). These things seem to indicate that Southeast Asians had a significant purchasing power, most probably through the export of China-bound items, which Chinese traders bought with silver. The Outer Islands (the territory of Dutch East Indies apart from Java and Madura) had a sizable export surplus in the nineteenth century, as shown in the following section, largely as a result of the growing export of natural products to China. Probably there were similar developments in the eighteenth century.

In terms of traders, Chinese junk traders and British country traders took part of the trade between South China coast and Southeast Asian ports. Apart from British traders, Europeans did not play an important role. British traders cooperated local and Chinese traders and commercial-military groups to trade (often clandestine) items in defiance of the VOC monopoly. For local and regional trade, Southeast Asian commercial-military groups played a crucial role in bringing natural products from the producing areas to local transit ports.

The shift in major Southeast Asian exports from small-volume high-value items to bulky mass-consumption items exerted powerful impacts on the producing regions. Different from the major exports in the previous centuries such as precious spices and wood, marine and forest products were collected spanning much larger areas. This means that the state control of the collection and trade of export products, as attempted in the Age of Commerce, became much less effective and therefore it was hardly conducted on the items such as rattan and shark's fin.[4] Without hardly any state monopoly, a much larger number of people came to be involved in commercial activities across wider areas. It seems very likely that local people became much more accustomed to commercial transactions, and became increasingly market-oriented through the collection of export items.

4.3.5 Commercial-Military Groups and States

The trade of forest and marine products made the role of the commercial-military groups more important. The producing and collecting areas of those products were usually far from state centers and state protection. Traders therefore had to arm themselves to defend their cargos and ships against attackers on seas and rivers. In order to obtain human captives to sell as slaves, military power was essential, while heavy armament was also advantageous to get an upper hand over commercial rivals. Maritime migrants such as the Bugis, Iranun, and Malay therefore tended to heavily arm themselves and organized commercial-military groups. These non-state groups obtained weapons, which were much more easily available than in the previous centuries. As mentioned earlier, British country traders brought Western weapons including firearms. Spanish and Dutch records tell that a number of commercial-military groups bought weapons from British traders in Sulu and the Malay waters (Warren 1981; Ota 2006).

The rise of commercial-military groups also had an impact on the state formation. States no longer played so prominent a role in the control of trade as they did in the Age of Commerce. States in this period often attempted to promote trade by establishing a strong connection with commercial-military groups. These groups were useful for states not only to obtain China-bound products, but also to gain military support for conflicts with their rivals. In return, states provided privileges such as a high official position and tax exemption. For example, Johor Kingdom, which had received waves of Bugis migrants after the Macassar War, gave influential Bugis families a hereditary position of Raja Muda (viceroy). The Sultan of Sukadana provided migrant groups with a place to settle down and tax exemptions, and granted their leader with a high official position (Trocki 1979; Ota 2010).

---

[4]There are records of state priority in the purchase of birds' nests in West Kalimantan, but the same records also indicate that the attempt was not very successful. The local chiefs of the producing region sold only a small part of the products to the state ruler, because of the weak state control (Ota 2010).

Some states were indeed established by the leaders of commercial-military groups. The founder of Mempawa in West Kalimantan was a legendary prince who took self-refuge after the Makassar War (Andaya 1995). The founder of Pontianak had been the leader of a notorious commercial-military group who had assaulted the south and east coasts of Kalimantan. After years of roaming, he went with his 200 followers to West Kalimantan, to establish the new state of Pontianak. His group consisted of a mixed group of people who were attracted to his charisma in his leadership in the successful trade and assaults (Ota 2010). This type of leadership to achieve economic success through commerce and violence formed a stronger basis of the legitimacy of the ruler in this period, than becoming a religious mediator or a promulgator of law codes, as was the case in the Age of Commerce.

States in the Age of the China-oriented trade were generally smaller, and they played a less prominent role to sustain the trade network than those in the Age of Commerce. It was rather commercial-military groups that played a larger role in the trade in insular Southeast Asia. Considering their role discussed above, it is possible to argue that commercial-military groups played a significant role in the continuation of local and regional trade, regardless of the rise and fall of states. For example, as I explained before, after the VOC conquest of Riau in 1784, trade continued using different hubs such as Sukadana and Pontianak. Lampung pepper was exported through commercial-military groups to China toward the end of the eighteenth century. These things mean that commercial-military groups took an initiative to continue trade under weak state control.

There is virtually no trace of capital accumulation among the commercial-military groups in this period. They were oriented not only to increase their economic wealth but also to enhance their military and political power, so that they did not always use their economic gain to accumulate capital nor to invest it in a new enterprise. They had to use large parts of their wealth for their armament and for military/political conflicts. Under the weak state authority there were neither effective state protection of safe commercial activities nor development of a legal framework to guarantee private properties. Local producers and collectors of China-oriented exports had a chance to get involved in small-scale commercial activities, but the economic environments were not so friendly for larger-scale entrepreneurs to increase their wealth.

4.4 Transition to Colonial Trade, c. 1830–1870

4.4.1 End of the Chinese Century?

In his edited volume discussing the "Chinese century," Anthony Reid and other contributors explored the development of local economy, state diplomacy, and commercial politics in the independent states in Asia. Many of them ended their discussions with the fall of the independent states during the colonial period. This gives an impression that the trade patterns of the Chinese century ended with the establishment of colonial rule, and they were taken over by the colonial trade. Indeed the new trade pattern developed soon after the establishment of British Singapore in 1819, and the regional trade of Southeast Asia was increasingly channeled to the one centered on Singapore throughout the nineteenth century, as Kobayashi discusses in the following chapter in this volume.

The rapid growth of Singapore, however, did not mean the disappearance of the China-oriented trade. On the contrary, the China-oriented trade steadily grew during the colonial period, at almost the same pace of the growing colonial trade bound for Western countries (Fig. 4.3). How was it possible?

4.4.2 Trade in the Outer Islands

I take the ports in the Outer Islands under the Dutch influence (hereafter the Dutch Outer Islands ports) for the examination of this question, as we have a standardized set of statistic records created by Dutch officials in a number of ports from Sumatra to Maluku. These ports include only those in which the Dutch authorities collected taxes, and therefore these sources do not include the trade of powerful independent states in Aceh and Bali, for example.[5] Figure 4.1 indicates the major exports from the Dutch Outer Islands ports from 1846 to 1869. In this figure, I categorize Southeast Asian export products into three groups, on the basis of producer, collector, or investor, as follows: "Local products" mean those collected or produced by local people, such as forest and marine products bound for China. "Chinese products" are mostly pepper, gambir, and tin produced by migrant Chinese workers and exported to China. "Colonial products" are those produced with Western investments and exported to Western countries for industrial use or for mass consumption, such as rubber, tobacco, and coffee. Until the 1850s tin and gambir were exported mainly to China and partly to other parts of Southeast Asia for traditional use (tin as explained before, and gambir as an ingredient of betel chewing), but in the 1860s a tin mine in Belitung and gambir gardens in Riau were reorganized on a much larger scale with Western investments for exports to Europe and the US for industrial use (tin for canned food,

---

[5]The interpretation of this set of statistics involves particular difficulties, which derives from the different degree of accuracy in the information collected from different places. For example, the volume of "the import from the Outer Islands to Java" collected in the Outer Islands is sometimes about three times larger than "the export from the Outer Islands to Java" collected in Java in 1846, although they refer to exactly the same trade. This resulted from the fact that the ability for the authorities to capture the trade in the ports in the Outer Islands was weaker than that in Java. In the Outer Islands, considerable number of traders seem to have evaded trade taxes by using small ports outside the Dutch control. Although this type of confirmation is possible only between Java and the Outer Islands as statistics are compiled in the same format, the same tendency probably took place in other places. We have to take into account this inaccuracy in the trade volume, but the trade trend, such as the distributions of exports to different destinations and those of different origins of import, is still reliable and deserves analysis. The ability of the port authorities to capture trade later improved, and by 1869 the volume of the trade measured in Java was only 1.2 times larger than that of the same trade measured in the Outer Islands (Ota 2013).

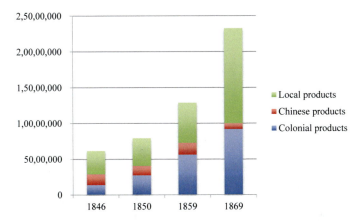

Fig. 4.1 Export from the Dutch ports in the Outer Islands, 1846–69 (Dutch guilders). *Sources* Direkteur der Middelen en Domeinen 1851–70

and gambir for leather tanning). Therefore, the export of these products is included in the "Colonial products" in 1869 of Fig. 4.1.

Local products and Chinese products in Fig. 4.1 were mostly exported to China, and these consists of various kinds of items such as tin, pepper, birds' nests, sea cucumber, and rattan, that is, typical items of mass consumption in China in the China-oriented trade. This figure thus clearly indicates that the China-oriented trade was growing from 1846 to 1869 as almost steadily as the export of colonial products, the great majority of which in this period was coffee from West Sumatra and North Sulawesi. In fact the export of colonial products skyrocketed after the 1870s, when the Dutch colonial government allowed private companies for more freedom in trade and production, and as a result the production of tobacco, sugar, and other products rapidly expanded in East Sumatra and some other places. Unfortunately it is impossible to analyze the trade trend in this phase in the same manner because of the significant changes in the format of statistics after 1870. It is very clear, however, that the China-oriented trade was still growing in the Outer Islands from 1846 to 1869, the period when the Singapore-centered regional trade was rapidly expanding and thus the colonial trade structure was being established (Ota 2013).

Figure 4.2 shows the trend of imports from various regions to the Dutch Outer Islands ports from 1846 to 1869, based on the same sources used in Fig. 4.1. This figure indicates that an increase of European products, among them textiles, was most remarkable. Most of them were British cotton textiles, the import of which expanded after the Dutch authorities accepted the British request to lower their discriminative customs against British products in Dutch East Indies in the 1820s (Kobayashi 2013). Indian textiles occupied about 10.8% of the total import in 1846, but in the following years the trade considerably shrunk. The "household items" was explained in the original sources to have come from China, Manila, and Siam, but considering the trade volume with these regions, most of them must have come from China. British cotton

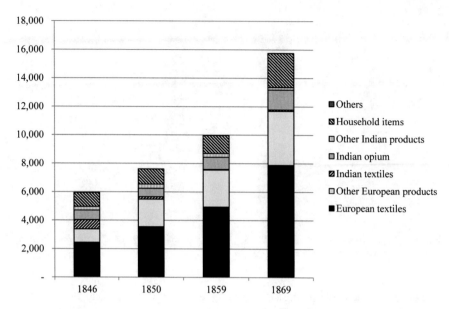

Fig. 4.2 Imports into the Dutch Outer-Islands Ports, 1846–1869 (1,000 Dutch guilders). *Sources* Direkteur der Middelen en Domeinen 1851–70

textiles were distributed almost exclusively via Singapore, while other items came mostly either via Singapore or Javanese ports such as Batavia and Surabaya, and the small remaining part via Manila and other ports (Ota 2013). These observations suggest that in imports, the Singapore-centered trade pattern increasingly incorporated the Outer Islands. Chinese and Indian imports no longer played a crucial role, while British cotton textiles seem to have taken over the demand for imported textiles.

The available statistical sources inform us, under the heading of "export destinations," of only the first ports to which items were sent, even though large parts of them were re-exported to other places. Nevertheless the "export destinations" deserve analysis, as a first step, in order to grasp the pattern of regional trade. Figure 4.3 indicates that the export to Java and Madura was steadily growing from 1846 to 1869. This is a result of the Dutch efforts to create Java-centered trade networks, redirecting the Singapore-centered trade to ports in Java, by offering favorable conditions such as tax reductions. Many traders, however, still preferred Singapore, where they were able to find items demanded in the Outer Islands, such as British cotton textiles, more easily. The result was almost the same pace of expansion of the trade to Straits Settlements (mostly Singapore) and the trade to Java. Second, the figure indicates the increasing importance of the long-distance trade. The largest increase took place in the export to Europe and the U.S. This is a result of the Dutch attempts to increase the direct export of coffee to the Netherlands first from West Sumatra, and then from North Sulawesi, in order to reduce the dependence on Singapore. In terms of export destinations, therefore, the increasing importance of the colonial setting is obvious. The Singapore was a powerful colonial port equipped with modern facilities such as

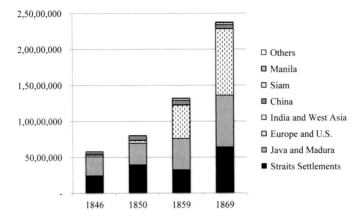

Fig. 4.3 Destinations of items exported from the Dutch ports in the Outer Island, 1846–69 (Dutch guilders). *Sources* Direkteur der Middelen en Domeinen 1851–70

large-scale harbors and advanced legal and financial systems, and so were Dutch ports like Batavia and Surabaya to a lesser degree. Large volumes of natural products were still exported to China, but traders now preferred these colonial ports as their transit ports. The Dutch effort to establish a Java-centered network was more successful than had been assumed so far,[6] while Singapore also increasingly attracted Outer-Islands exports. Trade hubs significantly shifted from dispersed numerous small ports in the Age of the China-oriented trade to a small number of modern ports in the colonial period.

The traders who participated in this changing trade pattern were a mixture of new and old actors. After the 1830s Chinese traders based in Singapore became influential in the trade between Singapore and various ports in the Outer Islands. Among them those who obtained Western sailing ships became important players (Wong 1960: 74–84; Reid 1993b: 28–29). In other words, newly emerged merchants in Singapore took a leading position, making use of new, if not the newest, technology. However, the Bugis who commanded *pinisi*, traditional sailing ships in East Indonesia, continued to play an important role especially between Surabaya and the eastern part of the Archipelago. These Chinese and Bugis traders carried products bound for the China and Southeast Asian markets to Singapore and major ports in Java, and in return redistributed various imported items, among them British cotton textiles, from these ports to various places in the Archipelago (Ota 2013; Kobayashi 2013).

What have been discussed in this section indicates that the China-oriented trade maintained its importance in Southeast Asian trade in the mid-nineteenth century, but it was conducted in the changing settings. Bugis traders continued to play an

---

[6]For example, Thomas J. Lindblad discusses that Dutch efforts to create a Java-centered trade network was not successful because Singapore continued to pull large parts of the exports from the Outer Islands, on the basis of the observations of colonial officials, but not of statistical sources (Lindblad 2002).

important role in the collection of early-modern types of Southeast Asian products, while they and the newly participated Singapore-based Chinese traders brought the products not to numerous small ports used in the previous decades but to Singapore and the major ports in Java. These traders distributed imported items to the producing regions of China-bound natural products, but the imported items were now not Indian textiles but mostly European items. Asian traders preferred Singapore, which now integrated the role of numerous small ports in nearby waters in the previous decades, while the Dutch authorities attempted to attract local traders to the major ports in Java. Under the new setting of the colonial economic structure, the China-oriented trade was maintained with some partial transformations. Some elements that facilitated the Chine-oriented trade, such as Chinese and Bugis traders and their networks, also buttressed the colonial trade structure.

Among the Singapore-based Chinese traders, some expanded the scale of their business and started to accumulate their capital, mainly through intermediation between British and Southeast Asian or Chinese traders (Kobayashi 2013). Some of them further expanded their wealth in the later decades. In this sense the continuing China-oriented trade provided the basis of the accumulation of Chinese capital in the high colonial era, although it did not work well among Bugis and other Southeast Asian entrepreneurs.

Why did the China-oriented trade continue to the colonial period? First, there was still strong Chinese demand on Southeast Asian natural products. Second, local people in the producing regions of China-bound items were market-oriented enough to respond to the demand on their products. Third, while these people had an increasing purchasing power through their export of natural products, they seem to have relied necessities such as textiles on import. The colonial trade structure focused on the producing regions of export products for the Western market, while the China-oriented trade continued to deal in the imports and exports in many other regions, where people had been well market-oriented and trade-dependent.

4.5 Conclusions

As mentioned at the beginning of this chapter, it is an interesting feature that Southeast Asia experienced brisk local and regional trade in the precolonial period. Although the patterns of the precolonial trade were constantly changing, the general trend in the early-modern era was the shift from state initiative to non-state initiative in the promotion of the trade. During the Age of Commerce (c. 1450–1680) states played a prominent role in the militarily protection of trade ports, creation of cosmopolitan port cities, promulgation of rules and regulations of commerce, and control of the production and trade of important export products. The state control of production and trade was possible and effective because they mainly dealt in small-volume, high-value items such as precious spices and wood, which were produced in very limited areas and traded in a small number of ports. After the Age of Commerce, the China-oriented trade started to develop in the mid-eighteenth century. During the

Age of China-oriented trade (c. 1750–1870), non-state commercial-military groups, often called pirates, played an important role in local and regional trade. Their heavily armed fleets were effective to collect marine and forest products demanded in China, in remote areas under weak state control. State control of production was no longer effective on these products, which could be collected in numerous coasts and forests. Many states attempted to maintain a good relationship with commercial-military groups, providing privileges in return for their commercial and military support.

The colonial trade pattern rapidly made a shape in the 1820s after the British establishment of Singapore (1819). The colonial trade patterns expanded to entire Southeast Asia, especially intensively to its insular part, buttressed by the modern port, legal, and financial facilities in Singapore, and the import of British cotton textiles, which now took over the demand for Indian textiles. However, the Singapore-centered trade pattern neither completely brought an end to the China-oriented trade nor imposed totally new systems. On the contrary, old systems survived in the new settings. It was existing Bugis trade network that distributed British cotton textiles to ports in the Outer Islands. People in these ports had purchasing power to consume imported items because of their export of China-bound products. The Singapore-centered trade patterns expanded, on the basis of the elements that had developed in the early-modern trade structure.

What sort of significance did the early-modern trade have in the economic history of Southeast Asia? First, large parts of Southeast Asia came to heavily depend on trade to obtain food and other necessities. In other words, they became trade-dependent and had to continue trade for their survival. Second, it made possible the gradual transition to modern trade patterns. The colonial trade pattern relatively smoothly penetrated the local society because it was able to make use of the existing trade structure. Third, during the Age of the China-oriented trade, the production/collection areas of major export items expanded to much wider areas in coastal and mountain areas. As a result, much larger areas of people were involved in commercial activities and they became more market-oriented. Commercial-military groups, who connected the producing areas to the transit ports were relatively independent from the states. As a result, when independent states fell one by one under the colonial rule, their network and commercial activities continued, because they chose alternative ports, either independent or colonial. The China-oriented trade was maintained, now making use of modern elements, such as British manufactured products, modern port facilities in colonial ports, and shipbuilding technology. In this manner, the colonial trade developed, by combining itself with the China-oriented trade, not by taking over the latter.

Considering the continuity from the early-modern to modern eras as discussed above, it is possible to argue that the basis of the Anglo-Dutch international order, in which free trade was pursued in colonial Asia (Sugihara 1996), had been created in the early-modern era. Southeast Asian and Chinese traders and producers preferred free trade, in which state intervention was minimum, to an increasing degree, from the Age of Commerce to the Age of the China-oriented trade. It was the tradition of trade-dependent and market-oriented society that made possible the pursuit of free trade without state protection.

The pursuit of free trade without state protection and legal framework to guarantee private properties also had its drawbacks. Until the colonial regimes brought legal framework to protect their business and properties, there was virtually no capital accumulation in insular Southeast Asia. States did not have enough experiences to promote commerce and trade through appropriate economic policy.

All these experiences and lack of experiences seem to have created the basis of Southeast Asian economy in the following periods until today. Society is trade-dependent and market-oriented, while capital accumulation was extremely limited until recent decades, except for those who were strongly connected to the state and outside capital. States were not really capable to conduct appropriate economic policy, and legal framework did not develop well to guarantee the safe and amicable business environment. Because of this basis the regional division of labor (between export item-producing regions and food-producing regions) developed in the high colonial period, while capital-intensive industrialization did not fully develop in the period after independence in most parts of Southeast Asia until quite recent decades, although micro-scale commerce has relatively well developed. The lack of capital accumulation and effective state economic policy were bottleneck of the economic development in many Southeast Asian states for several decades after independence. In recent years, however, while manufacturing industry stands still, micro-scale service industry based on internet facilities without large capital is mushrooming in several states. Southeast Asia seems to follow its historical path of economic development, and its market-oriented tendency embedded in society, without heavily depending on state protection, will perhaps have advantage in non-capital-intensive industries in the coming years.

References

Andaya, L. Y. (1995). The Bugis-Makassar diasporas. *Journal of the Malaysian Branch of the Royal Asiatic Society, 68*(1), 119–138.

Blussé, L. (1999). The Chinese century: The eighteenth century in the China Sea Region. *Archipel, 58,* 107–129.

Direkteur der Middelen en Domeinen. (1862–1870). *Overzigt van den handel en de scheepvaart in de Nederlandsche bezittingen in Oost Indie, buiten Java en Madura, over de jaren ...* [Overview of trade and shipping in the Dutch possessions in the East Indies, apart from Java and Madura, for the years ...]. Batavia: Landsdrukkerij.

Kobayashi, A. (2013). The role of Singapore in the growth of intra-Southeast Asian trade, c. 1820s–1852. *Southeast Asian Studies, 2*(3), 443–474.

Lindblad, J. T. (2002). The outer islands in the 19th century: Contest for the periphery. In H. Dick, V. J. H. Houben, J. T. Lindblad, & T. K. Wie, *The emergence of a national economy: An economic history of Indonesia, 1800–2000* (pp. 82–110). St Leonards: Allen & Unwin; Leiden: KITLV Press.

Ota, A. (2006). *Changes of regime and social dynamics in West Java: Society, state, and the outer world of Banten, 1750–1830*. Leiden and Boston: Brill.

Ota, A. (2010). The business of violence: Piracy around Riau, Lingga, and Singapore, 1820–40. In R. J. Antony (Ed.), *Elusive pirates, pervasive smugglers: Violence and clandestine trade in the Greater China Seas* (pp. 127–141). Hong Kong: Hong Kong University Press.

Ota, A. (2013). Tropical products out, British cotton in: Trade in the Dutch Outer Islands ports, 1846–69. *Southeast Asian Studies, 2*(3), 499–526.

Ota, A. (2014). Toward cities, seas, and jungles: Migration in the Malay Archipelago, c. 1750–1850. In J. Lucassen & L. Lucassen (Eds.), *Globalising migration history: The Eurasian experience (16th–21st centuries)*. (pp. 180–214). Leiden and Boston: Brill.

Pomerantz, K. (2000). *The great divergence: China, Europe, and the making of the modern world economy*. Princeton: Princeton University Press.

Reid, A. (1993a). *Southeast Asia in the age of commerce 1450–1680 Vol 2: Expansion and crisis*. New Haven and London: Yale University Press.

Reid, A. (1993b). The unthreatening alternative: Chinese shipping in Southeast Asia 1675–1842. *Review of Indonesian and Malaysian Affairs, 27*, 13–32.

Reid, A. (1997). Introduction. In A. Reid (Ed.), *The last stand of Asian autonomies: Responses to modernity in the diverse states of Southeast Asia and Korea, 1750–1900* (pp. 1–25). Basingstoke and London: Macmillan Press.

Sugihara, K. (1996). *Ajia kan boeki no keisei to kozo* (The Formation and structure of intra-Asian trade). Kyoto: Minerva Shobo.

Trocki, C. A. (1979). *Prince of pirates: The Temenggongs and the development of Johor and Singapore, 1784–1885*. Singapore: NUS Press.

Warren, J. F. (1981). *The Sulu Zone, 1768–1898: The dynamics of external trade, slavery, and ethnicity in the transformation of a Southeast Asian Maritime State*. Singapore: Singapore University Press.

Wong, L. K. (1960). The trade of Singapore, 1819–1869. *Journal of the Malayan Branch of the Royal Asiatic Society, 30*(4), 1–315.

Open Access This chapter is licensed under the terms of the Creative Commons Attribution-NonCommercial-NoDerivatives 4.0 International License (http://creativecommons.org/licenses/by-nc-nd/4.0/), which permits any noncommercial use, sharing, distribution and reproduction in any medium or format, as long as you give appropriate credit to the original author(s) and the source, provide a link to the Creative Commons licence and indicate if you modified the licensed material. You do not have permission under this licence to share adapted material derived from this chapter or parts of it.

The images or other third party material in this chapter are included in the chapter's Creative Commons licence, unless indicated otherwise in a credit line to the material. If material is not included in the chapter's Creative Commons licence and your intended use is not permitted by statutory regulation or exceeds the permitted use, you will need to obtain permission directly from the copyright holder.

Chapter 5
Growth of Regional Trade in Modern Southeast Asia: The Rise of Singapore, 1819–1913

Atsushi Kobayashi

5.1 Introduction

During the nineteenth century, Southeast Asian countries were progressively colonised by the West; their economic relations with the Western capitalist economy intensified through the expansion of long-distance trade. As a result, Southeast Asia was incorporated into the international division of labour, exporting a large amount of primary goods in exchange for capital investment and imports of manufactured goods (Cowan 1964; Drabble 2000; Maddison and Prince 1989). While long-distance trade grew in Southeast Asia, Singapore—the British colonial emporium—prospered as a trade hub by providing industrial products to the neighbouring Southeast Asian countries and re-exporting regional primary goods to industrial countries (Huff 1994; Wong 1960). In addition to trade articles, money, Western trading firms, and Asian merchants accumulated in Singapore, leading to remarkable trade growth based on the trade relationships with Southeast Asian countries. Thus, Singapore became the centre of international trade for Southeast Asia, which accelerated its regional integration into the West-led global economy. Singapore also played a pivotal role in connecting production and consumption within the region through the development of regional trade (Chiang 1978; Wong 1978). Unveiling such multifaceted trade development in Southeast Asia, this chapter intends to shed light on the growth of regional trade in Singapore during the nineteenth century.

Previous studies have stressed the significance of Singapore as a trading hub for the growth of Southeast Asian trade. However, it remains unclear how this port-city was singled out to develop into such a prominent trade centre in the region, and what kind of mechanism operated for the growth of its regional trade. One bias in the literature is that previous studies have considered the late nineteenth century as the watershed period for Singapore's trade growth, specifically with the opening of Suez Canal

---

A. Kobayashi (✉)
Osaka Sangyo University, Osaka, Japan
e-mail: koba@eco.osaka-sandai.ac.jp

© The Author(s) 2019
K. Otsuka and K. Sugihara (eds.), *Paths to the Emerging State in Asia and Africa*,
Emerging-Economy State and International Policy Studies,
https://doi.org/10.1007/978-981-13-3131-2_5

in 1869. The primary research relating to Singapore's economic history addressing before and after this period exists, but they have often been treated separately (Wong 1960; Chiang 1978; Huff 1994). As a result, the remarkable growth of Singapore's trade after the 1870s tended to be associated with the effect of the revolution of transport and communication driven by Western colonialism and the growing demand for raw material in Western industrial countries. The regionally specific mechanism of trade growth, running through the nineteenth century, has not been fully explored.

To reconsider the significance of Singapore's regional trade, we must re-examine its progressive development beyond the periodic gap before and after 1870. The present chapter tackles this assignment, and in so doing, we estimate the real growth rate of Singapore's trade from 1831 to 1913, suggesting the steady growth of its trade throughout the nineteenth century. In addition, we investigate the factors and mechanism for the long-term growth of this trade.

Singapore's regional trade was closely connected with each country's local trade. Manufactured goods transported into Singapore via long-distance trade were then carried to rural port-cities by regional trade, and further supplied to local inhabitants through internal local trade, such as coastwise and riverine trade (Warren 1981; Li 2004; Lindblad 2002). Therefore, the functional linkage of Singapore's regional trade with local trade in each country was significant in integrating Southeast Asia with the growing international economy. However, we are not familiar with how Singapore's regional trade built its connections with each country's local trade, and what sort of changes local trade underwent in response to the expansion of regional trade. Due to the lack of focus on local trade, we are not adequately able to assess the significance of Singapore's regional trade for the whole of nineteenth-century Southeast Asian economy. Therefore, we shed light on the process of consolidating the linkage between regional and local trade to comprehensively understand the regional trading system. Section 4 addresses this subject by focussing on the case of Sarawak.

The remainder of this chapter is organised as follows. Section 2 shows the long-term growth of Singapore's trade, and analyses the trade structure during the nineteenth century. It also discusses the factors that influenced the growth of regional trade with focus on trade policy and merchants' business. Section 3 highlights the emergence of the intra-regional circulation of consumer goods by analysing the changing commodity composition. Section 4 focuses on the expansion of Sarawak's trade to explore the connectivity of regional trade with local trade. Section 5 concludes the chapter.

5.2 Rise of Singapore's Regional Trade

Singapore was founded as a British colonial port in 1819 under the initiative of Thomas Stanford Raffles (Turnbull 1977; Trocki 1979). According to the Anglo—Dutch Treaty of 1824, Singapore was officially acknowledged as a British possession, and in 1826, it became one of the three colonial port-cities of the Straits Settlements.

5 Growth of Regional Trade in Modern Southeast Asia: The Rise …

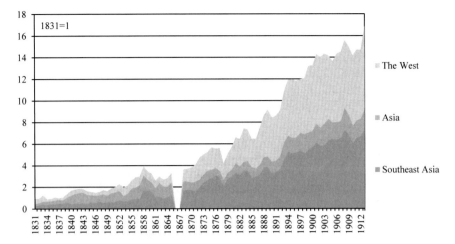

Fig. 5.1 Singapore's regional export index, 1831–1913. *Source Tabular Statements*, 1839–1865; *Blue Book*, 1868–1913. *Note* The export index is expressed in real terms and estimated by deflating the nominal export value by the export price index. The price index is adopted from Kobayashi (2017)

Throughout the nineteenth century, the colonial authority maintained the status of free port—no tariff and port dues—in Singapore, enticing Western trading firms and Asian merchants. Through the commerce of various mercantile parties, Singapore developed multilateral trade relationships with Western and Asian countries.

We first explore the growth in Singapore's trade during the century after its establishment. Figure 5.1 shows the regional exports from Singapore by three regional classifications: trade with Southeast Asia, trade with Asia (except Southeast Asia), and trade with the West. This export index represents growth trend in real terms. The figure indicates that Singapore's export index increased four-fold between 1831 and the early 1870s. It further increased from the rate of 4 in the early 1870s to 16 in 1913. It follows that Singapore's exports grew at 16 times during these 80 years. Figure 5.2, which depicts Singapore's import data, shows an increasing tendency as well, where the index increased from 1 to 4 during 1831–1870, and further grew to nearly 20 by 1913. This higher growth rate for imports suggests that the imports of consumer goods increased at a faster pace in response to the increasing local demand as a result of Singapore's rapid urbanisation and population growth, from about 10,000 in the 1820s to approximately 230,000 in the early twentieth century (Saw 1969).

Figure 5.1 also presents the destinations for Singapore's exports, aggregated by regional classification, that is, the West, Asia, and Southeast Asia. We see that, while Singapore had close trading relations with Southeast Asia, which was fundamental for its overall trade, the West, specifically Britain, was also a significant trading counterpart for the colony. According to the data, more than 40% of Singapore's exports were bound for Southeast Asia throughout the period examined. Exports to Asia, including India, China, Japan and the Middle East, reported a relatively large share

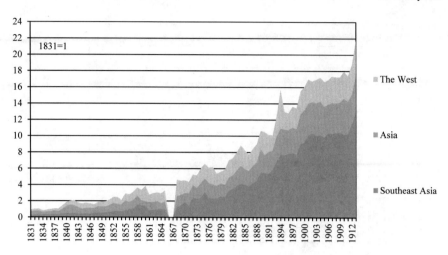

Fig. 5.2 Singapore's regional import index, 1831–1913. *Source Tabular Statements*, 1839–1865; *Blue Book*, 1868–1913. *Note* The import index is estimated using the same mean as that in Fig. 5.1

until the 1860s, suggesting that, during the early period of its trade growth, Singapore served as a transit port for the international circulation of commodities, including the re-exports of Chinese products to Britain. However, following the 1870s, with Asia's significance in Singapore's exports gradually diminishing, it appears that the port enhanced its function as a trading hub for Southeast Asian countries. In addition to export data, Fig. 5.2 shows the origins of Singapore's imports with three regional classifications. We see that Southeast Asia held a bigger share than that of Asia and the West, maintaining this share at more than 50% after the 1880s. Thus, Southeast Asian countries were significant trading counterparts in Singapore's trade during the colonial period.

The role of Singapore as a transit port began developing at the onset of its colonial history. When Raffles founded the East India Company's (EIC) factory at Singapore, he had two economic aims (Turnbull 1977). The first was the expansion of British trade with China via Singapore, and the other was the establishment of a British trade centre in Southeast Asia to confront Dutch colonial power. In terms of his first ambition, Singapore fulfilled the role of a transit port, offering the British mercantile community with a trade route to the Chinese market. Table 5.1 lists the ratios of Singapore's key import and export articles; we can see that 'East Asian goods', including Chinese raw silk and tea, occupied a relatively large share in both imports and exports before the 1840s. This indicates that Singapore was a depot for transit trade, importing Chinese articles and re-exporting them to Britain. However, this role was later assumed by Hong Kong, which was founded in 1842 as a British trading base in Southern China. Thereafter, Singapore's trade began to focus on trades with Southeast Asian regions to satisfy Raffles' second ambition. Table 5.1 also shows that the share of 'Southeast Asian foodstuffs', including rice, pepper, and sugar, and

5 Growth of Regional Trade in Modern Southeast Asia: The Rise …

Table 5.1 Imports and exports in Singapore's trade, 1822–1913

	1822	1828	1840	1862	1880	1900	1913
Imports							
Manufactured goods (%)	27.6	21.1	19.9	13.3	15.3	5.1	4.5
Opium (%)	22.1	10.8	20.7	12.9	10.9	5.3	2.1
East Asian goods (%)	4.5	20.1	9.2	6.0	8.0	7.1	5.1
S. E. Asian foodstuffs (%)	13.5	8.5	13.2	17.1	24.9	21.0	23.7
S. E. Asian raw materials (%)	10.2	4.6	5.7	11.3	19.0	28.7	29.1
Others (%)	22.0	34.9	31.3	39.4	21.9	32.7	35.5
Total imports	3,092,134	8,732,450	11,929,401	22,455,845	47,865,849	229,718,302	333,669,588
Exports							
Manufactured goods (%)	21.6	11.4	10.1	15.8	12.1	4.8	3.4
Opium (%)	22.6	8.9	20.1	12.5	9.9	5.3	1.8
East Asian goods (%)	5.1	19.6	11.4	3.2	3.6	2.1	1.6
S. E. Asian foodstuffs (%)	16.1	10.3	17.9	17.8	25.7	23.9	27.6
S. E. Asian raw materials (%)	13.7	6.0	8.6	18.6	24.6	38.0	39.5
Others (%)	20.9	43.8	31.9	32.2	24.1	25.9	26.0
Total exports	2,624,740	8,438,150	10,182,478	18,750,166	46,162,886	186,616,348	257,861,006

Source Data for 1822 is from *Sumatra Factory Records*; data for 1828 is from *Straits Settlements Factory Records*; data for 1840 and 1862 are from *Tabular Statements*; and those for 1880–1913 are from *Blue Book*

Notes 'Manufactured goods' include Indian and British cotton piece goods. 'East Asian goods' consist of silk piece goods and raw silk. 'S. E. (Southeast) Asian foodstuffs' comprise rice, salted fish, coconuts oil, sugar, tapioca, pepper, areca nuts, sago, tobacco, tea, and coffee. 'S. E. Asian raw materials' include tin, *gutta percha*, gambier, hides, rattan, *copra*, coal, petroleum, and rubber. The values are expressed in Straits dollars

'Southeast Asian raw materials', such as tin, forest produces, and rubber, increased over time.

In addition, Table 5.1 shows that, together with opium, the ratio of manufactured goods in Singapore's trade was relatively large during the mid-nineteenth century. In fact, before 1850, there was a shift in cotton products from Indian handloom textile to British industrial products in the trade of manufactured goods. The rise of British cotton products in place of Indian products was a driving force in the growth of Singapore's trade. The expansion of cotton goods' trade was augmented by two factors: the predominance of trade liberalisation and the vigorous reaction of local Asian merchants. Next, we examine these factors.

The expansion of free trade influence assisted the growth of British cotton products' trade in Singapore. Through the industrial revolution following the mid-eighteenth century, Britain achieved the import substitution of Indian fabrics, and began exporting cotton manufactured goods worldwide. When British cotton goods flowed into Southeast Asia, Singapore was becoming the gateway to the regional market. British articles were transported there via long-distance trade, and finally, re-exported to neighbouring countries through regional trade. However, the regional circulation of British cotton goods encountered an obstacle—the Dutch protectionist tariffs (Van der Kraan 1998; Kobayashi 2013). After the 1820s, the Dutch government set a discriminatively high tariff on the imports of British cotton goods from Singapore at Dutch colonial port-cities. In fact, during the mid-1830s, the tariff rate reached 70%, hindering Singapore's regional trade, which considerably relied on the exports of British cotton goods. These circumstances provoked British diplomatic protests against the Dutch discriminative tariff. By the early 1840s, the Dutch government amended the tariff rate against Singapore to 25%. Following the early 1840s, the exports of cotton goods from Singapore to the Dutch ruling places rapidly increased (Kobayashi 2013). Thus, after the mid-nineteenth century, British industrial cotton goods were widely circulated across Southeast Asia via Singapore, and promoted the growth of its regional trade. The rivalry over the Anglo–Dutch tariff policy and resultant free trade also defeated protectionism, and coordinated the institutional setting for the growth in Singapore's regional trade. Thereafter, the Dutch tariff on the imports of British cotton goods remained unaltered until the later 1860s, after which the tariff rate was progressively lowered to 16%. In 1874, the differential duties between British and Dutch products were corrected (Korthals-Altes 1991).

Another primary factor affecting the development of Singapore's regional trade was the reorganisation of commercial relationships among merchants. In Singapore, British trading firms and merchants imported industrial cotton products and purchased Asian produce that were in demand in their home country (Drabble and Drake 1981). Thus, they had to transact with Asian merchants to sell industrial fabrics and obtain native produces in Singapore. However, most British merchants were inexperienced in conducting transactions in local markets, and thus, required middlemen who could deal with the local traders. Chinese merchants who moved from Malacca to Singapore satisfied this requirement (Lee 1978; Wong 1960). Before moving to Singapore, Chinese merchants, whose ancestors immigrated from China's southern provinces, had a long history of trading in Southeast Asia. Therefore, they were familiar with local commerce and able to speak not only English, but also the vernacular languages of the Malay Archipelago. Since some of the merchants held an administrative position, it was easier to ensure themselves trustworthy for the Western community. Using these aptitudes, the Chinese middlemen purchased industrial products from British merchants, and in exchange, delivered local Southeast Asian produce.

Furthermore, the Chinese middlemen played a significant role in drawing local traders' commerce to Singapore and re-organising their diverse activities. Even after the collapse of the Johore–Riau Kingdom in the 1780s, while there seemed to be no influential trade hub in the Malay Archipelago, local traders, such as Bugis, Malay, and Chinese traders, were scattered across the region, and maintained active trading, based in tiny port-cities (see Chap. 4 of this volume). However, the emergence of

Singapore changed these circumstances. As Singapore began to function as a free port that offered lucrative business opportunities, such as a deal for British industrial products, the port started to attract local traders from across Southeast Asia. Bugis traders came to Singapore with abundant regional produce, such as forest and marine products from the petty ports in Borneo and Celebes, and Malay traders brought various agricultural and mineral produces from the Malay Peninsula and Sumatra. In addition, Chinese junks imported foodstuff, such as rice and sugar, from mainland countries like Siam and Cochin China. The local traders generally purchased their commodities from Chinese middlemen, who could offer merchandise ranging from British fabrics to regional foodstuffs (Kobayashi 2013). In other words, by trading with the Chinese middlemen, local traders who arrived at Singapore could acquire every commodity that was demanded in their homelands. Under the circumstances, an efficient deal warranted the alleviation of high transaction costs, and this in turn was likely to have enhanced the bargaining position of the Chinese middlemen. Thus, Chinese middlemen came to play a pivotal role in the circulation of commodities in Singapore at the onset of its trade growth.

Although Singapore was newly built in the early nineteenth century, its trade growth did not begin from nothing. For the development of Singapore's regional trade, it was significant that Chinese merchants who had accommodated to local commerce operated intermediary business not only between Western merchants and local traders, but also among the various local traders. The extra-regionally produced commodities, such as cotton manufactured goods, Indian opium, and Chinese goods, flowed into Southeast Asia via Singapore. In exchange for its exports, Southeast Asian produces were brought and further transported to consuming countries. Consequently, through these reciprocal linkages between long-distance trade and regional trade in Singapore, Southeast Asian trade grew, and the regional trading system was established by the mid-nineteenth century. This trade structure further developed after the 1870s, and led to the overall growth of Southeast Asian trade, as we see in the next section.

5.3 Mechanism of Demand Linkage in Southeast Asian Trade After the 1870s

Prior to the late nineteenth century, Singapore's trade mostly comprised the general pattern of transit trade. Extra-regional products brought into Singapore by long-distance trade were re-exported through regional trade, and regional products were transported overseas through reverse flows. However, this pattern changed following the 1870s. In particular, the change took place in the regional trade, and the new pattern of the regional commodity circulation fuelled the expansion of primary goods' exports from Southeast Asia. In this section, we discuss the development of Singapore's regional trade after the 1870s with focus on the mechanism of demand linkage.

After the 1850s, the expansion of Western economic influence further accelerated; regional economies were also affected by the movements of international trade. In particular, in Insular Southeast Asia, including Malay Peninsula, Dutch East Indies, and the Philippines, tin mines and plantations were developed under the surge of Western colonisation, and large exports of raw materials were initiated to the West. Exports of forest products, including resin, rattan, and oils, also expanded. In some inland regions, the livelihood of the local populations shifted towards market-oriented agricultural production and labour income at plantations (Lindblad 2002, 100–105; Murray 1980). However, because the population was relatively small in most island countries, immigrants became indispensable as labour in order to increase primary goods production. Chinese and Indian immigrants met this requirement. Following the 1870s, a large number of Chinese began to immigrate to Southeast Asia from China's southern provinces, such as Guangdong and Fujian; in fact, the average number reached approximately 200,000 per annum (Sugihara 2005). While most of them returned to China after saving a certain amount of income from working in the mines and plantations, some settled in Southeast Asia. Likewise, Indian immigrants worked in rubber plantations under the Kangani system in the Malay Peninsula (Sugihara 1996; McKeown 2004). This international movement of labour force reinforced the production of raw materials in Insular Southeast Asia, and products were exported to the West either directly or via Singapore. Table 5.2 shows that the ratio of Southeast Asian raw materials in Singapore's regional imports conspicuously increased after the 1860s, and the share of tin dramatically soared following the 1880s, suggesting the increasing production of raw materials in the neighbouring countries. Finally, they were re-exported from Singapore to the West by long-distance trade.

In mainland Southeast Asia, the Western colonies, British Burma, and French Cochin China (Indochina after 1899), were established, and the Kingdom of Siam barely remained independent. In those countries, the production of primary goods expanded in response to the growth of international economy. Nevertheless, the nature of primary goods produced there somewhat differed from that of primary goods in Insular Southeast Asia. Following the 1850s, the reclamation of the deltas in Burma, Siam, and Cochin China rapidly proceeded, and farmers began to settle there. As a result, the yield of rice increased in those lands. Consequently, local farmers began exporting surplus rice abroad on an unprecedented scale, and rice became the most significant export article from the mainland countries (Owen 1971). Although Europe imported some of the Burmese rice, which was used as starch for paper manufacturing, Asian countries imported most of the rice as a staple food item. Rice produced in the Burmese Irrawaddy Delta was shipped to vicinities, such as British India and the Straits Settlements, and rice reaped in the Chao Phraya Delta in Siam and the Mekong Delta in Cochin China was exported to Insular Southeast Asia, China, and Japan. Siamese and Cochin Chinese rice was exported through the country's emporiums, Bangkok and Saigon. The rice supply from the mainland countries facilitated the shift of labour force from the agricultural to export sector; in other words, it led to the rise of plantation and commercial agriculture in Asian countries. Thus, the exports of primary goods from the mainland mainly comprised foodstuffs, which supported the enhancement of productivity in the Asian economies.

Table 5.2 Imports and exports in Singapore's regional trade, 1828–1913

	1828	1840	1862	1873	1880	1900	1913
Regional imports							
Rice (%)	10.1	11.0	31.1	19.9	24.8	16.4	21.7
Manufactured goods (%)	2.3	4.3	4.6	4.8	0.6	1.0	0.4
Tin (%)	12.5	9.4	3.5	2.5	1.0	25.7	24.9
S. E. Asian raw materials (%)	4.5	3.3	8.9	24.3	26.7	23.7	19.9
S. E. Asian foodstuffs (%)	27.5	35.7	22.9	28.1	23.6	18.6	18.6
Others (%)	43.1	36.2	29.0	20.5	23.2	14.6	14.4
Total	2,122,933	3,105,673	5,944,146	16,749,822	20,804,862	127,974,215	186,899,242
Regional exports							
Cotton piece goods (%)	41.1	26.2	28.3	25.0	23.0	10.9	7.3
India and China products (%)	23.4	32.1	26.1	25.7	20.8	9.3	2.9
S. E. Asian raw materials (%)	0.9	2.8	1.5	2.2	2.2	3.4	1.3
Rice (%)	2.2	0.8	5.7	12.5	18.3	20.3	28.1
S. E. Asian foodstuffs (%)	4.5	6.3	3.9	6.1	8.7	15.5	18.1
Others (%)	27.9	31.8	34.5	28.5	27.0	40.6	42.3
Total	2,026,323	2,440,884	6,010,299	14,772,414	22,769,850	76,637,644	102,167,243

Source Data for 1828 is from *Straits Settlements Factory Record*; data for 1840 and 1862 are from *Tabular Statements*; and those for 1873–1913 are from *Blue Book*

Note The total values are expressed in Straits dollars

The food supply from mainland Southeast Asia was critical in the production of raw materials in Insular Southeast Asia. Numerous Chinese and Indian immigrants had arrived in the island regions, and this increasing population was likely to induce greater food demands. Without food supply, the immigrants could not engage in production in mines and plantations. Thus, the exports of foodstuffs from the mainland indirectly assisted the growth of raw materials exports in the island. In addition, Singapore played a central role as an emporium in the rise of the intra-regional circulation of foodstuffs.

Next, we explore the commodity compositions in Singapore's regional trade. Table 5.2 indicates that the percentage of rice in Singapore's regional imports increased by the 1860, and the high ratio of no less than 16% sustained till 1913. A certain share of rice imported into Singapore was locally consumed, while the majority was re-exported to neighbouring regions, such as the Malay Peninsula, Dutch East Indies, and British Borneo. The share of rice in Singapore's regional exports surged from less than 6% to more than 20% after the 1870s, replacing the commanding shares of cotton piece goods and Indian and Chinese products (Table 5.2). That is, a certain amount of mainland's rice was transported to Singapore, and distributed to the island regions, to satisfy the growing food demand by Chinese and Indian immigrants, as well as local inhabitants. In addition, Table 5.2 shows that the percentage of Southeast Asian foodstuffs, including sugar, oil, and salted fish, increased after the 1880s, suggesting the expansion of food distribution across Southeast Asia with Singapore as its hub. Thus, after the late nineteenth century, Singapore transformed from a transit port for long-distance trade between the West and Asia to an emporium coordinating intra-regional trade, and connecting production and consumption within Southeast Asia.

At the same time, there were several changes in Singapore's mercantile activities. Until the mid-nineteenth century, local traders, such as Bugis, Malay, and Chinese traders, carried regional produce from the neighbouring islands to Singapore, and transacted the merchandise with Western merchants through Chinese middlemen. The establishment of such a transaction system between Asian and Western merchants smoothed the commodity circulations between regional and long-distance trade in Singapore. However, within the realm of regional trade, newcomers from China were gradually expanding their businesses in place of native traders who were visiting Singapore from remote islands. After 1850, the port of Singapore was equipped with transport infrastructure: its harbour was upgraded to accommodate huge steamships, and regular steamship lines were inaugurated, with Singapore as a hub of maritime traffic (Bogaars 1956; Boon 2013). The new transport infrastructure in Southeast Asia was vigorously used for commerce by not only Western merchants, but also Asian ones (Tan 1902; Huff 1989; Boon 2013). Furthermore, the telegraph system was constructed after the late nineteenth century to promote communication among staple cities across the globe, for which Singapore was one of the network hubs (Latham and Neal 1983). The telegraph dramatically reduced the communication time between Asia and Europe, and facilitated the exchange of commercial and political information. These technological innovations benefitted Singapore's mercantile community, particularly Chinese merchants, by enabling them to extend their trade to the remote islands. Until then, native traders, such as Bugis and Malay traders, primarily conducted Singapore's regional trade with the eastern islands, such as Borneo, Celebes, and Sumatra. Following the 1850s, however, new transport and communication tools reduced the physical and temporal distance to the eastern islands, and alleviated hindrances faced by Singapore's traders who wanted to advance there in search of lucrative commerce.

In addition to improved trade infrastructure, social relationships were another advantage for Chinese traders. Chinese immigrants who came to Southeast Asia during the high-colonial period built a society on the basis of each home province, such as Fujian, Guangdong, and Teochew, and the fellowship of each provincial group was close and strong (Lee 1978). We assume that the mutual trust among the members mitigated the risk of undertakings in Southeast Asia, and provided the opportunity of business success, even for the newcomers from China. To explore trading operations by a Chinese petty trader, we cite an excerpt from a contemporary article that describes trading by a Chinese peddler in the late nineteenth-century Singapore (Tan 1902).

> A new-comer from China, or a return immigrant, would scrape together from friends and other accommodating creditors sufficient means to buy a cart-load of such necessaries as rice, salt, salt-fish, tobacco, kerosene, matches, sugar, biscuits, manufactured cotton goods, umbrellas, etc., and proceed to a distant village some miles from the nearest trading centre, and at once commence operations by building a hut and planting a small vegetable garden for his own requirements, and opening a "kedai [shop]". … His shop is soon the rendezvous of the natives, who resort thither on all occasions or when they have leisure. For such among them who possess jungle produce, such as gutta, garroo-wood, rattan, gum-damar, areca-nut, etc., the shopkeeper is ready to barter in exchange the goods of his shop. … The goods thus obtained are carefully stored until, after a few years' collection, the man finds he has sufficient to load two or three carts, when after first disposing of his shop, good-will, and stock-in-trade to a successor, he would start with his goods to the port of embarkation. Here [Singapore] he would dispose of them to the best advantage, pay off his creditors, and he is then ready to take a trip to China to enjoy a holiday with his family.

The above description suggests that Chinese expatriates who simply visited Southeast Asia could start their own trading business by raising funds from Chinese fellows and creditors without any collateral. We suppose that the trade-by-credit sale, which was based on the partnership among Chinese provincial groups, was aimed at expanding commerce from Singapore to the remote rural villages, although there may have been many defaults in the harsh milieu of business in Southeast Asia.

Thus, we suggest that the expansion of the geographical range of Chinese commercial activities through unique credit sale fuelled the circulation of merchandise between Singapore and Southeast Asian countries. In particular, Gregg Huff (1989) emphasises the significance of rice trade by Chinese mercantile groups in Singapore. According to Huff, Singapore's Chinese merchants who imported rice from Siam passed it to Chinese traders who exported consumer goods, including rice, to neighbouring islands in exchange for primary goods; the latter paid the former after earning a profit from the transaction. For these Chinese merchants, it is assumed that rice was a medium of exchange based on a solid partnership, and a way to cope with the deficiency of currency by providing liquidity for commerce. Such a chain of credit sales among the Chinese promoted the development of the intra-regional circulation of consumer goods centred on Singapore and raw materials exports. In sum, the formation of a transaction system for Chinese mercantile communities in Singapore and its expansion across the neighbouring countries accelerated the growth of regional trade in Southeast Asia.

5.4 Linkage with Local Trade: Pattern of Sarawak's Trade Development

In 1841, James Brooke, as Rajah appointed by the Sultan of Brunei, founded Sarawak Kingdom in North-Western Borneo. The ruling by the Brooke family lasted until World War II. After the second half of the nineteenth century, Brooke's Sarawak progressively took over the territory of Brunei, causing its trade to also grow (Ooi 1997; Kaur 1998). Various types of primary goods were exported from Sarawak in exchange for overseas imports, such as manufactured goods, foodstuffs, and money. A majority of Sarawak's overseas exports were sent worldwide via Singapore, which also served as a route for imports. We can assume that Sarawak's trade growth increased through the strong connection with the regional trading system centred in Singapore. However, this close relation with Singapore was not sufficient to maintain Sarawak's trade growth. Its trade development also critically hinged on the linkage between overseas and local trades.

The structure of Sarawak's trade was as follows. During its course of trade growth, Kuching—Sarawak's capital—established close trade relations with Singapore (Chew 1990; Kobayashi and Sugihara 2018). Manufactured goods and foodstuffs were imported into Kuching from Singapore, and in exchange, Sarawak's local primary goods were exported to the international market via Singapore. Asian merchants primarily engaged in overseas trade in Kuching, and Chinese merchants particularly traded with Singapore. At the same time, while some imports were consumed by inhabitants in Kuching and its hinterlands, the rest were shipped to rural cities through coastwise trade. Finally, these foreign products were transported to forest dwellers via a riverine from markets near an estuary to the inland villages. In the reverse commodity flow, forest and agricultural products delivered by local folks were bound for Kuching via riverine and coastal trade, and finally, exported abroad. Although the coastwise and riverine trade had allegedly been controlled by Malay traders, as Sarawak's trade grew and strengthened the connection with Singapore, Chinese traders began to overpower native traders in terms of business, and dominated internal trade (Chew 1990). Most Chinese traders were small-scale peddlers and had long-term commercial relationships with Chinese merchants in Kuching, who provided funds or commodities through credit sales. Likewise, Kuching's merchants were likely to hold business relations with Singapore's Chinese merchants. Thus, consumer products imported from overseas were circulated across Sarawak through the chain of transactions by the Chinese traders, and Sarawak's primary goods were remitted to industrial countries via Singapore. Moreover, the systematic linkage between foreign trade and domestic coastwise and riverine trade promoted trade growth in Sarawak.

Figure 5.3 depicts the trends of foreign trade and coasting trade in Kuching from 1860 to 1917. We see the synchronising growths between foreign and coasting trade; particularly, their volumes were more or less the same before the 1890s. This suggests that the growth of foreign imports led to that of coasting exports through the provision of external articles. The same relationship existed between coasting imports and foreign exports. Following the 1890s, however, a large amount of pepper produced on the outskirts of Kuching was exported without going through coasting trade, and from the 1910s, another commodity, a large amount of rubber was exported from Kuching and Sibu via direct steamship lines to Singapore. As a result, the growth of foreign trade left coasting trade behind, as seen in the widening gap in Fig. 5.3.

5 Growth of Regional Trade in Modern Southeast Asia: The Rise …

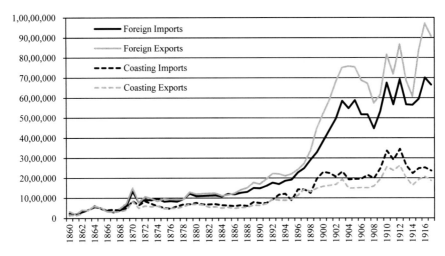

Fig. 5.3 Foreign trade and coasting trade in Kuching, 1860–1917. *Source Sarawak Gazette*, Sarawak Trade Returns; *Sarawak Government Gazette*, Sarawak Trade Returns. *Note* The units are expressed in Straits dollars

Nevertheless, the figure shows similar trends for foreign and coastwise trade after the beginning of the twentieth century.[1]

In addition, we explore commodities to gain deeper insight into the sectoral linkages of Sarawak's trade. Table 5.3 presents a general pattern for commodity compositions in foreign exports and coastal imports in Kuching during the late nineteenth century. Although Sarawak's trade statistics reported numerous local and extra-local products (a total of 119 articles) during 1870–1904, we aggregated them to specific items in the table. The upper half lists the percentages of items for foreign exports from Kuching, and indicates large shares of natural resins, forest products, and sago[2] before the 1890s, and also of minerals, if for a brief period,—mostly gold dust produced in the Kuching's hinterland. The lower half of the table shows that coastal imports that include similar items—such as natural resins; forest products, such as rattans; and sago—maintained a predominant share throughout the late nineteenth century. It suggests that most local products imported into Kuching via coastal trade were re-exported abroad. In the articles for foreign exports, the percentage of peppers substantially increased in the 1880s, and became a significant export item after the turn of the century. As discussed, the expansion of pepper production by Chinese immigrants in Kuching's vicinities created a gap in the trade growth between foreign and coastwise trade, which indicates that, with respect to the rest of commodities, foreign and coastwise trade had close linkages in Sarawak, and the commodities of coastal trade were probably transported through riverine trade, eventually reaching

---

[1] According to statistical data for Singapore's trade, Sarawak was a minor trading partner that maintained an approximate 5% share for Singapore's entire trade.

[2] Sago is a traditional starch food extracted from the indigenous palm in Insular Southeast Asia.

Table 5.3 Commodities of foreign exports and coasting imports in Kuching, 1870–1904

	1870	1875	1880	1885	1890	1895	1900	1904
Foreign exports								
Natural resins (%)	58.0	11.5	25.4	13.4	18.3	13.5	26.7	13.2
Rattans (%)	0.0	6.6	2.4	12.5	10.6	7.5	6.5	1.2
Forest products (%)	3.8	12.1	3.8	6.4	5.4	5.5	3.6	1.9
Gambier (%)	0.0	0.0	8.2	10.5	7.8	9.5	4.6	2.3
Peppers (%)	0.1	0.1	0.3	10.5	14.0	10.9	28.9	34.5
Sago (%)	8.9	32.4	28.8	19.2	20.2	31.1	17.3	11.0
Minerals (%)	6.1	16.0	12.1	8.3	7.9	8.9	3.0	24.8
Others (%)	7.2	11.8	9.2	10.0	10.9	7.8	5.1	6.9
Treasures (%)	15.8	9.6	9.6	9.1	4.9	5.3	4.2	4.2
Total	1,494,241	963,590	1,193,195	1,157,299	1,700,142	2,208,723	4,336,280	7,573,289
Coasting imports								
Natural resins (%)	58.2	16.2	33.7	23.3	31.6	28.8	42.4	38.0
Rattans (%)	0.0	3.3	0.3	17.6	14.1	12.2	9.9	4.2
Forest produces (%)	3.2	8.3	3.2	9.9	5.4	9.0	2.7	2.6
Pepper (%)	0.0	0.0	0.0	0.2	3.6	3.0	3.7	1.4
Sago (%)	11.1	38.0	34.2	20.6	23.0	23.0	27.4	24.4
Food (rice, fish, livestock) (%)	3.3	4.8	6.4	11.0	5.7	5.5	4.6	2.8
Minerals (%)	0.5	2.3	2.1	3.2	2.3	2.5	1.7	5.2
Others (%)	3.9	6.8	5.5	5.0	5.6	4.0	2.2	12.4
Treasures (%)	19.7	20.3	14.5	9.2	8.8	12.1	5.4	9.2
Total	855,882	515,637	762,957	632,570	751,044	872,565	2,307,416	1,925,170

Source *Sarawak Gazette*, Sarawak Trade Returns, 1870–1904
Note The total values are expressed in Straits dollars

inland forest dwellers. Such a functional linkage among the discernible trade sectors was established in Sarawak.

Nevertheless, the question remains of how the regional trading system centred on Singapore affected Sarawak's trade growth. As discussed, with growing raw material exports from Southeast Asia to Western industrialised countries, the intra-regional circulation of consumer goods also expanded in response to the increasing demand for primary goods' producers. In particular, following the 1870s, mainland Southeast Asian rice was transported on a massive scale to the island countries via Singapore's regional trade. The development of Singapore's regional trade was highly likely to have influenced Sarawak's trade growth because the former was the latter's most significant counterpart. Rice maintained an approximately 10–20% share in Sarawak's growing foreign imports during the pre-war period: most of the rice was supplied

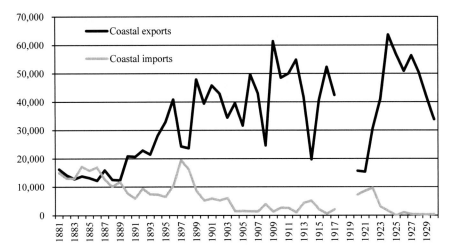

Fig. 5.4 Coastal rice exports and imports in Kuching, 1881–1930. *Source Sarawak Gazette*, Sarawak Trade Returns; *Sarawak Government Gazette*, Sarawak Trade Returns; *Sarawak Annual Report*. *Notes* The values are measured in piculs

from the mainland via Singapore. Once imported into Kuching, foreign rice widely circulated in Sarawak, and helped the country augment its primary goods' exports. Next, we explore how the internal circulation of rice developed in Sarawak.

Figure 5.4 depicts the coastal rice exports and imports in Kuching. It is assumed that coastal exported rice was originally imported from overseas, particularly from mainland countries via Singapore, and coastal imported rice was primarily produced by local Sarawak inhabitants. The figure also shows an increase in foreign rice exports from Kuching to the coastal areas, and a secular decline in the distribution of locally produced rice.

As for foreign rice, annual imports soared from about 60,000 piculs in the early 1880s, to about 170,000 piculs in the early 1900s, and finally reached roughly 420,000 piculs in the late 1930s (Trade Returns in *Sarawak Gazette* and *Sarawak Government Gazette*). According to these numeric values and the data presented in Fig. 5.4, while most foreign rice imported into Kuching was consumed by the city dwellers and neighbourhood, approximately 11–25% was likely to turn into coastwise exports. However, focussing on the early period in Fig. 5.4, it is evident that the volumes of coastal imported rice were comparable to those of coastal exports until the end of the 1880s. It is likely that the inland rice was transported to Kuching via coastal trade, and finally, consumed by its residents and surrounding inhabitants. While the unit price of foreign imported rice, on average, was 2.55 Straits dollars per picul during the 1880s, the coastwise imported rice was priced at 1.01 Straits dollars during the same period (Trade Returns in *Sarawak Gazette* and *Sarawak Government Gazette*). Foreign imported rice was priced higher most probably because its quality was superior to native rice like paddy—husked rice—produced by swidden agriculture. Meanwhile, it is likely that the cheaper native rice was provided to labourers in the primary goods' industry, and contributed to the competitiveness of export in Sarawak. Thus, its circulation remained in the domestic trade until the 1880s. Accordingly, we can assume that the domestic trade did not just work for the dynamism of international trade as an extension that carried foreign products to natives, but also exhibited sustained adaptability to regional demand. Until the 1880s, while the Sarawak economy was responsive to the growing world economy, it maintained an autonomous system of local trade.

Nevertheless, after the 1890s, Sarawak's economy eventually integrated into the Singapore-centred trading system. Figure 5.4 shows that the volume of coastal imported rice gradually decreased after the 1890s. Rice was scarcely imported via coastwise trade after 1900, although around 1920, its imports temporarily increased, possibly to cope with the fall in coastal rice exports. By contrast, the volume of coastal exported rice from Kuching to rural cities was increasing at a rapid rate, and was expected to facilitate the expansion of the production of primary goods, such as pepper, rubber, and forest products. Due to the massive inflows of foreign rice from Singapore, local rice was no longer demanded, and thus, its domestic circulation almost ceased. Therefore, a majority of the commercial productions in Sarawak's economy further focussed on industrial raw materials; the region intensively exported them to Western industrial nations in exchange for the imports of manufactured goods and regional foodstuffs. This was the effect of integration of Sarawak into the regional trading system centred on Singapore. Thus, Singapore served as an interface for Sarawak to connect with both long-distance trade with the West and regional trade with Southeast Asia.

5.5 Conclusions

The previous sections discussed one of the trade growth patterns in nineteenth-century Southeast Asia by focussing on Singapore's regional trade. This section summarizes the above discussion.

Following its foundation in 1819, Singapore's trade grew as a result of transit trade connecting long-distance and regional trades. The initial driving force for trade growth was the influx of British cotton goods. With Singapore at the centre, British cotton goods circulated across the region as reasonably priced consumer goods freely or even with the tariff barrier set by the Netherlands. The massive imports of industrial products induced the growth of primary goods' exports to the West, thus moving the terms of trade in favour of Southeast Asia (Kobayashi 2017). In other words, by initiating the inflows of industrial products, while preserving the momentum of China-oriented trade since the eighteenth century (see Chap. 4 of this volume), Southeast Asian trade progressively consolidated its trade relationship with the West in line with Singapore's trade growth. In addition, the vigorous commerce by Asian merchants who managed Singapore's regional trade was indispensable to the circulation of industrial products at this time. Asian merchants' reaction towards the emerging business opportunity, that is, the arrival of British industrial products, drove the trade growth of Singapore as a new-born emporium, and the trading system, centred on Singapore, flourished by the end of the mid-nineteenth century.

Following the second half of the nineteenth century, owing to the improvement of transport infrastructure, the geographical range of Chinese mercantile activities expanded to unexplored areas, such as the Malay Peninsula and Dutch ruling islands, where native traders dominated the commerce. Furthermore, after the 1870s, numerous Chinese and Indian immigrants began flowing into Insular Southeast Asia, and began to work in mines and on plantations. With the arrival of immigrants and expansion of raw materials production, the demand for consumer goods surged. To satisfy the rising demand for food, mainland Southeast Asia exported a large amount of rice to the island countries via Singapore. In exchange for the supply of foodstuffs, industrial raw materials were imported into Singapore and re-exported to the West.

The final section discussed the linkage between Singapore's regional trade and Sarawak's local trade. Sarawak's trade grew as a result of the connectivity between foreign and local trades. At a glance, Sarawak's local trade seemed to be a mere extension of the foreign trade. However, the internal circulation of rice, for example, indicates that local traders distributed the country's commodity to fulfil local demand. Singapore's regional trade could not exert a strong influence on Sarawak's local trade solely by providing industrial products. Eventually, after the 1890s, as the circulation of foreign imported rice expanded across Sarawak via local trade, the production of raw materials for industrial economies was reinforced. Thus, the development of Singapore's regional trade consolidated the linkage with each country's local trade, and as a result, the Southeast Asian economy strengthened the intra-regional trading relations and the connection with the West-led global economy.

References

Bogaars, G. (1956). The Tanjong Pagar Dock Company, 1864–1905. *Memoirs of the Raffles Museum, 3*, 117–244.
Boon, G. C. (2013). *Technology and entrepot colonialism in Singapore, 1819–1940*. Singapore: Institute of Southeast Asian Studies.
Chew, D. (1990). *Chinese pioneers on the Sarawak Frontier 1841–1941*. Singapore: Oxford University Press.
Cowan, D. C. (Ed.). (1964). *The economic development of Southeast Asia: Studies in economic history and political economy*. New York: Frederick A. Praeger Publishers.
Chiang, H. D. (1978). *A history of Straits Settlements foreign trade 1870–1915*. Singapore: Koon Wah Lithographers.
Drabble, J. H., & Drake, P. J. (1981). The British agency houses in Malaysia: Survival in a changing world. *Journal of Southeast Asian Studies, 12*(2), 297–328.
Drabble, J. H. (2000). *An economic history of Malaysia, c. 1800–1990: The transition to modern economic growth*. London: Macmillan Press Ltd.
Huff, G. W. (1989). Bookkeeping barter, money, credit, and Singapore's international rice trade, 1870–1939. *Explorations in Economic History, 26*, 161–189.
Huff, G. W. (1994). *The economic growth of Singapore: Trade and development in the twentieth century*. New York: Cambridge University Press.

Kaur, A. (1998). *Economic change in East Malaysia: Sabah and Sarawak since 1850*. London: Macmillan Press Ltd.

Kobayashi, A. (2013). The role of Singapore in the growth of intra-Southeast Asian trade, c. 1820s–1852. *Southeast Asian Studies, 2*(3), 443–474.

Kobayashi, A. (2017). Price fluctuations and growth patterns in Singapore's trade, 1831–1913. *Australian Economic History Review, 57*(1), 108–129.

Kobayashi, A., & Sugihara, K. (2018). Changing Patterns of Sarawak Exports, c. 1870–2013. In N. Ishikawa & R. Soda (Eds.), *Anthropogenic tropical forest, Chapter 27*. Singapore: Springer Nature.

Korthals-Altes, W. L. (1991). *Changing economy in Indonesia, Vol. 12a, General trade statistics 1822–1940*. Amsterdam: Royal Tropical Institute.

Latham, A. J. H., & Neal, L. (1983). The international market in rice and wheat, 1868–1914. *Economic History Review, 36*, 260–280.

Lee, P. P. (1978). *Chinese society in nineteenth century Singapore*. Kuala Lumpur: Oxford University Press.

Li, Tana. (2004). The late-eighteenth and early nineteenth-century Mekong Delta in the regional trade system. In N. Cooke & T. Li (Eds.), *Water frontier, commerce and the Chinese in the Lower Mekong Region, 1750–1880* (pp. 71–84). Singapore: Rowman & Littlefield Publishers Inc.

Lindblad, T. J. (2002). The outer islands in the 19th century: Contest for the periphery. In H. Dick, V. Houben, T. Lindblad, & T. Kian (Eds.), *The emergence of a national economy: An economic history of Indonesia, 1800–2000* (pp. 82–110). Honolulu: Allen & Unwin.

Maddison, A., & Prince, G. (Eds.). (1989). *Economic growth in Indonesia, 1820–1940*. Dordrecht: Foris Publications.

Mckeown, A. (2004). Global migration, 1846–1940. *Journal of World History, 15*(2), 155–189.

Murray, M. J. (1980). *The development of capitalism in colonial Indochina (1870–1940)*. Berkeley, Los Angeles, London: University of California Press.

Ooi, Keat Gin. (1997). *Of free trade and native interests: The Brookes and the economic development of Sarawak, 1841–1941*. Kuala Lumpur: Oxford University Press.

Owen, N. G. (1971). The rice industry of mainland South East Asia 1850–1914. *The Journal of the Siam Society, 59*(2), 75–143.

Sugihara, K. (1996). *Ajiakan Boeki no Keisei to Kozo (patterns and development of Intra-Asian Trade)*. Kyoto: Minerva Shobo.

Sugihara, K. (2005). Patterns of Chinese Emigration to Southeast Asia, 1869–1939. In K. Sugihara (Ed.), *Japan, China, and the Growth of the Asian International Economy, 1850–1949* (pp. 244–274). Oxford: Oxford University Press.

Saw, S. H. (1969). Population trends in Singapore, 1819–1967. *Journal of Southeast Asian History, 10*(1), 36–49.

Tan, T. S. (1902). Chinese local trade. *The Straits Chinese Magazine, 6*(23), 89–97.

Trocki, C. A. (1979). *Prince of pirates: The Temenggongs and the development of Johor and Singapore 1784–1885*. Singapore: NUS Press.

Turnbull, M. C. (1977). *A history of Singapore 1819–1975*. London: Oxford University Press.

Van der Kraan, A. (1998). Contest for the Java cotton trade, 1811–40: An episode in Anglo-Dutch rivalry. Occasional Paper No. 32, The University of Hull, Centre for South-East Asian Studies.

Warren, J. F. (1981). *The Sulu Zone 186–1898: The dynamics of external trade, slavery, and ethnicity in the transformation of a Southeast Asian maritime state*. Singapore: Singapore University Press.

Wong, L. K. (1960). The trade of Singapore 1819–69. *Journal of Malaysian Branch of Royal Asiatic Society, 33*(4), 1–135.

Wong, L. K. (1978). Singapore: Its growth as an entrepot port, 1819–1941. *Journal of Southeast Asian Studies, 15*(1), 50–84.

Statistical Sources

Blue book for the colony of the Straits Settlements, trade returns for the years, 1868–1913. Singapore: Government of the Straits Settlements.
Sarawak Gazette. Sarawak trade returns for the year, 1870–1907.
Sarawak Government Gazette. Sarawak trade returns for the year, 1908–1917.
Sarawak annual report of the Department of Trade and Customs for the year, 1920–1940.
Straits Settlements Factory Records, record no. G/34/160.
Sumatra Factory Records, record no. G/35/51.
Tabular statements of the commerce and shipping of Singapore, 1839–1865. Calcutta: Military Orphan Press.

Open Access This chapter is licensed under the terms of the Creative Commons Attribution-NonCommercial-NoDerivatives 4.0 International License (http://creativecommons.org/licenses/by-nc-nd/4.0/), which permits any noncommercial use, sharing, distribution and reproduction in any medium or format, as long as you give appropriate credit to the original author(s) and the source, provide a link to the Creative Commons licence and indicate if you modified the licensed material. You do not have permission under this licence to share adapted material derived from this chapter or parts of it.

The images or other third party material in this chapter are included in the chapter's Creative Commons licence, unless indicated otherwise in a credit line to the material. If material is not included in the chapter's Creative Commons licence and your intended use is not permitted by statutory regulation or exceeds the permitted use, you will need to obtain permission directly from the copyright holder.

Chapter 6
Labour-Intensive Industrialization and the Emerging State in Pre-war Japan

Masayuki Tanimoto

6.1 Introduction

It is widely asserted that the "success" of emerging states in Asia rested on the adoption of a development strategy based on export-oriented instead of import-substitution industrialization. In fact, the growth of export trade that started with labour-intensive products seems to have played a significant role in fostering the emerging economies and states beginning in the 1970s, especially in East and Southeast Asia.

On the other hand, it is also widely known that the Meiji government, established through the Meiji Restoration in 1868, adopted "*Shokusan-kogyo seisaku*", or the economic policy of encouraging new industries as a means of catching up with the "advanced" states in the West. In fact, the government tried to transplant brand-new industrial technologies and institutions, such as mechanized cotton spinning mills, iron works, shipyards, arsenals, and so on. It is clear that these newly transplanted and more or less capital-intensive industries targeted to promote import substitution. If they played a central role for Japan's economic development after the Meiji Restoration from 1868 onwards, how can we evaluate the role of export-oriented industrialization in Japan's development, a distinctive example of emerging state prior to WWII?

Based on the recent literature discussing the multi-layered nature of Japan's economic development,[1] this chapter reconsiders the significant role of labour-intensive industrialization in pre-war Japan. In doing so, the chapter specifically examines its

---

[1] In regard with the term "multi-layered nature of Japan's economic development", see Sawai and Tanimoto (2016), 148–149. I also keep the discussion about "balanced growth", initiated by Takafusa Nakamura, in mind. See Nakamura (1971/1983).

M. Tanimoto (✉)
Graduate School of Economics, Faculty of Economics, The University of Tokyo, Bunkyo-ku, Tokyo 113-0033, Japan
e-mail: tanimoto@e.u-tokyo.ac.jp

© The Author(s) 2019
K. Otsuka and K. Sugihara (eds.), *Paths to the Emerging State in Asia and Africa*, Emerging-Economy State and International Policy Studies, https://doi.org/10.1007/978-981-13-3131-2_6

role in import and export trade, to which the discussion of the development strategy mentioned above pays special attention. After an overview of the features of Japan's economic development, the chapter demonstrates the role of labour-intensive industrialization by exemplifying cases of cotton related industries, followed by a discussion on the changing pattern of export-oriented industries, with a focus on urban small-scale manufacturers. The last section touches on the prospects in the post-war period.

6.2 The Nature of Industrialization in Modern Japan

According to Fig. 6.1, Japan's per capita GDP nearly reached the level of those in industrialized Western states in the 1970s through the so-called "rapid growth era" in the late 1950s and the 1960s. Although this post-war economic growth is eye-catching, the figure also reveals the catching up process of Japan's per capita GDP before World War II, starting from a level of less than one-quarter of that of the U.K., the most advanced state in terms of economic development, and around 40% of those of France and Germany, relatively backward states which were trying to catch up to the U.K. in the 1870s and the 1880s. The pre-war economic growth achieved 40% of the GDP of the U.K. and around 50% of those of France and Germany in the 1930s. The speed of catching up was more rapid in terms of the state's total GDP, reflecting the relatively high population growth in Japan. Considering the destructive effect of World War II on Japan's economy, the post-war rapid growth can be positioned as the last stage of the long-term catching up process that continued from the second half of the nineteenth century. In other words, Japan can be regarded as an emerging state, at least in the early twentieth century, whose growth was "trapped" in the 1940s and the early 1950s. In this regard, Japan's pre-war experience deserves to be explored in light of the emerging state argument.

The next concern is a question as to whether the focus on labour-intensive sectors deserves a better understanding in Japan's industrialization. One way to approach this question is to consider the relative contribution of labour-intensive sectors to overall Japanese production. Since it is difficult to estimate the relative weight in value-added terms, we will use the contribution to employment as a way to approach this problem. Table 6.1 shows the estimated composition of manufacturing workers by employment size in 1909. Among 3,337 million people occupied in the manufacturing sectors, only 0.92 million workers were affiliated with "factories" employing five workers and more, or established by the government. In other words, approximately 70% of the manufacturing work force was working in industrial sites recognized as non-factory workshops. A similar estimation for the year after the rapid growth during World War I, based on the first national census of population carried out in 1920, also reveals the dominance of small workshops in manufacturing sectors. Among the total working population engaged in the manufacturing sectors, approximately 4.56 million, 62.9% of the total working population were engaged in non-factory workshops (Tanimoto 2006, 6). Since the strong positive correlation between firm

6 Labour-Intensive Industrialization and the Emerging State ...

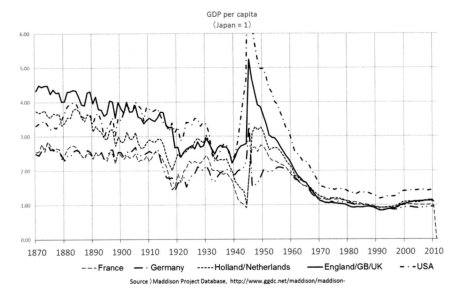

Fig. 6.1 GDP per capita in comparison with Japan

Table 6.1 Distribution of working population of manufacturing industries in 1909

	Total	Non-factory	Factory					
		Total	Private sector				Government-run factory	
			Total	5–9 employees	1,000 or more employees		Total	1,000 or more employees
Male	2,030,600	1,630,586	307,139	66,275	30,537		92,875	81,466
Female	1,306,500	788,618	493,498	42,141	80,742		24,384	23,528
Total	3,337,100	2,419,204	800,637	108,416	117,259		116,385	104,994
Proportion of female (%)	39.2	32.6	61.6	38.9	72.6		20.8	22.4

Source Noshomusho ed, *Kojotokeisohy, Noshomutokeihyo* and *Honpokogyoippan*, Umemura et al. (1988)

size and capital intensity is confirmed by the industrial survey conducted in 1932 in Tokyo, the prefecture comprising the largest manufacturing population from the 1920s onwards, it is plausible to use employment size as a proxy for labour intensity in working sites (Tanimoto 2013a, 156). Thus, it is clear that Japan's pre-war industrialization entailed the proliferation of labour-intensive sectors, at least in a quantitative sense.

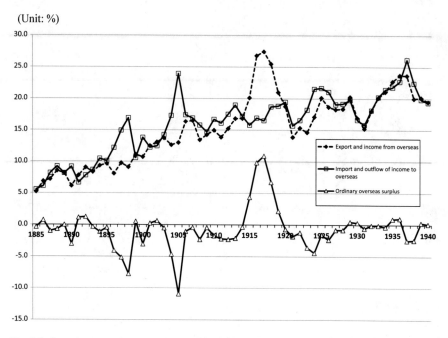

Fig. 6.2 Japan's export, import and trade balance against GNP. *Source* Ohkawa et al. (1974)

The contribution of labour-intensive sectors in Japan's international trade is also worth discussing. As Fig. 6.2 suggests, the degree of dependence upon foreign trade, the total value of export and import per GDP, rose along with GDP growth. On top of that, the trade balance tended toward imbalance except during specific periods, and the margin of the imbalance occasionally grew significantly. The structural change of trade is also worth noticing. According to the overviewing of the trade based on the estimated long-term statistics, the main import commodities changed from finished manufactured goods to intermediate and capital goods, followed by an increase in raw materials in tandem with the development of the manufacturing sectors. The expenditure for these imported commodities should have been financed by revenue from the export trade, from mining products such as copper and coal, to silk related commodities and newly developed manufactured products (Yamazawa and Yamamoto 1979: 5–9). The changing role of the labour-intensive sectors can be effectively examined by observing the trade related aspects, touching on a discussion of the effect of import-substitutive and export-oriented strategies.

6.3 The Role of Labour-Intensive Sectors in Pre-war Japan

6.3.1 The Cotton Industry for Import Substitution[2]

It is well known that the Opening of the Ports in 1859, the end of the "seclusion policy" of Tokugawa Shogunate, had a great impact on the cotton industry in Japan's archipelago. In fact, the increase in English cotton cloth grew to occupy nearly 40% of the domestic market for cotton cloth in the early 1870s. However, the proportion of imported cotton cloth to domestic cotton demand had begun to decrease in the mid-1870s, and fell to around 10% before 1880. On the other hand, as Table 6.2 shows, the volume of imported cotton yarn exceeded cotton cloth during the latter half of the 1870s. This transformation, from importing finished goods to intermediate goods, suggests a structural change in the production aspects of cotton goods in Japan's archipelago.

What happened were drastic re-organizations of the industry. The importation of cotton yarn almost eliminated domestic hand-spun yarn from the yarn market. Naturally, as it provided material for spinning, cotton cultivation also suffered. However, it was not before the late 1880s that cotton cultivation in Japan had clearly declined, since the self-use of cotton for spinning and weaving continued in a certain portion of peasant households. It was the penetration of 'new' cotton cloths produced in the domestic weaving districts, which were relatively cheap as well as suitable to consumers in Japan, that ruled out the self-use production of cloth in the rural areas. The appearance of these 'new' cloths showed the consequences of the re-organization of the cotton weaving districts, the other phase of re-organization of the cotton industry.

Unlike imported cloth, imported yarn that came from England at the early stage, followed by British Indian yarn in the next stage, provided weaving districts with the opportunity to survive, or even develop. The relative low price of machine-made imported yarn enabled the weaving districts to realize competitive prices compared to imported cloth, as well as to develop a new kind of cloth, whose quality was different from those made of hand-spun yarn (Tamura 2004). The import substitution of the cloths can be accounted for by the response of these weaving districts, and these districts could have been prosperous under the circumstances of the market expansion for cloth in the 1870s. Based on this transformation, Japan's cotton industry started development of both weaving and spinning sectors. The former provided the market that was indispensable for establishment of the latter. However, there was a huge difference in terms of the production form within the industry. Regarding this as a multi-layered structure, we will see their development from the 1880s onwards in the light of labour-intensive industrialization.

When it comes to the cotton weaving industry, producers were divided into two different categories. One comprised weaving mills that were attached to the cotton spinning companies that emerged in the late 1880s, at the earliest. Such mills were equipped with British or North American power looms, and they employed numerous

---

[2]The first half of this section is based on Tanimoto (2006, 2009).

Table 6.2 Trade and production of cotton goods in the late 19th century Japan (unit: 10,000 kin)

	Import			Domestic production		Export		Domestic consumption	Production/consumption		Production/consumption
	Yarn	Cloth	Raw cotton	Yarn	Cloth	Yarn	Cloth	Cloth	Cloth	Yarn	
	A	B	C	D	E	F	G	H = B + E − G	E/H	D/(A+D − F)	
1875	1,484	1,493	282	1,601	3,085		4	4,574	67.4%	51.9%	
	45.5%	45.8%	8.7%								
1880	3,146	1,817	146	2,815	5,961		12	7,766	76.8%	47.2%	
	61.6%	35.6%	2.9%								
1889	4,709	1,576	3,969	4,875	9,584		58	11,102	86.3%	50.9%	
	45.9%	15.4%	38.7%								
1899	903	1,953	33,935	29,129	18,772	11,260	1,175	19,550	96.0%	155.2%	
	2.5%	5.3%	92.2%								

Source Nakamura (1968) Appendix 3
Note The estimated values of yarn and cloth and raw cotton are converted into the weight of ginned cotton. *kin*. 1 kin ≒ 600 g

6 Labour-Intensive Industrialization and the Emerging State …

Table 6.3 Distribution of businesses and workers by production forms of weaving industry in 1905

	Total	Form of production			Piece rate weaving
		Independent business			
		Factory	Workshop	Clothier	
Number of business	448,609	3,097	138,833	14,370	292,309
Number of workers	767,423	91,279	229,446	58,591	388,107
Proportion of female workers	95.3	88.5	95.7	89.4	97.6
Worker per business	1.7	29.5	1.7	4.1	1.3

Source Noshomusho ed, *Noshomutokeihyo*

young female workers, just like the cotton spinning mills that we will discuss later. This type represents a factory system directly transplanted from Western countries (Takamura 1971; Nakaoka 2006). However, this production system produced at most only about one-third of the total output of cotton fabrics even in 1914 (Abe 1990: 24). The rest of the cotton weaving was carried out in regional industrial districts, *sanchi*, most of which originated in the production area prosperous in the 1870s or before. In these districts, clothiers and other manufacturers worked together in areas characterized by a highly concentrated presence of merchants dealing in products and materials. Even in 1905, as Table 6.3 shows, workers in "factory" production units employing 10 employees and more accounted for only 12% of the total number of workers in the entire industry. The statistics show that 30% of the workers were employed in workshops with less than 10 workers, and that 50% of the workers were in workshops organized under the putting-out system.[3] In addition, the average number of workers in these workshops was less than two. The power loom ratio (the number of power looms divided by the total number of looms) remained as low as 16% in 1914 (Abe 1989: 46).

We exemplify the development of these weaving districts by considering the *Iruma* region, which thrived at the turn of the twentieth century.[4] The Iruma region, a southwestern part of Saitama prefecture adjacent to Tokyo, was a cotton-weaving district developed immediately after the Opening of the Ports. By the 1880s, the driving force was import of machine-made cotton yarn from overseas. This was followed by domestic cotton spinning mills, which replaced the expensive hand-spun yarn provided by nearby rural areas. Production initially developed under the Kaufsystem,

---

[3] Considering the working hours of weavers in each category, namely fulltime workers in the large factories and the seasonal side line weavers in the small workshops, the factories seem to have occupied larger proportion in terms of volume of the production than that of number of workers.

[4] The historical facts on Iruma weaving districts are obtained from Tanimoto (1998), Chaps. 6 and 7.

where rural factors collected and purchased fabrics from weavers scattered around villages. At the end of the 1880s, however, the putting-out system, then a new way of organizing production in Japan, replaced the Kaufsystem. This was accompanied by an increase in the total volume of production. Putting-out continued to be the prevalent form of production organization until the mid-1920s. In this form, the direct producer, a *Chin-ori* (literally, a 'piece rate wage weaver') was supplied with dyed and warped yarn by the putting-out master, or clothier, and the producer wove fabrics according to a piece rate.

This transformation from the Kaufsystem to putting-out was triggered by competition in the market. Since cost reduction through the introduction of power looms was not a feasible choice because imported power looms were too expensive, it became vital for clothiers to enhance their competitive edge through improving the quality of their products. Under these circumstances, the putting-out system based on the supply of yarn served to improve the quality using standardized materials. Moreover, the clothier was able to provide wage-weavers with detailed market information, such as texture and design of fabrics, by supplying dyed, warped yarn, which played a pivotal role in the evaluation of product quality. The introduction and implementation of the putting-out system should then be seen as an adaptation strategy to emerging market conditions.

This case indicates that the newly introduced dispersed production system based on labour-intensive technology, weaving with a hand-loom, worked as a promoter of industrial development in modern Japan. It is also noticeable that this type of industrial growth was accompanied by a concentration of related traders within a relatively narrow area. The activities of clothiers were supported by merchants engaged in providing materials or selling products, dyers, and financial institutions, as well as trade associations and institutions of vocational education. Indeed, in Iruma, we can confirm the agglomeration of merchants and dyers in Tokorozawa town, a local centre in this area, together with the establishment of two trade associations and a local bank. The association also ran a small training school for dying skills in the 1900s. This was the formation of an industrial district, distinguished from a mere concentration of producers.

Around 1910, clothiers trying to introduce power looms emerged in certain weaving districts such as Izumi (Osaka prefecture), Chita (Aichi prefecture), Enshu (Shizuoka prefecture) (Abe 1989). Although this trend worked to transform the production form from putting-out to a factory system, it is worthwhile noticing that almost all power-looms introduced in these weaving districts were domestically manufactured machines whose prices were one third or less of imported British or North American power looms. Manufacturers near the leading weaving districts exploited low cost machines, substituting wooden staffs for metal parts to save expensive iron materials(Minami et al. 1982; Suzuki 1996). Since the relatively low price of domestic power looms lowered the barrier for clothiers to establish a machine equipped weaving factory, small scale factories proliferated in certain weaving districts from the 1910s onwards. Therefore, the introduction of domestic power-looms and establishment of small and medium sized factories in these cases, where the capital equipment rate was still lower than in full scale weaving factories, can be recognized as a continuous path of industrial development up to the 1930s, rather than a transformation from a labour-intensive to capital-intensive path.

In contrast, the Osaka Spinning Corporation was the first cotton spinning mill equipped with British spinning machines, comprising tens of thousands of spindles and employing several hundreds of spinners. Following its success, the proliferation of cotton spinning factories from the late 1880s onwards was apparently the capital-intensive path of industrialization, considering the amount of fixed capital required for machines and the facilities of a mill. In fact, almost all the spinning firms of this type adopted the newly introduced model of a joint stock company, rallying more than a hundred investors to cover the fixed cost. However, it is also worth emphasizing that the invested capital should have brought about high profits because the interest rate, or the price of capital, was relatively high in contemporary Japan, as is often the case in an industrializing economy. Continuous operation of factories was the key, and the assimilation of the technological knowledge by Japanese engineers, together with the provision of repair parts based on metal processing skills among domestic craftsmen, enabled the reduction of idle time caused by machine troubles (Nakaoka 2006, Chap. 5). On top of that, operation time was increased by adopting day and night shifts. Even though the night shift was costly because of the extra wage and the deterioration of workers' attentiveness, enhancing capital turnover was essential for higher return on equity (ROE). In other words, the capital-labour ratio of spinning mills tended to be lowered by increasing labour input through the double shift system (Takamura 1971; Sugihara 2013). It is also worth mentioning that the adoption of ring spindles from the late 1880s, which contributed to enhance total factor productivity of the spinning firms, was accompanied by the introduction of cotton mixing processes which required further labour inputs (Otsuka et al. 1988, Chap. 3). Thus, the labour-intensive nature can be discussed even in the case of exact transplantation of the Western factory system.

It is also noticeable that both sectors of the cotton industry, weaving and spinning, commonly depended on rural farming households as their source of workers. The order list of Takizawa Kumakichi, a leading putting-out master in Iruma, reveals that almost all the orders were directed to nearby farming villages, concentrating specifically in the middle layer of farming households there. In other words, piece weavers existed within the households that were inclined toward agriculture. In fact, the orders placed with the piece weavers by Takizawas showed strong and continuous seasonal fluctuations that clearly reflected the nature of this source of labour. Indeed, orders in May and June accounted for less than 10% of the yearly totals in almost all the years from 1896 to 1920. It is not surprising that the seasonal fluctuations in time devoted to weaving were inversely related to the labour demand for farming within peasant households. The May–June period was harvest time in the region for wheat and tea, and peak season for silkworm breeding (for springtime).

In contrast, workers in cotton spinning mills came from the lower layer of farming households, whose cultivating lands were smaller than those in the middle layer. The well-known industrial report, *Orimono Shokko Jijo* (The Working Conditions of Weaving Workers), published by the central government in 1903, pointed out a distinction between the 'factory' pattern of labour organizations and that of the "peasant's side-line business". The report stated that "It is more beneficial for local women to weave fabrics according to a piece rate at home than to work for the factory that binds them for a long period of time. Therefore, in general, female workers at weaving factories are looked down upon in villages".[5] The report also recognized two separate sources of labour in the following remark: "Today, most of the local women employed at factories seem to come from financially-pressed families" (ditto). In fact, spinning mills organized a recruiting system seeking juvenile female workers with low opportunity costs, who were expected to exist in the lower layer of farming households scattered among rural villages that were usually far away from the location of the spinning mills in urban areas. As factory statistics[6] reveal, the ages of female workers were highly concentrated under 25; in 1909, more than half were teenagers. The duration of their factory work was limited to their younger years, followed by re-inclusion in either farming or urban households as a household head's spouse, usually under the plural self-employment system. Although their working sites differed from home to factory, the underlying logic of labour provision was common, determined by the labour allocation strategy formed in each household.

Thus, the development of the cotton industry in late nineteenth to early twentieth century Japan strongly entailed the nature of labour-intensive industrialization being also effective for import substitution of cotton manufactured goods from Britain, British India, and other Western states. On the other hand, it is important to recall that the development of the cotton industry itself was a major factor in the growing trade imbalance. The key factor was importation of raw cotton from British India and the US, as already suggested in Table 6.2. The balance of payments for cotton related trade (the difference between the excess of exports in yarn and cloth and the excess of imports of raw cotton and cotton related machines) was apparently constantly negative, forming the major cause of the trade imbalance shown in Fig. 6.2 (Ushijima and Abe 1996). Although the cotton industry in those years could meet the growing domestic demand, it did not have a competitive edge in the rich market of Europe and North America. In this context, the significant role of export-oriented industries in financing the payments created by the growth of the import trade comes up. The next section discusses the dynamism of labour-intensive sectors in export-related industries.

6.3.2 Dynamism of Export-Oriented Industries[7]

It is well known that textiles constituted the largest part of Japan's export trade during the pre-World War II period. Raw silk (silk thread) was continuously Japan's single largest export until the early 1930s. The second largest export item shifted

---

[5]Cited from reprinted version; Noshomusho (1903/1998), vol. 2, p. 178.

[6]*Kojotokeihyo* (Statistical Tables of Factories) edited by Noshomusho (Ministry of Agriculture and Commerce).

[7]This section is mainly based on Tanimoto (2013a), 162–166.

from silk cloth to cotton yarn in the early 1890s, and then to cotton cloth after World War I. Despite their significant role, textiles did not monopolize exports. The sum of various consumer goods (hereafter, miscellaneous goods) other than textiles contributed a considerable proportion of manufactured exports, although individual categories accounted for only small proportions. Indeed, by the 1930s, the combined export output of the following products made them joint contenders with cotton cloth or yarn for the second biggest export position: matches, knitted goods, hats, footwear, buttons, accessories, ceramics, glassware, enamel ironware, straw plaits, fancy mats, Western-style umbrellas, brushes, trunks, and toys.[8]

Apart from the volume, the changing patterns in the composition of export-oriented miscellaneous industries were also noteworthy. We can roughly distinguish three categories among the miscellaneous exports in Fig. 6.3, defined by the timing of their respective places in the export supply. Ceramics and lacquerware comprised the first category, with exports beginning soon after Japan's opening of ports in 1859. The second category comprised goods whose exports surged in the 1880s, including matches, trunks, straw plaits, and fancy mats, and accounted for a significant part of aggregate exports from the 1880s to the 1900s. It is notable that the export of these goods commonly decreased sharply in the 1920s, and were unable to recover their position in the export trade throughout the interwar period. The third category comprised accessories, knitting goods, glassware, enamel ironware, and toys, exports of which increased gradually from the 1880s, surged during World War I, and maintained an almost constant level in the 1920s. In the 1930s, there was a rapid increase in the export of some of these goods; for instance, toys, which we will focus on later.

Behind the shifting composition of these sales, there was an evolutionary process in production, such as changes in technology or location. The miscellaneous goods exported soon after the opening of the ports were characterized as traditional craft products, which attracted an overseas consumer market with a particular taste for Japanese style. Their production system, including technologies, skills, and the nature of workers, must have been inherited largely from the Tokugawa period. On the other hand, the straw plaits and fancy mats that made up 40% of miscellaneous goods exports during the late 19th century were inferior goods to those available in overseas markets, such as carpets in the US. In addition, Japanese matches were regarded in South and East Asia as inferior goods to those imported from Europe. With regard to the system of production, a large portion of the output of straw plaits and fancy mats was produced as a side line by peasant households. Furthermore, even where the factory system had been adopted, it was established in the countryside and was based on handicraft technology with indigenous materials. In contrast, matches were produced mainly in urban settings, using imported technology. However, both types of production systems commonly involved a widely available source of labour—unskilled females—to produce relatively simple, uniform products. In this sense, they were typical labour-intensive industries but entirely different from the traditional crafts industry that employed skilled male workers.

---

[8] For the sources of historical information on each commodity, see the footnotes of Tanimoto (1995).

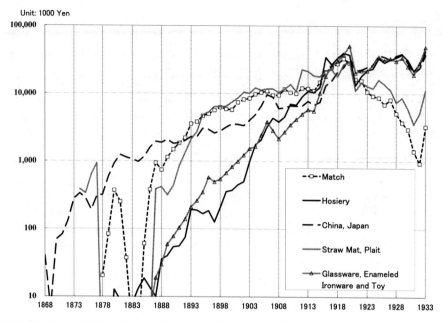

Fig. 6.3 Export of miscellaneous goods. *Source* Toyokeizai Shinposha (1935)

In contrast to these two categories, a distinct feature of the third category of export products was that they were 'new' items produced by 'transplanted' technology with 'new' materials, such as metals or chemical products, rubber, and celluloid. In addition, it is noteworthy that each individual industry in the third category manufactured various kinds of products with different uses or designs. Although the goods continued to be inferior in quality, their manufacturers were required not only to supply low-priced goods but also to respond to consumer tastes. In other words, these industries had to be able to acquire market information and hold 'skilled' labour, broadly defined, to reflect market information in the products.

Table 6.4 shows this direction of transformation from another angle. The table compares the export markets of industries with significant shares of total exports in 1937. The export markets are divided into four areas. A includes 'Manchuria' in northeast China and the 'Kwantung Leased Territory', also in China. B includes the rest of Asia, excluding the areas in the Japanese Empire, such as Korea and Taiwan. C includes Central and South America, Africa, Oceania, and the Middle East. D includes Europe and North America. For manufactured products, barriers to entry appeared to be highest in the case of markets in the industrialized countries in D. On the contrary, barriers to entry could have been lowered by Japanese political influence in area A. Barriers to entry in areas B and C were in between those two. In fact, machine-manufacturing industries, which were technologically backward compared with those in the Western industrialized countries of those years, mostly limited their market to area A. By contrast, almost all raw silk was exported to

Table 6.4 Japan's export trade in 1937

	Machinery and parts	Raw silk	Cotton cloths	Miscellaneous goods			
				Accessories	Ceramics	Lamps and parts	Toys
Sum of export trade (million yen)	227.7	407.1	573.1	15.5	54.0	22.0	83.2
(Proportion by areas)							
China (including Manchuria, Hong Kong): A	64.4	0.0	18.5	4.7	11.3	15.3	3.3
Other Asian countries: B	26.8	2.1	33.7	34.3	20.4	21.6	13.1
Rest of the world: C	4.3	2.9	39.6	26.5	22.1	21.2	18.6
Europe and North America: D	4.0	95.0	8.3	34.4	46.2	41.9	65.1
Total	100.0	100.0	100.0	100.0	100.0	100.0	100.0

Source Okrasho ed. *Dai-Nihon Boeki Nenpyo*

area D, particularly to the US, based on the tight ties between the weaving and knitting industries in that country, and their supplier of intermediate goods in Japan. Meanwhile, cotton cloth made up the largest volume of consumer goods exports. Less than 10% of cotton cloth exports were to area D. In contrast with all these categories of exports, a distinct feature of the miscellaneous goods was the relatively high proportion of exports to area D. In addition, this area was the largest market for toys, accessories, ceramics, and table lamps, and these goods almost matched the items included in the abovementioned third export category.

Therefore, the export-oriented development of Japan's miscellaneous industries during the interwar period was made possible by penetrating the markets of high-income countries in the face of competition from within those industrialized countries. This was one of the industrial frontiers for the Japanese economy in those years. The case of the toy industry discussed in the next section exemplifies this dynamism well.

6.3.3 The Development of Japan's Toy Export[9]

Toy exports increased continuously from the turn of the 20th century, declined after the Japan–Russo War, and soared from World War I to the period of the post-war boom. Exports dropped sharply in 1920 and stagnated during the first half of the 1920s, followed by a certain level of recovery in the latter half of the decade. Although there was a negative effect from the Great Depression around 1930, toy exports rose from 1932 up to 1938, when the war economy placed great limitations on the manufacture of 'non-necessities'. Comparing these export statistics to those of import and production, we can identify the distinct feature of toy manufacturing. First, the export-production ratio exceeded 100% in many years. This seemingly irrational percentage can be understood partly by considering the limits of the original statistics, such as coverage of the production data.[10] Still, it is realistic to assume that most toy products were manufactured for overseas markets. Second, it is important to mention that there were very few imports of toys from the late nineteenth century. Third, the breakdown of the materials used in exported toys also reveals that more than half were made of rubber, celluloid, and tin from 1920 onwards.

These facts suggest an intriguing argument in considering the relationship between trade patterns and industrial development. The development of the toy industry had been consistently led by the growth of export trade through the manufacture of newly developed items made from materials originating in foreign 'advanced' countries with very small importation of the original goods. Thus, toy manufacturing did not follow the typical 'flying geese model', where development patterns are a series of steps from importation to import substitution, and from saturation of domestic markets to exportation (Yamazawa 1984). It was the demand from overseas, not the domestic market, that formed the starting point for the toy industry. This pattern differs not only from the cotton industry, which fitted the flying geese model well by exemplifying efforts for import substitution discussed in the previous section, but also from the export-oriented raw silk industry, which exemplified the changing patterns of indigenous industries that had long been dependent on the domestic market, and started exporting after the opening of the ports in 1859.

Although Japanese toys occupied the US import market during World War I in the absence of Germany, a dominant provider to the international toy market, the share of Japanese toys in the US market fell drastically throughout the 1920s. These trends clearly reveal the lack of global competitiveness of Japanese toy manufacturing at that time. However, the situation changed from the late 1920s, when the share of Japanese toys in the US and UK markets started to rise gradually, and even soared in the 1930s, displacing German toys. It is noteworthy that the trend started to change before 1932, when the depreciation of the yen began to provide favourable conditions for export.

---

[9]The discussion in this section draws on Tanimoto (2017). For the sources of the following descriptions, see the footnotes and references in Tanimoto (2007).

[10]Although trade statistics covers, in theory, all exported toys, the most consistent statistics for production, *Kojotokeihyo* (Statistical Tables of Factories), covered factories and workshops employing five or more employees only.

6 Labour-Intensive Industrialization and the Emerging State ...

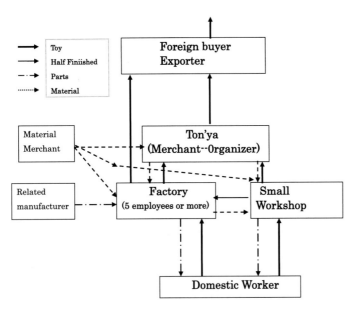

Fig. 6.4 Production organization of the toy manufacturing industry in Tokyo

This fact suggests that the competitive edge of Japanese toys rested not only on the deterioration of price, but also on improvement in the quality of the products. In fact, the foreign trade division of Shokosho (the Ministry of Commerce and Industry) stated in its trade reports[11] that the toy industry went beyond the emulation stage, and acquired the ability to create innovative designs. The focal point is the fact that this improvement was carried out under the context of labour-intensive industrialization.

Figure 6.4 illustrates the production organization of the toy manufacturing industry. The merchant organizers were located between manufacturing workshops and the export markets, connecting manufacturers to distributors. They often related to the production process by coordinating workshops for manufacturers, who took charge of the partial processes. It is notable that the number of non-factory workshops far exceeded the number of factories that employed more than four workers. The workforce was composed of employers, family workers, 'apprentices', and adult labourers. Based on their role in the organization of production, there are two categories of manufacturers: core manufacturers producing finished goods, and rather small workshops performing partial processes. The former tended to be associated with factories; however, it was not unusual for non-factory workshops to provide finished goods to wholesalers. In contrast, the work assigned to domestic workers was limited to partial processing or simple assembly, and even small workshops placed orders with domestic workers. In addition, the gender composition of the workforce differed by type of workers, as most domestic workers were female.

---

[11] *Honpo Gaikokuboekigaikyo* (The overview of the foreign trade of Japan) edited by Shokosho.

The origin of the competitive edge of the toy manufacturing industry lay in this organizational character. In fact, it was usual to economize labour cost by subcontracting to domestic workers. The employment of juvenile workers as 'apprentices' might have also had a similar effect on the labour cost of small-scale workshops. However, toys were not the kind of goods whose demand was determined mostly by price. They were subject to fashion, and supplier had to match or even develop the taste of consumers in order to increase their sales. In this context, it is rather notable that each category of actor—merchant organizer, factory workshop, and non-factory workshop—included firms that had the ability to design the goods. The records of the registration of designs and devices, held either at the National Patent Office or by the trade association of toy manufacturing, reveal that firms in each of these three sometimes succeeded in registering theirs ideas. In other words, several small workshops, as well as merchant organizers and "factories", were capable of creating the original models of products. Therefore, we should not simply assume that the relationship between merchant organizer and manufacturer, or between consigner and consignee among manufacturers, was complementary or exploited the division of labour. While the influential merchant organizer vertically coordinated the production process under its own control, there were manufacturers, including non-factory workshops, who designed and produced finished goods on their own accounts. These manufacturers sometimes held relatively strong positions in the negotiation processes with merchant organizers. The relationship between merchant organizers and manufacturers included competition on the same grounds, as well as transactions based on the vertical division of labour. Thus, the production organization of the toy manufacturing industry was by no means static for the traders, and this competitive nature among traders was maintained through vigorous new entries that resulted from the establishment of independent workshops, as a product of the life course of the workers.

In addition to the endogenous factor of the organization, we can point out some other external factors that support the competitive edge of the industry. One of the conspicuous features of the toy manufacturing industry was the agglomeration of the traders within a relatively small area. For example, in Tokyo, the centre of toy production from the 1920s onwards, the location of more than 40 merchant organizers in 1933 was almost entirely limited to only two blocks in the commercial area. Metal toy manufacturers were concentrated in three blocks, with 39 in one block (Umayabashi). The situation was almost the same for celluloid toy manufacturers. The highly concentrated location of traders suggests the positive effects of agglomeration, reminding us of the arguments of Alfred Marshall and others regarding the effects of external economies in industrial clusters (Marshall 1920). For instance, for merchant organizers, proximity to other traders engaged in the same industry might have increased their opportunities to acquire market information, which was indispensable for the sale of fashionable goods. The agglomeration also facilitated development of the division of labour among traders, which might have increased the productivity of the industry.

Moreover, it was noticeable that traders located within each cluster were not limited to toy traders. In fact, as the directory of celluloid traders of 1939 indicates, it is better to say that celluloid toy workshops were located within the agglomeration of traders of various celluloid goods. This appears to have been true of traders in metal or rubber toys as well. These facts suggest that the traders might have moved in among industries that used the same material. Indeed, by matching the trade directories of different years, we can confirm that several celluloid toy manufacturers changed their product to other celluloid goods during the course of time and vice versa. This flexibility among traders appears to have relieved the blows of market fluctuations. Although this buffer function was probably limited, as market trends of the industries would not have been inversely correlated to compensate for the slump of the other industry, it might have provided more opportunities to survive, at least for traders with a relatively high ability to respond to the unstable economic environment.

Meanwhile, the coexistence of related industries in the same area was important for the toy traders as well. Mould producers were a typical example. In order to acquire the fruits of product innovation, it was vital for traders to possess the moulds. However, a relatively high level of skills was required to produce the moulds, and it was rather difficult for the traders, particularly small workshops, to internalize this process. In this situation, the mould 'factories' generated within the agglomeration of metal-processing workshops near the agglomeration of toy traders, or the mould-processing workshops whose locations overlapped with those of celluloid toy manufacturers, played an important role in actualizing the originally generated ideas as real products. Similar roles were played in the areas of businesses that required relatively high skills, such as manufacturing springs and gears, and printing tin plates. The agglomeration of related industries provided complementary factors that were indispensable to the development of the dispersed production organization based on small workshops. Thus, the competitive edge of toy production was largely rooted in its location in urban settings, specifically the metropolis of Tokyo. In fact, as is seen in the following section, Tokyo became the largest industrial city comprising the agglomeration of various kinds of small scale workshops in the interwar period.

6.3.4 The Structure of Small-Scale Industries in Interwar Tokyo

Table 6.5 is based on data extracted from an industrial census conducted by the Tokyo Municipal Office in 1932 (*Kogyo Chosa-sho*).[12] It indicates the proportion of small workshops run on a self-employment basis in the manufacturing sector. In light of the number and composition of workers, workshops with 2,000–4,999 yen of capital appear to be the upper threshold for self-employment-based workshops. These workshops comprised 87.7% of all workshops and factories, and employed

---

[12]The following discussion on the structure of small-scale industries is a summary of Tanimoto (2013a), 154–162.

49.3% of all workers. It is apparent that family workers, including employers, played significant roles in the workforce. The high proportion of 'apprentices' recorded in the census is also striking. There were more 'apprentices' than 'labourers'. This implies that these workshops depended greatly on workers other than 'labourers', who were the main work force of the large factories. On the other hand, we can estimate by the industrial census that more than half of the workshops belonging to the layer of capital of 2,000–4,999 yen were equipped with prime movers. Although the difference in per capita fixed capital according to scale was clear, small workshops were not simple equivalents of the traditional handicraft manufacturing industry. Thus, not a few small workshops were engaged in processing newly introduced materials with relatively small fixed capital; in other words, resting their production more on labour than on capital when compared with large factories. In this sense, we can certainly regard small workshops as being labour-intensive. How then did labour-intensive workshops manage to survive or even develop in the face of the competition with capital-intensive factories? To tackle this question, let us focus on the nature of their workforce.

As mentioned above, small workshops had three types of workers: 'family workers', 'labourers', and 'apprentices'. With respect to gender, we should point out the high proportion of male workers, accounting for more than 70% in each type. This gender bias contrasts to that of the textile industries in both types of factories, as well as in side-line jobs, and suggests the different nature of the workforce in urban small-scale industries. On the other hand, it is noteworthy that the age range clearly differed according to the composition of the workforce. The number of 'apprentices', which is the highest among the three main categories of workers, was greatest among teenage workers, accounting for two-thirds of the workers in the same age group. In contrast, 'family workers', including employers, accounted for more than 80% of the workers over the age of 30. In between were the 'labourers', who accounted for the highest number of workers in their twenties, but the smallest number of workers overall. These facts enable us to suggest that a strong tendency existed to change one's industrial status from that of an 'apprentice' to 'labourer', and from 'labourer' to 'family worker (employer)'. The latter change implies the existing intention among employees to be independent by establishing their own workshops, and the former suggests the importance of skill formation to become a full-fledged worker.

According to an industrial survey carried out in 1936 in Tokyo,[13] more than 70% of the manufacturers across 26 trades replied that they required more than two years of training. In the case of six of these trades, more than 40% of the manufacturers claimed that a period of five years of training was necessary. This is in sharp contrast to the case of "domestic workers" in the same survey. Half of the domestic workers could work without any training, and another quarter could work with training of less than one month. These observations make it clear that a workforce with a certain level of skill was required for the small workshops, and this attribute of the workforce provided the foundation for an 'apprentice' being distinguished from a mere 'juvenile labourer'. We do not possess any concrete evidence to confirm that

---

[13] Tokyo Municipal Office ed. (1937).

Table 6.5 Content of workshops classified by the size of capital in Tokyo 1932

Class by capital	Number of workshops	Proportion of worker (%)	Workers per workshop						Value-added[a] per worker	Number of prime mover per worker
			Total	Employer and family		Employee				
				Male	Female	Adult		Apprentice		
			(Person)						(Index)	
Less than 100 yen	1,378	0.5	1.67	1.00	0.32	0.08		0.23	44.2	0.02
100–	16,396	7.5	2.06	1.09	0.28	0.15		0.49	63.7	0.09
500–	18,262	10.9	2.68	1.16	0.33	0.29		0.80	66.2	0.23
1,000–	19,929	14.4	3.24	1.19	0.31	0.46		1.11	82.3	0.40
2,000–	16,389	16.0	4.39	1.21	0.28	1.13		1.53	100.0	0.59
5,000–	4,903	7.4	6.76	1.17	0.20	2.82		2.03	146.5	0.81
10 thousands–	3,665	10.8	13.24	1.01	0.15	7.94		2.46	194.7	1.28
50 thousands–	641	3.9	27.31	0.82	0.12	18.97		2.54	240.2	3.09
100 thousands–	663	10.2	69.37	0.36	0.04	54.91		2.01	306.0	7.48
500 thousands–	282	18.3	292.14	0.35	0.13	222.15		2.90	417.0	55.49
Total	82,508	100.0	5.44	1.14	0.29	2.30		1.13		

Source Tokyo Municipal Office ed. (1934)
Note [a] Value-added = Revenue − Expenditure + Wage and Salary + Interest − Rental cost of capital (Capital × 0.08)

an institutionalized apprenticeship with a formal training period or restriction of job entry was effectively operating in these trades at that time. However, we can probably assume that substantial needs existed for the training of workers, and it was natural that some system, though not a formal institution, emerged to meet the demand. The fact that the word 'apprentice' was commonly used in the official investigation might be evidence that one existed.

An investigation of the "apprentices", which was conducted around 1938 and based on 3,768 samples, including 2,990 males, supports this speculation.[14] The investigation reveals that more than half of the male juveniles intended to undergo training at the workplace. Judging from the data on age, working period, and the experience of changing jobs, it appears that a majority of the male 'apprentices' had worked at the same workshop for at least two years. These findings are almost consistent with the data on the training period mentioned above. On the other hand, as we see in the following part of this section, the low wages of these juvenile workers were profitable for the employers. The employers also needed 'apprentices' for cheap labour. Though we do not possess any further information for analysing the equilibrium between the cost of training and low wages, we can probably assume that being trained as an 'apprentice' during their teens, albeit informally, was built into the early stage of the life course of the workers in the small-scale industries.

What was the outcome of these small workshops? Table 6.5 presents the average value-added labour productivity of the workshops in each layer. Since income data tended to be underreported for fear of tax liability, the calculated value-added may be understated. Despite this, great differences between the layers in value-added productivity are apparent. For example, the average productivity of the workshops (or rather, factories) with the largest capital of 500 thousand yen or more, was recorded as four times higher than those with capital of 2,000–4,999 yen. Labour productivity increased in accordance with the increase in capital employed. Therefore, the higher physical productivity of labour achieved by utilizing machines or prime movers might account for most of the productivity differential. In other words, the market value of the products of the small-scale workshops could not compensate fully for their relatively low physical productivity. Although some products might have realized higher market value based on unique technology or skills, in general, the small-scale workshops should be recognized as an industrial sector with relatively low productivity.

However, the difference in productivity was not the decisive factor undermining the competitiveness of the small workshops. Their earnings, after deduction of costs including wages, can be caluculated from this industrial census. It is clear that scale greatly influenced earnings, since the earnings of the small workshops were significantly below the wages of labourers employed in the large-scale factories. However, it should be noted that the earnings of workshops capitalized at 2,000–4,999 yen or more apparently exceeded the highest wages of the labourers employed. Even the earnings of the next layer down, with capital of 1,000–1,999 yen, almost equalled the second highest wage level of factory labourers. This level of earnings might not

---

[14]Tokyo Prefectural Office (1939).

have discouraged employed labourers from establishing their own workshops. In fact, the wages of employees in workshops whose capital were under 10,000 yen, and which employed more than half of the total employees, could not reach the level of earnings mentioned above. This implied that employees with lower wages had no chance of increasing their income as long as they remained employees, given the low possibility for workers to move from small workshops to large ones. Therefore, establishing one's own workshop must have appeared as a promising option, although it involved considerable risks. The differential wages according to the scale of workshops, which also reflected small workshops' use of juvenile workers as 'apprentices' (as mentioned above), enabled small workshops to earn a certain amount, although their value-added labour productivity was considerably lower than that of large-scale factories. On the other hand, this motivated adult labourers to establish their own workshops.

In summary, we may assume a particular life course of workers employed in urban industries. Teenaged males worked in small workshops, undergoing on-the-job training and acquiring a certain level of skills. After being employed in their twenties as adult labourers, some of them might succeed, possibly with some luck, in establishing their own workshops. It was this shared perspective of a certain life course that enabled the skill formation and low wage compatibility in urban industrial settings.

6.3.5 Prospects to the Post-war Development

Thus, the development of urban small-scale industries represented the dynamic nature of labour-intensive industrialization in pre-war Japan. Specifically, export-oriented manufacturing sectors such as toy making showed distinctive growth in the 1930s, driving the relatively faster recovery of the Japanese economy from the Great Depression.

On the other hand, it is plausible that the "success" of these export-oriented industries intrinsically entailed tension between Japan and its trading partners, or among trade rivals. In fact, it is well known that the expansion of cotton textiles exports to South and Southeast Asia in the 1930s resulted in a bilateral trade negotiation between Japan and Britain, British India and the Netherlands, the colony and the suzerain states. Regarding urban toys, the United States imposed more than 100% duties in 1930 (converted to an ad valorem tax). Even Britain, which had advocated a free trade regime, imposed 15–25% ad valorem duties on Japanese toys in the 1930s.[15] Furthermore, the progress of the controlled economy following the outbreak of Sino-Japan war from 1937 onwards suppressed the manufacturing sectors producing consuming goods irrelevant to military needs. In fact, the production of export-oriented goods such as toys, textile goods and ceramics deteriorated significantly under the war-economy from the late 1930s to 1945.

---

[15] Regarding duties imposed on Japan's exported toys, see Tanimoto (2013b), 61.

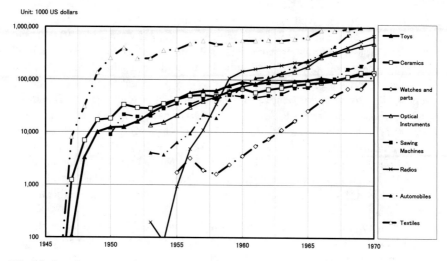

Fig. 6.5 Japan's export trades after World War II. *Source* Tsushosangyoseisakushi Hensaniinkai (1992)

Despite resulting in the disastrous situation, however, it is still important to notice the fact that the development of urban-based export-oriented industries during the interwar period can be regarded as one of the industrial frontiers for the Japanese economy, as mentioned in the previous section. The distinct feature was that their markets primarily targeted the demands of high-income countries, where they won a competition with their counterparts in those industrialized countries. It was not just the achievement of industrialization in the pre-war stage, but it also appears to have been the forerunner of industries exporting finished consumer products to Western industrialized countries after World War II.

According to Fig. 6.5, cotton textile goods led export trade soon after the end of WWII, followed by toys, ceramics, optical instruments (binoculars and cameras), and sewing machines as the second group. It is noticeable that the continuous export trends, such as toys and ceramics from the pre-war period, overlapped those of the latter two that newly emerged after WWII. Furthermore, this trend can be extended to the exportation of radios and watches in the 1960s by creating a category of "light machines",[16] from binoculars to sewing machines to radios.[17] In fact, these products can be categorized as finished goods targeting markets in high-income states, despite the differences in technological basis. Table 6.6 clearly shows that these finished goods, included under the headings of "machines" and "others" in this table, had largely helped compensate for the decline in raw silk in export trade to the US, which had formed more than 80% of Japan's exports to the US in 1929, but sharply deteriorated after the Great Depression. Recalling the growing weight of export trade

---

[16] Sawai and Tanimoto (2016) explicitly touches on, though briefly, the role of "light machine" in post war Japan (p. 386).

[17] Sawai (2013) discussed the development of Japan's export of binoculars from the 1950s to 1960s.

6 Labour-Intensive Industrialization and the Emerging State …

Table 6.6 Proportion of commodities in export to US

	1937	1960	1965
Food	8.2	5.6	2.9
Textile	66.1	26.7	18.4
Raw silk	51.2		
Clothing		8.4	5.8
Chemical goods	6.1	1.4	1.7
Nonferrous metals, mineral goods	3.8	5.4	3.9
Potteries	3.1	3.6	1.6
Metal and metal goods	1.1	14.2	25.7
Steel	0.0	5.6	17.3
Machinery	0.3	14.4	26.1
Sewing machines	0.0	2.0	1.3
Radio	0.0	5.7	3.8
Others	14.4	32.3	21.4
Toys	2.6	5.2	1.8
Optical instruments	0.1	3.0	3.3
Plywood	0.0	3.7	1.8
Total	100.0	100.0	100.0

Source Okurasho ed. *Dai-Nihon Boeki Nenpyo* and *Gaikoku Boeki Gaikyo*

to the US after WWII, we may recognize that the production of these finished goods embodied the direction of the industrialization that led post-war Japan's economic development. In that sense, the development of small scale urban-based industries, such as toys, was one of the distinct aspects of labour-intensive industrialization in pre-war Japan and continued through post-war Japan's rapid economic growth.

6.4 Concluding Remarks

Japan's pre-war economic development can be seen as the case of an emerging state, trying to catch up to the "advanced" west after the Opening of the Ports and Meiji Restoration. The concept of labour-intensive industrialization worked well to explain its development, specifically by considering the changing role of labour-intensive sectors. From the late nineteenth to early twentieth century, the rural-based dispersed cotton weaving industry played a significant role in substituting for imported cotton textiles typically factory-manufactured in "industrialized" states. The success of the transplantation of factory-based cotton spinning should also be explained, if partly, by the reduction in the capital-labour ratio through adoption of a double-shift system and a cotton-mixing technic required for introducing ring spindles. The invention of narrow-sized power-looms made from a mixture of iron and wood, saving the expensive iron parts, was another example of the capital-saving way of assimilating imported technologies.

On the other hand, the development of import-substitutive industries, such as cotton related manufacturing, had to be complemented by export-oriented industries to relax the trade imbalance caused by the increase in imports, consisting of raw materials and, in some cases, advanced machines; in the case of the cotton industry, these were raw cotton and spinning machines. The urban-based, export-oriented small-scale industries deserve special attention in this regard. Their growth in the interwar period supported the expansion of export trade, particularly in the 1930s, compensating for the decline of raw silk, which was previously the major component of exports. They based the labour force on male workers with a certain level of skills acquired by being a kind of apprentice when they were young. The potential possibilities of moving from employees to employers through the establishment of their own workshops encouraged juvenile workers to invest in skill formation, and made them tolerate relatively low wage levels, both supporting the competitiveness in the world market. Thus, the composition of the workforce was distinctively different from the textile industry, which had been the major labour-intensive industry up to the interwar period, endowing Japan's labour-intensive industrialization with its dynamic nature.

In fact, it was in a new wave of export trade targeting mainly the demands of high-income countries where they won a competition with their counterparts in those industrialized countries. On one hand, this achievement might have resulted in causing, at least partly, a rural-urban divide in domestic settings,[18] and trade conflict in an international sphere. This can be seen as comparable to the concept of the "middle income trap" in the contemporary emerging states argument, since Japan's economy became stagnant and even deteriorated from the late 1930s to 1940s because of the war economy. At the same time, the achievement of the pre-war stage can be regarded as the basis for industries exporting finished consumer products to Western industrialized countries after World War II, the emergence of new competitive products from binoculars to watches, and probably to home electronics appliance and transportation machines. In this sense, the perspective of labour-intensive industrialization is open to the post-war rapid economic growth, the last stage of the Japanese economy as an emerging state.

---

[18]There are quite a few discussions on this issue in diverse streams of literature from pre-war period to the present. For brief overviewing of the discussions underlying the literature, see Minami et al. (1998).

References

Abe, T. (1989). *Nihon niokeru Sanchi Menorimonogyo no Tenkai* (The development of cotton weaving districts in Japan). Tokyo: Tokyodaigaku Shuppankai.

Abe, T. (1990). Menkogyo (Cotton manufacturing industry). In S. Nishikawa & T. Abe (Eds.), *Nihonkeizaishi 4 Sangyoka no Jidai Jo*. Iwanami Shoten: Tokyo.

Marshall, A. (1920). *Principles of Economics* (8th ed.). London: Macmillan.

Minami, R., Ishii, T., & Makino, F. (1982). *Gijyutsu fukyu no shojoken: rikishokki no baai* (The conditions of the diffusion of technology: In cases of power looms). *Keizaikenkyu, Hitotsubashi University, 33*(4), 334–359.

Minami, R., Nakamura, M., & Nishizawa, T. (Eds.). (1998). *Demokurashi no Houkai to Saisei: Gakusaitekisekkin* (The collapse and restoration of democracy: An inter-disciplinary approach). Tokyo: Nihonkeizai Hyoronsha.

Nakamura, S. (1968). *Meijiishin no Kisokozo: Nihon Shihonshugi Keisei no Kiten* (Basic structure of Meiji restoration: The starting point of the formation of the Japanese capitalism). Tokyo: Miraisha.

Nakamura, T. (1971/1983). *Senzenki Nihon Keizaiseicho no Bunseki*, Tokyo, Iwanami Shoten translated into *Economic Growth in Pre-war Japan*. New Haven: Yale University Press.

Nakaoka, T. (2006). *Nihon Kindaigijyutsu no Keisei: "Dento" to "Kindai" no Dainamizumu* (The formation of the modern technology in Japan: Dynamism of "tradition" and "modernity"). Tokyo: Asahi Shinbunsha.

Noshomusho. (1903/1998). *Shokkojijo* reprinted by Iwanami Shoten.

Ohkawa, K. et al. (1974). *Choki Keizaitokei 1 Kokuminshotoku* (Estimates of long-term economic statistics of Japan since 1868, vol. 1 National income). Tokyo: Toyokeizai Shinposha.

Otsuka, K., Ranis, G., & Saxonhouse, G. (1988). *Comparative technology choice in development: The Indian and Japanese cotton textile industries*. London: Macmillan Press.

Sawai, M. (2013). 1950, 60 nendai no sogankyo kogyo to amerika shijo (The binocular industry in the 1950s & the 1960s and the US market). *Osakadaigaku Keizaigaku, 63*(1), 151–178.

Sawai, M., & Tanimoto, M. (2016). *Nihonkeizaihi: Kinsei kara Gendai made* (The economic history of Japan: From the early modern era to the present). Tokyo: Yuhikaku.

Sugihara, K. (2013). Labour-intensive industrialization in global history: An interpretation of East Asian experience. In G. Austin & K. Sugihara (Eds.), *Labour—intensive industrialization in global history* (pp. 20–65). London: Routledge.

Suzuki, J. (1996). *Meiji no Kikai Kogyo: Sono Seisei to Tenkai* (Machinery industry in Meiji: Its formation and development). Kyoto: Mineruva Shobo.

Takamura, N. (1971). *Nihon Bosekigyoshi Josetsu Jo* (The introduction to the history of cotton spinning industry in Japan, vol. 1). Tokyo: Hanawa Shobo.

Tamura, H. (2004). *Fasshon no Shakaikeizaishi* (The socio-economic history of fashion). Tokyo: Nihonkeizai Hyoronsha.

Tanimoto, M. (1995). Kindai nihon niokeru 'zairaiteki' keizaihatten to kogyoka: shonin, chushokigyo, meiboka (Industrialization and the "indigenous" economic development: Merchant, small and medium size enterprises and notables). *Rekisihyoron, 539*, 92–109.

Tanimoto, M. (1998). *Nihon niokeru Zairaiteki Keizaihatten to Orimonogyo: Shijokeisei to Kazokukeizai* (The indigenous economic development and the weaving industry: Market formation and household economy). Nagoya: Nagoyadaigaku Shuppankai.

Tanimoto, M. (2006). The role of tradition in Japan's industrialization: Another path to industrialization. In M. Tanimoto (Ed.), *The role of tradition in Japan's industrialization* (pp. 3–44). Oxford and New York: Oxford University Press.

Tanimoto, M. (2007). The development of dispersed production organization in the interwar period: The case of the Japanese toy industry. In T. Okazaki (Ed.), *Production organization in Japanese economic development* (pp. 167–208). London and New York: Routledge.

Tanimoto, M. (2009). Cotton and the peasant economy: Foreign fibre in early modern Japan. In G. Riello & P. Prasannan (Eds.), *The spinning world: A global history of cotton textile 1200–1850* (pp. 367–385). Oxford and New York: Oxford University Press.

Tanimoto, M. (2013a). From peasant economy to urban agglomeration: The transformation of labour-intensive industrialization in modern Japan. In G. Austin & K. Sugihara (Eds.), *Labour-intensive industrialization in global history* (pp. 144–175). London: Routledge.

Tanimoto, M. (2013b). Senkanki nihon no chushoshokogyo to kokusai shijo: Gangu yushutsu wo jirei toshite (Japanese small-scale manufacturing in the international market: Export-oriented toy business in interwar period). *Osakadaigaku Keizaigaku, 63*(1), 51–73.

Tanimoto, M. (2017). From emulation to innovation: Japanese toy export to high-income countries before World War II. In K. Furuta & L. Grove (Eds.), *Imitation, counterfeiting and the quality of goods in modern Asian history* (pp. 225–243). Singapore: Springer.

Tokyo Municipal Office (Ed.). (1934). *Kogyo Chosa-sho* (Census of Industry).

Tokyo Municipal Office (Ed.). (1937). *Tonyasei Shokogyo Chosa* (Survey on small manufacturing and processing workshops under the putting-out system).

Tokyo Prefectural Office (Ed.). (1939). *Chushokigyo no Keiei Jijo to Totei no Rodo Jijo* (An investigation on the management of small and medium firms and the working conditions of apprentices).

Toyokeizai Shinposha (Ed.). (1935). *Nihon Boeki Seiran* (Statistical book on Japan's oversea trade). Tokyo: Toyokeizai Shinposha.

Tsushosangyoseisakushi Hensaniinkai (Ed.). (1992). *Tsushosangyoseisakushi 16 Tokei Nenpyo hen* (The history of trade and industrial policy vol. 16 Statistics and chronological tables). Tokyo: Tsushosangyo Chosakai.

Umemura, M., et al. (1988). *Choki Keizaitokei 14 Rodoryoku* (Estimates of long-term economic statistics of Japan since 1868, vol. 2 Labour force). Tokyo: Toyokeizai Shinposha.

Ushijima, T., & Abe, T. (1996). Mengyo (Cotton industry). In S. Nishikawa, K. Odaka, & O. Saito (Eds.), *Nihon Keizai no 200 nen*. Tokyo: Nihon Hyoronsha.

Yamazawa, I. (1984). *Nihon no Keizaihatten to Kokusaibungyo* (Japan's economic development under the international division of labor). Tokyo: Toyokeizai Shinposha.

Yamazawa, I., & Yamamoto, Y. (1979). *Choki Keizaitokei 2 Boeki to Kokusaishushi* (Estimates of long-term economic statistics of Japan since 1868, vol. 14 Foreign trade and balance of payments). Tokyo: Toyokeizai Shinposha.

Open Access This chapter is licensed under the terms of the Creative Commons Attribution-NonCommercial-NoDerivatives 4.0 International License (http://creativecommons.org/licenses/by-nc-nd/4.0/), which permits any noncommercial use, sharing, distribution and reproduction in any medium or format, as long as you give appropriate credit to the original author(s) and the source, provide a link to the Creative Commons licence and indicate if you modified the licensed material. You do not have permission under this licence to share adapted material derived from this chapter or parts of it.

The images or other third party material in this chapter are included in the chapter's Creative Commons licence, unless indicated otherwise in a credit line to the material. If material is not included in the chapter's Creative Commons licence and your intended use is not permitted by statutory regulation or exceeds the permitted use, you will need to obtain permission directly from the copyright holder.

Chapter 7
Changing Patterns of Industrialization and Emerging States in Twentieth Century China

Toru Kubo

7.1 Introduction

It might be a problem whether we should study China as an emerging country, because she had her own history as a great empire. But it is obvious that after the middle of the 19th century, China started to struggle for industrial development and eventually achieved it. In particular, industrialization during Mao Zedong's era in the middle of the 20th century left us with such a distinctive impression. So we expect the study on the process of China's industrialization will shed light on the study of the nature of emerging states.

This chapter distinguishes four periods of China's industrialization, and discusses them by referring to the three factors that have shaped the economic development of modern China, the global economy, private enterprises, and the government. Such an understanding will help us to situate Mao's era in the whole process of China's industrialization. We will also make it clear that China had two types of industrialization with particular reference to the significance of the wartime controlled economy under the Nationalist government.

The first factor, the global economy, is mainly reflected on the roles of foreign trade and foreign investment. They include investments in railway construction and the development of domestic river shipping industry and mining and manufacturing industries, which have been beneficial for both the investor countries and China. The second factor, private enterprises, includes large enterprises in cities, smaller enterprises throughout the country, and lots of small-scale industrial activities in the countryside. The third factor is the government, which provided the infrastructure necessary for industrial development, managed state enterprises, and implemented

---

T. Kubo (✉)
Shinshu University, 3-1-1 Asahi, Matsumoto, Japan
e-mail: kubot@shinshu-u.ac.jp

© The Author(s) 2019
K. Otsuka and K. Sugihara (eds.), *Paths to the Emerging State in Asia and Africa*, Emerging-Economy State and International Policy Studies,
https://doi.org/10.1007/978-981-13-3131-2_7

various economic policies. In this chapter, I will examine the influences of these three factors in the following four periods of the economic development of modern China.

7.1.1 Development Led by the Global Economy, 1880s–1900s

Increasing demand for industrial materials and food stuffs in Europe stimulated Chinese exports of agricultural products. This increase allowed China to import more manufactured goods, including machines for industrialization (Table 7.1). Trade balance was also supported by overseas Chinese remittance and foreign investment (Table 7.2). Foreign investment promoted the development of the Chinese transportation system, especially railway and domestic river steamship lines, which in turn facilitated trade expansion further (Tables 7.3 and 7.4). China's relationship with the global economy stimulated economic development and increased the accumulation of capital, which created conditions fundamental to the development of import substitution industrialization policy. When the First World War began, imports of industrial products from European countries by Asian countries decreased drastically; however, this provided a wonderful opportunity for Asian countries to develop their own industries. China used this opportunity to enlarge several of its industries, such as the cotton and flour industries, and to promote import substitution industrialization.

Table 7.1 General trends of foreign trade, 1871–2013 (100 million US$)

Year	Export	Import	Balance	Index of quantity	
	(Average of three years)			Export	Import
1871–73	1.11	1.07	0.04	100	100
81–83	0.95	1.11	−0.16	123	132
91–93	1.14	1.50	−0.36	176	230
1901–03	1.31	2.00	−0.69	250	391
11–13	2.77	3.59	−0.82	385	564
21–23	5.40	7.38	−1.98	508	628
31–33	2.70	4.47	−1.77		
51–53	8.67	12.20	−3.53		
61–63	15.43	13.00	2.43		
71–73	39.66	34.07	5.59	100	100
81–83	221.94	208.99	12.95	348	325
91–93	828.71	827.75	0.95		
2001–03	3,433.10	3,171.60	261.50		
11–13	20,520.33	18,372.93	2,147.40		

Source Kubo et al. (2016: 138)

7 Changing Patterns of Industrialization and Emerging … 143

Table 7.2 General trends of foreign investment, 1902–2014. Million US$

Year	Total	Direct Investment (%)		Loan (%)	
1902	788	503	(63.9)	285	(36.1)
14	1,610	1,085	(67.3)	526	(22.8)
31	3,243	2,532	(78.1)	711	(21.9)
36	3,483	2,717	(78.0)	767	(22.0)
1985	22,947	6,060	(26.4)	15,547	(67.8)
90	69,602	20,691	(29.7)	45,673	(65.6)
95	230,665	134,868	(58.5)	91,255	(39.6)
2000	520,450	348,348	(66.9)	147,157	(28.3)
05	809,150	622,429	(76.9)	147,157	(18.2)
10	1,250,443	1,048,381	(83.8)	147,157	(11.8)
14	1,719,861	1,513,256	(88.0)	147,157	(8.6)

Source Kubo et al. (2016: 148)

Table 7.3 Sectoral composition of foreign investment, 1914 and 1931 (%)

Year	1914	1931
Industry	6.9	11.6
Mining	3.7	4.0
Transportation	33.0	26.1
Public Utility	1.7	4.0
Trade	8.8	14.9
Finance	0.4	6.6
Estate	6.5	10.5
Military and government	20.5	13.2

Source Kubo et al. (2016: 150)

7.1.2 Development Led by Private Enterprises Under Protectionist Policy, 1910s–1930s

Industrialization by private enterprises proceeded under the protectionist policy of the government of the early 20th century. The Industrial Production Index clearly shows marked industrial development from the 1910s to 1930s (Table 7.5, Fig. 7.1). The domestic supply of industrial goods increased during this period (Table 7.6). Many private industrial enterprises were established in China during this period. Such enterprises were successful during the First World War and throughout most of the 1920s. For example, as Chinese cotton mills produced good cotton yarn and low-cost products, they could compete with Japanese cotton mills in the Chinese market. At the same time, China recovered tariff autonomy, which allowed it to pursue a protective policy after 1928. International circumstances during the inter-war

Table 7.4 Railway construction, 1890–2014 (km)

Year	Distance in business	High speed railway	Foreign management (%)
1890	220	–	–
1900	1,066	–	–
10	8,233	–	3,718(45.2)
20	10,954	–	3,755(34.3)
30	13,807	–	4,145(30.0)
36	20,009	–	7,275(36.4)
40	24,383	–	10,229(42.0)
46	26,857	–	–
50	22,200	–	–
60	33,900	–	–
70	41,000	–	–
80	53,300	–	–
90	57,900	–	–
2000	68,700	–	–
10	91,200	5,133	–
14	111,800	16,456	–

Source Kubo et al. (2016: 76)

period helped Chinese industrialization. The development of domestic transportation and communication networks and commerce and banking systems were increasing, although the economic relationship with foreign countries did not develop much after the end of the First World War. During this time, Chinese industrialization was mainly limited to the light industry. Although heavy and chemical industries were starting to develop in some areas, they did not have an intimate connection with the domestic light industry. Nevertheless, heavy and chemical industries began to grow in importance as the possibilities of a Japanese invasion and a second world war increased.

7.1.3 *Development Under a Controlled and Planned Economy, 1940s–1970s*

During a period of successive wars (Sino-Japanese War, Second World War, Korean War, Cold War), Chinese economic development became strongly colored by the development of heavy and chemical industries. However, as heavy and chemical industries needed investment and a long lead time to develop, government aid was needed. Almost half of the companies established in Free China during the Sino-Japanese War were government-owned companies (Fig. 7.2). This trend became

Table 7.5 Industrial development, 1912–1949

Year	Index of industrial production	Value of industrial production	Quantity of industrial production								
			Cotton yarn	Cotton pieces	Silk	Silk goods	Flour	Cement	Iron	Coal
	1933 = 100	Million yuan/1933 price	1,000 bales	1,000 piculs	ton	1,000 piculs	1,000 bags	1,000 ton	1,000 ton	1,000 ton
1912	18.4	256	468	1,919	3,576	–	23,301	90	8	5,166
13	21.0	292	527	1,948	4,204	–	26,423	81	98	5,678
14	23.0	321	598	2,267	3,432	–	27,640	110	130	7,974
15	25.3	353	608	2,299	3,821	–	37,210	112	166	8,493
16	26.7	372	651	2,906	4,143	20	35,313	105	199	9,483
17	30.4	423	650	2,983	4,445	37	48,445	125	188	10,479
18	32.6	454	743	3,083	3,950	98	56,471	133	158	11,109
19	37.0	516	808	3,534	5,523	112	66,964	144	237	12,805
20	40.7	567	980	4,816	3,482	132	73,223	142	259	14,131
21	42.5	592	1,427	4,559	5,398	154	45,327	161	229	13,350
22	47.6	664	1,783	7,417	5,567	241	30,591	306	231	14,060
23	49.2	685	1,716	8,136	4,859	247	37,494	349	171	16,973
24	60.8	847	2,073	8,854	5,244	483	67,348	356	190	18,525
25	71.3	993	2,326	10,974	6,907	929	78,253	364	193	17,538
26	70.2	979	2,225	11,465	7,159	945	79,357	496	228	15,617
27	69.7	972	2,211	11,955	7,032	1,326	67,742	498	258	17,694

(continued)

Table 7.5 (continued)

Year	Index of industrial production	Value of industrial production	Quantity of industrial production							
			Cotton yarn	Cotton pieces	Silk	Silk goods	Flour	Cement	Iron	Coal
	1933 = 100	Million yuan/1933 price	1,000 bales	1,000 piculs	ton	1,000 piculs	1,000 bags	1,000 ton	1,000 ton	1,000 ton
28	77.3	1,077	2,334	16,399	8,351	1,504	76,354	608	298	17,980
29	79.8	1,113	2,381	16,423	8,279	1,539	80,116	755	301	18,854
30	79.3	1,105	2,393	16,975	6,951	1,816	69,445	691	376	19,892
31	93.3	1,301	2,556	22,205	6,268	2,354	112,154	687	345	21,093
32	90.0	1,254	2,590	24,441	3,482	1,864	91,357	621	413	20,213
33	100.0	1,394	2,715	25,260	4,524	2,868	105,000	727	471	22,075
34	102.7	1,432	2,780	28,215	3,173	2,306	99,506	838	521	25,801
35	110.4	1,539	2,635	29,462	4,160	2,197	108,105	1,027	648	30,093
36	121.1	1,688	2,920	35,978	3,690	2,578	90,127	1,243	670	33,794
37	88.1	1,228	1,447	25,341	3,739	1,533	79,256	1,072	831	31,387
38	92.5	1,289	1,773	28,534	2,267	969	62,516	1,236	910	27,703
39	119.6	1,667	1,979	43,688	3,360	1,760	102,991	1,337	1,124	36,156
40	113.3	1,579	1,764	43,690	3,182	1,113	36,609	1,482	1,156	40,728
41	105.6	1,472	1,620	26,695	2,290	988	11,913	1,534	1,345	48,747
42	98.3	1,370	1,036	11,536	627	473	3,709	1,953	1,803	49,956

(continued)

Table 7.5 (continued)

| Year | Index of industrial production | Value of industrial production | Quantity of industrial production |||||||||
| | | | Cotton yarn | Cotton pieces | Silk | Silk goods | Flour | Cement | Iron | Coal |
	1933 = 100	Million yuan/1933 price	1,000 bales	1,000 piculs	ton	1,000 piculs	1,000 bags	1,000 ton	1,000 ton	1,000 ton
43	97.5	1,359	809	8,532	148	438	28,814	1,882	1,897	48,581
44	82.8	1,154	590	5,335	116	357	22,910	1,491	1,395	46,011
45	48.9	682	411	2,610	107	330	16,718	839	316	28,690
46	80.0	1,115	1,543	37,210	777	463	80,341	292	29	16,342
47	94.3	1,315	1,974	47,625	638	850	55,080	749	34	17,538
48	81.4	1,135	1,680	35,561	548	1,132	54,895	550	40	12,420
49	79.9	1,114	1,803	30,178	363	1,120	6,954	661	246	30,984

Source Kubo (2012: 306)

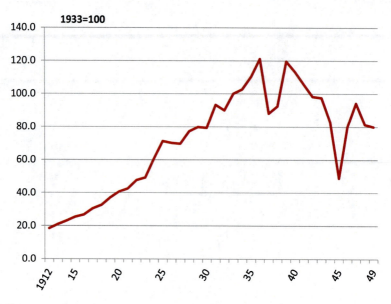

Fig. 7.1 Industrial production index, 1912–1949. *Source* Table 7.5

Table 7.6 Ratio of domestic supply of Chinese industrial production, 1890–1936 (%)

Year	Cotton yarn	Cotton pieces	Cement	Soda ash
1890	5.8	1	…	–
1900	40.4	7.4	…	–
10	38.4	8.2	…	–
20	68.9	19.4	59.9	–
30	102.3	55.3	84.6	35.6
36	102.3	86.5	92.0	52.7

Source Kubo et al. (2016: 23, 24, 52, 54)

clear when the Communist government emerged in 1949 in response to the Cold War. As heavy and chemical industries rapidly developed from the 1950s to the 1970s, the ratio of heavy and chemical industries of the whole economy markedly increased (Tables 7.7 and 7.8). This was Mao Zedong's era. It can be said that such a path of partial development was possible because light industry had already been sufficiently developed. However, during this period the economic relationship with foreign countries decreased, and the domestic commerce and banking systems declined. In addition, limited investment in the transportation and energy industries damaged them. This resulted in many problems within heavy and chemical industries, but ultimately resulted in marked economic development throughout the 1970s.

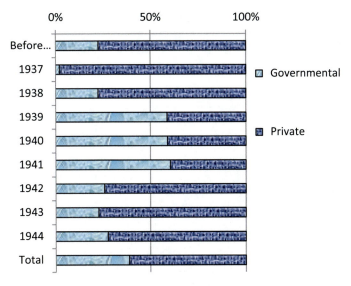

Fig. 7.2 Ratio of paid-in capital of governmental and private companies in free China, 1936–1944
Source Kubo (2004: 183)

Table 7.7 Composition of production, 1933–2014 (value added) (%)

Year	Agriculture	Manufacturing	Service	Total
1933	54.1	19.6	26.2	100.0
36	53.4	19.8	26.8	100.0
40	53.2	24.7	22.2	100.0
52	51.0	25.2	23.9	100.0
60	23.6	51.6	24.8	100.0
70	35.4	44.8	19.8	100.0
80	30.2	52.9	16.9	100.0
90	27.1	47.6	25.3	100.0
2000	15.1	52.1	32.8	100.0
10	10.1	51.4	38.5	100.0
14	9.5	51.7	38.8	100.0

Source Kubo et al. (2016: 19)

7.1.4 Further Development with the Global Economy, 1980s–2010s

The end of 1970s marked the start of the fourth period of economic development in modern China. The agriculture and light industries showed renewed development, and the bias toward development of heavy and chemical industries gradually waned. Improvements in the relationships with Western countries meant that economic rela-

Table 7.8 Composition of industrial production, 1933–1993 (%)

Year	1933	1953	1963	1970	1980	1985	1990	1993
Fiber industry	40.0	38.1	21.8	20.9	19.5	19.1	14.5	13.1
Food industry	34.5	35.1	26.5	16.4	14.7	13.4	14.8	12.7
Metal industry	4.0	6.6	15.1	14.8	11.6	9.3	12.8	17.9
Machine industry	4.3	7.6	17.8	24.4	26.9	31.5	30.4	27.8
Chemical industry	6.4	3.7	12.5	18.8	21.4	20.5	23.4	17.4
Pottery industry	2.5	2.8	2.5	2.9	4.4	4.9	6.4	8.3
Wood industry	0.9	6.0	3.9	1.9	1.5	1.3	1.1	1.8
Light industry	74.5	73.2	48.2	37.3	34.1	32.5	25.3	25.8
Heavy industry	14.7	17.9	45.3	57.9	59.9	61.3	63.9	63.1

Source Kubo et al. (2016: 73)

tionships with foreign countries rapidly increased, eventually reaching the highest level in China's history. The commerce and finance sectors became very active, and the transportation and energy industries also developed. As a result, contemporary China became the second largest economy in the world while maintaining a high rate of economic growth. However, throughout China's economic development, the disparity among provinces and social classes has increased and environmental pollution has become a serious issue, suggesting that economic development will not proceed so smoothly in the future.

7.2 Industrialization in China

Scholars generally agree that there are two types of industrialization—capital-intensive industrialization and labor-intensive industrialization. In China, we can find capital-intensive industrialization and labor-intensive industrialization proceeding simultaneously. In this section, as examples of capital-intensive industrialization, I will examine the development of the Chinese cotton and iron industries. Then, as an example of labor-intensive industrialization, I will discuss the development of small cotton mills in Jiangnan, a geographic area covering the lower Yangzi Delta.

7.2.1 Development of Machine-Made Cotton Yarn Industry in Big Mills as an Example of Capital-Intensive Industrialization in China

Increasing imports of foreign machine-spun cotton yarn in the latter half of the 19th century led several western businessmen in China to consider building cotton mills in Chinese open ports. For example, the business plan of British mercantile companies in Shanghai from the 1860s to 1870s was to produce machine-spun cotton products that imitated domestic cotton pieces to sell alongside domestic products in the cotton market. However, Chinese cotton merchants protested the plan because it threatened their interests. The Qing government ignored the plan because they were concerned for the livelihoods of the farmers engaged in small-scale weaving and wanted to avoid the promulgation of foreign-managed mills. Thus, ultimately, the plan of the British mercantile companies failed (Suzuki 1992).

The famous comprador and merchant Zheng Guangying (1842–1922) and his colleagues established the first Chinese cotton mill, called the Shanghai Machine-made Cotton Pieces Mill (Shanghai Jiqi Zhibuju), in 1880 with the support of Li Hongzhang (1823–1901), a high-class administrator of the Qing government. The mill began operation in 1890 producing machine-spun cotton yarn and woven products for the domestic market. The plan for the mill did not face any opposition from Chinese merchants dealing in domestic cotton pieces, and received the support of the Qing government (Hatano 1961). It was considered that reducing the imports of cotton products, which accounted for one-third of total imports, would improve the "red ink" in China's trade finances.

After the signing of the Sino-Japanese Peace Treaty in 1895, which granted foreign investors the right to build mills in Chinese open ports, several new cotton mills were established by western mercantile companies in Shanghai (Tanaka 1973). Chinese merchants were able to follow suit and establish their own cotton mills, which cost around C$200,000 each (approx. US$150,000 at the 1900 rate), because conditions by then had allowed them to accumulate sufficient capital. From the end of the 19th to the middle of the 20th century, the Chinese cotton industry developed rapidly, arriving at a level of self-supply. They could meet almost all of the domestic needs of machine-spun cotton yarn and about 80% of the domestic needs of cotton pieces in 1930s (Table 7.9). This kind of development was pursued mainly by Japanese and Chinese cotton mills, rather than by Western cotton mills (Fig. 7.3). In fact, most of the cotton mills established by western mercantile companies failed because of the high costs of management and low profits, and they were ultimately sold to Chinese merchants or Japanese companies (Nakai 1996).

There were several reasons that Japanese cotton mills were able to develop rapidly in China. For example, most Japanese cotton mills built in China had been competitive in the Chinese domestic market, because large Japanese cotton industrial companies had directly invested their capital and technology in China. Also, Japanese cotton companies needed to invest in China because the Japanese domestic market was shrinking. In addition, workers' wages were rising in Japan, a 5% customs tariff

Table 7.9 Production and trade of machine-made cotton yarn and cotton pieces, 1880–1990

Year	Production of cotton yarn	Import of cotton yarn	Production of cotton pieces	Import of cotton pieces	Export of cotton pieces
	10,000 tons	10,000 tons	1 million m²	1 million m²	1 million m²
1880	–	0.9	–	451.6	–
90	0.4	6.5	5.2	518.2	–
1900	6.1	9.0	42.3	531.6	–
10	8.6	13.8	50.5	566.5	–
20	16.8	8.0	160.4	670.5	2.2
30	44.0	1.0	565.3	500.7	43.9
36	39.7	0.5	1,203.1	196.5	8.1
50	43.7	–	2,520.0	–	27.7
60	109.3	–	5,450.0	–	591.7
70	205.2	–	7,800.0	–	695.5
80	292.6	–	8,710.0	–	1,086.3
90	462.6	–	10,825.0	–	2,221.6

Source Kubo et al. (2016: 24–25)

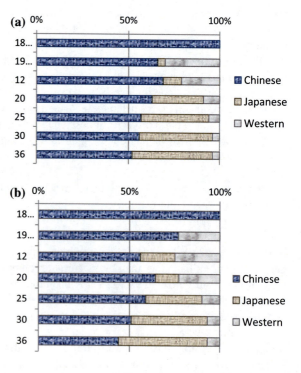

Fig. 7.3 **a** Proportion of spindles in Chinese and foreign cotton mills, 1894–1936, **b** proportion of weaving machines in Chinese and foreign cotton mills, 1894–1936 *Source* Kubo et al. (2016 :25)

Table 7.10 Geographical distribution of spindles of Chinese and Japanese cotton mills in China, 1922–36. Unit: 1,000 spindles; () index (1930 = 100)

Year	Shanghai		Yangzi Delta	North China, Costal Cities		North China, Inland
	Chinese	Japanese	Chinese	Chinese	Japanese	Chinese
1922	624	587	420	230	85	165
	(65)	(51)	(81)	(104)	(22)	(65)
1930	953	1,148	518	221	379	255
	(100)	(100)	(100)	(100)	(100)	(100)
1936	1,117	1,331	672	112	689	330
	(117)	(116)	(130)	(51)	(182)	(130)

Source Kubo et al. (2016: 27)
Notes Yangzi Delta includes Jiangsu and Zhejiang provinces. North China, Costal Cities includes Qingdao and Tianjin

was imposed in China, and the technical disparity between Japanese and Chinese cotton mills was closing, resulting in a loss of competitiveness of exports of Japanese cotton products made in Japan; thus, the Japanese cotton industry needed to invest in building mills in China (Takamura 1982).

Chinese cotton mills were in direct competition with Japanese mills in China. By classifying the number of spindles by location and mill-owner nationality, we can see that Japanese cotton mills were dominant only in the coastal cities in North China, which are areas where Japan was applying strong political and military pressure (Table 7.10). In Shanghai and other districts, Chinese cotton mills were dominant. Regarding profit rates, Chinese cotton mills (such as Yong-an or Shenxin in Shanghai, Huaxin in Xi County, and Jinhua in Yuci City), had profit rates comparable to those of Japanese mills (Fig. 7.4). Yong-an or Shenxin in Shanghai had stable management fundamentals and relatively advanced technology. In addition, they could use cheap raw cotton imported from foreign countries. In contrast, Huaxin in Xi County in Henan Province, Jinhua in Yuci City in Shanxi Province, and other such mills built in inner districts had a superior location to buy raw cotton directly from farmers and also to sell cotton yarn directly to weavers. Other factors important for the development of the Chinese cotton industry included (1) decreased imports due to the First World War, (2) implementation of a protective tariff policy implement by the Nationalist government from the end of the 1920s to the 1930s, (3) improved movement of raw cotton as a result of the cooperation between the government and private companies, and (4) increased domestic supply of spinning and weaving machines (Kiyokawa 1983).

In particular, the domestic supply of spinning and weaving machines had a very important affect on promoting the transfer of technical knowledge from developed countries to developing countries. The first generation of cotton mills established at the end of the 19th century imported all of their spinning and weaving machinery from the West and invited Western engineers to oversee operation of this machinery. How-

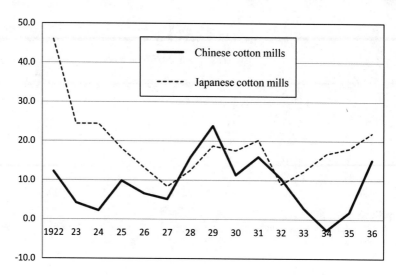

Fig. 7.4 Profit rates of Chinese cotton mills and Japanese cotton mills in China, 1922–36. *Source* Kubo et al. (2016: 28)

ever, this technological transfer had various knock-on effects from the 1920s to the 1930s. For example, Dalong Machinery Manufacturing in Shanghai began to make cotton-spinning machines from 1936, although the quality of these machines was somewhat low. However, technological developments by factories such as Zhongguo Fangzhi Jianshe Gongsi (Chinese Cotton Industry Constructing, CCIC) Shanghai No. 1 Machinery Manufacturing (formerly Toyoda Boshoku Sho Tekkobu, established in 1935), CCIC Shanghai No. 2 Machinery Manufacturing (formerly Naigaiwata Tekkosho, established in 1941), and CCIC Qingdao No. 1 Machinery Manufacturing (formerly Toyoda Tekkosho, established in 1938 with two others) continued the development of Japanese cotton mills in China.

The system for educating engineers was also developed with Dasheng Cotton Mill in Nantong and Shenxin Cotton Mill in Wuxi in the 1910s. The School of Spinning and Weaving (Fangzhi Chuanxisuo), a famous educational organization in modern China, was attached to Dasheng Cotton Mill in Nantong in Jiangsu Province in 1912, changed its name to Nantong College (Nantong Xueyuan) in 1930, and had educated 1,750 engineers by 1952. Beijing Business High School (Jingshi Gaodeng Xuetang), Beiyang University (Beiyang Daxue), and Tianjin Industrial High School (Tianjin Gaodeng Gongye Xuetang) were founded in northern China between the end of the Qing and the early Republican period, all of which had a major in spinning or weaving. At the same time, in Yangzi Delta, Suzhou Industrial High School (Suzhou Gongye Zhuanmen Xuexiao) and Hangzhou Industrial Business High School (Hangzhou Gaoji Gongye Zhiye Xuexiao) also started to educate spinning and weaving engineers (Zhongguo Jindai Fangzhishi Bianweihui 1996–1997). The spinning and weaving educational system developed in Shanghai when the cotton industry was expanding under the conditions created by the Sino-Japanese War.

These developments in the educational system provided valuable manpower for the Chinese cotton industry when the Japanese abandoned their cotton mills in China at the end of the Second World War.

The Sino-Japanese War also had a huge influence on the development of the Chinese cotton industry. Overall, the level of production decreased during the war not only because of direct war damage but also because of the removal of equipment by the Japanese Army. However, Japanese cotton mills in China were still able to make a profit during the war because of the rise in the price of cotton products. In addition, the Japanese Army assumed management of captured Chinese cotton mills (Takamura 1982). Despite the circumstances, Chinese cotton mills operating in the Shanghai settlement were still able to make a profit (Wang 1990). Moreover, many small cotton mills were able to escape being taken over by the Japanese Army. Newly established Chinese cotton mills in Free China, especially in Sichuan or Shanxi, also developed and were successful.

After the end of the Sino-Japanese War, the Nationalist Government took over the Japanese cotton mills as part of the reparation agreement and one state company, China Spinning and Weaving Construction Company (CSWCC; Zhongguo Fangzhi Jianshe Gongsi), began to manage all of the mills. Originally, the intention was to sell the mills to private companies after three years (Kawai 1987). However, before the three years had passed, the Nationalist Government fell and the People's Republic of China emerged. The central government of the People's Republic of China took over not only CSWCC but it also nationalized other private cotton mills until eventually all of the cotton mills in China were under government control. This was because the central government prioritized financing the national budget and supplying the population with clothes. According to trial accounts, the profit rate for cotton yarn reached 26%, which provided the central government with C$10 billion within five years (Onoe 1971). This prompted the central government to invest intensively in improving the equipment of the cotton industry, using from 80 to 90% of the total investment for the fabric industry. Particular attention was paid to develop the cotton industry in districts such as Xian or Shijiazhuang as part of the central government's economic strategy to develop inner China. Many engineers in the cotton industry were educated from the 1930s to the 1940s, and technology transfer progressed via Japanese cotton mills during the same period. Such achievements in the Republican period undoubtedly helped the government of the People's Republic of China pursue their policies.

7.2.2 Development of the Iron and Steel Industries Before 1949 as a Second Example of Capital-Intensive Industrialization in China

The starting point of China's development of iron and steel industries was the establishment of Hanyang Iron Foundry (Hanyang Tiechang) in 1894. The founder, Zhang

Zhitong, a high-class administrator of the Qing government, wished to develop an industrial base in Wuhan district, which was where he was posted at the time, and to supply steel for the construction of a railway between Wuhan and Beijing (Hatano 1961). However, because the Hanyang Foundry used the Bessemer process, which was not suitable for their phosphorus-rich iron ore, and they needed to import coke from Britain, and because Wuhan was far from the iron ore and coal mines, the iron produced by the Hanyang Foundry was very expensive and was not suitable for railway construction (Chuan 1972).

After the Hanyang Foundry introduced a Martin-Siemens open-hearth furnace, which was suitable for their Daye iron ore, and built a new railway to bring coal from Pingxiang coal mine, they finally succeeded in producing high-quality iron. At that time, Hanyang Foundry became part of a large united company called the Han-Ye-Ping Company (Han-Ye-Ping Gongsi) in 1908. However, such improvements needed additional investment, but since this was too much of a financial burden for the Qing government to accept, Han-Ye-Ping Company introduced private capital and Japanese debt.

However, the management of Han-Ye-Ping Company itself were experiencing problems. Private investors demanded high dividends, and the company did not have enough assets to strengthen its competitiveness. As soon as the post-war depression began after the end of the First World War, it faltered until finally it stopped production in 1925.

While the Han-Ye-Ping Company was in decline, the Japanese iron industry in Manchuria, including the Anshan Foundry and the Benxihu Foundry, was rapidly developing (Table 7.11). In Anshan, the Japanese attempted to get mining rights of iron ore under a joint Sino-Japanese company. China, which had enacted the law to protect domestic mining rights, saw that this joint venture was to be effectively under Japanese control, and resisted to grant the rights in April 1916. Aggressive negotiations by Japan continued, however, and eventually forced the compromise. A large Japanese state-owned company, South Manchuria Railway Company thus began to build the Anshan Foundry in October 1916, which started operation in April 1919 (Nakura 1984). In Benxihu, after Japan secured the rights to engage in mining there under the Sino-Japanese Agreement on Five Problems in Manchuria in September 1909, Benxihu Coal Mining Company, led by Okura Financial Group, was established in May 1910. The company changed its name to Benxihu Coal and Iron Company in October 1911 and started operation in January 1915 (Murakami 1982). This process shows that the Japanese iron industry in Manchuria was realized due to Japanese imperialistic policy pursued before and after the First World War.

The development of both foundries cannot be separated from the development of Japanese imperialism. Anshan Foundry had to invest heavily to deal with the low iron content of the ore it used. Nevertheless, South Manchuria Railway Company supported the foundry by supplying cheap coal, discounting railway fares, and providing a special low assessment of depreciation. In addition, South Manchuria Railway Company itself invested heavily in developing new methods to deal with the low iron content of the ore until high-output low-cost production could be achieved. In the case of Benxihu Foundry, because they were already producing high-quality

Table 7.11 Production of iron foundries, 1919–37 (1,000 tons)

Year	Mainland			Manchuria	
	Hanyang	Baojin	Yangzi	Anshan	Benxihu
1918	139	–	–	–	45
19	166	–	–	32	79
20	126	–	8	76	49
21	124	–	15	58	31
22	148	…	15	67	–
23	73	…	–	73	24
24	27	…	15	96	52
25	53	…	–	90	50
26	–	5	–	165	51
27	–	…	–	203	51
28	–	5	6	224	63
29	–	3	11	210	76
30	–	3	–	288	85
31	–	6	4	269	66
32	–	–	19	300	81
33	–	5	29	312	116
34	–	4	17	347	153
35	–	3	…	472	151
36	–	…	…	492	160
37	–	…	…	677	136

Source Kubo et al. (2016: 66)

steel for ship building and arms manufacture for the Japanese Navy due to their supplies of high-quality coal and iron ore, the foundry was able to secure a low-rate loan from the Japanese government to develop their management. Both of the Japanese foundries established in Manchuria developed under Japanese state organization and policy, exporting most of their products to Japan (Table 7.12). Thus, these products were not a part of China's national economy until Japan's defeat in 1945.

In mainland China, the Nationalist Government planned to establish new state-owned foundries after the decline of Han-Ye-Ping Company in the 1930s and 1940s. The plan to build a new foundry in Ma'anshan near Nanjing proceeded with German support before 1937; however, the location was changed to Zhuzhou in Hunan Province because of the threat of a Japanese invasion. But even this new plan could not be realized because of the outbreak of the Sino-Japanese War in 1937 (Hagiwara 2000). However, the Nationalist Government established several small foundries in Free China during the Sino-Japanese War and these foundries played a very important role in supporting China's resistance against Japan, even though their production was only 77,000 tons per year at its peak.

Japan's defeat fundamentally changed the situation of the Chinese iron industry. Former Japanese foundries in Manchuria were taken over by the army of the

Table 7.12 Sales of Anshan and Benxihu foundries (1,000 tons (%))

Year	Anshan Foundry			Benxihu Foundry		
	Total(A)	For Japan (B)	% (B/A)	Total(A)	For Japan (B)	% (B/A)
1923	77	57	(74)	24	15	(63)
24	81	62	(76)	53	37	(71)
25	113	87	(77)	51	39	(76)
26	147	121	(83)	49	37	(76)
27	208	175	(84)	53	37	(69)
28	212	172	(81)	62	38	(62)
29	200	160	(80)	76	52	(69)
30	163	120	(74)	74	48	(66)
31	277	227	(82)	65	51	(78)
32	350	309	(88)	88	74	(84)

Source Kubo et al. (2016: 68)

Union of Soviet Socialist Republics (USSR), and were requisitioned by the Resource Commission of Nationalist Government, finally becoming a very important part of state-owned enterprises in the People's Republic of China as a result of the 1949 revolution. The army of the USSR took over six of the nine furnaces in the Anshan Foundry and two of the four furnaces in the Benxihu Foundry. In spite of such big losses, 1,300,000 tons of iron was produced by the two foundries in 1953, which accounted for 60% of total Chinese iron production. The remaining Japanese engineers and newly dispatched Russian engineers cooperated with the Chinese to rebuild the foundries in Manchuria (Matsumoto 2000). In addition, Shijingshan Foundry and some other small foundries were developed in northern China by Japan during the Sino-Japanese War, and they too became part of the state-owned enterprises of the People's Republic of China.

7.2.3 Development of the Small-Mill Cotton Industry as an Example of Labor-Intensive Industrialization in China

One of the factors that supported the production of cotton yarn and products in the People's Republic of China was the development of many small cotton mills in the countryside. Despite the low-efficiency of their machinery, these small cotton mills used cheap labor in the countryside to realize cheap products that could compete in the market. In Jiangnan in the lower Yangzi Delta, small cotton mills moved from Japanese-controlled cities to the countryside during the Sino-Japanese War.

In Wuxi, one area in which these small mills developed, there were seven big modern cotton mills with the total of 237,000 spindles. However, three mills burned down and the other four mills were damaged in October 1937 in the midst of the Sino-Japanese War. Only 45,000 spindles of the Qingfeng and Zhenxin Cotton Mills were in operation in the summer of 1939 (Koain 1940: 294). The first response to this situation was to move the cotton mills to the foreign settlement in Shanghai, where they could continue to operate safely, using imported raw cotton and selling their products in Shanghai's large market. The second response was to reopen the mills under Japanese control in occupied cities. However, both responses produced limited results as foreign trade became difficult after the start of the Asia-Pacific War at the end of 1941. As a third response, some of the Chinese cotton mills moved their equipment to the countryside, separating it among many small mills. According to statistics published by the Preparatory Association of the Shanghai Cotton Industry in 1947, in Jiangnan district alone there were 16 large cotton mills each equipped with an average of 31,031 average spindles and 57 small cotton mills equipped with an average of 2,979 spindles (Shanghai-shi Mianfangzhi Gongye Tongyegonghui Choubeihui 1950).

Among the semi-official books on local history one finds explanations such as the following:

> Cotton mills in Shanghai, Wuxi, and Suzhou, one after another, removed a large proportion of their spinning machines and brought them to cotton-growing areas such as Changshu County to establish new small mills. Twenty small mills equipped with 41,092 spindles were established in Changshu County in Jiangsu Province. (Changshu shi Difangzhi Biansuan Weiyuanhui 1991: 337)

> In 1944, Litai Cotton Mill in Taicang County in Jiangsu Province used their equipment and capital to establish more than 10 new mills in different places. These small mills were each equipped with about 2,000 spindles. (Changshu shi Difangzhi Biansuan Weiyuanhui 1991: 272)

Small mills built in cotton-growing areas could easily obtain cheap raw cotton and then supply cotton products during the wartime period, thereby securing large profits (Zhongguo Jindai Fangzhishi Bianweihui 1996–1997: II 34). With these small mills increasing their demand for cotton yarn, small dye houses and weaving mills also profited and were able to develop. These mills got good results because most of them were located in old, cheap buildings and used simple equipment such as charcoal engines (Zhongguo Jindai Fangzhishi Bianweihui 1996–1997: I 277–278). Most of them were equipped with cheap secondhand spinning machines, although some of them introduced a new simplified spinning machine called a Xinnong shi Fangjiji (Xinnong-type Spinning Machine) (Zhongguo Jindai Fangzhishi Bianweihui 1996–1997: I 43). It should be noted that appreciation for the significance of such small mills was spreading among Chinese engineers. For example, when Zhang Fangzuo, (1901–1980, graduate of Tokyo Technical High School), manager of Xinyu Cotton Mill in Shanghai, wrote a textbook to educate engineers, he recommended establishing a small mill equipped with 1,200 spindles. He pointed out that such small mills were suitable for meeting contemporary demand, were easy to start a new business, and were beneficial for the rural economy (Zhang 1945: 127–128). Thus, such viewpoints began to act as footlights for the arrival of the People's Republic of China.

However, small mills in the countryside lost their competitive edge after the end of the Sino-Japanese War, when the electricity supply was returned to the cities and cheap raw cotton could be imported from America. In addition, as the transportation system was disturbed as a result of the civil war, it became difficult to bring raw cotton from Jiangbei to the cotton market in Jiangnan. These conditions put pressure on cotton mills in Wuxi district to stop operation (Zhenhuai 1946) and it seemed that the era of small mills was over. Many small mills moved back to the cities from the countryside and were merged with big mills. For example, in Changshu, a famous mill district in the countryside, Jinfeng Mill moved to Hankou, Fusheng Mill moved to Weinan, Taishan Mill and Changan Industrial Company moved to Nanjing, Dakang Mill was merged with Anda Mill in Shanghai, and Yongfeng Mill and Home Industrial Company were merged with Qingfeng Mill in Wuxi (Changshu shi Difangzhi Biansuan Weiyuanhui 1991: 338). In Taicang, another famous mill district in the countryside, most of the small cotton mills were merged with big cotton mills in cities and only one cotton mill, Litai Cotton Mill, existed in 1956 (Taicang xian Xianzhi Biansuan Weiyuanhui 1991: 272).

Nevertheless, many small cotton mills in Jiangnan revived at the end of 1950s. Many small mills reopened when the Department of the Cotton Industry of the central government of the People's Republic of China transferred the right to establish mills to local governments on 7 March 1958, the eve of the Great Leap Forward (Guojia Jingji Maoyi Weuyuanhui 2000: 313–314). In the case of Jiangyin County, most small cotton mills managed by the Peoples Commune emerging from the end of the 1950s to the 1960s used old equipment and could make only coarse yarn (Jiangyin xian Xianzhi Biansuan Weiyuanhui 1992: 370). It is likely that the level of technology of such small mills was similar to those established during the Sino-Japanese War.

Small cotton mills began to revive in Jiangnan in the 1970s. Many small cotton mills came and went in accordance with demand and supply. Such factors certainly continued to support the production of cotton products in the People's Republic of China since 1950s. In the background, there was the experience during Sino-Japanese War. Undoubtedly, some of the policy makers in the Department of the Cotton Industry and the other governmental organizations intentionally revived the industrialization process during the War. Thus Zhang Fangzuo, the engineer who stressed the importance of small cotton mills during the war, became a leading figure at the Institute of Spinning and Weaving Science in the People's Republic of China.

7.3 Wartime Controlled Economy Under the Nationalist Government: The Controlled and Planned Economy Before Mao's Era

Economic policy played a very important role in China's economic development. With regard to a controlled economy, in particular, the attitudes of modern Chinese governments went through significant changes. Such changes could not be explained away by the difference between the Nationalist government and the Communist government, as under the Nationalist government, there was a period of controlled economy and a period of open economy. After the Communist government emerged, the range of changes in economic policy became much wider than the period of the Nationalist government. In a controlled economy the state puts most economic activities under its direct control. By contrast, in an open economy intervention in economic activities by the state is kept to a minimum and the open market plays an important role. Needless to say, there are various economic systems between these two extremes. Furthermore, in a planned economy the state decides various economic targets to ensure that the economy develops according to a predetermined plan. A planned economy is closely related to a controlled economy and this was a characteristic of the USSR type of socialism in the 20th century (Elleman 1979).

7.3.1 Economic Construction by the Nationalist Government on the Eve of War

As most western countries adopted controlled economy policies to defend against economic depression and the Union of Soviet Socialist Republics spread propaganda hailing the success of their planned economy, many countries began to consider the idea of a controlled and planned economy during 1930s. The idea of a controlled or planned economy also became active in China under the Nationalist regime. However, the economic policies of the Nationalist government originally proceeded along the lines of a protective tariff policy to promote domestic industries and currency reform to unite and stabilize the Chinese currency (Kubo 1999). No one was thinking of a controlled and planned economy, including the former leader of the Nationalist Party, Sun Yatsen, in his grand plan for economic construction written in 1910s. As a result, in spite of many calls for implementing a controlled and planned economy, the Nationalist government refused.

The National Economic Committee established under the National Government in 1931 was very active from 1933 to 1938, when it was absorbed into the Department of Economy. The committee comprised officials in the relevant government departments, famous entrepreneurs in private enterprises, and specialists and engineers from industry. The NEC succeeded in improving the quality of the raw cotton, cocoon, and tea, constructing national highways, expanding the irrigation system by using foreign aid, including American loans, and cooperating with the League of Nations (Kawai 1982). Thus, the NEC was instrumental in promoting economic development led by private enterprises in the light industry in the 1930s.

The vice-chairman of the NEC, Song Ziwen, in his address to the members of the committee, stressed that the state would help private enterprises. Although he specifically mentioned a controlled economy, his position was far from supporting a true controlled economy. At that time, one of the economists criticized the NEC, saying that it was not the organization to implement a controlled economy and that this interest in a controlled economy was only a passing fad. In reality, although a controlled economy was often mentioned, their real intentions were actually closer to an open economy (Kubo 1996).

In contrast, the Resource Commission, led by the many technocrats in the Nationalist government, clearly announced their intention to promote development under a controlled and planned economy from the latter half of the 1930s to the 1940s. At first, the Resource Commission was a secret commission, established as the Defense Planning Committee under the General Staff of the Nationalist Army in 1932; however, it was reorganized as the Resource Commission under the Military Committee of the Nationalist Government in 1935. In 1938, the Resource Commission was again reorganized and enlarged under the Department of the Economy. The Resource Commission promoted the establishment of a controlled and planned wartime economy, attaching importance to heavy and chemical industries, strengthening development of inner districts, and using barter trade comprising the export of strategic materials and import of machinery and equipment. This viewpoint helped the Resource Commission achieve its aim (Zheng et al. 1991; Ishikawa 1991).

Weng Wenhao, the Head of the Resource Commission, was a respected geologist in China, receiving his doctoral degree from Ruben Catholic University in Belgium. He was appointed Secretary of Executive-Yuan by the Nationalist government in 1935 and led Chinese economic policy during the very difficult period during and after the Sino-Japanese War. In 1933, before his appointment, Weng already knew about the five-year plan of the USSR and its economic system, and had criticized the economic policy of the Nationalist government saying that it did not have systematic planning (Kubo 1996).

The leading organization of the economic policy of the Nationalist government changed from the NEC to the Resource Commission in the 1930s, and the basic thought on economic development changed from an open economy to a controlled economy accordingly. The outbreak of the Sino-Japanese War accelerated this change. The Nationalist government had other organizations related to economic policy, including the Construction Committee, which mainly supervised power stations, and the Department of Industry, which promoted an export-orientated policy under Chen Gongbo until 1937, but the basic trend was not influenced by the activities of such organizations.

7.3.2 Wartime Economy Under the Nationalist Government

The Nationalist government moved from Nanjing to Chongqing, the preliminary capital, to continue its resistance against Japan. The government promoted the establishment of new factories in inner districts such as Sichuan or Yunnan to strengthen Chinese economic power for the Resistance War, and some of the industrial factories in the coastal districts moved to inner districts. The Chongqing government invested state funds to establish modern iron foundries, machine factories, electronic factories, and chemical factories, which supported the state-owned munitions industry. The Resource Commission played a decisive role in these activities. According to statistical data, industrial production in Free China increased more than 50% from 1938 to 1942. However, in spite of such growth, the ratio of Free China's industrial production of the total national industrial production reached only about 10% and the quality of industrial products was poor (Kubo 2004). Nevertheless, the historical perspective that China could resist invasion by developing a state-owned munitions industry in its inner districts seriously influenced the management of China's economy after the end of the Sino-Japanese War.

Policies for trade control were an important aspect of the controlled economy of the Nationalist government. First, the government tried to stop trading with Japanese-occupied areas after the Sino-Japanese War started. At the same time, it established the Trade Adjustment Commission under the Military Committee in October 1937, conducting collective purchases and sales for exporting agricultural products and ores through their three state-owned trade companies. The Trade Adjustment Commission was reorganized to become the Trade Commission under the Department of Finance in February 1938. The Trade Commission aimed to maintain a trade balance to continue importing munitions and securing foreign loans. Although several problems occurred, such as corruption of officials, the controlled trade system allowed the government to use transportation efficiently and adjust trading price adequately (Zheng 2004).

However, the situation changed after the outbreak of the Asia-Pacific War. Because trade routes between Free China and the outside world were almost stopped, the lack of various materials became more serious in Free China. So the Chongqing government changed the aim of its trade policy to acquire materials, promulgating a new act on 11th May 1942. This loosened the control of trade to allow the imports of materials essential for the construction of defense base and the daily necessities of the population.

Another control policy concerned the control of price and production. As the amount of food and cotton goods in the market decreased, their price increased in Free China. The Chongqing government tried to limit the price of several foodstuffs and cotton goods in the largest cities. In addition, the government pursued collective purchase and sale of such materials; however, the results were limited. For example, in the case of raw cotton, as the supply decreased, the production of cotton yarn also decreased. Cotton farmers did not want to sell their raw cotton for the low price decided by the government, and so a considerable amount of raw cotton flowed out from Free China to Japanese-occupied areas. Furthermore, under the controlled economy, private cotton mills ceased operation (Feng 1948).

Thus, the policies of a controlled economy realized by the Chongqing government obtained limited results, because the government was not powerful enough to pursue the necessary policies and the wartime circumstances limited the supply of materials.

7.3.3 Other Phases of the Wartime Economy

It was not only in Free China that the number of state companies increased and a controlled economy developed. Powerful policies of a controlled economy were executed in Manchuria and north China by Japan while under the Japanese occupation. In Manchuria, the Japanese Kanto (Guandong) Army decided on a "Five-year industrial development plan" to establish a "Manshu koku (State of Manchuria)" in the lead up to the outbreak of the Sino-Japanese War. However, after the war started, the Japanese government demanded enlargement of the original plan to supply sufficient materials such as steel, coal, and magnesium for the production of munitions. Japan invested five billion yen and made intensive efforts for the exploitation of several resources (Yamamoto 2003). However, although the steel and coal industries developed, only a partially developed industrial structure was built, and left as a legacy after the war.

In central China, the state-owned development company Naka-Shina Shinko Kabushiki Kaisha, capitalized with 100 million yen, was established by Japan in August 1938. The Japanese government invested half of the capital and private Japanese companies invested the other half. Naka-Shina Shinko Kabushiki Kaisha wanted to develop and manage the transportation, communication, electricity, mining, and fishery industries in occupied areas of central China. Similarly, Kita-Shina Kaihatsu Kabushiki Kaisha, capitalized with 350 million yen, was also established in north China in November 1938. Subsequently, supported by both these state-owned companies, many Japanese private companies came to China to run their business. In north China, iron foundries reached a production capability of 756,000 tons per year and a large electricity transmission network was constructed (Ju and Zhang 1997). This electricity network played an important role in the controlled and planned economy of the People's Republic of China (Tajima 2008).

The trend to develop state companies and adopt a controlled economy increased in Free China, Manchuria, and Japanese-occupied areas of China. The content and range of control differed in these areas and they could not usually get good results, except for the Resource Commission's activities in Free China and the partial industrial development in Manchuria. Nevertheless, the experience of economic development by state companies and controlled economy during the war period influenced Chinese management of the post-war economy.

7.4 Concluding Remarks

One of the historical roots of industrialization in China was certainly the investments and various economic policies made by the state, but the role of the state was limited in the 19th century. The influence of the global economy, including foreign trade and investment, strongly promoted Chinese industrialization in its early stage.

China's struggle toward becoming a modern nation state started at the end of the Qing dynasty and continued through the Republican period. Many private enterprises developed under the various protectionist policies pursued by the newly emerging nation state. In particular, the protective tariff and currency reform of the Nationalist government played a decisive role.

Two kinds of industrialization can be seen in modern China from the 19th to the 20th century—capital-intensive industrialization characterized by the development of the large cotton mills in Shanghai and the Japanese iron foundries in Manchuria, and labor-intensive industrialization characterized by the development of the small cotton mills in Jiangnan, and both types of industrialization proceeded simultaneously.

The sphere of the state's economic activities widened from the 1940s to the 1970s under a controlled and planned economy, as China adopted a wartime economy first against the Japanese invasion and then against the United States of America and the Union of Soviet Socialist Republics. The development of state companies and adoption of a controlled economy increased in Free China, Manchuria, and Japanese-occupied areas during the Sino-Japanese War, and this trend was continued and strengthened during Mao Zedong's era. As a result, although heavy industries and munitions industry developed, the process of industrialization faced many problems. At the end of the 1970s, after China opened its door to the world again, industrialization in China began to proceed under an intimate relationship with the global economy. It also involved a much greater number of private enterprises, ranging from large enterprises in cities and smaller enterprises throughout the country to lots of small-scale industrial activities in the countryside.

References

Changshu shi Difangzhi Biansuan Weiyuanhui. (1991). *Changshu-shi Zhi* (History of Changshu-city). Shanghai: Shanghai Renmin Chubanshe.
Chuan, H. (1972). *Han-ye-ping Gongsi Shilue* (A brief history the Han-ye-ping Iron and Coal Mining and Smelting Company 1890–1926). Hong Kong: The Chinese University of Hong Kong.
Elleman, M. (1979). *Socialist Planning*. Cambridge: Cambridge University Press.
Feng, S. (1948). Minyuanlai woguo zhi mianfangzhi gongye (Cotton industry in China from 1912). In S. Zhu (Ed.) *Minguo Jingjishi* (The economic history of Republican China). Shanghai: Yinhang Zhoubao She.
Guojia Jingji Maoyi Weuyuanhui (National Economic and Trade Committee). (2000). *Zhongguo Gongye wushi nian* (The fifty years of China's industry). Beijing: Jingji Chubanshe.

Hagiwara, M. (2000). *Chugoku no Keizaikensetsu to Nicchukankei: Tainichikosen heno Jokyoku 1927–1937nen* (China's economic construction and Sino-Japanese relationship: a prelude for the resistance war against Japan, 1927–1937). Kyoto: Mineruva Shobo.

Hatano, Y. (1961). *Chugoku Kindai Kogyoshi no Kenkyu* (A study on the history of Chinese modern industry). Kyoto: Toyoshi Kenkyukai.

Ishikawa, Y. (1991). Nankinseifu-jiki no gijutsu-kanryo no keisei to hatten: Kindai-Chugoku gijutsusha no keifu (The formation and development of technocrats in the Nanjing Government Era). *Shirin, 7*(2).

Jiangyin shi Xianzhi Biansuan Weiyuanhui. (1992). *Jiangyin-shi Zhi* (History of Jiangyin-city). Shanghai: Shanghai Renmin Chubanshe.

Ju, Z., & Zhang, L. (1997). Riben zai Huabei Jingji Tongzhi Luetuo-shi (The history of Japanese plunder and economic control in North China). Tianjin: Tianjin Guji Chubanshe.

Kawai, S. (1982). Zenkokukeizaiiiinkai no seiritsu to sono kaiso o meguru ici-kosatsu (A survey on the establishment and reorganization of the National Economic Committee). *Toyoshi Kenkyu, 40*(4).

Kawai, S. (1987). Sengochugoku boshokugyo no keisei to Kokuminseifu: Chugoku boshoku konsu no seiritsukatei (The formation of China's cotton industry and the National Government after the World War II: The process of the establishment of the Chinese cotton industry constructing Company). *Kokusaikankeiron Kenkyu, 6*.

Kiyokawa, Y. (1983). Chugoku senyi-kikai kogyo no hatten to zaikabo no igi (The development of China's fiber machine industry and the meaning of Japanese cotton mills in China). *Keizaikenkyu, 34*(1).

Koain. (1940). *Mushaku Kogyo Jittaichosa Hokoku-sho* (A survey report of Wuxi Industry). Tokyo: Koain Seimubu. Chosashiryo 18.

Kubo, T. (1996). Kin-gendai Chugoku ni okeru kokka to keizai: Chuka minkoku-ki keizai seisakushiron (State and economy of modern and contemporary China: Understanding the history of economic policy of the Republican period). In T. Yamada (Ed.) *Rekishi no nakano Gendai Chugoku* (Contemporary China in the History). Tokyo: Keiso Shobo.

Kubo, T. (1999). *Senkanki Chugoku < Jiritsu eno Mosaku > : Kanzei Tsuka Seisaku to Keiza Hhatten* (China's quest for sovereignty in the interwar period: Tariff policy and economic development). Tokyo: Tokyo Daigaku Shppankai.

Kubo, T. (2004). Senji no kogyo seisaku to kogyo hatten (Industrial policy and development during the war-time). In N. Ishijima & T. Kubo (Eds.) *Jukei Kokuminseifushi no Kenkyu* (History of the Chongqing National Government). Tokyo: Tokyo Daigaku Shuppankai.

Kubo, T. (Ed.). (2012). *Chugoku Keizaishi Nyumon* (An introduction to China's economic history). Tokyo: Tokyo Daigaku Shuppankai.

Kubo, T. et al. (2016). *Tokei de Miru Chugoku Kin-gendai Keizaishi* (Economic history of modern China: An approach based on statistical data). Tokyo: Tokyo Daigaku Shuppankai.

Matsumoto, T. (2000). *"Manshu-koku" kara Shin Chugoku e: Anzan Tekkogyo karamita Chugokutohoku no Saihenkatei, 1940–1954* (From "the state of Manchuria" to New China: Reorganizing process seen from the Anshan Steel Industry 1940–1954). Nagoya: Nagoya Daigaku Shuppankai.

Murakami, K. (1982). *Okura Zaibatsu no Kenkyu: Okura to Tairiku* (A study on Okura Financial Group: "Okura" and Mainland). Tokyo: Kondo Shuppansha.

Nakai, H. (1996). *Choken to Chugoku Kindai Kigyo* (Zhang Jian and Chinese Modern Enterprise). Hokkaido: Hokkaido Daigaku Tosho Kankokai.

Nakura, B. (1984). *Nihon Tekkogyoshi no Kenkyu* (A study on the history of Japanese Steel Industry). Tokyo: Kondo Shuppansha.

Onoe, E. (1971). *Chugoku Sangyoricchi no Kenkyu* (A study on regional distribution of China's Industry). Tokyo: Institute of Developing Economies.

Shanghai-shi Mianfangzhi Gongye Tongyegonghui Choubeihui (Preparatory Association of the Shanghai Cotton Industry). (1950). *Zhongguo Mianfang Tongji Shiliao* (Historical statistics of China's Cotton Industry). Shanghai.

Suzuki, T. (1992). *Yomu Undo no Kenkyu* (A study of the westernization movement in China in the latter half of the nineteenth century). Tokyo: Kyuko Shoin.

Taicang xian Xianzhi Biansuan Weiyuanhui. (1991). *Taicang-xian Zhi* (History of Taicang County). Nanjing: Jiangsu Renmin Chubanshe.

Tajima, T. (2008). *Gendai Chugoku no Denryoku Sangyo* (Electric power industry of contemporary China). Kyoto: Showado.

Takamura, N. (1982). *Kindai Nihon Mengyo to Chugoku* (The modern Japanese cotton industry and China). Tokyo: Tokyo Daigaku Shuppankai.

Tanaka, M. (1973). Nisshin senso-go no Shanhai kindai "gaisho" boseki-gyo to Chugoku shijo (Shanghai foreign-owned modern cotton industry and Chinese market after Sino-Japanese War of 1894). In H. Yamada (Ed.), *Shokuminchi Keizaishi no Shomondai* (Several problems in the history of colonial economies). Tokyo: Institute of Developing Economies.

Wang, Z. (1990). Gudao-shiqi de minzu mianfang gongye (National cotton industry in the so-called solitary island era). In *Zhongguo Jindai Jingjishi Yanjiu Ziliao* (Materials of Chinese modern economic history) 10. Shanghai: Shanghai Shehui Kexueyuan Chubanshe.

Yamamoto, Y. (2003). *"Manshu-koku" Keizai-shi Kenkyu* (A study on economic history of "The State of Manchuria"). Nagoya: Nagoya Daigaku Shuppankai.

Zhang, F. (1945). *Mianfangzhi Gongchang zhi Sheji yu Guanli* (Plan and management of cotton mill). Shanghai: Kaiming Shudian.

Zhenhuai. (1946). Zuijin Wuxi fangzhiye de gaikuang (Recent outlook of cotton industry in Wuxi). *Jingji Zhoubao, 2*(2).

Zheng, H. (2004). Boeki tosei seisaku (The policy of controlled trade). In N. Ishijima & T. Kubo (Eds.) *Jukei Kokuminseifushi no Kenkyu* (History of the Chongqing National Government). Tokyo: Tokyo Daigaku Shuppankai.

Zheng, Y., et al. (1991). *Jiu-Zhongguo de Ziyuan Weiyuanhui (1932–1949): Shishi yu Pingjia* (The Resource Commission in Old China, 1932–1949: Facts and estimation). Shanghai: Shanghai Shehuikexue Chubanshe.

Zhongguo Jindai Fangzhishi Bianweihui. (1996–1997). *Zhongguo Jindai Fangzhishi (shang-ce, xia-ce)* (History of Chinese modern fabric industry (1)–(2)). Beijing: Fangzhi Chubanshe.

Open Access This chapter is licensed under the terms of the Creative Commons Attribution-NonCommercial-NoDerivatives 4.0 International License (http://creativecommons.org/licenses/by-nc-nd/4.0/), which permits any noncommercial use, sharing, distribution and reproduction in any medium or format, as long as you give appropriate credit to the original author(s) and the source, provide a link to the Creative Commons licence and indicate if you modified the licensed material. You do not have permission under this licence to share adapted material derived from this chapter or parts of it.

The images or other third party material in this chapter are included in the chapter's Creative Commons licence, unless indicated otherwise in a credit line to the material. If material is not included in the chapter's Creative Commons licence and your intended use is not permitted by statutory regulation or exceeds the permitted use, you will need to obtain permission directly from the copyright holder.

Chapter 8
Historical Roots of Industrialisation and the Emerging State in Colonial India

Chikayoshi Nomura

8.1 Introduction

Following a clear shift towards economic liberalisation in economic policy in the early 1980s, India's economic growth rate rose from the notorious 'Hindu growth rate' of 3% to over 6%, helping improve the welfare standard of its one billion plus population, while providing market opportunities to producers and investors elsewhere in the world. The high growth rate resulted in the awakening of India, which has received worldwide attention.

One of the driving forces of the high growth rate is the expansion for 3 decades in the activities of private industrial enterprises, whose origins date back to the colonial era. By the time of independence, India already had various 'modern' industrial sectors covering mining, textile, iron and steel, and chemical. Some had even reached global standards in terms of production and employment, although the overall industrialisation level was far from sufficient. The history of active private industrial enterprise has formed one of the important foundations of the current high rate growth of Indian economy since the early 1980s. This chapter reviews India's industrialisation in the colonial era, focusing on its stagnated nature and three known hypotheses on the causes of the stagnation.

The chapter consists of six sections. Section 8.2 reviews the stagnated nature of colonial India's industrialisation. The next three sections review three hypotheses on the possible causes of the stagnated industrial development in colonial India. Section 8.3 addresses the common hypothesis proposed by scholars such as

---

I cordially appreciate encouraging and illuminating comments I received from the editors and contributors of this book for the past 2 years. Needless to say, all responsibility of any possible errors solely rest upon me.

C. Nomura (✉)
Graduate School of Literature and Human Science, Osaka City University, Osaka, Japan
e-mail: chikayoshi_nomura@hotmail.com

M.D. Morris, which argues that India's limited progress in industrialisation can be explained by its labour abundant and capital scarce mix of factor endowments. Section 8.4 deals with another well-known hypothesis advanced by scholars such as A.K. Bagchi, which argues that the adoption of laissez-faire economic policies, which was part of a pivotal framework of British rule in colonial India, explains the stagnated industrial growth based on the understanding that proactive government interventions in economic activities can promote industrialisation. Section 8.5 addresses a persuasive hypothesis advanced mainly by Japanese economists (Kiyokawa 1976a, b, 1983; Otsuka et al. 1988) that compared growth in cotton textile industries in colonial India and imperial Japan, and conclude that India's stagnated industrialisation can be explained by factors related to its insufficient adoption and innovation of useful technological knowledge. They argue that institutional and organisational factors, such as the weak technical education system or insufficient long-term perspective of management, conditioned colonial India's sluggish technology transfer and innovation. The final section offers conclusions.

8.2 Stagnated Industrialisation in Colonial India

'Modern' industrial enterprises in colonial India started to grow in the mid-19th century. The derivation of the monopolistic status of East India Company in the early 19th century fostered buoyant private economic activities in India, where modern industrial enterprises financed both by British and Indian capital were set up in various fields. The cotton milling business grew steadily throughout the second half of the 19th century, achieving high international competitiveness as early as the end

Table 8.1 Top seven cotton spindle holding countries (1,000)

	U.K.	U.S	Germany	France	India	Russia	Japan
1875	n.a.	n.a.	4,700	5,000	*1,100*	n.a.	n.a.
1880	n.a.	*10,653*	4,800	4,800	*1,464*	4,400	n.a.
1890	40,512	*14,384*	6,071	5,040	*3,274*	6,000	*358*
1900	n.a.	*19,472*	*8,031*	n.a.	*4,945*	n.a.	*1,274*
1910	53,400	28,000	9,900	6,700	6,058	7,900	1,955
1925	57,200	37,937	9,500	9,428	8,500	n.a.	5,292
1930	55,200	34,031	11,070	10,250	8,907	7,624	7,072
1935	42,700	30,110	n.a.	10,157	9,613	9,800	9,944

Source Mitchell (1980, 1982, 1983, 1988). Bombay Millowners' Association. *Report of the millowners' association*, Bombay
Note 1 The table are sorted by descending order in 1930
Note 2 Data in italic are from Bombay Millowners' Association

Table 8.2 Top nine pig iron producers (1,000 metric tons)

	U.S	France	Germany	U.K.	Russia	Belgium	Czechoslovakia	India	Japan
1900	14,011	2,714	7,550	8,960	2,937	1,019	n.a.	n.a.	30
1910	27,742	4,038	13,111	10,012	3,047	1,852	n.a.	n.a.	72
1915	30,396	584	10,190	8,794	3,764	68	n.a.	250	321
1925	37,289	8,494	10,177	6,262	1,309	2,543	1,166	902	697
1930	32,261	10,035	9,695	6,192	4,964	3,365	1,437	1,199	1,188
1935	21,715	5,789	12,846	6,424	12,490	3,030	811	1,490	1,965

Source Mitchell (1980, 1982, 1983, 1988)
Note 1 The table is sorted by descending order in 1930

Table 8.3 Manufacturing production 1926–28

	Manufacturing (million US$)	Imports of manufactured articles (million US$)	Exports of manufactured articles (million US$)	Manufacturing per head (US$)
U.S.	42,200	1,064	2,027	350
Germany	11,500	512	2,001	180
U.K.	9,400	1,069	2,790	190
France	6,600	336	1,356	160
USSR	4,300	175	53	30
Italy	3,300	259	401	80
Japan	2,500	241	451	40
Canada	2,400	627	336	250
Belgium	1,900	209	448	240
Czechoslovakia	1,600	156	395	110
Australia	1,400	510	30	220
India	1,200	684	305	4

Source League of Nations (1945, p. 84)

of the 19th century.[1] Jute mills also expanded rapidly in Calcutta in response to a mounting global demand for ropes and other products, occupying a large share of the international market by the late 19th century. In addition, brewing, paper-milling, leather-making, matches, and rice-milling industries also developed during the century, while heavy industries such as the iron industry were also established as early as 1814 by British capital.

Due to progress in modern industrial enterprises, some industries reached global standards by the beginning of the 20th century. The cotton mill industry in India had 9 million spindles in the 1930s, which placed India fifth globally in terms of the number of spindles (Table 8.1). The Indian jute mill industry was the largest in the world in terms of the amount of raw jute consumed for production at the end of the 19th century. India's iron industry was ranked eighth in the world in terms of output in 1930 (Table 8.2). Just before the Great Depression, India was ranked as the twelfth largest industrialised country measured by the value of manufacturing products (Table 8.3).

This comparatively steady progress of industrial production in colonial India was not accompanied by a general transformation in its economic structure, which is, according to Kuznets, represented by a rise in the share of the manufacturing sector against GDP/NDP. Kuznets shows that the industry share in the UK rose from 34% in 1841 to 40% in 1901. In the US, which was late to industrialisation, the share rose from 31% in 1839 to 51% in 1879 (Kuznets 1966). India's industrial growth

---

[1] The Indian cotton mill industry's high international competitiveness in the second half of the 19th century is reviewed in Sect. 8.4 of this chapter.

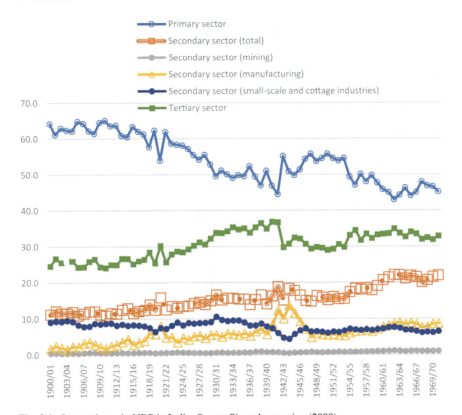

Fig. 8.1 Sector shares in NDP in India. *Source* Sivasubramonian (2000)

was insufficient to bring such general transformation in its economic structure, and the net domestic product (NDP) share of the manufacturing sector (excluding small scale and cottage industries) barely reached 7% even in 1946. India's slow progress is conspicuous in comparison to the astonishing progress of another early industrialising country in Asia, Japan. According to Fig. 8.1, the share of the manufacturing sector in India (total of manufacturing and small scale and cottage industries) in total NDP grew gradually from approximately 10% in the early 20th century to over 20% in the 1960s. On the other hand, Japan's manufacturing sector share, which also includes the shares of large- and small-scale industrial manufacturing enterprises, reached over 30% as early as in the 1930s (Fig. 8.2). Considering its slow progress, the share of factory employment in India was also small (i.e. 0.4% of the total population in 1900 and 1.4% in 1941). In Japan, it was 1.6% in 1900 and reached 9.9% in 1940 (Umemura et al. 1988). The slow transformation of the economic structure formed the foundation of the long-held understanding that India's industrialisation stagnated under the British colonial regime.

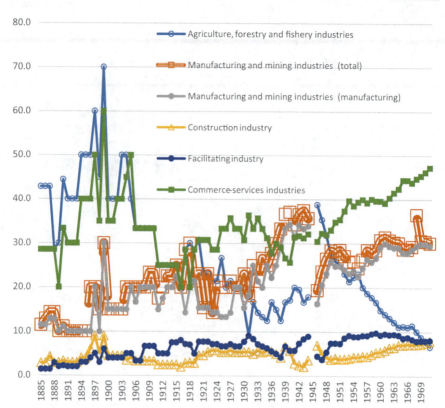

Fig. 8.2 Sector shares in GDP in Japan. *Source* Okawa et al. (1974)

8.3 Factor Endowment Hypothesis

8.3.1 Overview

In the mainstream economic history of colonial India, there are two main hypotheses that explain its stagnated industrialisation. The first hypothesis assumes factor endowment as the main cause, while the second considers the laissez-faire economic policy of the colonial government. In the following two sections, we review the general features of the two hypotheses and assess them.

Morris David Morris, a leading proponent of the factor endowment hypothesis, assumes that the Indian economy was driven by market forces led by private initiatives. Morris wrote, 'the Indian economy in the 19th and first half of the 20th centuries was pre-eminently a private enterprise economy…(whose) economic decisions… were made by private individuals, households, and groups' (Morris 1987). Morris also assumes that the colonial government played only a limited role in economic affairs in the one and half century of British rule. According to Morris, 'In no decade between 1872 and 1947 did the state's annual share of GNP average more than 10%; usually it was less than that' (Morris 1983). Based on the market based understanding of economic activity in India, Morris construes its abundant labour and scarce capital factor endowment as the main causes of stagnated industrialisation. Morris writes,

> [Modern economic growth in colonial India had] very serious inhibitions on the supply side… most factors of production were costly… Only raw labour was cheap and on occasion – as in the jute and cotton industries – it provided an industrial advantage. But cheap labour typically worked against mechanisation. The expansion of demand for a product did not necessarily put pressure on labour supply or on labour cost relative to other costs. To the contrary, the businessman was encouraged to expand existing organisation rather than shift to techniques where capital requirements were relatively greater. And even where mechanised industries grew up, they invariably used more cheap labour per unit of capital than was true in the West. All this was a rational response to relative factor price relationships but it slowed the expansion of factory organisation (Morris 1983).

According to Morris, due to its particular factor endowment characteristics, India had less incentives to seek capital-intensive economic growth, which was essential for industrialisation. The view that factor endowment is the main cause of India's stagnated development has been espoused by other recent economic historians, such as Roy and Gupta (Roy 2005, 2006; Gupta 2016).

8.3.2 Statistical Analysis

How robust is the hypothesis? We validate the hypothesis by using historical data of recent works, such as Sivasubramonian (2000). More specifically, we compare the wage-rental ratio of colonial India and imperial Japan for several decades from the beginning of the 20th century. Comparing the wage-rental ratios trends in the two early Asian industrialising countries is a worthy first step to test the factor endowment hypothesis for the following two reasons. First, as is well-known, the important features of factor endowment of a specific area/year are well represented by the wage-rental ratio, which is the nominal wage divided by nominal interest rate.[2] In other words, India's wage-rental ratio should have been relatively lower if it really had abundant labour and capital scarcity in comparison to other countries whose economic development level was higher. Second, the comparative study could aid our assessment of the level of wage-rental ratio in India as India and Japan started industrialisation at almost the same time in the second half of the 19th century. Despite the similarity in its initial starting point for industrialisation, Japan's economy succeeded in growing rapidly from the end of the 19th century, and eventually, its industrialisation outpaced India's from the early 20th century. Clear differences in wage-rental ratios trends between the two countries would indicate that the hypothesis is a good

---

[2] To be precise, rental price is equal to 'machine price × real interest rate + depreciation rate'. Here, we assume that (1) machine prices in colonial India and imperial Japan were the same or had same trends, and (2) deprecation rates in both the countries were the same.

explanation for the sluggish mechanisation and industrialisation of the Indian economy. If there is no such difference, the hypothesis will need to be supplemented by further explanations.

Analysing wage-rental ratio trends requires interest rate and nominal wage data for the long-term. India had three distinct interest rates for short-term lending/borrowing, reflecting the risks involved: bank rate of the quasi-central bank, the *hundi* rate, and the bazaar rate. The bank rate of the quasi-central bank was the rate charged for short-term lending by, for instance, the Bank of Bengal, the Imperial Bank of India, or the Reserve Bank of India, all of which functioned as a bank of bank note issuer, as a bank of the East India Company prior to the mid-19th century, and of the British government of India subsequently, and as a deposit bank under strict regulation of the East India Company and the British government. These quasi-central banks supplied short-term capital to leading financial and commercial agencies using a discount rate, which is called the bank rate. Bagchi mentions that the discount rate was higher than 2% of the bank rate of the Bank of England, and was influenced by the bank rate of the central bank in London (Bagchi 1997). The *hundi* rate was used by large-scale local bankers for their short-term lending to small-scale manufactures and traders. The bazaar rate was charged by money lenders for short-term lending to the wider public, and was generally much higher than the other two types of interest rates.

Banking and Monetary Statistics (BMS), published in 1954 by the Reserve Bank of India, the central bank of independent India, included data on these interest rates, some of which date back to the early 20th century. According to the BMS, discount rates of the Bank of Bengal (January–June) remained relatively stable at 6% prior to the end of the 1910s (average 6.44%; min. 5.56% in 1904; max. 7.25 in 1915) (Fig. 8.3). The corresponding rates in the 1920s (bank rate of the Imperial Bank of India) hiked in the 1920s, reaching 8.05% in 1924 when the Indian money market experienced shortage of market liquidity owing to the Indian government's joint use of the retrenchment policy and increase in government bond issue. The discount rates gradually returned to pre-war levels after the mid-1920s, reaching 6.02% in 1932. In 1933, the rate plunged to 3.5% and remained at the level throughout the 1930s. *Hundi* rates, whose data is available for 1909 and after, were generally lower than the bank rates of the quasi-central bank of colonial India in the 20th century. It was approximately 4% before WW1, rose to 5–7% for almost 15 years after the outbreak of the war, and sharply decreased to 3% after 1933. For bazaar rates, whose data is available only after 1922, the BMS shows that the rates were much higher than the other two. For instance, the Calcutta bazaar rate in June remained approximately 9–10% for a decade from 1922. Even after 1933 when the above two rates plummeted, the bazaar rate in Calcutta remained as high as 7.5%, although it decreased to 5.5% in 1936.

In terms of nominal interests, we observe that India did not suffer from a shortage of short-term capital in comparison to Japan. Japan had two short-term lending/borrowing interest rates: the bank rate of the Bank of Japan and the market rates of major private banks. The two Japanese rates correspond to the first two interest rates in India. Bank rates of the Bank of Japan, the central bank of Japan, were used for money lent for securities and roughly corresponds to the bank rate in India. The

8 Historical Roots of Industrialisation …

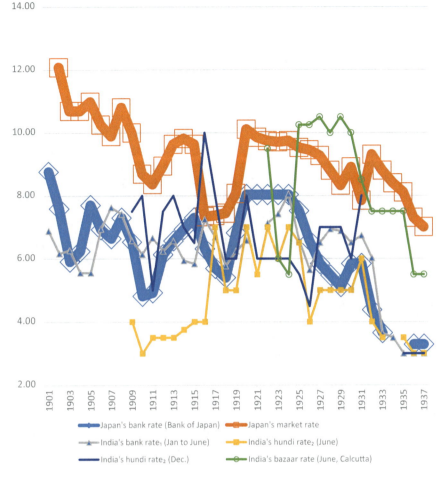

Fig. 8.3 Nominal short term interest rates (%). *Sources* Nomura (2018). *Note 1* India's bank rates from Jan. to June were generally higher than those from July to Dec. *Note 2* India's *hundi* rates in June were generally equivalent to the average annual rates

market rate, which was used by major private financial institutions for short-term lending (less than 3 months), roughly corresponds to the *hundi* rate of colonial India. According to *The Oriental Economists Yearbook* (*Keizai nenkan*), the bank rates in the 1900s were approximately 6%, as were the Indian bank rates, although there were relatively larger fluctuations (average 6.55%; min. 4.82 in 1910; max. 8.76 in 1901) (Fig. 8.3). The bank rate rose to 8.03% in 1920 and remained at that rate until 1924. Subsequent to 1925, the rate started to decrease gradually and reached 5.84 in 1931, then it suddenly dropped to 4.38% in 1932, 3.65% in 1933, and 3.29% in 1936. These bank rate trends in Japan indicate that there were no clear differences in bank rates of the central/quasi-central banks in Japan and India.

Considering the market rate, the rates in Japan were in general higher than the *hundi* rates, the corresponding Indian rates. *The Oriental Economists Yearbook* shows that the Japanese market rate remained over 10% in the 1900s, except for 9.89% in 1907 (Fig. 8.3). The rate decreased to approximately 7–9% throughout the 1910s; however, it rose again to over 9% in the first half of the 1920s. Subsequent to the mid-1920s, the rates started to decrease gradually from 9.45% in 1926 to 7.85 in 1931, and rose again in 1932 to reach 9.31, although the rates gradually declined again after that year to 7.01% in 1937. Overall, the Japanese market rate trends clearly indicate that leading private financial institutions charged higher interest rates for their short-term lending than India's financial institutions. Surprisingly, Japanese market rates in the 1930s were higher than India's bazaar rates, which have been notorious among economic historians of colonial India for its exploitive nature.

This clearly indicates that India suffered from short-term capital supply less seriously than Japan throughout the first half of the 20th century when the two countries started to show distinct patterns of industrial development.

To test the factor endowment hypothesis, we not only compare interest rate trends, but also nominal wage trends in India and Japan. For data on long-term nominal wages in manufacturing in India, we use Sivasubramonian's estimation of daily nominal wages of skilled and unskilled labour at 'small-scale and cottage industries' spanning 47 years from 1900/01 (Sivasubramonian 2000). Sivasubramonian defines carpenters, blacksmiths, and masons as skilled labour, and weavers and potters as unskilled labour. Unfortunately, Sivasubramonian did not estimate similar long-term nominal wage trends of workers in 'modern' manufacturing sectors, such as the cotton mill industry. However, we can assume that wages at 'small-scale and cottage industries' approximate wages at similar posts in modern manufacturing sectors as India already had high labour mobility in general by the end of the 19th century, as Bagchi stresses (Bagchi 1972).

After carefully analysing several historical wage data utilised by economic historians, Sivasubramonian estimated that the nominal daily wages of urban skilled labour, most of whom were adult male, grew steadily from Rs. 0.51 in 1900 to Rs. 0.90 in 1917 (Fig. 8.4). After 1918, wages started increasing marginally, rising from Rs. 0.99 in 1918 to Rs. 1.60 in 1925. After peaking in 1925, the nominal daily wages of urban skilled labour in India began to decrease gradually in the 1920s and rapidly in the 1930s, returning to the level of 1918, Rs. 1.01, in 1939. Sivasubramonian also estimated the nominal daily wages of unskilled labour and those of cotton weavers, most of whom were adult male. Both unskilled labour and cotton weavers, who may have be 'slightly better off than the agricultural labourers in the rural areas' (Sivasubramonian 2000), received almost half of the wages of urban skilled workers. The nominal daily wages of unskilled labour steadily grew from Rs. 0.25 in 1900 to Rs. 0.48 in 1917. After 1918, it rose marginally, as did for urban skilled labour. The wages rose from Rs. 0.53 in 1918 to Rs. 0.82 in 1925. Further, the wage started to decrease from Rs. 0.80 in 1926 to Rs. 0.46 in 1939, gradually in the 1920s and rapidly in the 1930s. The nominal daily wages of cotton weavers, whose data are available only for 11 years from 1910, were similar to the wages of unskilled labour, which validated Sivasubramonian's classification of weavers as unskilled labour.

8 Historical Roots of Industrialisation …

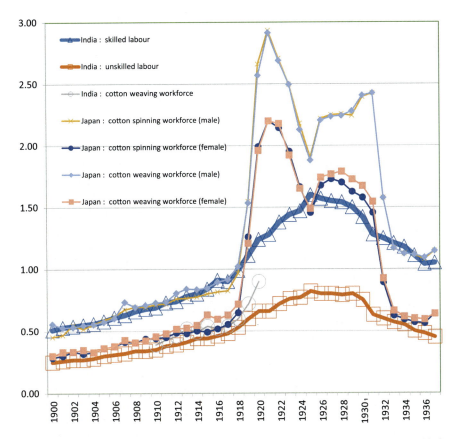

Fig. 8.4 Nominal daily wages for manufacturing labours (in Indian rupee). *Sources* Nomura (2018)
Note 1 The sharp drop in wages in Japan during the 1930s was due to a marked decline in yen-based nominal wages and a sudden depreciation of the yen against the rupee after 1931 (Rs./Yen decreased from 1.47 in 1931 to 1.05 in 1932 and 0.79 in 1933)

The nominal daily wages in India was not so different from that in Japan in the first and last years of the first half of the 20th century. According to Fujino (Fujino et al. 1979), a pioneering compilation work of economic statistics of modern Japan, rupee-based nominal daily wages of male workers of the cotton spinning and weaving sector of Japan, which was one of the leading 'modern' manufacturing sectors in Japan, were at similar levels to India's urban skilled workers in small-scale and cottage industries before 1918 and after 1933 (Fig. 8.4). Additionally, Sivasubramonian (2000) and Fujino (Fujino et al. 1979) jointly show that rupee-based nominal daily wages of 'female' workers of the Japanese cotton and spinning sector in two periods (before 1918 and after 1933) were only approximately 10–20% higher than the rupee-based nominal daily wages of Indian unskilled adult worker, who were 'slightly better off than the agricultural labourers in the rural areas' (Sivasubramonian 2000). Wage trends in the two countries diverged for 15 years after 1918, although the difference disappeared completely in the early 1930s due to the sharp decline in Japanese yen-based nominal wages in Japan, and a marked depreciation of the Japanese yen against the Indian rupee after 1931 (Rs./Yen decreased from 1.47 in 1931 to 1.05 in 1932, and 0.79 in 1933).

We should pay special attention to two facts in assessing the above-mentioned wage trends in the two countries. First, female workers were the majority in some leading 'modern' manufacturing sectors in Japan, such as the cotton mill industry, while adult males constituted the majority in most of the 'modern' as well as traditional manufacturing sectors in India. Second, as was pointed out previously, Indian skilled and semi-skilled workers at 'modern' business enterprises and those at 'small-scale and cottage industries' could be construed to have received approximately similar wages for the following reasons. *Prices and Wages*, one of the most well-known historical statistics of colonial India, indicates that both sizers in the sizing department and slubbers in the card-room department of India's cotton mills received approximately similar wages to those of blacksmiths and carpenters working at Indian railway companies in the early 20th century. Assuming that blacksmiths and carpenters working at railway companies and those working at small-scale or cottage industries received similar wages in a highly mobile labour market due to similarity in job specifications, Indian male adult workers at skilled or semi-skilled posts of 'modern' manufacturing sector, such as slubbers in the card-room department of cotton mills, may have received, at least, similar nominal wages to that of skilled labour such as blacksmiths or carpenters as shown in Fig. 8.4. Based on these two facts, we conclude that Indian workers in manufacturing received no less than the amount of nominal daily wages received by workers at 'modern' manufacturing sector in Japan in the two periods (before 1918 and after 1933).

Comparing interest rates and nominal wages in India and Japan does not lead to the conclusion that India was capital scarce and labour abundant at least in comparison to Japan in the early 20th century. Rather, India's factor endowment was similar to that of Japan in the time period. Despite the similarity, India failed in achieving similar pattern of 'labour intensive' industrialisation that Japan achieved since the end of the 19th century, during which time, the labour intensive industrialisation led Japan's modern economic growth in its early phase. What could explain the causes of the failure of colonial India's labour intensive industrialisation? We will check with another hypothesis that has been proposed to answer the question.

8.4 Laissez-Faire Economic Policy Hypothesis

8.4.1 Overview

Based on the understanding that governments can lead industrialisation through comprehensive interventions in economic activities, scholars such as Amiya Kumar Bagchi stress that India could have developed its industries more robustly if the colonial government had taken interventionist policies to boost overall industrial development (Bagchi 1972). They assume that the colonial government had no intention or capacity to undertake such interventionist economic policies as the government considered laissez-faire policies as its pivotal policy framework to protect British interests in colonial India. Under the common acceptance of market mechanisms guided by the 'invisible hand', the colonial government assumed that laissez-faire policies merited both British and Indian interests. Additionally, this framework was welcomed by the colonial government as it significantly limited the scope of colonial governance and left wide-ranging, sometimes bothersome, business matters in the hands of private entities. This non-interventionist philosophy is well summarised by Morris David Morris, who wrote that 'there can be no question that in India during the century and a half of British rule the market was given its head. British India was one of the great social experiments in letting self-interest and market forces do virtually everything' (Morris 1987). The laissez-faire economic policy framework, according to Bagchi and others, resulted in stagnated industrialisation in colonial India.

8.4.2 Statistical Analysis

Testing the entire scope of the laissez-faire economic policy hypothesis is beyond the capacity of this short essay. On the one hand, the assertion that weak government intervention caused stagnation in industrialisation is a challenging hypothesis to prove, considering the weak performance in the post-colonial era when interventionist policies were adopted. On the other hand, we also know that some types of interventions into the economy could help promote industrial growth from the case study of Asian Miracle stories in South Korea after 1960s and Southeast Asian countries after the 1970s, when developmental directorships played a part in raising the growth rate of the manufacturing sector in these countries. A full assessment requires an in-depth investigation on government interventions that could have potentially affected industrial growth. This requires a full-fledged analysis on an optimal interventionist policy portfolio, and any negative influence by laissez-faire policies on such a portfolio. Such an analysis is far beyond the scope of this short essay. Leaving the full-fledged analysis for future work, this section describes the basic features of India's laissez-faire economic policy framework as an initial step in verifying this hypothesis. Similar to the above section, we use historical data that have been compiled by recent scholars.

An important feature of the Indian laissez-faire policies was the limited share of government revenue in the total GDP, which Morris refers to in his quote mentioned above, and is verified by historical data. Figures 8.5 and 8.6 indicate the shares of total government revenue in the total GDP/NDP for India, Japan, and the UK prior to the 1940s. The figures clearly indicate the limited annual financial capacity of the Indian government in comparison to the other two countries. Figure 8.5 also indicates that India's limited capacity declined until the end of the 1920s, although it increased

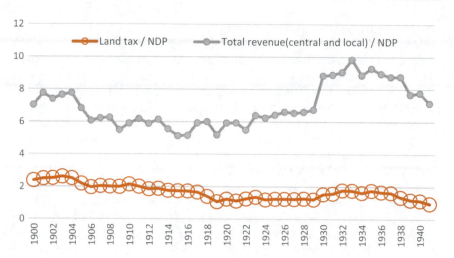

Fig. 8.5 India's share of government revenue against NDP. *Source* Data of NDP from Sivasubramonian (2000). Data of British India's government revenue from Reserve Bank of India (1954). Data of population size of British India and princely states from Government of India. *Statistical Abstract of British India*. New Delhi: Department of Commercial Intelligence and Statistics. *Note 1* The government revenue includes revenues of both British India's central and local government of, which was separated from the central government after an enactment of the Government of India Act 1919. *Note 2* Original data of the government revenue in *Banking and Monetary Statistics* includes only central and local government revenue of British India, while excluding data on revenue of princely states. We estimate the government revenue of the princely state based on their relative size of population. According to *Statistical Abstract of British India*, total population in British India and princely states are as follows. 231 million and 63 million in 1901, 244 million and 70 million in 1911, 247 million and 71 million in 1921, and 271 million and 81 million in 1931. Based on these figures, we assume that the government revenue of the princely states were 22% of the government revenue of British India throughout the period of the figure. On the assumption, we firstly estimated total government revenue of India. And then, to figure out the India's revenue share in NDP, the estimated government revenue of India was divided by Sivasubramonian's total India's NDP, which includes NDP data of both British India and princely states

in the 1930s largely owing to the sharp drop in NDP in the decades following the Great Depression.

In addition to the relative scale of government revenue in the total GDP/NDP, the absolute scale of India's government revenue was smaller, for instance, than that of Japan. As Fig. 8.7 indicates, initially, India's revenue gradually grew at a similar pace to that of Japan. This may lead some to conclude that the relatively smaller share of Indian revenue against its NDP should not be overemphasised. However, as the figure also indicates, Japan's revenue scale outpaced India's after the early 1920s when its revenue scale stagnated. More importantly, India's government revenue maintained the welfare standard of its population, which was more than 200 million as early as in the 20th century, when the population in Japan was only approximately 60 million. Moreover, the Indian government was required to spend approximately 30% of its revenue on defence, part of which was used to maintain British troops inside and

8 Historical Roots of Industrialisation … 183

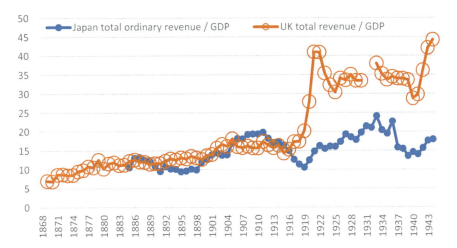

Fig. 8.6 Japan and the UK's share of government revenue against GDP. *Source* Data of Japan's government revenue from Emi and Shionoya (1966). Data of Japan's GDP from Okawa et al. (1974). Data of the UK from Mitchell (1988). *Note 1* The government revenues include revenues of both central and local government in the respective countries

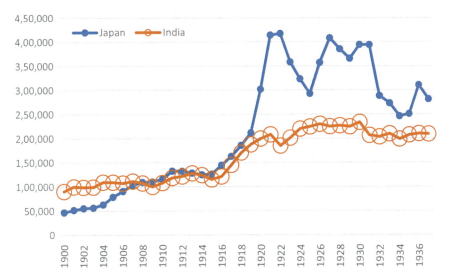

Fig. 8.7 Government revenue (absolute figure in million rupee). *Source* Data of exchange rate from same source with Fig. 8.4. Other data are from same sources with Figs. 8.5 and 8.6

outside India. Overall, the Indian government's revenue was, as acknowledged by economic historians, small not only in its relative scale, but also in absolute terms.

One of the leading causes of the limited capacity of government revenue is the land tax assessment system called the 'permanent settlement system', which was applied to the leading part of the colony from the early stage of colonial rule in the late 18th century. Under the system, land tax per acre was fixed at the initial stage of colonial governance in the late 18th century. It was fixed to avoid costs related to reassessment of the rates, as well as insurgency risks by taxpayers against any reassessments. As a result, government revenue, as is clearly shown in Fig. 8.5, suffered from a gradual decline in real terms owing to the steady rise in general prices throughout the colonial period (Kumar 1983). The inability to raise revenue from lands through a reassessment may imply limited legitimacy of the colonial government to govern its subjects.

The Indian government's limited financial capacity is also observed in Fig. 8.8, which shows the shares of the central government's public debt against GDP/NDP of India, Japan, and the UK until the 1940s. According to the figure, India's share (total of debt in rupees and in sterling) was higher than its counterparts in the early 1900s. This is owing to the UK's strict observance of liberalisation economic policies, as well as Japan's weak capacity to borrow from abroad at that time. However, the Indian government strengthened its conservative debt policy throughout the period, while its counterparts expanded their debt, particularly after WW1.

Attempts by the Indian government to limit its public debt to a 'necessary minimum' are well-known among economic historians as an important feature of its 'imperial commitment'. For instance, Brian Tomlinson, a well-known economic historian of colonial India, explained it as follows. '[as a colonial state forming a part of British empire], irreducible minimum' for Government of India were 'to provide a market for British goods, to pay interest on the sterling debt and other charges that fell due in London, and to maintain a large number of British troops from local revenues and make a part of the Indian army available for imperial garrisons' (Tomlinson 2013). Tomlinson called this irreducible minimum an 'imperial commitment', which shaped British policy foundation in India. Tomlinson argues that the Indian government adopted an automatic, self-regulating system of currency management to protect British investor interests. Imperial commitment resulted in Indian officials not playing an active role in matters important to the domestic economy, as seen in the limited public debt during the colonial period, which in other words, indicates India's strict observance of conservative fiscal policy throughout the colonial period.

The significance of the imperial commitment is also observed in India's exchange rate policy, which has also received wide scholarly attention. Before the end of the 19th century, India employed the silver standard, while the UK employed the gold standard. Subsequent to the early 1870s, when silver prices began to decline due to the decisions of leading European countries to employ the gold standard, the rupee exchange rate declined abruptly against the sterling pound. To tackle the decreasing value of the rupee against the sterling pound and to stabilise international finance, the Indian government decided to introduce the gold exchange standard by the early 20th century. Figure 8.9 shows that the rupee exchange rate against the sterling pound remained stable for over a century since the early 19th century, despite the difference in the economic growth rate between India and the UK in the period. On the one hand, the stable exchange rate trend helped British investments by reducing the exchange rate risk in India, which occupied a large part of British overseas investment since

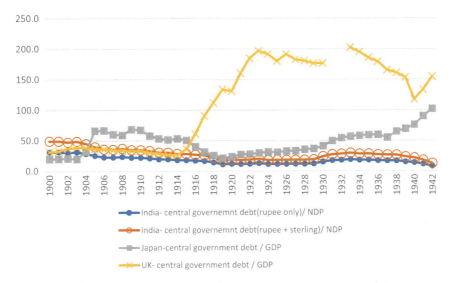

Fig. 8.8 Shares of central government's public debt against GDP/NDP. *Source* Data of India's NDP from Sivasubramonian (2000). Data of British India's central government debt from Reserve Bank of India (1954). Data of Japan's GDP from Okawa et al. (1974). Data of Japan's central government debt from Emi et al. (1988); Toyo Keizai Shinposha, *The Oriental economist* (Toyo Keizai Shinposha), Tokyo: Toyo Keizai Shinposha. Data of the UK from Mitchell (1988). *Note 1* As was the case of Fig. 8.5, original data of the government revenue in *Banking and Monetary Statistics* includes only central government debt of British India, excluding data on princely states' debt. Again, using the population size, we assume that the princely states' government debt were 22% of the government debt of British India. On the assumption, we estimated total central government debt of India. And then, to figure out the India's central government debt share in NDP, the estimated central government debt of India was divided by Sivasubramonian's total India's NDP, which includes NDP data of both British India and princely states

the mid-19th century, while on the other hand, the stabilised exchange rate limited the flexibility in managing fiscal and financial policies for the colonial government.[3]

Under the non-interventionist, 'experimental' laissez-faire policies, the Indian government limited its intervention to the minimum, leaving the coordination of economic transactions to the market. Among the market fundamentalist economic policies, the tariff policy is well-known. For instance, general import duty was reduced from 10% in the early 1860s to zero in 1882. India's tariff rate remained low at approximately 5% before the 1920s, while the rate rose drastically after that due

---

[3] Figure 8.9 also shows the exchange rate trends of Japanese yen against sterling pound since 1895. The figure indicates that Japanese yen gradually decreased its value against the Indian rupee in the 1920s and abruptly in the 1930s. The relative decrease in the Japanese yen value against the Indian rupee roughly went along with the positive debt policy of imperial Japan after WW1, which is shown in Fig. 8.8.

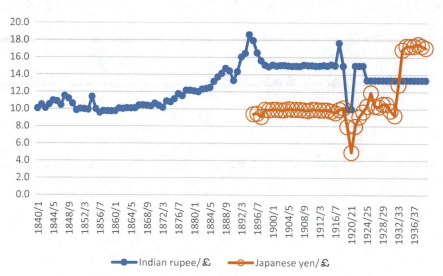

Fig. 8.9 Exchange rate of Indian rupee and Japanese yen against Sterling pound. *Source* Indian rupee data before 1918/19 from Shirras (1920). Indian rupee data after 1919/20 from Government of India. *Statistical Abstract of British India*. New Delhi: Department of Commercial Intelligence and Statistics. Japanese yen data from Government of Japan (1949)

to various reasons, one of which was the fiscal stringency of the colonial government (Fig. 8.10).[4]

Another significant policy under the laissez-faire policy framework was the policy to invest in transportation facilities to promote free trade. One of the most influential transportation facilities was the railway network. An initial attempt to construct railway networks dates back to the 1840s, when the then Governor-General of India proposed the construction of a railway network to promote trade, administrative, and military efficiency. Under his leadership, the first railway company was incorporated in 1849, which was followed by additional networks, and resulted in the Indian railway networks ranking fourth in operated lines globally in 1913.

The historical data based test on Indian policy choices validate the hypothesis that it operated under a strict laissez-faire policy framework. The colonial government limited its commitment to the economy to a lesser extent than the Japanese or British governments, while the private sector thrived under this framework.

The free rein given to private business entities formed a foundation for the growth of modern industrial enterprises in India. However, it is also clear that these policies led to limited industrial development. This recognition may have led to the adoption of proactive government interventionist policies after independence. As we have already mentioned, fully addressing the impact of the laissez-faire economic policy framework on stagnated industrialisation is left for future work.

---

[4]Figures 8.5 and 8.10 jointly indicate that custom revenue helped the government to maintain its revenue share among NDP, particularly after WW1.

8 Historical Roots of Industrialisation ...

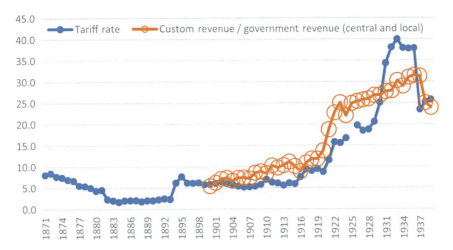

Fig. 8.10 Import tariff rate and custom revenue share among total government revenue in India (%). *Source* Tariff rate data from Mitchell (1995). Custom revenue and total revenue data from same sources with Fig. 8.5. *Note 1* Tariff rate is estimated by custom revenue *divided by* total imports

8.5 Sluggish Technical Transfer Hypothesis

In addition to the two hypotheses mentioned above, there is another hypothesis to explain colonial India's stagnated industrialisation, which has mainly been proposed by Japanese economists, such as Kiyokawa (1976a, b, 1983) and Otsuka et al. (1988). Examining the rapid withdrawal of Indian cotton mills from the international market in the early 20th century, the studies argue that factors affecting technology choice had a profound influence on the stagnated growth of the Indian cotton mill industry, which was a representative industry of colonial India. They argue that the underlying factors include India's institutional and organisational challenges that go beyond factor endowment or colonial government laissez-faire based economic policies.

The cotton mill industry led industrial development in both India and Japan in the initial phase of their industrialisation. In India, the first steam-powered cotton mill was founded near Calcutta in 1817/18 by an Englishman, although the foreign capital-led attempt failed to achieve steady growth. The first successful attempt was made in the 1850s in Bombay by C.N. Davar, a wealthy Parsee merchant and his associates. The cotton milling business grew steadily throughout the second half of the 19th century, particularly from the 1870s, achieving high international competitiveness by the end of the 19th century. The success can be observed in the drastic rise in India's coarse yarn export to China. Indian export of coarse yarn grew rapidly from 6 million lbs in 1876 to 18 million lbs in 1878, 141 million lbs in 1894, and to 254 million lbs in 1899. Considering that the 1899 figure amounted to almost five times the Indian finer-count yarn import from the UK, Kiyokawa comments that the miraculous growth deserves more academic attention (Kiyokawa 1976a). However, the miraculous growth in the Chinese market suddenly came to an end in the early 20th century. Export to China plummeted from 243 million lbs in 1905 to 172 million lbs in 1910 and 87 million lbs in 1913 (ibid., p. 238).

Japanese cotton mills supplied coarse yarn to China from the 1910s, replacing Indian export. While the first modern cotton mill was founded in Japan in 1867 under the leadership of the Satsuma-*han*, one of the most powerful feudal loads under the Tokugawa shogunate, it was only after the 1880s that Japanese cotton mill industries started to show the signs of success. Under the leadership of Eiichi Shibusawa, known as the 'father of Japanese capitalism', Japanese cotton mills grew rapidly and steadily to form one of the foundations of Japan's industrial development by the end of the 19th century. Otsuka et al. (1988) indicates that Japanese yarn exports to China and Hong Kong increased from 15.3 million lbs in 1895 to 102.4 million lbs in 1910 and to 170.3 million lbs in 1915. Japanese coarse yarn found its market even in India after the 1910s. Otsuka et al. (1988) shows that Japanese yarn exports to India increased from null in 1905 to 1.4 million lbs in 1915, 13.7 million lbs in 1920, and 26.0 million lbs in 1925. The divergence in the development of the cotton mill industry in India and Japan continued further after the early 1920s. India's cotton mill industry confined its outlet to the domestic market, while Japan extended its reach to countries in East, Southeast, and South Asia.

According to Kiyokawa and Otsuka et al., a salient factor that differentiated the developmental pattern of cotton mill industries in the two countries was their attitudes towards technological adaptation and innovation in the spindle section. Spindle section, which forms the final process of yarn production, occupies more than 30% of the cotton mill's entire production facility. Hence, Kiyokawa writes, 'technical progress in spinning frames has a crucial effect, and even a slight improvement in them leads to a great increase in productivity as a whole' (Kiyokawa 1983).

As explained by Kiyokawa (1976a, b, 1983) and Otsuka et al. (1988), cotton mill industries in India and Japan had two types of spindles, mule and ring spindles. Mule spindles could produce high quality yarn and had long been used in the UK due to its strong preference for high quality yarn. On the other hand, ring spindles could produce coarse yarn that was dominantly consumed in both countries for a long time. In the initial phase of cotton yarn production before the 1870s, mule spindles dominated yarn production in both countries as they both imported spindles from the UK. However, over time, ring spindles replaced mule spindles due to cost efficiency in both the Asian countries where capital was scarce and labour abundant in comparison to the factor endowment structure in the UK. Otsuka et al. summarises the advantage of ring spindles as follows, 'The ring machinery had a clear advantage over mules in requiring less skilled labour. Moreover, by adding workers to tie the broken yearn, rings could be run at higher speeds. Consequently, for any given yarn count up to at least the 40s rings are much more labour-intensive than mules' (Otsuka et al. 1988).

Despite the advantage of ring spindles over mule spindles, Indian cotton mills were slow in making the transition. The slow transition is apparent in comparison to the speedy diffusion of ring spindles in Japan, as shown in Figs. 8.11 and 8.12. Ring spindles started being used by the 1880s in both countries. However, it was only

8 Historical Roots of Industrialisation ...

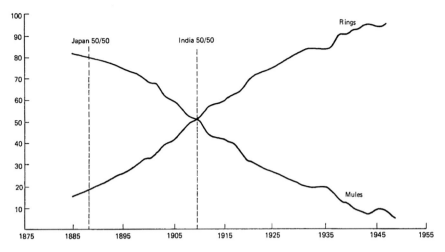

Fig. 8.11 Percentage of rings and mules: India. *Source* Otsuka et al. (1988, p. 9)

after the late 1930s when ring spindles dominated more than 90% of Indian mills. It took 20 years to reach a point where 50% of the spindles were replaced in India. Surprisingly, there were even cases of new installation of mule spindles in the early 20th century when the advantage of ring spindles over mule spindles was obvious. In Japan, as Fig. 8.12 indicates, the 50% replacement mark was reached as early as at the end of the 1880s, only a few years after replacement attempts began in the mid-1880s. Furthermore, more than 90% of mule spindles were replaced by ring spindles by the end of the 19th century. According to Otsuka et al. (1988), the speedy diffusion of the ring spindles in Japan explains 55–80% of total factor productivity growth of Japanese cotton mills in the 1890s, when its cotton mill industry experienced magnificent growth that formed the foundation for booming export to China in the 1900s.[5]

What explains the slow transition in colonial India? Both Kiyokawa (1976a, b, 1983) and Otsuka et al. (1988) focus on organisational and institutional factors to explain the cause. By examining the cotton mill's depreciation allowance policy, Kiyokawa (1976a, b) clarifies that India's slow transition was due to the poor depreciation allowance policy adopted by its myopic management. In his work in 1983, Kiyokawa also focuses on the continuing installation of mule spindles in the early 20th century as a sign indicating another salient feature of slow transition in India. Based on a rigorous statistical analysis, Kiyokawa shows that 'the high Mule ratio reflected the joint presence of foreign (British) staff in both top and middle managements supported by the mediating function of a foreign manager' (Kiyokawa 1983). Kiyokawa concludes by stating that, 'This analysis confirms the important role of

---

[5]Otsuka (1995) also clarifies that capital-output ratio (spindle/ton) of Indian cotton mills came to be more than double in comparison to Japanese mills by 1900, while there was much less differences between the ratios in the two countries around the 1890s.

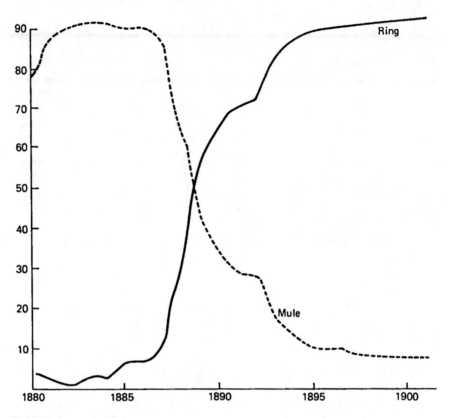

Fig. 8.12 Percentage of rings and mules: Japan. *Source* Otsuka et al. (1988, p. 10)

foreign technicians in the decision-making on choice of technique …they (British technicians) were generally inclined to stick with old but familiar technology based upon their experience in Great Britain… In short, technological adaptation in India was greatly influenced by the British experience and by British patterns of technological development (ibid.)'. Kiyokawa also referred to India's slow development in technical education as a factor in the heavy reliance on British technical experts. He added, 'While it cannot be denied that the government was not especially eager to advance technical education in India, the Indian top management class has to share the responsibility as well for not having promoted technical education in real earnest by encouraging a more open and meritocratic society in the industrial world' (ibid.).

Otsuka et al. (1988) sheds light on the different aspects of India's institutional and organisational specificities to explain the slow transition. Initially, they argued that prices, such as factor prices and domestic prices under tariff protection, influenced the speed of technical diffusion. For instance, they mentioned that 'The price distortions commonly observed in developing countries are likely to result in both "inappropriate" choices of technology and an "inappropriate" direction for technology change' (Otsuka et al. 1988). However, they assert that rigorous statistical examination 'permit us, moreover, to proceed beyond the simple factor price distortion story in explaining comparative technological performance'. After pointing out the importance of Japan's innovative activities in fields such as cotton mixing procedures for the efficient adaptation of ring spindles to the lower average staple length, they point out that 'the choices made by an individual Japanese entrepreneur [of cotton mills], in contrast to his Indian counterpart, illuminate the importance of differences in institutional and organisational environments (ibid.)'. In terms of the institutional and organisational environment in Japan, they focus on the existence of competitive pressure in the domestic market influenced by business associations, the availability of 'formal education and learning by opportunity', and 'the legal convenience of a petty patent system' (ibid.), none of which sufficiently existed in India.

Overall, Kiyokawa (1976a, b, 1983) and Otsuka et al. (1988) focus on the influence of institutional and organisation factors that were established both by private and public initiatives to explain the divergence of cotton mill industries in India and Japan, which were leading sectors of modern industrial growth in both countries.

8.6 Conclusions

After surveying the stagnated industrialisation nature of colonial India, this chapter reviewed three hypotheses to explain this phenomenon: the factor endowment hypothesis; the laissez-faire economic policy hypothesis; and the sluggish technical transfer hypothesis. In the review, we also briefly examined the first two hypotheses using historical data compiled by recent scholars. This chapter reveals that the factor endowment hypothesis needs to be supplemented by further investigations, while the laissez-faire economic policy hypothesis requires further analysis on how laissez-faire policies negatively affected India's industrialisation. Augmenting the two hypotheses may require further analysis, for instance, on the effects of fiscal stringency under laissez-faire policies on India's institutional and organisational development for mass and vocational education, patent system, or industrial financing system as it could have affected the performance of industrial enterprises through raising efficiency in labour or capital transactions. Further clarification on India's institutional and organisation development, on which Kiyokawa (1976a, b, 1983) and Otsuka et al. (1988) strongly focused, would help us deepen our understanding on factors underlying the stagnated nature of industrialisation in colonial India. However, this is an agenda for future work.

References

Bagchi, A. (1972). *Private investment in India, 1900–1939*. Cambridge: Cambridge University Press.
Bagchi, A. (1997). *The evolution of the state bank of India: The era of the presidency banks, 1876–1920*. New Delhi: Sage Publications.
Bombay Millowners' Association. (various years). *Report of the millowners' association*. Bombay: Bombay Millowners' Association.
Emi, K., Ito, M., & Eguchi, H. (1988). *Estimates of Japan long term economic statistics series volume 5 savings and currency*. Tokyo: Toyo Keizai Shinposha.
Emi, K. & Shionoya U. (1966). *Estimates of Japan long term economic statistics series volume 7 government expenditure*. Tokyo: Toyo Keizai Shinposha.
Fujino, S., Fujino, S., & Ono, A. (1979). *Estimates of Japan long term economic statistics series volume 11 textiles*. Tokyo: Toyo Keizai Shinposha.
Government of India. (various years). *Prices and wages in India*. Calcutta: Superintendent Government Printing.
Government of India. (various years). *Statistical abstract of British India*. New Delhi: Department of Commercial Intelligence and Statistics.
Government of Japan. (various years). *Statistical abstract of imperial Japan*. Tokyo: Toyo Shorin.
Government of Japan (1949) *Japan statistical year-book*. Tokyo: Executive Office of Statistics Commission, Statistics Bureau of the Prime Minister's Office.
Gupta, B. (2016). The rise of modern industry in colonial India. In L. Chaudhary, B. Gupta, T. Roy, & A. Swamy (Eds.), *A new economic history of colonial India*. London: Routledge.
Kiyokawa, Y. (1976a). *Indo menkōgyō ni okeru gijyutsu to shijyō no keisei ni tsuite (1)* (Technology and market formation in the cotton mill industry of India: A comparison with the cotton industries of Japan and China). *Keizai kenkū, 27*(3), 234–249.
Kiyokawa, Y. (1976b). *Indo menkōgyō ni okeru gijyutsu to shijyō no keisei ni tsuite (2)* (Technology and market formation in the cotton mill industry of India: A comparison with the cotton industries of Japan and China). *Keizai kenkū, 27*(4), 307–322.
Kiyokawa, Y. (1983). Technical adaptations and managerial resources in India: a study of the experience of the cotton textile industry from a comparative viewpoint. *The Developing Economies, 21*(2), 97–133.
Kumar, D. (1983). The fiscal system. In D. Kumar (Ed.), *The Cambridge economic history of India* (Vol. 2, p. c.1757–c.1970). Cambridge: Cambridge University Press.
Kuznets, S. (1966). *Modern economic growth*. New Haven: Yale University Press.
League of Nations. (1945). *Industrialization and foreign trade*. Geneva: League of Nations.
Mitchell, B. R. (1980). *European historical statistics, 1750–1975*. London: Macmillan.
Mitchell, B. R. (1982). *International historical statistics: Africa and Asia*. London: Macmillan.
Mitchell, B. R. (1983). *International historical statistics: The Americas and Australasia*. London: Macmillan.
Mitchell, B. R. (1988). *British historical statistics*. Cambridge: Cambridge University Press.
Mitchell, B. R. (1995). *International historical statistics: Africa, Asia & Oceania 1750-1988* (2nd ed.). New York: Macmillan.
Morris, M. D. (1983). The growth of large-scale industry to 1947. In D. Kumar (Ed.), *The Cambridge economic history of India, 2, c.1757–c.1970*. Cambridge: Cambridge University Press.
Morris, M. D. (1987). Indian industry and business in the age of laissez faire. In D. Tripathi (Ed.), *State and business in India: A historical perspective*. Manohar: New Delhi.
Nomura, C. (2018). *The house of Tata meets the second industrial revolution: An institutional analysis of Tata Iron and Steel Co. in colonial India*. Singapore: Springer.
Okawa, K., Takamatsu, N., & Yamamoto, K. (1974). *Estimates of Japan long term economic statistics series volume 1: National income*. Tokyo: Toyo Keizai Shinposha.
Otsuka, K. (1995). Technology choice, employment, and development. *Asian Development Review, 13*(2), 105–137.

Otsuka, K., Ranis, G., & Saxonhouse, G. (1988). *Comparative technology choice in development: The Indian and Japanese cotton textile industries.* Basingstoke: Macmillan.

Reserve Bank of India. (1954). *Banking and monetary statistics of India.* Bombay: The Reserve Bank of India.

Reserve Bank of India. (various years). *Report on currency and finance.* Bombay: Reserve Bank of India.

Roy, T. (2005). *Rethinking economic change in India: Labour and livelihood.* London: Routledge.

Roy, T. (2006). *The economic history of India 1857–1947* (2nd ed.). New Delhi: Oxford University Press.

Shirras, G. F. (1920). *Indian finance and banking.* London: Macmillan.

Sivasubramonian, S. (2000). *The national income of India in the twentieth century.* New Delhi: Oxford University Press.

Tomlinson, B. (2013). *The economy of modern India: From 1860 to the twenty-first century* (2nd ed.). Cambridge: Cambridge University Press.

Toyo Keizai. (various years). *The Oriental economist year book (Keizai nenkan).* Tokyo: Toyo Keizai Shinposha.

Umemura, M., Akasaka, K., Minami, R., Nii, G., Ito, S., & Takamatsu, N. (1988). *Estimates of Japan long term economic statistics series volume 2 manpower.* Tokyo: Toyo Keizai Shinposha.

Open Access This chapter is licensed under the terms of the Creative Commons Attribution-NonCommercial-NoDerivatives 4.0 International License (http://creativecommons.org/licenses/by-nc-nd/4.0/), which permits any noncommercial use, sharing, distribution and reproduction in any medium or format, as long as you give appropriate credit to the original author(s) and the source, provide a link to the Creative Commons licence and indicate if you modified the licensed material. You do not have permission under this licence to share adapted material derived from this chapter or parts of it.

The images or other third party material in this chapter are included in the chapter's Creative Commons licence, unless indicated otherwise in a credit line to the material. If material is not included in the chapter's Creative Commons licence and your intended use is not permitted by statutory regulation or exceeds the permitted use, you will need to obtain permission directly from the copyright holder.

Chapter 9
Industrial Policy, Industrial Development, and Structural Transformation in Asia and Africa

Yuki Higuchi and Go Shimada

9.1 Introduction

Industrial policy has long been a controversial issue among researchers and policymakers. Proponents of industrial policy, including early development economists like Hirschman (1958), Nurkse (1953), and Rosenstein-Rodan (1943), argue that big push-type policy to promote industrial development is central to economic development. Opponents argue that such interventionist policy will distort markets, and have a deleterious effect on economic growth (e.g., Baldwin 1969; Krueger and Tuncer 1982; Lal 1983). According to Newman et al. (2016, Chap. 2), the international trend of industrial policy can be divided into three phases. The first phase took place in the 1960s and 1970s, when the industrial policy was favorably accepted in the post-independence countries. In this period, import substitution industrialization (ISI) policies were adopted to promote certain domestic industries by means of tariffs and subsidies in many African countries under socialist regimes, such as, Ghana, Tanzania, and Zimbabwe. The ISI policies, however, failed to promote industrial development because these policies lacked linkages with markets and ignored the comparative advantage of the economy.[1]

---

[1] The failure of African industrial policy in the 1960s and 1970s is similar to the experience of post-independence India, briefly discussed by Nomura (2018) in this volume. In both post-independence India and Africa, the government did not support labor-intensive industries, in which the country had comparative advantage.

Y. Higuchi (✉)
Graduate School of Economics, Nagoya City University, Nagoya, Japan
e-mail: higuchi@econ.nagoya-cu.ac.jp

G. Shimada
Meiji University, Tokyo, Japan
e-mail: go_shimada@meiji.ac.jp

The second phase took place in the 1980s and the 1990s, when the Washington Consensus became an international norm, and structural adjustment programs (SAP) were adopted by the Bretton Woods Institutions, including the World Bank and the International Monetary Fund (IMF).[2] In this second phase, the failure of ISI policies provoked harsh backlash against governmental intervention in industries, and the SAP program was favorably accepted, partially because of the widespread worldwide support for neoliberal regimes. The proponents of SAP policies emphasized the risk of government failure and political capture.

The third phase began in the 2000s when industrial policies were reconsidered as an important policy tool for economic development, as the rise of emerging economies like China, India, Brazil, and South Korea was observed. In this phase, the importance of narrowly defined industrial policy, in the form of previously failed ISI policies, has been muted, but the importance of policy to promote industrialization in general and to reform investment climate has been recognized. Although there is no universally accepted definition of industrial policy, the scope of industrial policy has expanded to include the selection and promotion of an industry in which a country has comparative advantage (e.g., Hausmann et al. 2005; Lin 2012) and even broader measures to correct market failures, including information asymmetry, externality, and coordination failure. The latter includes infrastructure development, job training, and research and development support to promote the industrial sector as a whole, not just specific industries (Harrison and Rodríguez-Clare 2010; Stiglitz et al. 2013). In this chapter, we do not formally define industrial policy, but we discuss the general importance of industrial policy and its potential in Africa.

The renewed attention to industrial policy in recent years has been called "the return of industrial policy" by Rodrik (2010), and a series of influential books have been published by Noman and Stiglitz (2015, 2016). The reasons behind the rising interest in industrial policy include the general recognition of the importance of job creation in the developing world, particularly after the Arab Spring, when unemployed educated youths started an economically motivated riot that ignited a political movement (World Bank 2012). In addition, a recent sign of successful industrialization in Ethiopia and Rwanda illustrated that industrial policy can promote structural transformation from the agricultural to the non-agricultural sector in Africa (Oqubay 2015; Noman and Stiglitz 2015; Dinh et al. 2012).

Furthermore, the importance of industrial policy in the history of the U.S. and Europe was rediscovered in recent studies (e.g., Chang 2007; Reinert 2007), and nascent literature empirically investigates the effect of industrial policies (Aghion et al. 2017; Criscuolo et al. 2012). Admitting that the literature is still emerging and not yet conclusive, Nunn and Trefler (2010) run a cross-country growth regression, and find that subsidies targeted to skill-intensive sectors promote economic growth, suggesting the ubiquitous role of industrial policy both in developed and developing countries. Lane (2017) attempts to establish causal impacts on industrial policy by

---

[2]The only international donor against the SAP was Japan. In 1993, the Overseas Economic Cooperation Fund (OECF, now JICA) published a paper in favor of industrial policy (OECF 1993). It caused controversy between the OECF and the World Bank (Mosley et al. 1995; Wade 1996).

examining the case of Korea's big-push industrial policy from the 1970s. Using newly digitized data, and exploiting the unexpected beginning and sector-choice of the policy, Lane (2017) finds that industries targeted by the policy had significantly higher growth rates even after the termination of the policy, which also had a positive spillover effect on downstream industries.

In this chapter, we first discuss how industrial policy can help industrial development and economic growth using a simple conceptual framework. Based on our framework, we illustrate that industrial policy contributes to economic growth by enhancing labor productivity and reallocating labor from low productivity to high productivity sectors. Second, we use macroeconomic data from Asian and sub-Saharan African countries to present a sharp contrast between the two economies. Asian economies successfully achieved economic growth, which was led by the industrial development, particularly in labor-intensive sectors, whereas African economies have long been stagnant since independence, which can be attributed to the failure of industrialization. We also conduct decomposition analysis to show that the degree of labor reallocation is particularly limited in Africa. Lastly, we argue that managerial capacity is missing in Africa, and introduce a feasible strategy that has potential to stimulate African economic growth.

9.2 Conceptual Framework

We denote Y as the real GDP and L as the population of a country so that Y/L indicates the country's GDP per capita.[3] Furthermore, we denote Y_k as the real GDP in sector k, where $k =$ agriculture (*agr*), industry (*ind*), or service (*ser*), and L_k as the employment in sector k. Now, we obtain the following equation:

$$Y/L = (Y_{agr} + Y_{ind} + Y_{ser})/L = \Sigma(Y_k/L) = \Sigma\{(Y_k/L_k) * (L_k/L)\} \quad (9.1)$$

In the last expression, Y_k/L_k represents intra-industry labor productivity and L_k/L represents sectoral share of labor. Assuming the standard production function where output is a function of labor and capital with a given level of technology, the intra-industry labor productivity is a function of capital per capita (that is, capital deepening) and technology.

In this framework, industrial policies can enhance the intra-industry labor productivity or reallocate labor from a low productivity to a high productivity sector. The intra-industry productivity will be enhanced by infrastructure investment, institutional reform, and technology borrowing. In the agricultural sector, the land endowment is fixed, and thus, an increase in agricultural share of labor (L_{agr}/L) reduces

---

[3] We assume that the whole population is employed, but the main discussion remains the same if we define GDP per capita as Y/N, where N is the total population. Then, Y/N is the product of Y/L and L/N, where the latter term represents the employment share of population. Under our assumption, we hold L/N constant at one because the availability of the employment share data is limited.

agricultural labor productivity (Y_{agr}/L_{agr}) because of diminishing marginal product of labor. Although agricultural productivity may be improved by irrigation, land reform, or the use of improved agricultural technology and inputs, the value-added of share of agriculture (Y_{agr}/L) does not dramatically increase because of these offsetting effects.

In contrast, an increase in industrial share of labor (L_{ind}/L) does not necessarily reduce industrial labor productivity (Y_{ind}/L_{ind}) because the industrial sector is not constrained by land endowment. In particular, development of labor-intensive industries will increase both industrial productivity and industrial share of labor, so that the value-added of share of industry (Y_{ind}/L) will dramatically increase. In addition, holding the service sector constant, the increase in industrial share of labor reduces agricultural share of labor, which in turn, increases agricultural labor productivity by reallocating surplus labor from the agriculture to industrial sector.

Indeed, the importance of the labor reallocation, or it can be stated as structural transformation, has received increasing attention both by researchers (e.g., Diao et al. 2017; Herrendorf et al. 2014; Hsieh and Klenow 2009; McMillan et al. 2014) and policymakers. A leading example is the Nairobi Declaration adopted after the Sixth Tokyo International Conference on African Development (TICAD VI) in 2016, where the heads of 54 African countries assembled. One of the three pillars of the declaration for future African economic development is "promoting structural economic transformation through economic diversification and industrialization.[4]" Hence, Eq. (9.1) illustrates the role of industrial policy in productivity improvement and labor reallocation.[5]

The service sector has traditional sub-sectors, mostly consisting of non-tradable goods and services, and modern sub-sectors, including finance and ICT-based services (Jensen 2011). An improvement in productivity in the former sub-sector is limited because of fixed local demand for non-tradable goods and services, whereas the latter sub-sector has potential for productivity increase. The modern sector, however, employs a small number of educated and highly skilled workers, and thus, the labor absorption capacity is limited (Goswami et al. 2011). Although the service sector is not constrained by land endowment, it is difficult to increase both service share of labor (L_{ser}/L) and service productivity (Y_{ser}/L_{ser}). Taken together, the development of the industrial sector, particularly the labor-intensive industrial sector, is the most important channel for economic growth, particularly for countries that have comparative advantage in labor-intensive industry with abundant unskilled labor.

The wage structure in Africa is characterized as dual, in which a small number of highly skilled and educated workers earn high wage, whereas the rest earn low (Hino and Ranis 2013). In addition, fertility rates are still high in African countries so that they can take advantage of the population bonus. Hence, Africa has comparative

---

[4]http://www.mofa.go.jp/af/af1/page3e_000543.html (retrieved on November 23, 2018).

[5]Estudillo et al. (2018) in this volume discuss the labor allocation from agriculture to non-agriculture (i.e., industry and service sectors taken together) in Asia and Africa. They argue that the development of the non-agricultural sector was a key component of Asian economic growth and poverty reduction, whereas the majority of Africans are still engaged in the agricultural sector, and the structural transformation was slow.

advantage in its unskilled labor with low wage, even compared with Asian countries whose recent economic growth puts upward pressure on wage. Importantly, the educational system has been developed and many African countries started to adopt free primary or even free secondary education programs, and thus, their labor force, which is not highly educated, but educated enough to be employable in the industrial sector, is increasingly available at relatively low cost.

Lastly, using Eq. (9.1), we adopt a canonical shift-share decomposition, originally developed by Fabricant (1942) and applied by McMillan et al. (2014) and De Vries et al. (2015) among others, to decompose the economic growth. The growth rate of GDP per capita can be decomposed as follows:

$$\Delta(Y/L) = \Sigma\{\Delta(Y_k/L_k) * (L_k/L)\} + \Sigma\{(Y_k/L_k) * \Delta(L_k/L)\} \\ + \Sigma\{\Delta(Y_k/L_k) * \Delta(L_k/L)\}, \qquad (9.2)$$

where the first term on the right-hand side represents the within-industry labor productivity growth, the second term represents the static labor reallocation, and the third term represents the dynamic labor allocation. We conduct decomposition analysis based on Eq. (9.2) to examine the importance of labor productivity growth in each sector and structural transformation in the histories of Asia and Africa.

9.3 Empirical Analyses

9.3.1 Sectoral GDP Per Capita

We use GDP per capita data from the Penn World Table (PWT) version 8.1 (Feenstra et al. 2015) and sectoral share data from the World Bank's World Development Indicators (WDI). Combining the two datasets, Fig. 9.1 shows changes in sectoral GDP per capita (in 2011, constant USD at purchasing power parity) in log scale. We include 17 major Asian countries for analyses in this chapter: Bangladesh, China, Hong Kong, Indonesia, India, Japan, Cambodia, South Korea, Laos, Sri Lanka, Malaysia, Nepal, Pakistan, Philippines, Singapore, Thailand, and Vietnam. However, the sectoral share data for 1970 (and other years) is not available for Hong Kong, Cambodia, Laos, Singapore, and Vietnam, and thus, these five countries are excluded from Fig. 9.1 so that we can remove influences from the inclusion of sample countries, and focus on time-series changes of sectoral GDP per capita (see Appendix for data availability of our sample countries). In addition, the economic development of Japan, which started in the 1950s, was exceptional among the Asian countries, and thus, Japan's changes in sectoral GDP are separately presented in Panel B, whereas weighted averages of other emerging Asian countries are presented in Panel A.

Similar to Japan, South Africa was exceptional compared to other sub-Saharan African economies because, for instance, its GDP in 1970 accounted for a quarter of total GDP of all 45 sub-Saharan African countries. Therefore, weighted averages of sub-Saharan countries, excluding South Africa, are presented in Panel C, whereas Panel D presents the numbers for South Africa. In Panel C, we restrict our sample to 26 sub-Saharan African countries whose sectoral share data for 1970 is available.

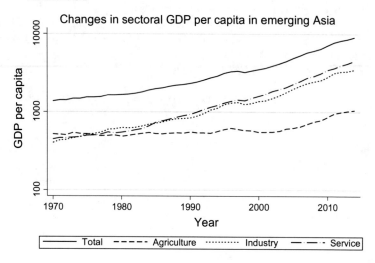

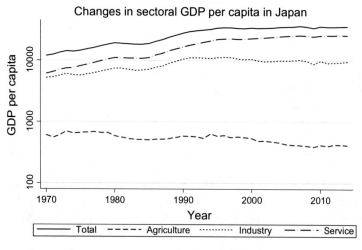

Fig. 9.1 Changes in sectoral GDP per capita in Asia and Sub-Saharan Africa. *Source* Penn World Table, World Development Indicators. *Note* GDP per capita is in USD (in PPP-adjusted 2011 constant price) and is presented in log scale. Panel A presents weighted averages (weight by population) of BGD, CHN, IDN, IND, KOR, LKA, MYS, NPL, PAK, PHL, and THA and Panel B presents numbers in JPN. Similarly, Panel C presents weighted averages of BDI, BEN, BFA, CAF, CIV, CMR, COG, GHA, GNB, KEN, LSO, MDG, MLI, MRT, MWI, NER, RWA, SDN, SLE, SWZ, TCD, TGO, UGA, ZMB, and ZWE and Panel D presents numbers in ZAF

Panel C: Sub-Saharan Africa (excluding South Africa)

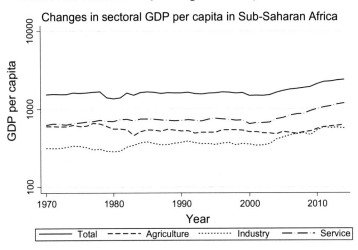

Panel D: South Africa

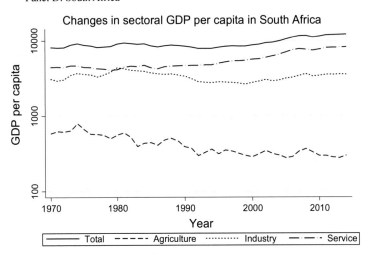

Fig. 9.1 (continued)

Although we limit our analyses to the 26 countries, the average level of GDP per capita is similar in Panel C and Fig. 9.2, which includes all the 45 sub-Saharan African countries for which GDP data is available, at around 2,000–3,000 USD, and thus, these 26 countries give a representative picture of the entire sub-Saharan African region.

Figure 9.1 corresponds to the second expression in Eq. (9.1), and presents a sharp contrast in the economic development of Asian and African economies. Panels A and C illustrate that the GDP per capita was at a similar level in 1970 in Asia and Africa. In

1970, for instance, Korea's GDP per capita was 2,088 USD, which was comparable to that of Congo (2,281 USD) or that of Tanzania (1,750 USD), and was much lower than that of Ghana (2,843 USD). The two regions' economies have diverged, and the stagnation of African economies in the 1970s and 1980s, as discussed by Easterly and Levine (1997) among others, is evident in Panel C. The increase in Asia's GDP per capita seems to be a result of the increase in industrial GDP per capita and service GDP per capita, whereas the industrial GDP remained stagnant in Africa.

Using the same data as Fig. 9.1, Table 9.1 presents sectoral GDP per capita and the contribution of each sector in selected years. There are three major points to note. First, the agricultural GDP per capita is almost constant in the last four decades, particularly in Africa. As Gollin et al. (2014) find, the increase in agricultural productivity is cancelled out by the decrease in the labor share in agriculture, and thus, the agricultural GDP per capita did not increase despite the productivity improvement. This supports our argument in the previous section that economic growth cannot be achieved only by developing the agricultural sector.

Secondly, similar to the agricultural sector, the industrial GDP per capita has been stagnant at a low level over the past four decades in Africa. This suggests that neither the ISI policies adopted in the post-independent era of the 1960s and 1970s nor the SAP policies in the 1980s and 1990s helped industrialization in Africa. The SAP comprised market-oriented policies without governmental intervention, which can be considered an absence of industrial policy. The absence of industrial policy and subsequent failure in industrialization in Africa in the 1980s and 1990s is reminiscent of India's experiences as discussed by Nomura (2018) in this volume. Using data from Nigeria, Austin (2014) argues that the failure, as well as the absence, of industrial policies resulted in the failure of labor-intensive industrialization despite its potential for offering ample employment opportunities.[6]

In contrast, Asian economies experienced a rapid increase in industrial GDP per capita, which led to Asian economic growth. Otsuka et al. (2017a) discuss that industrial development played a critical role in Asian economies by increasing income without expanding inequality because labor-intensive industrial sectors created ample job opportunities. Similarly, Tanimoto (2018) and Kubo (2018) in this volume illustrate that labor-intensive industrialization took place in the early stage of economic development, which was followed by the development of capital-intensive industries in Japan and China, respectively. Stiglitz and Uy (1996) and Wade (1990) argue that such economic "miracle" of Asia, led by Japan and followed by Asian Tigers (Hong Kong, South Korea, Singapore, and Taiwan), was a consequence of industrial policies not in the form of ISI policies that ignored the comparative advantage but in the form of export-oriented policies that was friendly with markets and took advantage of the comparative advantage.

---

[6]We admit that there are other factors, other than industrial policy, that hampered African industrialization. For instance, Frazer (2008) empirically finds that influx of used-clothing donation, which ended up being sold in Africa, had large negative impacts on apparel production. Discussing all possible factors that affected a specific industry is beyond the scope of this chapter, and we focus our discussion on industrial policy.

Table 9.1 GDP per capita and contribution of each sector in the selected years

Panel A: Asia

	1970	1975	1980	1985	1990	1995	2000	2005	2010
Agriculture (%)	525 (27)	531 (24)	492 (19)	528 (19)	556 (16)	597 (14)	550 (12)	619 (10)	848 (10)
Industry (%)	673 (34)	798 (36)	979 (38)	1,027 (37)	1,266 (37)	1,651 (37)	1,727 (37)	2,285 (38)	3,069 (38)
Service (%)	766 (39)	909 (41)	1,086 (42)	1,233 (44)	1,623 (47)	2,160 (49)	2,430 (52)	3,134 (52)	4,243 (52)
Total	1,963	2,238	2,557	2,788	3,445	4,409	4,707	6,038	8,160

Panel B: Sub-Saharan Africa

	1970	1975	1980	1985	1990	1995	2000	2005	2010
Agriculture (%)	599 (23)	611 (22)	558 (22)	525 (19)	505 (19)	476 (19)	478 (19)	483 (17)	528 (16)
Industry (%)	767 (29)	856 (31)	928 (36)	894 (33)	817 (31)	714 (28)	692 (28)	795 (28)	892 (28)
Service (%)	1,243 (48)	1,274 (46)	1,232 (48)	1,305 (48)	1,298 (50)	1,378 (54)	1,342 (54)	1,598 (56)	1,821 (56)
Total	2,609	2,741	2,569	2,724	2,620	2,568	2,494	2,876	3,240

Source Penn World Table, World Development Indicators

Note GDP per capita is in USD (in PPP-adjusted 2011 constant price). Panel A presents weighted averages (weight by population) of BGD, CHN, IDN, IND, JPN, KOR, LKA, MYS, NPL, PAK, PHL, and THA and Panel B presents weighted averages of BDI, BEN, BFA, CAF, CIV, CMR, COG, GHA, GNB, KEN, LSO, MDG, MLI, MRT, MWI, NER, RWA, SDN, SLE, SWZ, TCD, TGO, UGA, ZAF, ZMB, and ZWE

Third, the service GDP per capita increased both in Asia and Africa. In particular, the modest growth of GDP per capita after 2000 in Africa has been led by service sector growth. The GDP per capita increased from 2,494 USD in 2000 to 3,240 USD in 2010, and most of the increase can be attributed to the service sector growth. This phenomenon is known as premature deindustrialization (Haraguchi et al. 2017; Rodrik 2016) and premature shift to service industries (Page 2012). In Asia, Philippines and India are examples of economic growth driven by service sector growth, and a similar pattern is observed in Rwanda and Senegal. The labor absorption capacity, however, is limited in the service sector, particularly in modern service sectors like finance and ICT without backward and forward linkages in industries. These countries experience widening inequality within each country, and thus, this pattern of economic development seems to be unsustainable.

9.3.2 Sectoral Employment

Next, we show the sectoral share of employment in Table 9.2. As the data availability is severely limited, we replace a missing observation with the nearest observation of the same country within the four-year interval.[7] We must note, however, that the number of observations is still small, particularly in the early period in our analyses. Our data shows that the agricultural share of employment has continuously decreased both in Asia and Africa, whereas the service sector share has continuously increased.

Admitting that sample countries do not overlap, Tables 9.1 and 9.2 suggest that industrial productivity has increased in Asia, but decreased in Africa, where the increase in employment share exceeds the increase in industrial GDP per capita. This stands in contrast to Duarte and Restuccia (2010) and Rodrik (2013), who find that manufacturing labor productivity unconditionally converges all over the world. Such exceptional absence of industrial productivity growth in Africa illustrates the failure of industrial development. At the same time, however, the low industrial productivity and global convergence suggests that there is potential room for increasing industrial labor productivity through industrial policies.

9.3.3 Finer Sectoral Classification

In order to analyze the contribution of specific industries to economic growth, we alternatively denote k in Eq. (9.1) as narrowly defined industries, such as mining, manufacturing, trade, and finance, rather than the broadly defined industrial sector vis-à-vis agriculture and service sectors. We use data taken from the Groningen Growth and Development Centre (GGDC) 10-Sector Database (Timmer et al. 2014), which categorizes economic activities into ten groups, which are comparable across

---

[7] For instance, the employment share data of Burkina Faso is replaced with its 1994 value for years 1990 and 1995, but the observations are missing for 1985 and earlier (see columns toward right in Table 9.5 in Appendix).

Table 9.2 Sectoral share of labor in selected years

Panel A: Asia

	1980	1985	1990	1995	2000	2005	2010
Agriculture (%)	38	38	41	44	39	32	33
Industry (%)	24	23	22	19	19	21	21
Service (%)	37	37	35	35	40	46	45
N	11	12	14	17	16	16	17

Panel B: Sub-Saharan Africa

	1985	1990	1995	2000	2005	2010
Agriculture (%)	84	75	68	62	57	53
Industry (%)	5	6	7	9	11	13
Service (%)	10	15	20	27	29	34
N	2	6	7	13	17	14

Panel C: Sub-Saharan Africa (including all countries)

	1980	1985	1990	1995	2000	2005	2010
Agriculture (%)	55	67	60	56	53	54	45
Industry (%)	11	8	10	11	12	11	14
Service (%)	32	24	27	30	34	32	40
N	3	6	16	17	22	28	26

Source Penn World Table, World Development Indicators
Note Simple averages in Asia and Sub-Africa are presented. Asia includes BGD, CHN, HKG, IDN, IND, JPN, KHM, KOR, LKA, MYS, NPL, PAK, PHL, SGP, THA, and VNM and selected Africa includes BDI, BEN, BFA, CAF, CIV, CMR, COG, GNB, KEN, LSO, MDG, MLI, MRT, MWI, NER, RWA, SDN, SLE, SWZ, TCD, TGO, UGA, ZAF, ZMB, and ZWE

countries and over time. Although the GGDC data has advantages over comparable and finer classifications of industries, the data coverage is limited. The sample Asian countries include China, Hong Kong, Indonesia, India, Japan, South Korea, Malaysia, Philippines, Singapore, and Thailand (nine of the original 16 sample countries) and the sample African countries include Botswana, Ethiopia, Ghana, Kenya, Mauritius, Malawi, Nigeria, Senegal, Tanzania, South Africa, and Zambia (11 of the original 45 sample countries).

Table 9.3 shows the sectoral contribution to GDP per capita and employment. The agricultural share of GDP per capita has decreased, and the share of the service sector has increased, particularly the finance sector both in Asia and Africa. In the previous sub-sections, the industrial sector included both mining and manufacturing sectors. The share of mining sector is larger in Africa than in Asia, particularly because the African sample countries incudes Botswana and Nigeria, resource-rich countries with relatively high per capita GDP in Sub-Saharan Africa. The employment share of mining, however, is small because the sector is intensive in capital-use and the employment creation is limited.

The manufacturing sector, which is represented by labor-intensive industries and absorbs large amounts of labor, presents clear contrast in the two regions. The manufacturing share of value added in Asia was already much higher than in Africa at 18.9% in 1970, and further increased to 23.3% in 2010 so that almost a quarter of Asian value-added is from the manufacturing sector today whereas the share in Africa has been stagnant at around 10%. Moreover, the value-added share of the manufacturing sector has increased more than the employment share in Asia, indicating that the labor productivity in the manufacturing sector has increased. Therefore, the manufacturing sector creates numerous high value-adding jobs, and contributes to Asian economic growth.

9.3.4 Decomposition Analysis

Table 9.4 shows the results of decomposition analyses based on Eq. (9.2). Row (A) corresponds to the first term on the right-hand side, and represents within-industry labor productivity growth. Both in Asia and Africa, this accounts for a large proportion of labor productivity growth. Row (B) represents static labor reallocation, whereas row (C) represents dynamic labor allocation. In Africa, the latter is negative and large in magnitude. Africa is experiencing urbanization and expansion of urban slums, and the urban service sector, mostly in informal economy, absorbs labor from rural areas. The productivity of such sector, however, remains low. On the other hand, the reduction of surplus agricultural labor increases agricultural labor productivity. Therefore, the contribution of dynamic labor reallocation is negative because the labor shifts away from agriculture, whose productivity increases, to other sectors—mostly the service sector, where the productivity does not increase.

We combine rows (B) and (C) to examine the total effect of labor reallocation. In Asia, the contribution is positive. Between both 1990–2000 and 2000–2010, labor reallocation contributes to about 1% of annual productivity growth. However, the contribution of labor reallocation is negative in Africa. In other words, the structural transformation does not account for economic development. Although the labor shifts from agricultural sector to other sectors, the productivity is low in these sectors.

Table 9.3 Sectoral GDP per capita and share of labor in selected years

Panel A: Asia

	1970	1975	1980	1985	1990	1995	2000	2005	2010
GDP per capita									
Agriculture (%)	504 (12.7)	570 (9.9)	570 (7.1)	576 (6.9)	601 (5.1)	622 (4.4)	581 (3.6)	644 (3.1)	739 (3.2)
Mining (%)	222 (5.6)	212 (3.7)	275 (3.4)	277 (3.3)	265 (2.2)	316 (2.2)	304 (1.9)	354 (1.7)	375 (1.6)
Manufacturing (%)	752 (18.9)	1,045 (18.1)	1,629 (20.3)	1,612 (19.3)	2,518 (21.3)	2,984 (21.2)	3,581 (22.2)	4,447 (21.6)	5,342 (23.3)
Public utility (%)	55 (1.4)	85 (1.5)	125 (1.6)	155 (1.9)	232 (2.0)	310 (2.2)	390 (2.4)	528 (2.6)	546 (2.4)
Construction (%)	341 (8.6)	428 (7.4)	604 (7.5)	570 (6.8)	874 (7.4)	1,030 (7.3)	897 (5.6)	987 (4.8)	1,103 (4.8)
Trade (%)	734 (18.5)	1,145 (19.8)	1,710 (21.4)	1,715 (20.5)	2,595 (22.0)	3,077 (21.9)	3,514 (21.8)	4,300 (20.8)	4,640 (20.3)
Transportation (%)	219 (5.5)	449 (7.8)	593 (7.4)	638 (7.6)	964 (8.2)	1,118 (7.9)	1,406 (8.7)	2,143 (10.4)	2,199 (9.6)
Finance (%)	244 (6.1)	515 (8.9)	852 (10.6)	1,030 (12.3)	1,546 (13.1)	1,962 (13.9)	2,356 (14.6)	3,421 (16.6)	3,875 (16.9)
Government service (%)	516 (13.0)	588 (10.2)	743 (9.3)	737 (8.8)	879 (7.4)	1,057 (7.5)	1,125 (7.0)	1,323 (6.4)	1,582 (6.9)
Other (%)	387 (9.7)	746 (12.9)	905 (11.3)	1,051 (12.6)	1,335 (11.3)	1,606 (11.4)	1,943 (12.1)	2,481 (12.0)	2,511 (11.0)
Total (%)	3,974 (100)	5,784 (100)	8,006 (100)	8,361 (100)	11,809 (100)	14,080 (100)	16,097 (100)	20,627 (100)	22,912 (100)
Employment share (%)									
Agriculture	50.3	44.7	40.0	36.8	33.6	29.3	27.2	25.2	22.6
Mining	0.6	0.6	0.6	0.6	0.5	0.5	0.4	0.4	0.4
Manufacturing	13.8	17.0	17.7	17.1	17.8	16.9	15.6	14.8	13.8
Public utility	0.4	0.5	0.5	0.5	0.5	0.6	0.5	0.5	0.5
Construction	3.5	3.9	4.7	5.6	5.8	6.7	7.3	6.9	7.6
Trading	12.5	13.8	14.5	16.4	17.2	18.4	19.6	20.7	21.4
Transportation	4.5	4.3	4.7	5.0	5.5	6.1	6.4	6.7	6.8
Finance	2.3	2.9	3.3	4.0	4.7	6.2	6.8	7.7	9.0
Government service	6.1	8.2	9.3	9.3	9.1	9.0	9.4	10.1	11.0
Other	8.0	5.9	6.6	6.6	7.0	8.2	8.7	9.2	9.2

(continued)

Table 9.3 (continued)

Panel B: Sub-Saharan Africa

	1970	1975	1980	1985	1990	1995	2000	2005	2010
GDP per capita									
Agriculture (%)	590 (30.4)	607 (28.0)	533 (25.5)	585 (25.4)	460 (24.2)	433 (25.5)	447 (24.8)	519 (23.1)	618 (21.0)
Mining (%)	473 (12.1)	552 (11.3)	563 (13.0)	598 (13.9)	406 (11.9)	370 (10.6)	438 (9.8)	634 (9.5)	471 (7.3)
Manufacturing (%)	358 (11.0)	415 (12.3)	445 (12.1)	471 (12.0)	560 (12.8)	585 (12.2)	641 (11.8)	607 (11.1)	696 (10.8)
Public utility (%)	30 (1.1)	40 (1.5)	49 (1.9)	60 (2.0)	62 (2.0)	71 (2.1)	82 (2.0)	91 (2.0)	94 (1.9)
Construction (%)	187 (9.0)	207 (8.3)	175 (6.6)	147 (5.0)	179 (5.5)	173 (4.6)	197 (4.7)	223 (5.3)	330 (6.3)
Trade (%)	394 (15.1)	434 (15.2)	453 (15.6)	465 (14.5)	516 (15.6)	560 (15.6)	649 (16.2)	731 (16.5)	985 (18.0)
Transportation (%)	161 (5.8)	188 (6.5)	198 (6.4)	209 (6.6)	235 (6.8)	276 (7.0)	346 (7.5)	420 (8.8)	579 (10.6)
Finance (%)	84 (2.5)	117 (3.5)	129 (4.0)	153 (4.4)	208 (5.3)	268 (6.6)	383 (7.5)	469 (8.1)	586 (8.5)
Government service (%)	301 (10.2)	340 (10.7)	423 (12.8)	471 (13.7)	498 (12.9)	533 (12.7)	570 (12.0)	635 (12.0)	710 (11.9)
Other (%)	74 (2.7)	82 (2.7)	77 (2.2)	87 (2.4)	115 (2.9)	142 (3.2)	165 (3.3)	203 (3.5)	260 (3.7)
Total (%)	2,652 (100)	2,982 (100)	3,045 (100)	3,246 (100)	3,239 (100)	3,411 (100)	3,918 (100)	4,532 (100)	5,329 (100)
Employment share (%)									
Agriculture	69.3	65.7	63.1	62.1	59.6	59.0	56.6	53.4	49.7
Mining	1.5	1.5	1.8	1.6	1.5	1.3	1.0	0.9	0.9
Manufacturing	5.8	6.9	7.2	7.4	8.3	7.9	8.3	8.1	8.4
Public utility	0.4	0.5	0.6	0.6	0.5	0.5	0.4	0.4	0.4

(continued)

Table 9.3 (continued)

Panel B: Sub-Saharan Africa

	1970	1975	1980	1985	1990	1995	2000	2005	2010
Construction	2.6	3.3	3.2	2.6	3.4	3.2	3.4	3.5	3.7
Trading	6.8	7.4	8.4	9.4	10.7	11.6	12.7	14.7	16.6
Transportation	2.1	2.5	2.4	2.5	2.5	2.5	2.6	2.9	3.3
Finance	0.7	0.8	1.0	1.2	1.5	1.8	2.1	2.6	3.4
Government service	4.9	5.4	6.2	6.7	6.8	7.3	8.1	8.6	8.9
Other	6.3	6.5	6.8	6.6	5.8	5.6	5.7	5.5	5.4

Source Penn World Table, GDCC

Note GDP per capita is presented in USD, presented in PPP-adjusted 2011 constant price and simple averages in Asia and Sub-Saharan Africa are presented. Asia includes CHN, HKG, IDN, IND, JPN, KOR, MYS, PHL, SGP, and THA and Sub-Saharan Africa includes BWA, ETH, GHA, KEN, MUS, MWI, NGA, SEN, TZA, ZAF, and ZMB

9.4 What Is Missing?

The comparison of macroeconomic data of Asia and Africa shows a sharp contrast between the two regions' economies. Admitting that there are various differences in the two regions, in terms of population (Asia with 4 billion and Africa with 1 billion) and land size (Asian countries spread over a vast area, and African countries, many of them landlocked, are concentrated in relatively small areas), Asia successfully achieved economic growth led by industrialization, and Africa's economies have long been stagnant. Although African economies have recently achieved modest growth because of the expansion of the service sector and improved agricultural productivity (mostly because of the declining share of agricultural employment), this is not a sustainable way of economic growth. The land endowment is limited, and subsequently, labor absorption capacity is limited in the agricultural sector, and the modern service sector also has limited capacity for labor absorption. If only the modern service sector grows and creates high-income jobs for a handful of educated and highly skilled workers, the problem of inequality will be a social concern. Therefore,

Table 9.4 Decomposition of GDP per capita growth

Panel A: Asia (excluding Japan)

	1990–2010	2000–2010
Annual GDP per capita growth (%)	4.0	5.2
(A) Within sector labor productivity growth	3.1	4.3
(B) Static labor reallocation	0.8	0.9
(C) Dynamic labor reallocation	0.2	−0.0
N	12	16

Panel B: Sub-Saharan Africa

	1990–2010	2000–2010
Annual GDP per capita growth (%)	1.5	3.0
(A) Within sector labor productivity growth	1.7	3.8
(B) Static labor reallocation	1.3	0.9
(C) Dynamic labor reallocation	−1.5	−1.6
N	9	16

Source Authors' calculation using Penn World Table and WDI

Note Asia includes BGD, CHN, HKG, IDN, IND, JPN, KHM, KOR, LKA, MYS, NPL, PAK, PHL, SGP, THA, and VNM and Sub-Saharan Africa includes BDI, BEN, BFA, CAF, CIV, CMR, COG, GHA, GNB, KEN, LSO, MDG, MLI, MRT, MWI, NER, RWA, SDN, SLE, SWZ, TCD, TGO, UGA, ZAF, ZMB, and ZWE development of the labor-intensive sector is important for sustainable and equitable development.

Recent empirical studies find that firms' managerial capital is missing in the developing countries, particularly in Africa (e.g., Bloom et al. 2012). Although firms are the drivers of industrial development, firm owners and managers have limited capacity to manage their firms and workers, and consequently, their business is unstable and short-lived. A number of recent studies, however, find that such managerial capacity can be taught by training, consultation, or coaching (e.g., Higuchi et al. 2015; McKenzie and Woodruff 2014; Shimada and Sonobe 2017). Hence, the capacity building of firms is an important policy tool for promoting industrialization.

Otsuka et al. (2017b) further advance the discussion, and propose the training-infrastructure-finance (TIF) strategy as a plausible set of policies for stimulating economic growth in Africa.[8] Unlike failed industrial policies in the past that ignored the comparative advantage, the TIF strategy aims to upgrade the existing industries, rather than developing new industries. Sonobe and Otsuka (2011) find that there are numerous industrial clusters of labor-intensive industries, such as apparel, shoemaking, food processing, and metalworking, which were spontaneously formed in the developing world. These industries survive in markets because they take advantage of abundant labor, but their products are usually of low-quality because of the limited capacity of firms in developing countries, particularly in Africa. Therefore, the TIF strategy aims to support and upgrade these existing industries.

The essence of the TIF strategy is to provide training, infrastructure, and finance as a strategic sequence. The first of the sequence is to provide training to invest in human capital in general and managerial human capital of firm owners and managers in particular, and then, to invest in infrastructure, particularly the establishment of industrial parks or zones, and lastly, to provide financial support for competent entrepreneurs.[9] This strategy begins with identifying potential entrepreneurs and nurturing their managerial capital, which eventually increases L_{ind}/L. Together with the investment in human capital, investment in infrastructure helps increase productivity, Y_{ind}/L_{ind}. The establishment of industrial parks, in particular, helps increase industrial productivity by taking advantage of agglomeration economies, such as knowledge spillover, input-output linkages, and skilled-labor market formation. This, in turn, further increases L_{ind}/L by creating not only entrepreneurial jobs, but also hired employment. The financial support further helps to create hired employment and improve productivity by supporting promising enterprises.

---

[8]Similar industrial policies are recommended by Shimada et al. (2013) and Dinh et al. (2012), although the importance of sequence is not emphasized. Otsuka et al. (2017b) emphasizes the importance of sequence in providing training, infrastructure, and finance as a strategic set of policy instruments.

[9]Hashino and Otsuka (2016) find from the Japanese history that governmental support for industrial clusters was an effective policy to enhance productivity.

9.5 Conclusion

This chapter compares the performance of Asian and African economies in the past half century. Starting with almost similar levels of GDP per capita at around 2,000 USD in 1970, the Asian economies experienced rapid economic growth and GDP per capita increased almost to 10,000 USD in 2015. On the other hand, the African economies had long been stagnant, and GDP per capita in 2015 was about 3,500 USD. We argue that Asia's economic success can, at least partially, be attributed to the industrial development, which increased the industrial productivity and the share of employment in the industrial sector.

Africa largely lacks industrial productivity growth and structural shift to the industrial sector. Now that Asian countries are losing comparative advantage in labor-intensive industries because of the increasing wage rates, Africa has a chance for industrialization. In particular, China, which used to be the world's factory, is shifting away from labor-intensive industries. Hence, decent industrial policies, including the TIF strategy, are expected to stimulate African industrial development so that Africa can be a next production base of labor-intensive products.

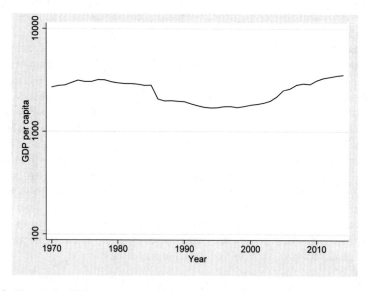

Fig. 9.2 Changes in GDP per capita in all Sub-Saharan African countries. *Source* Penn World Table, World Development Indicators. GDP per capita is in USD (in PPP-adjusted 2011 constant price) and is presented in log scale. All Sub-Saharan countries, whose GDP data is available are included

Appendix

See Fig. 9.2 and Table 9.5.

Table 9.5 Data availability

Code	Country	PWT	Value added share (WDI)	Employment share (WDI)
Asian countries in sample				
BGD	Bangladesh	1959–2014	1960–2015	1980, 84–86, 89–91, 95–96, 2000, 02–03, 05, 10
CHN	China*	1952–2014	1960–2015	1985, 87–2011
HKG	Hong Kong*	1960–2014	2000–2014	1980–2008, 10
IDN	Indonesia*	1960–2014	1960–2015	1980, 82, 85–2014
IND	India*	1950–2014	1960–2014	1990, 94–95, 2000, 05, 10, 12–13
JPN	Japan*	1950–2014	1970–2014	1980–2010, 12–13
KHM	Cambodia	1970–2014	1993–2015	1995, 98, 2000–01, 04–05, 08, 10
KOR	South Korea*	1953–2014	1965–2015	1980–2013
LAO	Laos	1970–2014	1989–2015	1995–2010
LKA	Sri Lanka	1950–2014	1960–2015	1980–81, 85, 90–98, 2000, 02–14
MYS	Malaysia*	1955–2014	1960–2015	1980–93, 95–2014
NPL	Nepal	1960–2014	1965–2015	1990–91, 95, 99–2001, 05, 08, 10, 13
PAK	Pakistan	1950–2014	1960–2015	1980–2011, 13–14
PHL	Philippines*	1950–2014	1960–2015	1980–2014
SGP	Singapore*	1960–2014	1975–2014	1980–2006, 10
THA	Thailand*	1950–2014	1960–2014	1980–2013
VNM	Vietnam	1970–2014	1985–2015	1995–2006, 10, 12–13
Sub-Saharan African countries in sample				
AGO	Angora	1970–2014	1985–2001	1992

(continued)

Table 9.5 (continued)

Code	Country	PWT	Value added share (WDI)	Employment share (WDI)
BDI	Burundi	1960–2014	1970–2015	1998
BEN	Benin	1959–2014	1960–2015	2003, 10
BFA	Burkina Faso	1959–2014	1960–2015	1994, 2003, 05–07
BWA	Botswana*	1960–2014	1960–66, 1975–2015	1985, 96, 98, 2000–01, 03, 06, 10
CAF	Central African Republic	1960–2014	1965–2015	N.A.
CIV	Côte d'Ivoire	1960–2014	1960–2015	N.A.
CMR	Cameroon	1960–2014	1965–2015	1986, 2001
COD	D.R. of the Congo	1950–2014	1991–2015	N.A.
COG	Congo	1960–2014	1960–2015	2005
COM	Comoros	1960–2014	1980–2014	N.A.
CPV	Cabo Verde	1960–2014	1980–2015	N.A.
ETH	Ethiopia*	1950–2014	1981–2015	1994, 2004–06, 2011–13
GAB	Gabon	1960–2014	2001–2015	1993, 2005
GHA	Ghana*	1955–2014	1960–2015	1992, 99, 2006, 10, 13
GIN	Guinea	1959–2014	1986–2015	1994, 2009–12
GMB	Gambia	1960–2014	2004–2014	1993, 2014
GNB	Guinea-Bissau	1960–2014	1970–2014	N.A.
GNQ	Equatorial Guinea	1960–2014	N.A.	1983
KEN	Kenya*	1950–2014	1960–2015	2005
LBR	Liberia	1964–2014	N.A.	2007, 10
LSO	Lesotho	1960–2014	1960–2014	1996–97, 99, 2008
MDG	Madagascar	1960–2014	1966–2015	2003, 05, 12
MLI	Mali	1960–2014	1967–2015	2004, 06
MOZ	Mozambique	1960–2014	1980–2015	2003
MRT	Mauritania	1960–2014	1960–2014	N.A.
MUS	Mauritius*	1950–2014	1976–2015	1990, 92, 94–2007, 2011–14

(continued)

Table 9.5 (continued)

Code	Country	PWT	Value added share (WDI)	Employment share (WDI)
MWI	Malawi*	1954–2014	1960–2015	2013
NAM	Namibia	1960–2014	1980–2015	1991, 97, 2000, 04, 08, 10–13
NER	Niger	1960–2014	1960–2015	2005
NGA	Nigeria*	1950–2014	1981–2015	1983, 86, 2004, 07
RWA	Rwanda	1960–2014	1965–2015	1989, 2005, 12
SDN	Sudan (former)	1970–2014	1960–2015	2011
SEN	Senegal*	1960–2014	1980–2015	2001, 06, 11
SLE	Sierra Leone	1961–2014	1964–2015	2003, 04
STP	Sao Tome and principe	1970–2014	2001–2014	1980–84, 91, 2000, 12
SWZ	Swaziland	1970–2014	1960–2015	N.A.
SYC	Seychelles	1960–2014	1976–2014	2011
TCD	Chad	1960–2014	1960–2015	1993
TGO	Togo	1960–2014	1960–2015	2006
TZA	U.R. of Tanzania*	1960–2014	1990–2015	1991, 2001, 02, 06, 07, 14
UGA	Uganda	1950–2014	1960–2015	2002, 03, 05, 09, 13
ZAF	South Africa*	1950–2014	1960–2015	2000–14
ZMB	Zambia*	1955–2014	1965–2015	1990, 98, 2000, 05, 08, 12
ZWE	Zimbabwe	1954–2014	1965–2015	1999, 2004, 11
North African countries excluded from sample				
DZA	Algeria	1960–2014	1965–2015	2001, 03, 04, 11
EGY	Egypt	1950–2014	1965–2015	1980–84, 1989–2013
TUN	Tunisia	1960–2014	1965–2014	1980–82, 89, 2007–14
MAR	Morocco	1950–2014	1980–2014	1990–93, 1995–2012

Note Countries indicated with * are included in GGDC data

References

Aghion, P., Cai, J., Dewatripont, M., Du, L., Harrison, A., & Legros, P. (2017). Industrial policy and competition. *American Economic Journal: Macroeconomics, 7*(4), 1–32.

Austin, G. (2014). Labour-intensity and manufacturing in West Africa, c.1450–c.2000. In G. Austin & K. Sugihara (Eds.), *Labour-intensive industrialization in global history* (pp. 201–230). New York: Routledge.

Baldwin, R. E. (1969). The case against infant industry tariff protection. *Journal of Political Economy, 77*, 295–305.

Bloom, N., Genakos, C., Sadun, R., & van Reenen, J. (2012). Management practices across firms and countries. *Academy of Management Perspective, 26*(1), 12–33.

Chang, H. J. (2007). *Bad Samaritans: The myth of free trade and the secret history of capitalism*. New York: Bloomsbury.

Criscuolo, C., Martin, R., Overman, H. G., & van Reenen, J. (2012). *The causal effects of an industrial policy*. Working paper 17842, National Bureau of Economic Research.

De Vries, G., Timmer, M., & De Vries, K. (2015). Structural transformation in Africa: Static gains, dynamic losses. *Journal of Development Studies, 51*, 674–688.

Diao, X., McMillan, M., & Rodrik, D. (2017). *The recent growth boom in developing economies: A structural change perspective*. Working paper 23132, National Bureau of Economic Research.

Dinh, H. T., Palmade, V., Chandra, V., & Cossar, F. (2012). *Light manufacturing in Africa: Targeted policies to enhance private investment and create jobs*. Washington, DC: World Bank.

Duarte, M., & Restuccia, D. (2010). The role of the structural transformation in aggregate productivity. *Quarterly Journal of Economics, 125*, 129–173.

Easterly, W., & Levine, R. (1997). Africa's growth tragedy: Policies and ethnic divisions. *Quarterly Journal of Economics, 112*, 1203–1250.

Estudillo, J. P., Cureg, E. F., & Otsuka, K. (2018). *Transformation of rural economies in Asia and Africa*. In K. Otsuka & K. Sugihara (Eds.) Paths to the Emerging State in Asia and Africa. (This Volume).

Fabricant, S. (1942). *Employment in manufacturing, 1899–1939*. National Bureau of Economic Research.

Feenstra, R. C., Inklaar, R., & Timmer, M. P. (2015). The next generation of the Penn World Table. *American Economic Review, 105*, 3082–3150.

Frazer, G. (2008). Used-clothing donations and apparel production in Africa. *Economic Journal, 118*, 1764–1784.

Gollin, D., Lagakos, D., & Waugh, M. E. (2014). The agricultural productivity gap. *Quarterly Journal of Economics, 129*, 939–993.

Goswami, A. G., Mattoo, A., & Sáez, S. (2011). *Exporting services: A developing country perspective*. Washington, DC: World Bank.

Haraguchi, N., Cheng, C. F. C., & Smeets, E. (2017). The importance of manufacturing in economic development: Has this changed? *World Development, 93*, 293–315.

Harrison, A., & Rodríguez-Clare, A. (2010). Trade, foreign investment, and industrial policy for developing countries. In D. Rodrik & M. R. Rosenzweig (Eds.), *Handbook of development economics* (Vol. 5, pp. 4039–4214). Amsterdam: Elsevier.

Hashino, T., & Otsuka, K. (2016). *Industrial districts in history and the developing world*. Singapore: Springer.

Hausmann, R., Rodrik, D., & Velasco, A. (2005). *Growth diagnosis*. Cambridge: Harvard University.

Herrendorf, B., Rogerson, R., & Valentinyi, A. (2014). Growth and structural transformation. In P. Aghion & S. N. Durlauf (Eds.), *Handbook of economic growth, Volume 2B*. Amsterdam: Elsevier.

Higuchi, Y., Nam, V. H., & Sonobe, T. (2015). Sustained impacts of kaizen training. *Journal of Economic Behavior & Organization, 120*, 189–206.

Hino, H., & Ranis, G. (2013). *Youth and employment in Sub-Saharan Africa: Working but poor*. Washington, DC: World Bank.

Hirschman, A. O. (1958). *The strategy of economic development*. New Haven: Yale University Press.
Hsieh, C. T., & Klenow, P. J. (2009). Misallocation and manufacturing TFP in China and India. *Quarterly Journal of Economics, 124*, 1403–1448.
Jensen, J. B. (2011). *Global trade in services*. Washington, DC: Peter G. Peterson Institute International Economics.
Krueger, A. O., & Tuncer, B. (1982). An empirical test of the infant industry argument. *American Economic Review, 72*, 1142–1152.
Kubo, T. (2018). *Changing patterns of industrialization and emerging states in twentieth century China*. In K. Otsuka & K. Sugihara (Eds.) Paths to the Emerging State in Asia and Africa. (This Volume).
Lal, D. (1983). *The poverty of development economics*. London: Institute of Economics Affairs.
Lane, N. (2017). Manufacturing revolutions: Industrial policy and networks in South Korea. Job Market Paper.
Lin, J. (2012). *New structural economics: A framework for rethinking development and policy*. Washington, DC: World Bank.
McKenzie, D., & Woodruff, C. (2014). What are we learning from business training and entrepreneurship evaluations around the developing world? *World Bank Research Observer, 29*(1), 48–82.
McMillan, M., Rodrik, D., & Verduzco-Gallo, I. (2014). Globalization, structural change, and productivity growth. *World Development, 63*, 11–32.
Mosley, P., Harrigan, J., & Toye, J. (1995). *Aid and power: The World Bank and policy-based lending, Volume 1: Analysis and policy proposals*. New York: Routledge.
Newman, C., Page, J., Rand, J., Shimeles, A., Söderbom, M., & Tarp, F. (2016). *Made in Africa: Learning to compete in industry*. Washington, DC: Brookings Institution Press.
Noman, A., & Stiglitz, J. E. (2015). *Industrial policy and economic transformation in Africa*. New York: Columbia University Press.
Noman, A., & Stiglitz, J. E. (2016). *Efficiency, finance, and varieties of industrial policy: Guiding resources, learning, and technology for sustained growth*. New York: Columbia University Press.
Nomura, C. (2018). *Historical roots of industrialisation and the emerging state in Colonial India*. In K. Otsuka & K. Sugihara (Eds.) Paths to the Emerging State in Asia and Africa. (This volume).
Nurkse, R. (1953). *Problems of capital formation in underdeveloped countries*. Oxford: Oxford University Press.
Nunn, N., & Trefler, D. (2010). The structure of tariffs and long-term growth. *American Economic Journal: Macroeconomics, 2*(4), 158–194.
Oqubay, A. (2015). *Made in Africa: Industrial policy in Ethiopia*. Oxford: Oxford University Press.
Overseas Economic Cooperation Fund (OECF, now JICA). (1993). Issues related to The World Bank's approach to structural adjustment: Proposals from a major partner. Occasional Paper No. 1, OECF.
Otsuka, K., Higuchi, Y., & Sonobe, T. (2017a). Middle-income traps in East Asia: An inquiry into causes for slowdown in income growth. *China Economic Review, 46*, s3–1s16.
Otsuka, K., Mieno, F., Sonobe, T., Kurosaki, T., Shimada, G., Kitano, N., et al. (2017b). *Training-infrastructure-finance (TIF) strategy for industrial development in Sub-Saharan Africa*. Tokyo, Japan: International Cooperation Agency (JICA) Research Institute.
Page, J. (2012). Can Africa industrialise? *Journal of African Economies, 21*, 86–124.
Reinert, E. S. (2007). *How rich countries got rich and why poor countries stay poor*. London: Constable.
Rodrik, D. (2010). The return of industrial policy. Project Syndicate, 12.
Rodrik, D. (2013). Unconditional convergence in manufacturing. *Quarterly Journal of Economics, 128*, 165–204.
Rodrik, D. (2016). Premature deindustrialization. *Journal of Economic Growth, 21*, 1–33.
Rosenstein-Rodan, P. N. (1943). Problems of industrialisation of Eastern and South-Eastern Europe. *Economic Journal, 53*, 202–211.

Shimada, G., Homma, T., & Murakami, H. (2013). Industrial development of Africa. In Japan International Cooperation Agency (Ed.), *For inclusive and dynamic development in Sub-Saharan Africa*. Tokyo: JICA Research Institute.

Shimada, G., & Sonobe, T. (2017). *Impacts of Kaizen management on workers: Evidence from the Central America and Caribbean Region*. Working Paper. Tokyo: JICA Research Institute.

Sonobe, T., & Otsuka, K. (2011). *Cluster-based industrial development: A comparative study of Asia and Africa*. New York: Palgrave Macmillan.

Stiglitz, J. E., Lin, J. Y., & Patel, E. (2013). *The industrial policy revolution II: Africa in the twenty-first century*. New York: Palgrave Macmillan.

Stiglitz, J. E., & Uy, M. (1996). Financial markets, public policy and the East Asian miracle. *World Bank Research Observer, 11*, 249–276.

Tanimoto, M. (2018). *Labour-intensive industrialization and the emerging state in pre-war Japan.* In K. Otsuka & K. Sugihara (Eds.) Paths to the Emerging State in Asia and Africa. (This Volume).

Timmer, M. P., De Vries, G. J., & De Vries, K. (2014). *Patterns of structural change in developing countries*. GGDC Research Memorandum 149.

Wade, R. (1990). *Governing the market: Economic theory and the role of government in East Asian industrialization*. Princeton: Princeton University Press.

Wade, R. (1996). Japan, The World Bank, and the art of paradigm maintenance: The East Asian miracle in political perspective. *New Left Review* (May–June).

World Bank. (2012). *World development report 2013: Jobs*. Washington, DC: World Bank.

Open Access This chapter is licensed under the terms of the Creative Commons Attribution-NonCommercial-NoDerivatives 4.0 International License (http://creativecommons.org/licenses/by-nc-nd/4.0/), which permits any noncommercial use, sharing, distribution and reproduction in any medium or format, as long as you give appropriate credit to the original author(s) and the source, provide a link to the Creative Commons licence and indicate if you modified the licensed material. You do not have permission under this licence to share adapted material derived from this chapter or parts of it.

The images or other third party material in this chapter are included in the chapter's Creative Commons licence, unless indicated otherwise in a credit line to the material. If material is not included in the chapter's Creative Commons licence and your intended use is not permitted by statutory regulation or exceeds the permitted use, you will need to obtain permission directly from the copyright holder.

Chapter 10
Transformation of Rural Economies in Asia and Africa

Jonna P. Estudillo, Elyzabeth F. Cureg and Keijiro Otsuka

10.1 Introduction

Economic transformation, rapid growth, and improvements in living standards are central features of emerging economies, which are characterized by a shift away from heavy reliance on agriculture and raw materials exports towards an emphasis on the manufacturing and service sectors. Escaping from low incomes and poverty is the main motivation driving emerging states to venture into rapid industrialization and service sector development as a strategy to achieve rapid aggregate income growth.

Emerging economies are undergoing the so-called "economic transformation," which is defined broadly as a process in which the foci of economic activities shift away from the farm and toward the manufacturing and service sectors. Economic transformation is always accompanied by aggregate economic growth, which serves as the main driver of household income growth and poverty reduction (Dollar and Kraay 2002; Zhuang and Ali 2010). Rapid economic growth is the main reason why Asia was able to reduce its proportion of poor people to less than one-half much earlier than in other regions of the world, in line with the Millennium Development Goals (United Nations 2015).

J. P. Estudillo (✉)
National Graduate Institute for Policy Studies, 7-22-1 Roppongi, Minato-ku,
Tokyo 106-8677, Japan
e-mail: jonna@grips.ac.jp

E. F. Cureg
Center for Local and Regional Governance (CLRG-NCPAG),
University of the Philippines, Diliman, Quezon City 1101, Philippines
e-mail: ely_cureg@yahoo.com

K. Otsuka
Graduate School of Economics, Kobe University, 2-1 Rokkodai, Nada, Kobe,
Hyogo 657-8501, Japan
e-mail: otsuka@econ.kobe-u.ac.jp

© The Author(s) 2019
K. Otsuka and K. Sugihara (eds.), *Paths to the Emerging State in Asia and Africa*,
Emerging-Economy State and International Policy Studies,
https://doi.org/10.1007/978-981-13-3131-2_10

This chapter explores the causes and consequences of the long-term process of economic transformation that triggered the evolution of emerging economies in Asia. This chapter also assesses to what extent the Asian experience is being replicated in Africa. By "evolution," we mean sustained household income growth and poverty reduction. We explore the role of three drivers—population pressure, the development of modern agricultural technology, and human capital formation—in the process of economic transformation.[1] Our hypothesis is that, while human capital is a fundamental determinant of economic growth (Otsuka et al. 2017), population pressure on limited cultivable land is a major factor in the deteriorating economic wellbeing of rural populations in the early stage of economic development, which can be overcome through the development of land-saving and labor-using modern agricultural technology (Hayami and Ruttan 1985; Otsuka and Runge 2011).

We examine the Philippines, Vietnam, Myanmar, the Lao People's Democratic Republic (Lao PDR), Bangladesh, and Sri Lanka in Asia and Mozambique, Kenya, Uganda, and Ethiopia in Africa because we have a compilation of panel datasets drawn from repeated surveys of households in Asia beginning in the mid-1980s and in Africa beginning in the early 2000s. Bangladesh, the Philippines, and Vietnam are among the so-called "Next Eleven" (N-11) countries that could exert a BRIC-like impact and rival the G7 due to their large populations (Goldman Sachs 2007).[2] While it is difficult to identify emerging economies or states (Tsunekawa 2017), we consider all our focus countries in this chapter as emerging economies by virtue of their rapid income growth and population size. Finally, we present a special case study of Central Luzon in the Philippines before and after the Green Revolution for a period encompassing nearly half of a century to demonstrate that agricultural development is a necessary condition for take-off into a rapid-growth era.

The rest of this chapter has four sections. Section 10.2 describes the nature and consequences of economic transformation, while Sect. 10.3 explores the role of the three drivers of economic transformation. Section 10.4 presents a comparative case study of the transformation of rural villages in our focus countries in Asia and Africa and illustrates how households in Central Luzon have changed their sources of livelihood. Finally, Sect. 10.5 presents a summary and conclusion.

---

[1] We consider infrastructure to be another important driver. However, reliable data on infrastructure such as electricity, roads, and telephones remain scanty in our focus countries. This issue is particularly serious in the case of roads.

[2] The gross domestic product (GDP) of these three countries accounted for more than 1% of the GDP of the United States in 2015.

10.2 Economic Transformation

10.2.1 Characteristic Features

Here, we discuss the size, composition, and growth rate of gross domestic product per capita (GDPPc) and labor force composition from the 1980s onward. We chose the 1980s as our benchmark because of the emergence during that period of newly industrializing economies (NIEs) in East Asia, such as Singapore, Taiwan, Hong Kong, and South Korea, which helped trigger the evolution of today's newly emerging economies. During the 1980s, the NIEs began a major shift toward the production of more sophisticated, high-value products using capital-using methods corresponding to their sharp wage increases while shifting labor-intensive industrial sectors to Southeast Asian countries, where wages were relatively low at that time.

Emerging economies are characterized by high economic growth rates, as is evident in the five focus Asian countries. The annual growth rate of real GDPPc from 2010 to 2015 is close to 5% in the Philippines, Vietnam, and Bangladesh and greater than 5% in Sri Lanka and Lao PDR (see Table 10.1). These economies started to boom in the 1990s, and many of them peaked between 2010 and 2015. Sri Lanka and the Philippines have the highest GDPPc, although Vietnam showed the greatest increase, of more than four times between 1985 and 2015 (see Table 10.1, Cols. A, B, and C), likely due to Vietnam's *Doi Moi* (or liberalization policy) implemented in 1986. Ethiopia, Mozambique, and Uganda have GDPPc rates that are only about one-sixth that of Sri Lanka. Annual real GDPPc growth rates are high in Ethiopia (7.69% from 2010 to 2015) and Mozambique (4.02%). Sustained high economic growth appears to have started in our focus Asian countries in the 1990s and in our African countries about 10 years later, in the 2000s.

A rapid transformation away from agriculture and toward industry and services is occurring, except in Myanmar, where the agricultural share of total gross domestic product (GDP) rose (see Fig. 10.1). The GDP of the Philippines and Sri Lanka are increasingly made up of services, while manufacturing dominates in Vietnam. The agricultural share of GDP has declined furthest in Lao PDR. Similar to the situation in Asia, Africa has experienced rapid economic transformation, except in Kenya, where the GDP composition remained the same between 1985 and 2005. Agricultural GDP declined furthest in Uganda and Mozambique and declined only modestly in Ethiopia. In our focus countries in both Asia and Africa, the GDP share of the service sector is rising more than that of manufacturing.

Agriculture accounted for more than 70% of total employment in Lao PDR and close to 50% in Bangladesh in 2010 (see Table 10.2). Labor is moving out of agriculture and into the service sector in the focus Asian countries. The increasing importance of the service sector is also evident in Ethiopia, where manufacturing had a share of only about 7% of total employment in the 2000s. The agricultural labor force is expected to decline in the long run, primarily because of the low income elasticity of demand for food. To sum up, economic transformation and economic growth are faster in Asia than in Africa, though the importance of the service sector is also increasing in African countries.

Table 10.1 Growth rate of per capita gross domestic product (GDPPc) in selected countries in Asia and Africa, 1980–2015

Country	Real GDPPc (constant 2010 US$)			Average annual growth rate of real GDPPc (constant 2010 US$)			
	1985 (A)	2015 (B)	Ratio (C = B ÷ A)	1980–1989 (D)	1990–1999 (E)	2000–2009 (F)	2010–2015 (G)
Asia							
Lao PDR	436	1,538	3.52	1.22	3.74	5.18	6.14
Myanmar	na	na	na	na	na	na	na
Philippines	1,381	2,635	1.90	−0.70	0.38	2.56	4.51
Vietnam	396	1,685	4.25	2.14	5.63	5.41	4.88
Bangladesh	379	973	2.56	0.81	2.44	3.96	4.94
Sri Lanka	1,100	3,638	3.30	2.58	4.26	4.22	5.58
Africa							
Ethiopia	190	486	2.55	−0.82	−0.66	5.13	7.69
Kenya	842	1,133	1.34	0.44	−0.68	0.92	3.18
Uganda	281	673	2.39	−0.36	3.57	3.69	2.00
Mozambique	134	510	3.80	−0.60	4.36	4.64	4.02

Data source World Development Indicators database

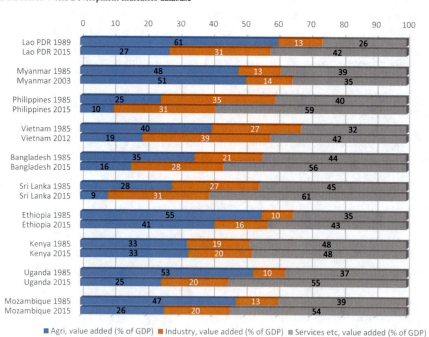

Fig. 10.1 Sectoral composition of gross domestic product in selected countries in Asia and Africa, 1985–2015. Drawn using data from World Development Indicators database

Table 10.2 Sectoral composition of total employment in selected countries in Asia and Africa, 1980–2014

Country		Percentage of total employment		
		Agriculture	Industry	Services
Asia				
Lao PDR	1995	85.40	3.50	7.90
	2010	71.30	8.30	19.50
Myanmar	1980	67.10	9.80	na
	1990	69.70	9.20	na
	1998	62.70	12.00	na
Philippines	1980	51.80	15.40	32.80
	1997	40.40	16.70	42.90
	2014	30.40	15.90	53.60
Vietnam	1996	70.00	10.60	19.40
	2004	57.90	17.40	24.80
	2013	46.80	21.20	32.00
Bangladesh	1984	58.80	11.00	24.20
	2000	62.10	10.30	23.50
	2010	47.50	17.70	35.30
Sri Lanka	1981	45.90	18.60	29.30
	2002	34.50	22.40	37.90
	2014	30.40	25.50	43.40
Africa				
Ethiopia	1994	89.30	2.30	7.60
	2005	79.30	6.60	13.00
	2013	72.70	7.40	19.90
Kenya	2005	61.10	6.70	32.20
Uganda	2002	65.50	6.50	22.10
	2009	73.80	7.10	19.10
	2013	71.90	4.40	20.20
Mozambique	2003	80.50	3.40	16.10

Data source World Development Indicators database

10.2.2 Consequences

GDPPc is greater and growing faster in emerging economies that are more diversified (e.g., Sri Lanka, Vietnam, Philippines), where the manufacturing and service sectors are more important (see Table 10.1 and Fig. 10.1). The high growth rate of GDPPc in Lao PDR is largely explained by the nation's expanding mining and quarrying sectors, whose share of GDP rose from less than 1% in 2002 to more than 6% in 2008. Poverty reduction is greater in economies with higher growth rates, indicating that economic

Table 10.3 Poverty and inequality in selected countries in Asia and Africa, 1983–2012

	Year	Headcount ratio at $1.90/day (2011 PPP)	Poverty gap at $1.90/day (2011 PPP)	Gini index of income inequality
Asia				
Lao PDR	1992	42.61	11.03	34.31
	2002	42.73	11.79	34.66
	2012	29.95	7.76	37.89
Philippines	1985	32.71	9.32	41.04
	2000	18.41	4.44	46.17
	2012	13.11	2.74	43.04
Vietnam	1992	49.21	14.95	35.65
	2002	38.78	10.37	37.32
	2012	3.23	0.58	38.7
Bangladesh	1983	69.55	22.37	25.88
	2000	59.97	18.81	33.06
	2010	43.65	11.15	31.98
Sri Lanka	1985	13.27	2.55	32.47
	1995	8.85	1.6	35.4
	2009	2.42	0.41	36.2
Africa				
Ethiopia	1981	69.26	24.32	32.42
	1995	67.9	27.07	44.56
	2010	33.54	9.04	33.17
Kenya	1992	23.08	7.93	57.46
	1997	21.5	5.59	46.3
	2005	33.6	11.7	48.51
Uganda	1989	87.95	53.13	44.36
	2002	62.21	24.47	45.17
	2012	33.24	10.13	42.37
Mozambique	1996	85.36	47.28	44.41
	2002	80.36	41.53	47.04
	2008	68.74	31.41	45.58

Data source World Development Indicators database

growth has benefited the poor. A high degree of poverty reduction occurred in focus countries in Asia and Africa (see Table 10.3). Ironically, the poverty headcount ratio (HCR) rose in Kenya by 10% from 1992 to 2005 because of the negative growth rate from 1990 to 1999 (see Tables 10.1 and 10.3). Poverty reduction was slow in Sri Lanka, which had the lowest HCR from the mid-1980s.

As is shown by the Gini index of income inequality reported in Table 10.3, the focus countries in Asia and Africa have experienced only a modest increase in income inequality, which indicates that rapid growth does not necessarily promote inequality. Kenya is unusual in that, because its poverty is increasing, its inequality is declining, and economic transformation is slow. Overall, economic transformation is inclusive of the poor in emerging economies because high economic growth rates have accompanied the expansion of employment opportunities for the poor without increasing income inequality substantially, as shown by Estudillo and Otsuka (2016).

10.3 Drivers of Economic Transformation

We explore the impacts of three drivers of economic transformation: (1) population pressure, (2) modern agricultural technology, and (3) human capital. In the course of economic transformation, these three drivers exert their impacts sequentially, from population pressure to the development of modern agriculture technology and then to investments in human capital, which, in turn, stimulates the development of nonfarm sectors.

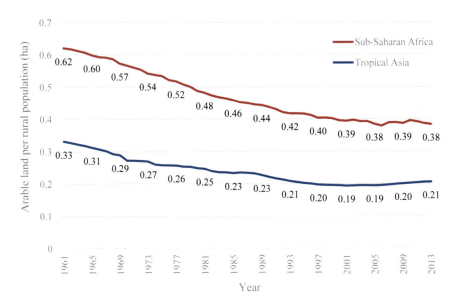

Fig. 10.2 Arable land per rural population in tropical Asia and sub-Saharan Africa, 1961–2013. Figure was drawn using data from FAOStat and World Population Prospects (United Nations, Department of Economic and Social Affairs, Population Division 2015); "Tropical Asia" refers to Southeast Asia and South Asia

10.3.1 Population Pressure

Arable land per rural population is a crude proxy for population pressure. Arable land per rural population was about 0.6 ha in sub-Saharan Africa and about 0.3 ha in tropical Asia in the early 1960s (see Fig. 10.2). This value declined by more than one-half from 1961 to 2013 because of a population explosion, which increased the scarcity of farmland. As Table 10.4 indicates, the growth rate of the rural population has been declining in tropical Asia but not in sub-Saharan Africa. In fact, rural population growth in our focus African countries was roughly double that of the growth of arable land.

According to Chamberlain et al. (2014), while sub-Saharan Africa is typically regarded as land-abundant, the region's underutilized land resources are concentrated in a small handful of countries, many of which are fragile states. The region's surplus land is currently under forest cover and the conversion of forests to cropland could entail a serious environmental cost. People, markets, and governments seem to have been responding to the rising rural population densities with agricultural intensification, diversification to nonfarm activities, rural-to-urban migration, and reduced fertility rates, which is consistent with the Boserupian thesis (Jayne et al. 2014). The low level of industrialization coupled with population pressure in rural areas across most parts of the African continent indicate an urgent need for economic growth through diversification into industries by utilizing Africa's ample endowment of unskilled labor outside agriculture (Macmillan et al. 2014).

Table 10.4 Growth rates of arable land and population in selected countries in Asia and Africa, 1961–2013

Country	Arable land (% growth per year)		Rural population (% growth per year)	
	1961–85	1986–2013	1961–85	1986–2013
Asia				
Lao PDR	1.14	2.65	1.86	0.91
Myanmar	−0.21	0.53	2.14	0.63
Philippines	0.48	−0.04	2.12	0.22
Vietnam	0.29	0.82	2.22	0.66
Bangladesh	0.28	−0.79	1.85	1.04
Sri Lanka	1.2	1.34	1.88	0.94
Africa				
Ethiopia	0.37	1.38	na	2.53[a]
Kenya	0.64	0.56	3.17	2.39
Uganda	1.29	1.38	2.84	3.11
Mozambique	1.04	2.34	1.74	2.17

Source Growth rates of arable land are authors' calculations from the FAOStat; population annual growth rates were taken from the World Development Indicator database
[a] Data from 1993

10.3.2 Modern Agricultural Technology

Hayami and Ruttan (1985) pointed out that population pressure induces not only land-saving technological innovations but also institutional innovations, which evolve because of the development of new technologies. Asia's intensification of land use started as early as the 1950s, with the closure of the land frontier and massive investment in irrigation. The Green Revolution (GR) started in 1966, when the International Rice Research Institute (IRRI) in the Philippines released IR8 (the first high-yielding variety of rice). The term "Green Revolution" is intended to express an epochal change in which "Third World agriculture was embraced in the process of modern economic growth" (Hayami and Otsuka 1994, 15). Land-saving GR technology was launched against the backdrop of a huge technology gap in agriculture between temperate and tropical countries and the fear of famine in Asia in the 1950s due to the population explosion that occurred after World War II and the region's stagnant agricultural productivity (see Chap. 2).

The four technological pillars of the GR are (1) seed-fertilizer technology, (2) irrigation systems, (3) mechanical technologies, and (4) knowledge-intensive management practices (Estudillo and Otsuka 2013). Modern rice varieties (MVs) are broadly classified into two generations: (1) first-generation MVs (MV1), which are short in stature and potentially higher yielding than traditional rice varieties (TVs); and (2) second-generation MVs (MV2), which are designed for yield stability, as they feature improved resistance to pests and diseases, better grain quality, and an early maturity period. Later MVs were designed to withstand unfavorable climatic conditions due to extreme weather events such as floods and drought. Hybrid rice and genetically modified rice are the most recent improved varieties of rice. Knowledge-intensive crop management practices, such as the timely application of fertilizer to replenish deficient nutrients, were recently introduced and have started to replace chemical inputs, thereby improving input efficiency.

In Asia, GR used to focus on irrigated rice land, as it produces 70% of the world's rice output. The GR was successful in this continent because it invested heavily in irrigation well before the advent of IR8. Fertilizer application has risen, partly because the yield of MVs is highly responsive to high fertilizer use and partly because of the use of fertilizer subsidies, which have reduced fertilizer prices in the domestic market. Yield growth has become the main source of rice production growth in Asia since the release of IR8, while the expansion of the rice-planted area has contributed modestly (see Chap. 2). The exceptions are Lao PDR and Myanmar where arable land is still expanding.

Is the Asian rice GR transferable to Africa? Irrigation investment appears to be one of the most important conditions for a successful GR. Figure 10.3 shows that tropical Asia had a large irrigated area as early as the 1960s and that its irrigated area continued to increase, while the irrigated area in sub-Saharan Africa rose only modestly. As a result, the area planted with MVs in tropical Asia rose rapidly and more visibly in the mid-1970s with the advent of IR36 (the first pest- and disease-resistant MV; see Fig. 10.4). By contrast, GR is slow to take off in sub-Saharan Africa

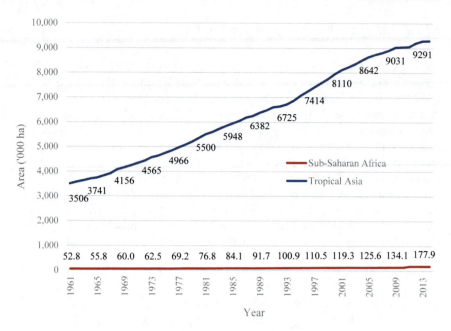

Fig. 10.3 Total area equipped for irrigation in selected countries in Asia and Africa, 1961–2013. Drawn using data from FAOStat; "Tropical Asia" refers to Southeast Asia and South Asia

because of the broader mix of crops grown in the region, agroecological complexities, and the region's heterogeneity, among other factors (World Bank 2008; Otsuka and Larson 2013, 2016).

Figure 10.5 shows the yields of major staple crops, such as rice, maize, wheat, millet, cassava, and sorghum, in tropical Asia and sub-Saharan Africa. Yields in tropical Asia are higher and continuously rising, indicating a widening technology gap between the two continents. However, tropical Asia and sub-Saharan Africa have similar yields of wheat, even as early as the 1960s. Wheat is grown in only a limited area in sub-Saharan Africa, though, as it can be grown in only a temperate zone. The yield gap is high for maize, millet, cassava, and sorghum but less high for rice, indicating that the Asian GR that occurred in rice could now be in the early stage in Africa. Otsuka and Larson (2013, 2016) point out that, unlike the technology for other crops, Asian rice technology is highly transferable to Africa, including in favorable rainfed lowland areas, which are found in moist and fertile valley bottoms.

10.3.3 Human Capital

The adoption of seed-fertilizer technology increases farm income through higher yields and increased cropping intensity, as MVs are short-matured and photo-period

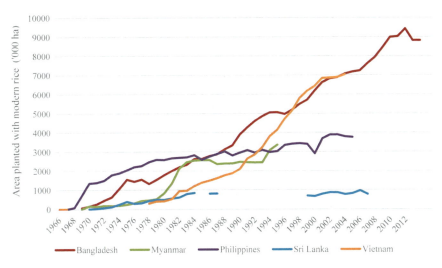

Fig. 10.4 Area planted with modern rice varieties in selected countries in Asia, 1966–2012. Drawn using data from World Rice Statistics

insensitive. Improvements in grain quality, on the other hand, contribute to higher farm income through higher market prices. Farm income and total household income rose, leading to a greater investment in human capital [in terms of education, as was pointed out by Otsuka et al. (2009)]. The discussion below compares the trends in education outcomes between Asia and Africa.[3]

Enrolment in both primary and secondary schools has risen almost everywhere in the developing world. A 100% primary school enrolment rate had been attained even before the 1970s in the Philippines, Vietnam, and Sri Lanka; this was attained in 1979 in Lao PDR and in 1992 in Myanmar (see Fig. 10.6). In Africa, a 100% primary school enrolment rate was attained in 1974 in Kenya, in 1977 in Mozambique, in 1997 in Uganda, and in 2014 in Ethiopia. All our focus countries have implemented a universal primary education policy, which means that primary education is free to all. We consider that free primary education is one of the reasons primary school enrolment rose so rapidly.

Secondary school enrolment is higher in Asia, but Africa is catching up. Among Asian nations, the Philippines and Sri Lanka had the highest rate (about 80% in the 2000s); in Africa, Kenya had the highest rate, whereas Mozambique and Uganda had the lowest (less than 40% in 2012). Nevertheless, a consistently rising trend is observed in Fig. 10.7. The high secondary school enrolment in the Philippines could be partly attributable to the Republic Act 6655 of 1988, which declared that the State shall provide for free public secondary education to all qualified citizens

---

[3] While health cannot be ignored, our discussion of investment in human capital is only on education because the literature shows a strong relationship between the advent of Green Revolution and investment in child schooling.

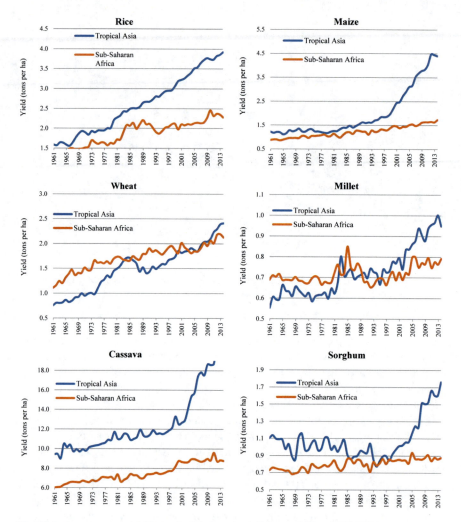

Fig. 10.5 Average crop yield in tropical Asia and sub-Saharan Africa, 1961–2014

and promote quality education at all levels. Mozambique is expected to increase its secondary school enrolment through the implementation of the first 12 years of public schooling at no cost and its recent increased investment in classroom construction and teachers. In 2007, Uganda's government established a free universal secondary education (USE) policy, the first among sub-Saharan nations.

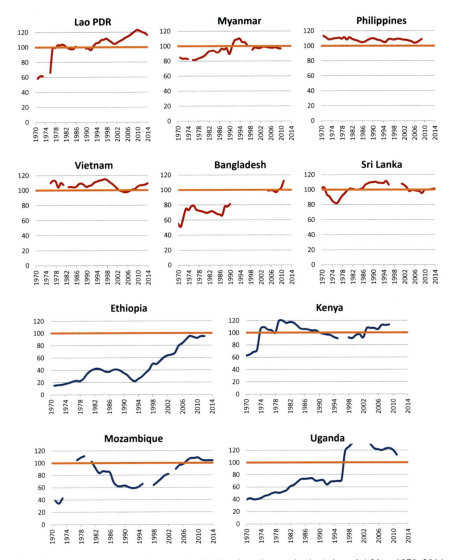

Fig. 10.6 Gross primary enrolment ratio (%) in selected countries in Asia and Africa, 1970–2014

10.3.4 "Push" and "Pull" Forces

The drivers of economic transformation can serve as either "push" or "pull" forces propelling the growth of emerging economies. The role of each driver as a propeller of growth appears to be fairly similar between Asia and sub-Saharan Africa.

Asia's high population growth on a closed land frontier, coupled with stagnant agricultural productivity in the 1960s, induced technological and institutional inno-

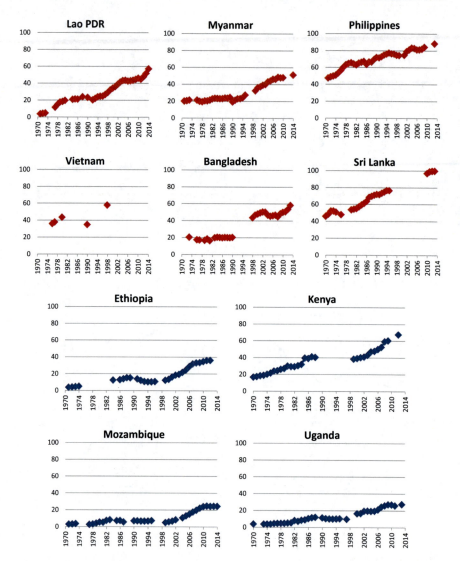

Fig. 10.7 Gross secondary enrolment ratio (%) in selected countries in Asia and Africa, 1970–2014

vation in response to changing relative factor prices (see Fig. 10.8). Since land is becoming a scarce factor in Asia, land-saving GR technology started to spread in response to the increasing price of land. Through this induced institutional innovation, institutions are changing in order to internalize the gains being made via the new technology.

The GR in rice started with the release of IR8 in 1966 and continued with the spread of newer and higher-yielding MVs in the 1970s and 1980s, which led to rapid growth in global rice production. As a consequence, rice prices

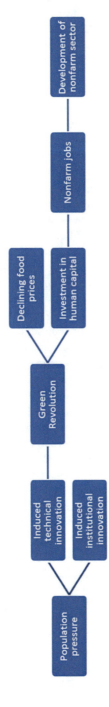

Fig. 10.8 Interrelationship between population pressure, Green Revolution, and the development of nonfarm sector

declined in the late 1970s after reaching an all-time high in the early to mid-1970s, as political conflict between the Soviet Union and the US led to chaos in the grain trade (see Fig. 2.5). Except for a one-time increase in 1980/81 (due to an oil price increase), rice prices were generally lower from 1980 to 2005 (hovering around US$400 per ton in 2010 US$) than in the 1960s and 1970s. Because of the global food crises from 2006 to 2008, rice prices increased but remained substantially lower than their 1974 peak of US$1,374. The declining rice prices from 1980 to 2005 made rice farming less lucrative. Employment opportunities in agriculture declined, as did income from rice farming.

The decline in rice prices would have served as a push factor inducing people to explore employment opportunities outside the rice industry in the nonfarm sector and to migrate to local towns and cities, or even overseas. Meanwhile, industrialization and the development of the service sector started in the mid-1970s, partly due to globalization via business process outsourcing and trade in tasks and partly due to the economic liberalization policies that began in the mid-1980s in Southeast Asian countries such as the Philippines, Lao PDR, and Vietnam. The "push" of declining rice prices and the "pull" of manufacturing and service sector development induced farm households to invest in the human capital represented by the younger generation, who prefer to work in the nonfarm sector and migrate to cities, strengthening the transformation process (Otsuka et al. 2009; Estudillo and Otsuka 2016). It thus seems reasonable to assume that population pressure and GR served as the early stimuli for the growth of emerging economies in Asia through an outmigration of the educated labor force from agriculture to nonfarm sectors (see Fig. 10.8).

Compared with Asia, population pressure in Africa was weak from the 1960s to the mid-1990s (see Fig. 10.2), which coincides with a period of low grain prices (e.g., rice and maize prices: see Fig. 2.5). In all likelihood, GR did not take off in sub-Saharan Africa primarily because of the disincentive effects of such low grain prices. Consequently, employment opportunities in agriculture declined because of stagnant technology as well as low grain prices. There was therefore a "push" to migrate from rural to urban areas. Meanwhile, the industrial sector did not develop fast enough to create jobs for the urban migrants. Industrialization was slow on the continent for a number of possible reasons: (1) a lack of human capital, (2) weak infrastructure (e.g., poor roads, congested ports, lack of electricity), or (3) regional leaders' failure to pursue appropriate economic policies supporting the labor-intensive industry sector, which could have facilitated the transfer of advanced technology and management practices from more advanced regions (see Chap. 9; Sonobe and Otsuka 2011, 2014). As a result, African countries have striven to industrialize in recent years.

Population pressure in sub-Saharan Africa appears to have become strong in the early 2000s owing to the closure of the land frontier and high population growth. After the 2006–2008 world food crises, there was a "push" for GR as rising income and urbanization slowly and steadily increased the demand for food. A rising trend emerged in the share of African imports of rice from tropical Asia, which is expected to continue and may affect world rice prices. Strong population pressure and urbanization are creating a need for GR, which is expected to trigger investments in agricultural research and human capital, as in Asia (Otsuka and Larson 2016). Human capital could, in turn, serve as the "fuel" for industrialization and service sector development. In brief, similar to the Asian story, population pressure and GR have the potential to serve as a strong base for the emergence of African economies. What is also needed is an appropriate strategy for African industrialization (Otsuka et al. 2018).

10.4 Economic Transformation in Rural Villages

We explore the features of economic transformation at the household level by analyzing the shift of household income structure away from farm toward nonfarm activities. Such a shift involves a dynamic process of labor allocation, which, interestingly, shows similar patterns across emerging economies in Asia and Africa.

10.4.1 Changes in Household Income and Their Sources in Asia

We trace changes in the sources of livelihoods among rural households in Myanmar, the Philippines, Vietnam, and Bangladesh. The datasets drawn from the Philippines, Vietnam, and Bangladesh constitute panel data with the replacement of households whose heads have died with successor households. We exclude Lao PDR in this section because its household income data were collected in 2010 only.[4] Data for Myanmar are repeated cross-section data from households living in the same villages. We divide the sample into farmer and landless household groups in Myanmar and the Philippines because the landless households, being the poorest in the village communities, are more geographically mobile and are more likely to have responded quickly to new employment opportunities. The sample villages in Asia were traditional rice-producing areas, and thus particularly suitable for exploring the role of modern agricultural technology during the process of "take-off" into emerging economies.

The sample villages in Myanmar are located in Ayeyawady Division (the country's rice granary), south of the main city of Yangon. A total of 739 households were interviewed in 1996 (Garcia et al. 2000) and 900 were interviewed in 2012 (Estudillo and Otsuka 2016). Four villages were studied in the Philippines: two are located in Central Luzon (the "rice bowl" of the country) and two are in Panay Island. A total of 632 sample households in the four villages (474 farmer households, 158 landless households) were interviewed in the benchmark survey in 1985. Estudillo and Otsuka (2016) conducted a unique survey that traced the children of the original 632 households in 1985; they were able to locate 527 married children from the

---

[4]Cross-border migration from Lao PDR to Thailand is an interesting issue (Estudillo and Otsuka 2016, Chap. 2).

original 474 farmer households and 129 married children from the original 158 landless households. In Vietnam, the sample villages are located in Hanoi and Thai Nguyen in the north and in Long An and Can Tho in the south. We examined 376 households in 1996 and 344 in 2009, which were divided almost equally between the north and the south. Ut et al. (2000) conducted the benchmark survey in 1996, followed by a resurvey of the same households by Estudillo and Otsuka (2016) in 2009.

The Bangladesh panel data cover most parts of the country and comprise information from 1,240 randomly selected households in 1988 and 2,010 households in 2008 (Hossain and Bayes 2009). The first survey in 1988 was conducted by the IRRI when MVs had just started to spread in Bangladesh. Data for Sri Lanka come from the Household Income and Expenditure Survey (HIES), a nationally representative dataset collected by the Department of Census and Statistics of Sri Lanka. The earliest round of surveys in 1990/91 consisted of 18,246 households, and the latest round in 2006/07 consisted of 18,363 households (Kumanayake et al. 2014). The HIES classified households into urban, rural, and estate. We used only the rural households from the HIES because of our focus on agriculture.

We divided household income into farm and nonfarm sources. Farm income is obtained from farming and agricultural wage employment. Wage employment refers to off-farm labor activities, primarily in transplanting, weeding, harvesting, and threshing in rice farming; these are characterized by low remuneration and high seasonality. The major share of farm income accrues from crop production (e.g., rice, vegetables, and fruits), livestock and poultry propagation, and fishing. Nonfarm income comes from four sources: (1) formal wage employment, (2) informal wage employment, (3) self-employment, and (4) remittances and other miscellaneous income. Nonfarm self-employment income is derived from retail and trade, transport, rural restaurants, the renting of self-owned equipment and vehicles, handicraft shops, and other sources. Remittances come mainly from family members (e.g., unmarried children) working abroad or locally in big cities and towns. Other income sources include pensions, gifts, and other forms of transfer payments. In Africa, other income sources include the wages from migrant workers. Poverty measures were estimated using the FGT index, with US$1.25 per capita per day in PPP 2005 based on private consumption used as the poverty line.

Myanmar Total household income (US$ PPP in 2005) rose by about 1.8 times for farmers and 2.0 times for the landless from 1996 to 2012 (see Table 10.5). Agricultural income is becoming less important: the share of agricultural income of farmer households declined from 91 to 82% and that of the landless from 68 to 38%. The major sources of income growth were rice farming and formal wage work for farmers, as income from formal work became the dominant source of nonfarm income in 2012. Income from rice farming rose because of the increase in rice yields (which rose from 1.8 to 2.8 tons per ha) and the abolition of government production quotas (mandatory selling of 0.5 tons of paddy to the government), which increased the prices received by farmers by about 50%. Recently, nonfarm income has increased in importance because the more educated children of farm households prefer to work in the formal wage sector in Yangon. Nonfarm informal wage work and nonfarm self-employment activities were the main sources of income growth for the landless. Landless households appear to have substituted informal wage work and self-employment activities for agricultural wage work in 2012, presumably because of the declining labor employment opportunities in rice farming due to decreasing farm size coupled with low cropping intensity. Poverty decreased moderately among both landless and farmer households, although the headcount ratio remained high for the landless (74% in 2012). Given the rising importance of nonfarm income, it is reasonable to surmise that the development of the nonfarm sector has become an important driver of household income growth and poverty reduction in rural Myanmar.

Philippines We have income data for two generations of households in the Philippines: respondents' generation (G1) and the married children of respondents (G2). In 1985, a substantial portion of G1 household income (76% for the farmer, 49% for the landless) came from agricultural sources (e.g., production of rice, nonrice crops, and livestock; see Table 10.5). The income of farmer households for G1 in 1985 was about twice that of landless households, and thus poverty was much higher among the landless (65%) than among the farmer households (42%). Interestingly, nonfarm income has become the major source of income for G2 (83% for farmer children and 92% for landless children in 2008). Income disparity between farmer and landless children appears to have disappeared for G2 when nonfarm income became the major driver of income growth: the ratio of farmer to landless income is only 1.22 for G2 compared with 2.10 for G1. While G2 incomes have largely equalized, poverty incidence among landless children remained higher but, with a mere eight percentage points difference, compared favorably with that of their parents, for whom poverty stood at 23% points higher among the landless class. Landless children who migrated to local towns and big cities were able to increase their income more than farmer children could. Such migration was facilitated by the earlier decision of landless parents to invest in their children's schooling. In brief, participation in the nonfarm labor market and migration to local towns and big cities are major strategies for moving out of poverty for the landless poor in the Philippines.

Vietnam We divided our sample villages into "northern villages" (referring to Hanoi and Thai Nguyen provinces) and "southern villages" (referring to Long An and Can Tho). Household income (US$ PPP in 2005) in the northern villages rose from $1,547 in 1996 to $4,093 (2.64 times) in 2009, whereas, in the southern villages, income rose from $2,896 to $11,748 (4.05 times; see Table 10.5). The most important source of income growth in the northern villages was nonfarm formal wage work (which almost doubled). An interesting gender specialization can be observed: women in the northern villages are left on the farms producing high-value products (e.g., citrus, cut flowers, vegetables, tea, poultry, and pigs), whereas the men work in factories in the cities and local towns, returning home in the rural villages during weekends (Estudillo and Otsuka 2016). In the southern villages, the major source of income growth was rice farming (which rose 4.8 times) because of the increase in rice yield and, importantly, because of high rice prices in 2009, which captured the rice

Table 10.5 Sources of rural household income in selected countries in Asia, 1985–2010

Source	1996	2012
Asia		
Myanmar: Farmer households		
Farm income	2,207 (91%)	3,602 (82%)
Nonfarm income	209 (9%)	785 (18%)
Total annual household income (US$ PPP in 2005)	2,416 (100%)	4,387 (100%)
Poverty headcount ratio (%)	51	39
Poverty gap ratio (%)	18	19
Myanmar: Landless households		
Farm income	736 (68%)	833 (38%)
Nonfarm income	340 (32%)	1,330 (62%)
Total annual household income (US$ PPP in 2005)	1,076 (100%)	2,163 (100%)
Poverty headcount ratio (%)	85	74
Poverty gap ratio (%)	44	42
Philippines: respondents' generation (G1)	Farmer households in 1985	Landless households in 1985
Farm income	1,446 (76%)	448 (49%)
Nonfarm income	449 (24%)	460 (51%)
Total annual household income (US$ PPP in 2005)	1,895 (100%)	908 (100%)
Poverty headcount ratio (%)	42	65
Poverty gap ratio (%)	20	25
Philippines: Married children of respondents (G2)	Farmer households in 2008	Landless households in 2008
Farm income	1,367 (17%)	565 (8%)
Nonfarm income	6,774 (83%)	6,063 (92%)
Total annual household income (US$ PPP in 2005)	8,141 (100%)	6,628 (100%)
Poverty headcount ratio (%)	26	34
Poverty gap ratio (%)	12	16
Vietnam: Northern villages		
Farm income	1,056 (68%)	1,454 (36%)
Nonfarm income	491 (32%)	2,639 (64%)
Total annual household income (US$ PPP in 2005)	1,547 (100%)	4,093 (100%)
Poverty headcount ratio (%)	62	26
Poverty gap ratio (%)	28	23

(continued)

Table 10.5 (continued)

Source	1996	2012
Vietnam: Southern villages		
Farm income	2,162 (75%)	9,400 (81%)
Nonfarm income	733 (25%)	2,348 (19%)
Total annual household income (US$ PPP in 2005)	2,896 (100%)	11,748 (100%)
Poverty headcount ratio (%)	35	19
Poverty gap ratio (%)	19	11
Bangladesh	1988	2008
Farm income	718 (56%)	1,665 (43%)
Nonfarm income	555 (44%)	2,169 (57%)
Total annual household income (US$ PPP in 2005)	1,273 (100%)	3,834 (100%)
Poverty headcount ratio (%)	83	42
Poverty gap ratio (%)	45	16
Sri Lanka: rural households	1990	2006
Farm income	796 (34%)	948 (18%)
Nonfarm income	1,544 (66%)	4,319
Total annual household income (US$ PPP in 2005)	2,340 (100%)	5,268
Poverty headcount ratio (%)	60	14
Poverty gap ratio (%)	24	5
Africa		
Ethiopia	2004	2006
Farm income	275 (90%)	318 (88%)
Nonfarm income	31 (10%)	44 (12%)
Total annual household income (US$ PPP in 2005)	306 (100%)	362 (100%)
Poverty headcount ratio (%)	82	76
Poverty gap ratio (%)	47	46
Kenya	2004	2007
Farm income	527 (60%)	665 (61%)
Nonfarm income	351 (40%)	426 (39%)
Total annual household income (US$ PPP in 2005)	878 (100%)	1,091 (100%)
Poverty headcount ratio (%)	42	40
Poverty gap ratio (%)	18	17
Uganda	2003	2009

(continued)

Table 10.5 (continued)

Source	1996	2012
Farm income	272 (73%)	431 (78%)
Nonfarm income	100 (27%)	122 (22%)
Total annual household income (US$ PPP in 2005)	372 (100%)	553 (100%)
Poverty headcount ratio (%)	78	57
Poverty gap ratio (%)	47	28
Mozambique	2002	2005
Farm income	565 (80%)	495 (71%)
Nonfarm income	142 (20%)	203 (29%)
Total annual household income (US$ PPP in 2005)	707 (100%)	698 (100%)
Poverty headcount ratio (%)	79.9	76.1
Poverty gap ratio (%)	48.3	48.2

Data sources Estudillo and Otsuka (2016), Table 2.4 on p. 33 for Lao PDR; Table 3.4 on p. 60 for Myanmar; Table 4.4 on p. 83 and Table 4.5 on p. 86 for the Philippines; and Fig. 5.2 on pp.103–104 for Vietnam; Debnath (2016) and Estudillo et al. (2013, Table 3 on p. 22) for Bangladesh; Kumanayake (2011, Table 4.3 on p. 100) for Sri Lanka; Estudillo et al. (2013), Table 3 on pp. 23–24 for Kenya, Uganda, and Ethiopia; and Cunguara and Kajisa (2009), Table 8.1 on p. 177 for Mozambique

price increase during the world food crises. Concomitant with the rising household income was a remarkable decline in poverty—36% points in the northern villages and 16% points in the southern villages. Clearly, household activities are increasingly concentrated on rice farming in the southern villages, while household activities have diversified away from rice farming and toward nonfarm formal wage work in the northern villages, where farms are much smaller than in the south.

To sum up, as in the Philippines and Myanmar, the migration of rural labor has become a major strategy for income growth in Vietnam's northern villages, whereas commercial agriculture, which is linked to international rice markets, has served as the driver of household income growth in the southern villages. Modern rice technology in the southern villages and urbanization and human capital in the northern villages appear to be important motors of income growth in Vietnam.

Bangladesh Farm income, particularly from rice farming, was by far the most important source of income in rural Bangladesh in 1988. The share of agricultural income dropped, however, from 56% in 1988 to 43% in 2008 (see Table 10.5), partly because of the decline in casual labor employment opportunities in rice farming. The major drivers of the decline were the rapid adoption of mechanical technology for land preparation and threshing and increased employment opportunities in the rural transport sector because of the development of rural roads (Hossain and Bayes 2009). Remittance income rose because of the expansion of the garment industry and construction booms in the cities, as well as increasing overseas migration.

Incomes almost tripled, and poverty declined from 83 to 42%. Taking up jobs in the nonfarm sector has been facilitated by the earlier decisions of parents to invest in their children's schooling, particularly for their girls, which was, in turn, induced by household income increases and government policies favoring girls (e.g., food for education program, cash for education program, and scholarships for girls; Estudillo and Otsuka 2016). It seems clear that investment in human capital is an integral part of the long-term and dynamic process of household income growth in rural Bangladesh.

Sri Lanka Nonfarm wage income was the dominant source of rural household income as early as 1990, and its importance had increased by 2006 (see Table 10.5). This indicates that rural households are increasingly allocating labor away from agricultural activities to nonfarm wage employment in the formal wage sector. The educated children of rural households are those involved in formal wage employment, as returns to education are bound to be higher in the sector. As a result, the share of farm income among the rural households declined significantly from 1990 to 2006. Concomitant with the rise in the share of nonfarm wage income is the increase in the annual household incomes of rural households by more than 2.4 times and a decline in the poverty headcount ratio from 60% in 1990 to 14% in 2006.

Sri Lanka has households living in estates that continue to be poor, whereas rural households experienced upper economic mobility when they participated in activities that produce nonfarm formal wage income. Low and stagnant wage income in the estate sector in the face of constant cost-of-living increases is the main factor preventing estate people from moving out of poverty (World Bank 2005). Kumanayake et al. (2014) argue that remoteness is another factor, because basic infrastructure in the estates remains largely underdeveloped, preventing estate people from taking advantage of emerging economic opportunities in the nonfarm sector. In other words, people in estates are examples of "hard-to-reach groups," those left behind in the course of the economic development of emerging economies.

To summarize, rural households in our focus countries in Asia have shifted their main livelihood sources away from farming to nonfarm work and, importantly, nonfarm formal wage work, as well as to overseas migration, as in the Philippines and Bangladesh; this shift is being accompanied by income growth and poverty reduction. This story is fairly similar across our focus countries in Asia: the development of the nonfarm sector has served as a springboard for economic mobility in rural communities.

10.4.2 Changes in Household Income and Their Sources in Africa

Rural household surveys in Ethiopia, Kenya, and Uganda were conducted as part of a research project, the Research on Poverty, Environment, and Agricultural Technology, or RePEAT (Matsumoto et al. 2009). The benchmark survey in Ethiopia was conducted in 2004, covering 420 households from the central to the southern region. The first survey in Uganda covered 94 local councils 1 (LC1s), the smallest administrative unit (comparable to a village in Asia), and 940 households in most of the country, except in the northern regions, where there were security concerns. The benchmark survey in Kenya was conducted in 2003 and covered 99 sub-locations, an administrative unit that may include a few villages, and 934 households in the central and western regions. Stratified random sampling of communities was used in the target regions, and about 10 households for every selected community were randomly chosen. Data on Mozambique were collected from the two rice-growing provinces of Zambezia and Sofala, extracted from the National Agricultural Survey in 2002 and 2005. There were 1,140 households in 2002 and 928 households in 2005; 928 households were included in both surveys (620 from Zambezia and 308 from Sofala; Cunguara and Kajisa 2009).

Ethiopia In Ethiopia, agricultural income (crop farming and livestock income) in 2006 accounted for as much as 88% of the total household income (see Table 10.5). Nonfarm income accounted for only 12% of total income, reflecting the low-return and low-productivity activities in the nonfarm sectors in this predominantly agrarian economy. Total income rose by only 1.18 times, and the poverty headcount ratio was high, declining only modestly from 82% in 2004 to 76% in 2006.

Kenya Farm income in Kenya accounted for 60% of the total household income in 2004. The remittances and earnings of migrant workers were an important portion of nonfarm income, comprising 40% of total income, which reflects the relatively developed nonfarm sectors in Kenya compared with other countries in Africa. This indicates the importance of migration as a strategy for increasing household income. There was a modest increase in total household income (from US$878 in PPP in 2004 to US$1,091 in PPP in 2007). Household incomes in Kenya are comparable to the incomes of landless households in the Philippines and Sri Lanka and those of small farmers in northern Vietnam and Bangladesh. Both the poverty headcount ratio and poverty gap ratio remained essentially the same from 2004 to 2007.

Uganda From 2003 to 2008, farm incomes in Uganda comprised about 70% of total household income (crop farming had a 60% share, livestock 10%), whereas nonfarm income, mainly from self-employment, comprised 30%. Total annual household income rose about 1.5 times from 2003 to 2007, primarily due to crop farming. Nonfarm wage employment was not very important, indicating that the nonfarm labor markets are not yet well-developed. The poverty headcount ratio declined from 78 to 59%. A more recent phenomenon is so-called "mobile money," which, since emerging in Uganda in 2009, has been used by more than 35% of the adult population. Its rate of penetration is rapidly increasing. Mobile money enables unbanked households to have access to financial services (important for sending remittances) at a reduced cost.

Mozambique Farm income (mainly from crop production) is by far the most important source of household income. Partly because of a drought during the 2002–2005 survey period, the share of farm income declined from 80% in 2002 to 71% in 2005 (Cunguara and Kajisa 2009). Surprisingly, poverty declined modestly when the share of nonfarm income rose. It appears that engaging in nonfarm activities is an important risk-coping mechanism for households in this country. Migration is not common in the study sites (remittance income comprised only about 3% of total income), and income from livestock is small (only about 2%). In brief, diversification out of the farm and into the nonfarm sector appears to enable people to avoid poverty, but this opportunity is limited in Mozambique to nonfarm activities that are undertaken when agricultural labor demand is low.

To sum up, farm income remains the most important source of rural household income in Africa. Nonfarm income in Africa is increasingly made up of remittances and the earnings of migrant workers, indicating the growing economic importance of nonfarm income associated with migration. Nonfarm self-employment activities are largely informal and home-based, intricately tied up with agricultural production (e.g., brewing of homemade beverages in Mozambique). Although we found that the shift of livelihood away from farm to nonfarm activities has taken place in both Asia and Africa, it is occurring much faster in Asia. The main driver in Asia is the development of the formal nonfarm sector and migration, including overseas migration. In Africa, the main driver appears to be domestic migration coupled with employment in informal nonfarm sectors, as livelihood opportunities within the nonfarm sector are largely confined to the informal sector in urban areas, which tend to wane in the course of economic development.

10.4.3 Conditions for "Take-off:" A Retrospective View from Central Luzon in the Philippines

We discuss below the underlying mechanisms behind the rise of Central Luzon (CL) as an emerging region in the Philippines, in an analysis made possible thanks to the availability of unusually long-term household data. We describe the socioeconomic conditions before and after the GR in CL, the most progressive rice-producing area of the country. The dataset comes from periodic surveys performed at an average interval of four years beginning in 1966 conducted by the Social Sciences Division of the International Rice Research Institute. The main aim of the survey is to monitor changes in the adoption of new rice technology, land tenure, mechanization, and labor practices. The dataset is called the "Central Luzon Loop Survey" because the respondents are located along a loop of the major highways stretching north of Manila through the provinces of Bulacan, Nueva Ecija, Pangasinan, Tarlac, and Pampanga (see Fig. 10.9). These provinces are frontrunners in the adoption of modern varieties of rice in the country. CL, contiguous to the National Capital Region (where the city of Manila is located), has become one of the fastest-growing regions in the nation.

This is the only dataset drawn from tropical Asia that offers information on household socioeconomic conditions as far back as half a century ago. The original sam-

Fig. 10.9 Location of Central Luzon, the Philippines

ple comprised 92 respondents (see Table 10.6), all rice farmers (excluding landless households). The original sample was intended to be maintained, but its size gradually declined because of retirements from farming and deaths. New samples from the same villages were added in the 1986 and 2011 surveys.

Table 10.6 Technology adoption, demographic characteristics, and income sources of sample households in Central Luzon, the Philippines, 1966–2011

Description	1966	1986	1998	2011
Technology adoption				
Number of sample households	92	120	79	93
Average farm size (ha)	2.1	1.8	1.5	1.6
Adoption of new technology				
Modern rice (% area)	0	100	100	100
Irrigation (% area)	60	68	65	61
Rice yield (tons per ha)	2.3	3.6	3.4	3.9
Demographic characteristics				
Average age of head (years)	46	49	58	59
Average schooling of head (years)	4.6	6.5	7.7	9
Average schooling of children (22 years old and older) (years)	na	9.9	11.2	11.9
Occupation of children 22 years old and older				
Farmer (%)	na	3	16	13
Wage work in agriculture (%)	na	2	1	1
Nonfarm self-employed (%)	na	1	3	2
Nonfarm formal work (%)	na	34	27	25
Nonfarm informal work (%)	na	14	25	21
Housekeeping/unemployed/retired (%)	na	45	28	38
Total (%)	na	100	100	100
Sources of household income[a]	1966–67	1986–87	1998–99	2011–12
Agriculture (%)	73	62	37	NA
Rice (%)	57	45	23	NA
Nonrice (%)	16	17	14	NA
Nonfarm (%)	27	38	63	NA
Total (%)	100	100	100	NA
Total household annual income (pesos per year, nominal)	2,011	30,056	113,545	NA

[a] Refers to June 1966 to May 1967, June 1986 to May 1987, June 1998 to May 1999, and June 2011 to May 2012

Source Authors' calculations from the Farm Household Survey Database of the International Rice Research Institute (http://ricestat.irri.org/fhsd/)

Our discussion on the emergence of CL revolves around a simple story that begins with population pressure as a trigger for the adoption of modern rice technology. The GR started in CL in 1966 with the release of IR8. The land reform (LR) program was implemented in the mid-1970s, when the adoption of modern rice varieties had reached high level. The LR program converted share tenants into owner cultivators or leasehold tenants while holding amortization fees and leasehold rents fixed at below the market return to land. Thus, farmers were able to internalize the gains from the rice yield growth that occurred under LR, leading to an increase in farm income. Farmers then invested the increased farm income in children's schooling induced by the growing availability of jobs for skilled and semi-skilled workers when the NIEs delocalized and outsourced some of their production processes to the Philippines. Educated children moved out of the villages and obtained nonfarm work in local towns, cities, and even overseas, while sending remittances back home. Household income from nonfarm sources has become the main contributor to sustained total household income growth and poverty reduction. The CL saga underscores the importance of modern agricultural technology as a springboard of economic transformation in the early stage of development.

Population Pressure and Modern Agricultural Technology The average cultivation size of farms has consistently declined from 2.1 ha in 1966 to 1.6 ha in 2011 (see Table 10.6). The decline in farm size can be partly explained by the changes in the composition of sample farms but is more fundamentally due to population pressure on the closed land frontier in CL. Inheritance is an institutional mechanism for the transfer of land across generations. It is common for parents in CL to divide the land equally among heirs or among male heirs only. Due to relatively large family sizes and, in some cases, secondary marriages, landholdings have become fragmented as an outcome of equal inheritance. When rice farming is the only source of income in a regime of small landholdings and stagnant technology, impoverishment becomes common.

In 1966, all sample farmers were planting only traditional varieties of rice. The first MV, IR8, was released in CL in November 1966. Earlier MVs released prior to the mid-1970s were the "first-generation" MVs (MV1), which are highly susceptible to pests and diseases. By 1986, all sample farmers had shifted exclusively to the "second-generation" MVs (MV2), which have strong resistance to against multiple pests and diseases. Such a shift has been facilitated by the opening of Pantabangan Dam in 1977, which provides water for irrigation and electricity via hydroelectric power generation. As a result, there was a significant increase in rice yield from 2.3 tons/ha in 1966 to 3.6 tons/ha in 1986, partly because of the shift from MV1 to MV2 and partly because of increased fertilizer application. The total irrigated area rose from 60% to around 70% between 1966 and 1998.

Over the years, the adoption of labor-saving technologies such as the use of tractors and threshers and direct seeding increased in response to increases in wages. During the 1980s, the Asian NIEs ventured into delocalization and the outsourcing of labor-intensive production processes in Southeast Asian countries to take advantage of the low wages. At the same time, there was a diversion of international division of labor for low-technology and labor-intensive products from high-performing countries in Southeast Asia to other low-wage countries in Asia, including the Philippines. These phenomena have created jobs for the semi-skilled and skilled workers in CL, raising the returns to schooling investments. Moreover, CL saw a growth of small cities, namely Cabanatuan, San Jose, and the Science City of Munoz, and a growth in population in the so-called *poblacion* (town centers) in each municipality. Small cities emerged partly because of the relocation of industries away from Metro Manila, which has become congested, thereby pushing up production costs.

History of Land Tenure System and Land Reform Implementation In the 1800s, during the Spanish colonial period, three modes of land acquisition contributed to the pervasive landlordism in CL: royal grants, purchase of *realengas*, and *pacto de retrovenda* arrangements (McLennan 1969). *Realengas* is the outright purchase at a low price of real estate from a badly-in-need peasant or from the public domain. Royal grants and *realengas* resulted in the proliferation of huge private *haciendas* (large blocks of consolidated landholdings) in Nueva Ecija, Tarlac, eastern Pangasinan, and northern and western Pampanga. *Pacto de retrovenda* was equivalent to today's mortgage system (*sangla*), whereby a moneylender (commonly a Chinese *mestizo* or Chinese merchant) lent a peasant some money and secured protection for his loan by taking immediate control of the land, allowing the peasant to remain but as a sharecropper under the Chinese *mestizo*. Seldom able to pay the loan at the appointed time, the peasant often relinquished his claim to the land due to his debt. *Pacto de retrovenda* extended landlordism in the form of the *kasamajan* (sharecropping) system, which resulted in a pattern of land ownership characterized by scattered, unconsolidated landholdings that was common throughout much of Pampanga and Bulacan, central Pangasinan, and, in the nineteenth century, in southern and central Nueva Ecija.

It was in the *haciendas*, in the growing depersonalized atmosphere of absentee landlordism (landlords lived in Manila), where peasants became discontented and began to clamor for land reform. Ferdinand Marcos issued Presidential Decree No. 27 in 1972 declaring the entire Philippines a land reform area, notwithstanding the fact that only rice and corn land was included. Under the "land-to-the-tiller" program, landholdings of more than 7 ha were to be purchased by the government and sold to individual tenants (up to 3 ha for irrigated land or 5 ha for non-irrigated land). Tenants would amortize for the value of the land over a 15-year period. Under the "operation leasehold" program, sharecroppers on holdings of less than 7 ha were to be converted to leaseholders, paying a fixed rent every cropping season.

Since the implementation of the LR program coincided with yield growth, due to the spread of modern seed-fertilizer technology, amortization fees and leasehold rents prescribed and fixed by law fell below the prevailing rental value of land, creating an economic rent that accrued to the land reform beneficiary. Indeed, according to Otsuka (1991), the LR program in the Philippines (particularly in CL) succeeded because of the heightened economic interest of tenants in land reform arising from the divergence of the rental value of land from leasehold rent and amortization fees prescribed by the LR law. Estudillo and Otsuka (1999) reported that the proportion of land area in the sample villages in the Central Luzon Loop survey under owner cultivation increased from 12% in 1966 to 24% in 1994 while that under share tenancy declined from 75% in 1966 to only 9% in 1994, attesting to the successful conversion of share tenants to amortizing owners and leaseholders due to land reform in CL.

Investments in Human Capital Farm households appear anxious to invest in the schooling of their children. Household children 22 years old and above had obtained significantly longer years of schooling than the household heads had (see Table 10.6). The proportion of adult children with tertiary schooling (more than 10 years of schooling) increased from 40% in 1986 to 67% in 2011; this is an underestimation because the more educated children had migrated and were not included in the list of children living in the households. Only 13% of adult children living in the household in 2011 were engaged in rice farming, whereas 46% were engaged in nonfarm work, including work in the formal sector. The average age of household heads rose from 46 in 1966 to 59 in 2011, which indicates that the heads of selected households remained the same for many years. Clearly, farming remains the main occupation of the household head, whereas the more educated children are engaged in nonfarm work.

According to Estudillo et al. (2009), farm income in the early years of the GR were used to finance investments in children's schooling at a time when new jobs in the nonfarm sector were created in the Philippines. These new jobs raised the returns to schooling, inducing land reform beneficiaries to invest in higher levels of schooling for their children.

Sources of Household Income The CL respondents have shifted their main source of livelihood away from farm toward nonfarm activities, as shown by the declining income share of agriculture (from 73% in 1966 to 37% in 1998/99) and the subsequent growth in the share of nonfarm income (see Table 10.6). Remittance income is an important component of nonfarm income; it has gained importance in recent years because of the increasing participation of the younger generation in nonfarm work in cities and overseas, made possible by earlier investments in schooling. Clearly, CL has experienced the same process of economic transformation as that seen in our focus countries, but this case highlights the importance of modern agricultural technology as a force behind economic transformation in its early stage.

10.5 Summary and Conclusions

Emerging economies are in developing countries that are rapidly growing and gaining an increasing share of the global economy. However, little is known about the underlying mechanisms of how these economies have actually evolved. This chapter explored three drivers of the evolution of emerging economies: population pressure, modern agricultural technology, and human capital. We performed a comparison between selected countries in Asia and sub-Saharan Africa; the former is the more dynamic region, and the latter has the potential to follow suit. The three drivers are distinct in their interaction yet define a common regional path for the emerging state, wherein agricultural development could serve as a strong stimulus for economic transformation (or the expansion of the nonfarm sector) through higher farm income and a subsequent growth in investments in human capital.

The CL case is clearly consistent with the Boserupian thesis that high population pressure can induce the adoption of labor-intensive agricultural technology. The GR and the simultaneous implementation of land reform have led to growth in the farm income of land reform beneficiaries. Meanwhile, rising wages in the newly industrializing economies in East Asia have induced the outsourcing and delocalization of labor-intensive production processes to Southeast Asia, including the Philippines, creating jobs for skilled and semi-skilled workers and opportunities for profitable investments in human capital. Farmers used their farm income to finance investments in the schooling of their children, who, upon receiving higher education, migrated out of the villages to small towns, cities, and abroad, thereby contributing to the development of nonfarm sectors and improvements in farm households' income (Estudillo et al. 2009). Nonfarm wage income and remittances became the main contributors to sustained household income growth and poverty reduction in rural areas.

What lessons can Africa learn from Asia? Our analysis shows that, to stimulate the development of the entire economy, it is necessary to first develop agriculture during the early stage of development. Following the Asian path, a robust agriculture sector in Africa is expected to stimulate the development of the nonfarm sector, which can eventually lead the entire economy into rapid growth. The Asian pathway is represented by the advent of the GR, followed by profitable investments in human capital inspired by the rising demand for semi-skilled and skilled workers as globalization proceeds. Since Africa is still in an early stage of development and population pressure has begun, agricultural development could serve as the critical first step toward sustained income growth and poverty reduction, as occurred in Asia about half a century ago.

Acknowledgements This work was partially supported by JSPS KAKENHI Grant Number JP25101002. The authors are grateful to Katrina Miradora for her excellent research assistance.

References

Chamberlain, J., Jayne, T. S., & Heady, D. (2014). Scarcity amidst abundance? Reassessing the potential for cropland expansion in Africa. *Food Policy, 48,* 51–65.

Cunguara, B., & Kajisa, K. (2009). Determinants of household income and schooling investments in rice-growing provinces in Mozambique, 2002–5. In K. Otsuka, J. Estudillo, & Y. Sawada (Eds.), *Rural poverty and income dynamics in Asia and Africa* (pp. 174–195). London: Routledge Taylor and Francis Group.

Debnath, D. (2016). Changing determinants of household income by source: Evidence from rural households in Bangladesh, 1988–2008. Unpublished manuscript, National Graduate Institute for Policy Studies, Tokyo, Japan.

Dollar, D., & Kraay, A. (2002). Growth is good for the poor. *Journal of Economic Growth, 7,* 195–225.

Estudillo, J. P., & Otsuka, K. (1999). Green revolution, human capital, and off-farm employment: Changing sources of income among farm households in Central Luzon, 1966–94. *Economic Development and Cultural Change, 47*(3), 497–523.

Estudillo, J. P., Sawada, Y., & Otsuka, K. (2009). Income dynamics, schooling investment, and poverty reduction in Philippine villages. In K. Otsuka, J. Estudillo, & Y. Sawada (Eds.), *Rural poverty and income dynamics in Asia and Africa* (pp. 1985–2004). London: Routledge Taylor and Francis Group.

Estudillo, J. P., & Otsuka, K. (2013). Lessons from the Asian green revolution. In K. Otsuka & D. Larson (Eds.), *An African green revolution: Finding ways to boost productivity on small farms* (pp. 17–42). New York: Springer.

Estudillo, J. P., Matsumoto, T., Hayat, C. Z. U., Kumanayake, N. S., & Otsuka, K. (2013). Labor markets, occupational choice and rural poverty in selected countries in Asia and Sub-Saharan Africa. Background paper for the World Development Report 2013 "Jobs," World Bank, Washington, D.C.

Estudillo, J. P., & Otsuka, K. (2016). *Moving out of poverty: An inquiry into the inclusive growth in Asia.* London: Routledge Taylor and Francis Group.

Garcia, Y. T., Garcia, A. G., Oo, M., & Hossain, M. (2000). Income distribution and poverty in irrigated and rainfed ecosystems: the Myanmar case. *Economic and Political Weekly, 35*(52/53), 4670–4676.

Goldman Sachs. (2007). The N-11: More than an acronym, Global Economics Paper no. 153. Goldman Sachs Economic Research. New York, NY.

Hayami, Y., & Otsuka, K. (1994). Beyond the green revolution: Agricultural development strategy into the new century. In J. Anderson (Ed.), *Agricultural technology: Policy issues for the international community.* Wallingford: CAB International.

Hayami, Y., & Ruttan, V. W. (1985). *Agricultural development: An international perspective.* Baltimore: Johns Hopkins University Press.

Hossain, M., & Bayes, A. (2009). *Rural economy and livelihoods: Insights from Bangladesh.* Dhaka: A. H. Development Publishing House.

Jayne, T. S., Chamberlain, J., & Heady, D. (2014). Land pressures, the evolution of farming systems, and development strategies in Africa: A synthesis. *Food Policy, 48,* 1–17.

Kumanayake, N. S. (2011). Structural transformation and poverty reduction: A view from three sectors in Sri Lanka. Unpublished Ph.D. dissertation, National Graduate Institute for Policy Studies, Tokyo, Japan.

Kumanayake, N. S., Estudillo, J. P., & Otsuka, K. (2014). Changing sources of household income, poverty, and sectoral inequality in Sri Lanka, 1990–2006. *Developing Economies, 52*(1), 26–51.

McLennan, M. (1969). Land and tenancy in the Central Luzon Plain. *Philippine Studies, 17*(4), 651–682.

Macmillan, M., Rodrik, D., & Verduzco-Gallo, I. (2014). Globalization, structural change, and productivity growth. *World Development, 63,* 11–32.

Matsumoto, T., Kijima, Y., & Yamano, T. (2009). Role of nonfarm income and education in reducing poverty: Evidence from Ethiopia, Kenya, and Uganda. In K. Otsuka, J. Estudillo, & Y. Sawada (Eds.), *Rural poverty and income dynamics in Asia and Africa.* London: Routledge Taylor and Francis Group.

Otsuka, K. (1991). Determinants and consequences of land reform implementation in the Philippines. *Journal of Development Economics, 35*(2), 339–355.

Otsuka, K., Estudillo, J. P., & Sawada, Y. (2009). *Rural poverty and income dynamics in Asia and Africa*. London: Routledge.

Otsuka, K., Higuchi, Y., & Sonobe, T. (2017). Middle-income traps in East Asia: An inquiry into causes for slowdown in income growth. *China Economic Review, 46*(S), S3–S16.

Otsuka, K., Jin, K., & Sonobe, T. (2018). (forthcoming). *Applying Kaizen in Africa: A new avenue for industrial development*. New York: Palgrave Macmillan.

Otsuka, K., & Runge, C. F. (Eds.). (2011). *Can economic growth be sustained? The collected papers of Vernon W. Ruttan and Yujiro Hayami*. Oxford: Oxford University Press.

Otsuka, K., & Larson, D. (2013). *An African green revolution: Finding ways to boost productivity on small farms*. Dordrecht: Springer.

Otsuka, K., & Larson, D. (2016). *In pursuit of an African green revolution: Views from rice and maize farmers' fields*. Dordrecht: Springer.

United Nations. (2015). *The Millennium development goals report 2015*. New York: United Nations.

Sonobe, T., & Otsuka, K. (2011). *Cluster-based industrial development: A comparative study of Asia and Africa*. Hampshire: Palgrave Macmillan.

Sonobe, T., & Otsuka, K. (2014). *Cluster-based industrial developments: Kaizen management for MSE growth in developing countries*. Hampshire: Palgrave Macmillan.

Tsunekawa, K. (2017). Globalization and the emerging state: Past advance and future challenges. Paper prepared for the Emerging State Project Workshop held at the National Graduate Institute for Policy Studies, Tokyo, Japan, January 21, 2017.

Ut, T. T., Hossain, M., & Janaiah, A. (2000). Modern farm technology and infrastructure in Vietnam: Impact on income distribution and poverty. *Economic and Political Weekly, 35*(52–53), 4638–4643.

World Bank. (2005). *Moving out of poverty in the estate sector in Sri Lanka: Understanding growth and freedom from the bottom up*. Sri Lanka: Centre for Poverty Analysis.

World Bank. (2008). *World development report 2008: Agriculture for development*. Washington, DC: World Bank.

Zhuang, J., & Ali, I. (2010). Poverty, inequality, and inclusive growth in Asia. In J. Zhuang (Ed.), *Poverty, inequality, and inclusive growth: Measurement, policy issues, and country studies*. London: Anthens Press.

Open Access This chapter is licensed under the terms of the Creative Commons Attribution-NonCommercial-NoDerivatives 4.0 International License (http://creativecommons.org/licenses/by-nc-nd/4.0/), which permits any noncommercial use, sharing, distribution and reproduction in any medium or format, as long as you give appropriate credit to the original author(s) and the source, provide a link to the Creative Commons licence and indicate if you modified the licensed material. You do not have permission under this licence to share adapted material derived from this chapter or parts of it.

The images or other third party material in this chapter are included in the chapter's Creative Commons licence, unless indicated otherwise in a credit line to the material. If material is not included in the chapter's Creative Commons licence and your intended use is not permitted by statutory regulation or exceeds the permitted use, you will need to obtain permission directly from the copyright holder.

Chapter 11
Agricultural Market Intervention and Emerging States in Africa

Masayoshi Honma

11.1 Introduction

Agricultural policies used to be regarded as determined by political institutions peculiar to each country. However, broad international comparisons of agricultural policy and economic performance reveal several common patterns. One is that countries tend to impose negative policies (taxation) on agriculture in the early stage of economic development while adopting positive policies (protection) for agriculture as the economy develops.

In the early stages of economic development, agriculture is the biggest industry and employs a large workforce. If economic development is promoted, as Petty-Clark's Law says, the agricultural sector shrinks in relative terms and the agricultural labor force also decreases. Taxation is imposed on agriculture despite the fact that it is the biggest industry with many workers. On the other hand, when development progresses, the agricultural sector is protected despite the fact that it shrinks. This phenomenon is called the "developmental paradox" (De Gorter and Swinnen 2002).

Starting in the 1980s, various models have been proposed to explain agricultural protection levels.[1] Furthermore, extensive research has been conducted to enable international comparison of protection levels as well as analysis of the domestic political economy of agricultural protection and international trade policies. There has been a rich accumulation of data in this area.[2]

---

[1] See e.g. Anderson et al. (1986), Honma and Hayami (1986), Gardner (1987), Krueger et al. (1988, 1991), Bates (1989), Tracy (1989), Lindert (1991), Swinnen et al. (2001), and Anderson (2009).

[2] Also, there have been important developments on political economy in the economics profession. See e.g. Grossman and Helpman (1994, 2002), Shleifer (1997), Persson and Tabellini (2000), and Acemoglu et al. (2001).

M. Honma (✉)
Department of Economics, Division of International Economics, Seinan Gakuin University, Fukuoka, Japan
e-mail: m-honma@seinan-gu.ac.jp

© The Author(s) 2019
K. Otsuka and K. Sugihara (eds.), *Paths to the Emerging State in Asia and Africa*, Emerging-Economy State and International Policy Studies,
https://doi.org/10.1007/978-981-13-3131-2_11

The agricultural policies of African countries have been analyzed quantitatively in a World Bank project published as a single volume (Anderson and Masters 2009). There are also a couple of comprehensive studies on the political economy of intervention in African agricultural trade (e.g. Bates and Block 2010).[3] However, there remains considerable scope to explore the determinants of agricultural policy in Africa.

The "developmental paradox" arises when politicians seek to maximize their votes in the political market. The outcome is far from optimal from an economic viewpoint and presents an obstacle to agricultural development. Correcting this paradox is indispensable for economic growth. The purpose of this chapter is to clarify whether the "developmental paradox" applies to African agricultural policy and to discuss the proper strategy of economic growth for Africa's emerging economies.

11.2 Distortion of Agricultural Markets in Africa

Many agricultural policies intervene in the market, pushing down or pushing up the prices of agricultural products, which causes distortion in agricultural markets. The greatest distortion is caused by import duties and export taxes imposed by governments at the border. Border measures have the effect of isolating the domestic market from the international market and thus weaken the influence of changes in the international market. Therefore, the difference between the domestic and international prices of agricultural products is an indicator of how much the market is distorted.

Various studies have been conducted to measure agricultural protection levels. The most comprehensive is the National and Global Estimates of Distortions to Agricultural Incentives 1955–2011 by the World Bank. It measures agricultural protection levels in 75 countries over more than 50 years and creates protection indices not only for distortions by border measures but also by domestic measures such as subsidies and assistance in non-agricultural sectors.

What was observed was that, as expected, agricultural protection levels varied depending on the stage of economic development. Agriculture was taxed in the early stages of development, but as the economy developed, agriculture became subject to protection. This trend was also found in African countries. However, it was not as readily apparent as in rapidly industrializing East Asian countries, especially in those African countries where economic development remained low (Anderson and Masters 2009).

An important indicator showing the level of protection is the nominal rate of assistance (NRA). The NRA is defined as the percentage by which government policies have raised gross returns to farmers above what they would be without government intervention (or have lowered them, if the NRA is negative). The NRA is measured for individual agricultural products. In addition, in order to estimate the country level of protection, a weighted average of the NRA of individual agricultural

---

[3] See also Block and Bates (2011), Hoeffler (2011), and Poulton (2014).

11 Agricultural Market Intervention and Emerging States in Africa

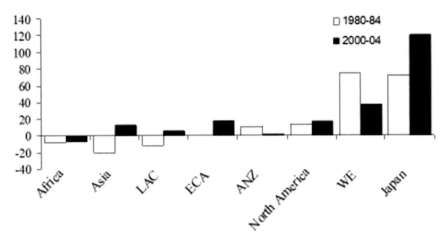

Fig. 11.1 Nominal rates of assistance to agriculture, by regions, 1980–84 and 2000–04 (percent). *Source* Anderson (ed.) (2009). *Note* LAC is Latin America and Caribbean, ECA is Europe and Central Asia, ANZ is Australia and New Zealand, and WE is Western Europe

products is calculated with weights of gross values of production at unassisted prices. Furthermore, the NRA by region is obtained as a weighted average of the NRA for each country in the region.

Figure 11.1 shows the NRA by region for the two periods of 1980–84 and 2000–04. Among developed country regions, the NRA of Western Europe (WE) and Japan are high, indicating that agricultural protection is prevalent. In fact, the figures show that Japan increased its protection level between the two periods while Western Europe's agricultural protection level was on a downward trend. Other developed regions—North America and Oceania (ANZ)—which are agricultural exporting areas, show low levels of agricultural protection.

On the other hand, in developing country regions, the NRA was negative in 1980–84, indicating that agriculture was taxed. Asia, which was heavily taxed in 1980–84, however, turned to positive in 2000–04, revealing a switch to agricultural protection. Africa was only the region where agricultural taxation remained in 2000–2004, indicating that it was impeding agricultural development.

Using NRA data in the World Bank database, Fig. 11.2 shows trends in Africa's NRA from 1955 to 2010 along with trends in Asia. Together with Asia, Africa shows negative values until the mid-1980s, indicating that the agricultural sector had been suppressed more than the international market price. However, the degree was lighter than in Asia. Asia was in the range of −20 to −30%, whereas in Africa it was in the −10 to −20% in range. Agricultural policies in Asia also turned to positive values, i.e. protection policy, in the late 1980s. On the other hand, domestic prices of agricultural products in Africa were still lower than international prices even in later years. In both areas, the level of agricultural protection in recent years has fluctuated greatly

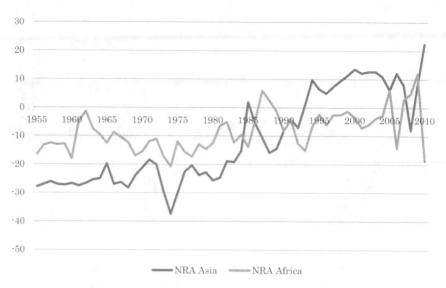

Fig. 11.2 Nominal rate of assistance (NRA) in Africa and Asia, 1955–2010. *Source* World Bank, National and Global Estimates of Distortions to Agricultural Incentives 1955–2011

from year to year, but looking at the overall trend for the past 50 years, it is clear that agricultural deprivation policy weakened and gradually switched to protection.

The overall trend in the weighted average of the NRA in Africa obscures a number of significant variations. The African continent can be divided into three regions: resource-rich countries, landlocked countries, and coastal countries. Bates and Block's analysis of agricultural trade intervention makes a number of important observations in this regard. African governments, with the exception of those in landlocked countries, have tended to protect food crops, raising the level of domestic prices above those prevailing in world markets, while taxing cash crops. The distortions introduced by government policies have eroded over time, with nominal rates of assistance for cash crops converging toward zero. Within the region, governments of resource-rich countries tend to provide the most favorable policy environment for producers of both food and cash crops, while the governments of landlocked countries tend to impose the least (Bates and Block 2010).

The major reductions in taxation of farmers have been in such countries as Ghana, Uganda, Tanzania, Cameroon, Senegal and Madagascar, while in Mozambique, and to a lesser extent Kenya, there has been a transition from taxing to supporting farmers. The opposite transition, from slight support to slight taxation, has occurred in Nigeria, while the degree of taxation is still heavy in Cote d'Ivoire, Zambia and Zimbabwe (Anderson and Masters 2009).

In the past, many studies have analyzed the relationship between agricultural protection or taxation and economic development. A common understanding is the change in the political environment accompanying economic development. In the early stage of economic development the government is required to tax agriculture,

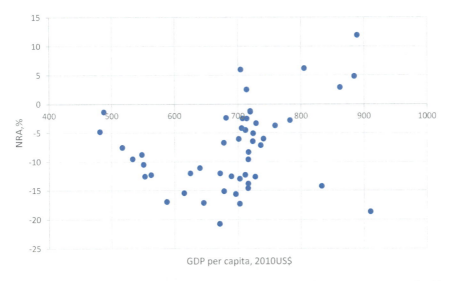

Fig. 11.3 Rerationship between GDP per capita and NRA in Africa, 1961–2010. *Source* World Bank, National and Global Estimates of Distortions to Agricultural Incentives 1955–2011

which is the largest industry in the economy. Also, in promoting industrialization, it is desirable to keep wages and food prices low. Food prices are an important factor determining wages in the early stage of development with a high Engel coefficient.

Figure 11.3 shows the relationship between the NRA and GDP per capita in Africa. Although it is not very clear, a positive correlation can be observed as a tendency. In Africa, as economic development progresses, the level of agricultural taxation moderates, and it seems that there is a tendency towards agricultural protection.

Another variable representing the change in the political environment accompanying economic development is the political power of the agricultural sector. Many workers are farmers in the early stages of development, but because farmers are scattered throughout the country, a free-rider problem arises (Olson 1965). According to the theory of collective action, it is difficult for farmers to lobby for favorable policy outcomes in agriculture. They have no political power to challenge the government's tax policy. However, as the number of farmers declines as economy develops, lobbying against agricultural taxation can be conducted more efficiently, and if their number declines further, farmers succeed in introducing protection policies.

Figure 11.4 shows how this hypothesis is applied to Africa. The NRA is compared with the political power of agriculture in terms of the share of rural population in the total population. In this case, a negative correlation is observed between the NRA and the rural population share. It shows that the degree of agricultural taxation weakens as the share of rural population decreases, that is, as economic development progresses, and agricultural taxation tends to turn into agricultural protection over the long term. As a determinant of agricultural policies the share of rural population seems to work.

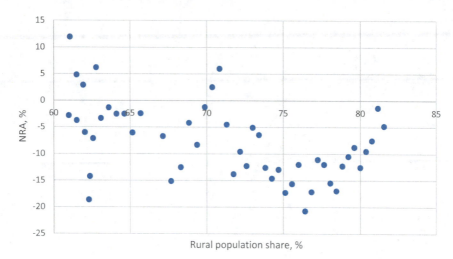

Fig. 11.4 Relationship between rural population share and NRA in Africa, 1961–2010. *Source* World Bank, National and Global Estimates of Distortions to Agricultural Incentives 1955–2011

However, GDP per capita or rural population share alone is not the sole determinant of agricultural policies, which depend on many other factors. Moreover, the numerical value of the NRA shown here is a weighted average that summarizes Africa as a whole in a single index. It is reasonable to consider that many different trends in different countries are hidden in the single NRA and unique characteristics by country may offset each other. Therefore, more detailed analysis is required.

Now, we focus on individual countries in Africa. Table 11.1 shows the average GDP per capita and NRA for agriculture for 20 Sub-Saharan Africa countries in the two periods of 1975–79 and 2006–10 (years varied by country) with the annual growth rate between the two periods. Excluding South Africa, GDP per capita in these countries is in the 200–600 dollar range in 2000 US dollars in the recent years. Although this is still at a low level, many countries grew from the late 1970s with a positive growth rate between the two periods. Six of 20 countries show annual growth rates exceeding 1%. Ethiopia, Mozambique and Uganda had a high growth rate of 1.72, 2.89, and 2.65%, respectively.

On the other hand, the NRAs for agriculture show many countries' negative values in the 2000s, indicating that agricultural taxation policies prevailed. Only five countries—Chad, Mozambique, Nigeria, South Africa and Sudan—had a positive NRA. However, looking at the annual rate of increase in the NRA between the two periods, 13 out of the 20 countries show positive values. This means that the degree of agricultural taxation declined, and some countries switched from taxing to protecting agriculture.

In the 1975–79 period, 11 countries had an NRA of minus 10% or less. Seven of the 11 are in coastal regions. Most of the coastal countries exported agricultural products on which governments imposed export tax. However, this trend in the NRA

11 Agricultural Market Intervention and Emerging States in Africa 259

Table 11.1 NRA and GDP per capita in 20 African countries

County (Region[a])	Period	GDP per capita[b]	NRA (%)[c]
Benin (C)	1975–79	276	−0.50
	2001–05	321	−0.12
	Growth rate	0.58	0.01
Burkina Faso (L)	1975–79	159	−1.51
	2006–10	263	−7.19
	Growth rate	1.64	−0.18
Cameroon (R, C)	1975–79	638	−14.35
	2005–09	695	−1.67
	Growth rate	0.29	0.42
Chad (L)	1975–79	197	−4.70
	2001–05	220	0.13
	Growth rate	0.42	0.19
Cote d'ivoire (C)	1975–79	1051	−34.71
	2005–09	565	−29.74
	Growth rate	−2.05	0.17
Ethiopia (L)	1981–85	123	−18.69
	2006–10	188	−4.65
	Growth rate	1.72	0.56
Ghana (C)	1975–79	238	−25.58
	2006–10	328	−3.91
	Growth rate	1.03	0.70
Kenya (C)	1975–79	402	−1.66
	2006–10	455	−1.20
	Growth rate	0.41	0.01
Madagascar (C)	1975–79	346	−27.06
	2006–10	248	−2.37
	Growth rate	−1.08	0.80
Mali (L)	1975–79	251	−2.18
	2006–10	276	−4.52
	Growth rate	0.31	−0.08
Mozambique (C)	1981–85	176	−29.74
	2006–10	359	7.33
	Growth rate	2.89	1.48
Nigeria (R, C)	1975–79	439	6.34
	2006–10	492	1.85
	Growth rate	0.37	−0.14

(continued)

Table 11.1 (continued)

County (Region[a])	Period	GDP per capita[b]	NRA (%)[c]
Senegal (C)	1975–79	495	−22.74
	2001–05	475	−1.11
	Growth rate	−0.16	0.83
South Africa (R, C)	1975–79	3296	3.83
	2006–10	3702	2.38
	Growth rate	0.38	−0.05
Sudan (L)	1975–79	313	−24.33
	2006–10	515	0.77
	Growth rate	1.62	0.81
Tanzania (C)	1976–80	n.a.	−44.80
	2006–10	402	−1.58
	Growth rate	n.a.	1.73
Togo (C)	1975–79	314	−0.40
	2006–10	265	−4.24
	Growth rate	−0.55	−0.12
Uganda (L)	1981–85	173	−6.79
	2006–10	332	−15.83
	Growth rate	2.65	−0.36
Zambia (R, L)	1975–79	506	−37.29
	2001–05	335	−14.02
	Growth rate	−1.57	0.89
Zimbabwe (L)	1975–79	594	−28.60
	2001–05	492	−37.96
	Growth rate	−0.72	−0.36

Source World Bank, National and Global Estimates of Distortions to Agricultural Incentives 1955–2011

Note
[a]Region is classified as follows: C is coastal, L is landlocked, and R is resource-rich
[b]GDP per capita is in 2000 US dollars and growth rate is annual compounded gwowth rate between the two periods
[c]Growth rate of the NRA is the annual average of increases between the two periods

diminished by the 2000s. Coastal countries are just one of four that show a nominal rate of protection (NRP) of minus 10% or less in the 2000s. It is notable that coastal countries show larger increases in the NRA per year during the two periods than other regions; eight of 13 countries that have a positive annual increase rate are coastal countries. In other words, distortions by market intervention in agriculture have been corrected in coastal countries, which were subject to agricultural taxation.

African countries have adopted policies to tax agriculture for a long time, which contributed to state finances and kept food prices low, thereby preventing wage

11 Agricultural Market Intervention and Emerging States in Africa 261

rises. However, in recent years the agricultural taxation trend weakened and the price distortion was corrected to some degree. Furthermore, as seen from the Asian experience of emerging economies, the income disparity between agriculture and industry tends to expand and become a social and economic problem in some African countries. Agricultural policy has to deal with that problem.

11.3 The Relationship Between Economic Development and Agricultural Protection Policy

A formal model showing the relationship between the NRA and economic development is presented in this section. First, it is assumed that politicians (or political parties) seek to maximize votes in elections.

The level of protection (taxation) desirable for politicians is, therefore, the level that maximizes their political power by maximizing the number of votes in elections. Even those who benefit from a policy or those who suffer losses express their intention by voting. Thus, it is necessary to examine the relationship between the costs and benefits for politicians who set the level of agricultural protection.

Politicians calculate how many votes they will secure by raising the level of agricultural protection. These votes will be cast by farmers. On the other hand, they also have to calculate how many votes will be lost by choosing the same policy. Those who previously supported the politicians may change their minds and not vote for them if they do not like an increase in the level of agricultural protection. They are most likely consumers.

Politicians calculate votes earned and votes lost in order to maximize their total vote. Maximizing votes then becomes a matter of setting the agricultural protection level at the point where the marginal benefit coincides with the marginal cost of the policy. The marginal benefit is an increment in the votes gained by increasing a unit of agricultural protection level while the marginal cost is a decrement of votes lost by the same policy.

Figure 11.5 shows the marginal benefit curve (MB) and the marginal cost curve (MC), which change along the level of agricultural protection. MB is described as a line with a downward slope to the right because the marginal utility (gain) of farmers declines as the level of protection is raised. On the other hand, MC is a line with an upward slope to the right because the marginal dis-utility (pain) of consumers increases as food prices are raised. Politicians can maximize votes by setting the protection level at T at which point MB and MC are intersected shown at point E.

While the level of protection desirable for politicians is not necessarily the socially desirable level of protection, it is not easy to break this equilibrium because the determination of the protection level is built into the structure of politics. Market failure can be caused by monopolies, the provision of public goods, the existence of externalities and information asymmetries, but not only the market but also governments and politics can fail.

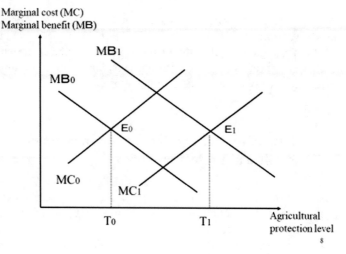

Fig. 11.5 Political determination of agricultural protection level

In the early stages of economic development, many farmers benefit from agricultural protection, but there is no organizational capacity or ability to make politicians increase their supporting votes. The proportion of the products for market sale is small so that there are few incentives to ask for price support. For politicians, the increment in support obtained from agricultural protection policy is small and therefore the marginal benefit curve is low. On the other hand, political pressures from industrial sector leaders who oppose agricultural protection are strong and well organized. Also, as agricultural price rises put pressure on the lives of urban workers and even cause riots, there are a large number of potential votes lost by increasing the level of agricultural protection. That is, the marginal cost curve for agricultural protection is set high. As a result, the level of agricultural protection in developing countries is extremely low, and in some cases, there is a negative protection level. Even agricultural deprivation measures are introduced.

However, as economic development progresses, the political environment also changes. First, as commercialization of agricultural products progresses, farmers' income becomes more dependent on prices of agricultural products because they sell the products in the market. The educational level of farmers also increases, and as transportation and communications develop, farmers become conscious of the gap in the standard of living between urban and rural areas, which expands in the process of industrialization. Therefore, farmers have greater desire for agricultural protection than before.

Voices calling for protection of agriculture are united through agencies such as agricultural organizations and become political pressures. As the industrial sector expands, the agricultural sector shrinks and the number of farmers also decreases, but in reality, this phenomenon itself increases the farmers' political power. When a group collectively tries to do something for a purpose, the smaller the members of that group, the higher the participation rate in that action and therefore the higher the efficiency. The reason is that if the number of people is large, the role of an individual is small, and there is a tendency to think that they have no influence on the whole. But if the group is smaller, this free rider problem can be prevented. This is what Olson pointed out in *Theory of Collective Action* (Olson 1965).

In this way, farmers' groups, which become more efficient at lobbying as the economy develops, can promise politicians to gain larger numbers of supporting votes in exchange for stronger agricultural protection. Also, fertilizer and other agricultural input material industries that depend on agricultural production support agricultural protection. Therefore, as the economy develops, the marginal benefit curve to politicians for supplying agricultural protection shifts higher upwards.

How about opposition to agricultural protection? As per capita income increases with economic development, the proportion of food expenses in total consumption declines. Rising grocery prices do not have as much impact on workers' lives as before, and their resistance to agricultural protection diminishes. Also, since the industrial structure itself shifts from labor-intensive to capital-intensive, the importance of wages is small for management and capitalists. Thus, their consciousness of prices of agricultural products diminishes. Furthermore, as the non-agricultural sector expands, the number of enterprises also increases, and even if they try to act jointly, the free rider phenomenon described above occurs and cooperation cannot be achieved at previous levels.

Most people engage in non-agricultural sectors in the developed-country stage. The cost of protecting agriculture is very small for non-agricultural people on a per capita basis. The costs necessary to provide the same protection to the small number of farmers drop drastically so resistance is reduced accordingly. In addition, at this stage, the importance of the non-economic value of agriculture such as conservation of green space and maintenance of country scenery in rural areas is increasingly asserted. Thus, protection of agriculture tends to be easy to accept. These changes shift the marginal cost curve of agricultural protection for politicians downwards.

For politicians, the marginal benefits from agricultural protection are strengthened and the marginal costs are reduced, resulting in both MR and MC curves shifting to the right and agricultural protection levels at the developed-country stage rising.

11.4 Determinants of the Agricultural Protection Level

This section presents a mechanism to determine the agricultural protection level based on the above model. An important variable that directly affects the number of votes cast for a politician in terms of agricultural protection policy is the relative farm household income in comparison with workers' income of the industrial sector. The income disparity between the agricultural and industrial sectors is neglected in the early stages of development. But, as development progresses, remediation of income disparity becomes a policy issue.

The labor wage rate is used as the most important variable representing income. The demand curve for labor is derived as marginal labor productivity: that is, the physical marginal labor productivity multiplied by the product price. The wage rate is determined at the level where the labor demand curve intersects with the labor supply curve. If the labor market is competitive, the wage rate is the same in agriculture and industry. However, production resources invested in the agricultural sector are mostly specific to agriculture and the migration and shifting of agricultural resources to the industrial sector are difficult and impose a large transaction cost including psychological costs. Therefore, the wage rate is determined differently between agriculture and industry equalizing it to the marginal value productivity of labor in each sector as follows:

$$Wa = Pa\ MLa \tag{11.1}$$

$$Wm = Pm\ MLm \tag{11.2}$$

where Wa and Wm are the agricultural and industrial wage rates, respectively. Pa and Pm are the price of agricultural and industrial products, respectively. MLa and MLm represent the physical marginal productivity of agricultural and industrial labor, respectively.

As economic development progresses, the income disparity between the agricultural and industrial sectors expands, and it becomes a policy issue to keep this gap at a certain level. Therefore, in order to balance the wage rate in agriculture with that in industrial sector at a certain level politically, the following relationship must be satisfied.

$$Wa^* = k\ Wm \tag{11.3}$$

where Wa^* is a politically desirable level of the wage rate in agriculture and k is a parameter indicating how much the government intends to rectify the income disparity. Politicians expect to increase the number of votes cast by strengthening the protection of agriculture, namely raising k, while it decreases the number of votes cast by groups who oppose agricultural protection such as consumer groups. The value of k is determined so as to equalize the marginal benefit and the marginal cost for politicians.

The marginal benefit curve, MB, shifts upward because of the strengthening political power of the agricultural sector as the economy develops. The share of rural population in total population (SA) is an indicator that shows the political power of the agricultural sector. On the other hand, the marginal cost curve, MC, shifts downward owing to the rising social tolerance of agricultural protection. As an indicator of the marginal cost, GDP divided by rural population (GA) is used. The variable GA needs to be explained as follows.

The marginal cost of increasing the level of agricultural protection for politicians is the marginal loss of votes from consumers. As income goes up, consumers tend not to be conscious of food prices because the Engel coefficient decreases. Also, if the share of farmers in total population declines, the total cost of protecting agriculture is reduced. Thus, consumers' tolerance of agricultural protection is a function of GDP per capita and the share of farmers who are protected. The variable GA is introduced as a proxy to indicate consumers' tolerance, which is GDP per rural population calculated by GDP per capita (GDP/N) multiplied by the reciprocal of the share of rural population in total population (N/Na), where N is total population and Na is rural population.

Then, MR and MC are expressed as follows.

$$MB = f(k, SA) \tag{11.4}$$

$$MC = g(k, GA) \tag{11.5}$$

Since the value of k is determined at the point where MB and MC are equalized in equilibrium, k is expressed by the exogenous variables SA and GA.

$$k = k(SA, GA) \tag{11.6}$$

The domestic price is the international price PW multiplied by the nominal protection coefficient (NPC), which is the nominal rate of protection (NRP, the difference between domestic and foreign prices divided by foreign price) plus 1. Therefore, Eq. (11.1) becomes as follows.

$$Wa = NPC\ PWa\ MLa \tag{11.7}$$

If the NRP is politically manipulated by politicians who try to correct the income disparity between the agricultural and industrial sectors, the nominal protection coefficient of the domestic agricultural products can be expressed as follows, using Eqs. (11.2), (11.3), (11.6) and (11.7).

$$NPC = NRP + 1 = k(SA, GA)\left(\frac{PWa}{Pm}\right)^{-1}\left(\frac{MLa}{MLm}\right)^{-1} \tag{11.8}$$

The level of agricultural protection depends on the share of rural population (SA), the GDP per capita of rural population (GA), the terms of trade of agricultural products to industrial products in international trade (PWa/Pm), assuming no distortions in industrial sector, and the marginal productivity ratio of the agricultural sector to the industrial sector (MLa/MLm).

An important fact is that as long as the marginal labor productivity gap between agriculture and industry is expanding, the level of agricultural protection needs to continue to rise to correct it. If economic growth accompanies industrialization and productivity in industrial sector continues to rise, agricultural protection will continue to be strengthened. In other words, even if the agricultural protection level is kept high, the political objective cannot be achieved unless the protection level is raised continuously. Agricultural protection has to grow under this mechanism.

11.5 Regression Analysis of Agricultural Protection Level

Based on Eq. (11.8), a regression analysis is conducted using pool data of 20 Sub-Saharan African countries for 1961–2010. Countries in the sample are Benin, Burkina Faso, Cameroon, Chad, Cote d'Ivoire, Ethiopia, Ghana, Kenya, Madagascar, Mali, Mozambique, Nigeria, Senegal, South Africa, Sudan, Tanzania, Togo, Uganda, Zambia, and Zimbabwe. The number of years for which data are available is different by country.

Data for the NRP used in the dependent variable are nra_tott (NRA, all primary agriculture, total for covered and non-covered) from the series of World Bank's National and Global Estimates of Distortions to Agricultural Incentives, 1955–2011. The data include domestic subsidies as well as the value of differences between the domestic and international prices of the products. For the country level of protection, a weighted average of the NRA of individual agricultural products is calculated with weights of gross values of production at unassisted prices.

Data used for the explanatory variables are as follows. The share of rural population to total population (SA) and the GDP per capita of rural population (GA) are available in the World Development Indicators of the World Bank, where GDP is expressed in 2010 constant US dollars. For the variable of the terms of trade (PA = PWa/Pm), data of the import price (unit value) index of agricultural products for each country are used for PWa while date of the export price (unit price) index of Africa as a whole are used for Pm. Data are available in the Trade Indices of the United Nations. For the variable of the marginal productivity ratio of the agricultural sector to the industrial sector (LA = MLa/MLm), the ratio of average labor productivity in agriculture to that in the non-agricultural sector is used because data for marginal labor productivity are not available. The labor productivity of agriculture is derived from the added value of the agricultural sector divided by rural population while the labor productivity of the non-agricultural sector is derived from the non-agricultural GDP divided by the non-rural population. Data are available in the World Development Indicators of the World Bank, where GDP is expressed in 2010 constant US dollars.

The equation for estimation is expressed as follows:

$$\ln(1 + NRA_{it}) = \beta 0 + \beta 1 \ln SA_{it} \\ + \beta 2 \ln GA_{it} + \beta 3 \ln LA_{it} + \beta 4 \ln PA_{it} + \gamma i + \varepsilon it \qquad (11.9)$$

where i is a subscript that represents a country, t is a subscript that represents a year, γi indicates the fixed effect of a country unchanged with respect to time, and $\varepsilon\, it$ is an error term. The expected signs of the coefficients are $\beta 1 < 0$, $\beta 2 > 0$, $\beta 3 < 0$ and $\beta 4 < 0$.

The results of the regression analysis using the fixed effect model are summarized in Table 11.2. First, looking at the relationship between rural population share and agricultural protection level in estimation (1), it is found that there is a statistically significant relationship between them. The correlation was not clear in Fig. 11.1,

Table 11.2 Results of regressions of nominal protection coefficient (NPC) in Africa

	(1)	(2)	(3)	(4)
Rural pop share	−0.2508***	−0.3757***	−0.2793***	−0.3204***
ln(SA)	(0.0500)	(0.0731)	(0.0957)	(0.0200)
GDP per rural pop			0.0566	0.0115**
ln(GA)			(0.0351)	(0.0072)
Labor productivity ratio		−0.0451**	−0.0351*	−0.0398***
ln(LA)		(0.0194)	(0.0205)	(0.0040)
Relative price				−0.0324***
ln(PA)				(0.0035)
Constant	−0.1045***	−0.2189***	−0.5105***	−0.2549***
	(0.0330)	(0.0572)	(0.1909)	(0.0399)
Observations	869	745	735	655
Adjusted R²	0.440	0.428	0.427	0.511

Source Author's calculation
Note Standard errors in parentheses
*Significant at 10%; **significant at 5%; ***significant at 1%

which showed the relationship between the share of rural population and the NRA in a weighted average for Africa as a whole. But the regression result in the country fixed-effect model here confirms a negative relationship between them.

Next, in estimation (2), the variable of the labor productivity ratio is added to the rural population share. The coefficient of this variable is also statistically significant as well as that of the rural population share. It shows that if labor productivity in the agricultural sector falls behind the nonagricultural sector, the level of agricultural protection rises. Thus, the hypothesis of the political correction of income disparity in the course of economic development is proven.

Furthermore, in estimation (3), which adds another political variable—GDP per capita of rural population—the coefficient takes a positive value as expected, but it is not statistically significant. This variable indicates whether the people are vital to protecting agriculture or not, but it could not be confirmed in Africa.

Finally, the relative price variable is added in estimation (4), which includes all the variables of the model presented in the previous section. The number of observations used for estimation is reduced because countries and years for which relative prices cannot be obtained are excluded. In the estimation of the full model, all the coefficients show signs as expected, and are statistically significant except for the GDP per capita of rural population variable.

The result of the full model estimation (4) confirms the relationship between the agricultural protection level and political and economic factors is relevant to politicians' behavior in seeking to maximize votes. In African countries, if the rural population share decreases by 1%, it may cause 0.32% increases in the agricultural protection level. That is, taxation on agriculture is reduced in the course of economic development. If the GDP per capita of the rural population increases by 1%, the protection level may increase by 0.1%. However, this relationship is not statistically significant. In other words, if other conditions are kept constant, it can be argued that in Africa the economy is not growing sufficiently to become tolerant of agricultural protection. In other words, African consumers and governments have changed the level of agricultural taxation for other reasons.

An important variable in relation to economic development is the relative labor productivity of agriculture. The source of economic development is often the growth in the industrial sector. The rapid growth of the industrial sector expands the disparity in labor productivity between agriculture and industry, resulting in income disparity. Although the value of the coefficient is small, the estimation result shows that the expansion in this productivity gap lowered agricultural taxation and, as seen in recent years, it turned into agricultural protection.

The variable of the relative price is also statistically significant, indicating that if the terms of trade become disadvantageous to agriculture, the agricultural protection level rises slightly but clearly. However, in this estimation, the price of the industrial sector is represented by Africa's total export unit value index. An analysis with data showing more accurate terms of trade would be desirable.

There are a number of residual problems in the statistical estimations. First, the independent variables of the estimated equations are not mutually independent. The share of rural population, GDP per capita of rural population, and relative labor productivity are all indicators that show economic development and are related to each other. Therefore, a problem of multiple-collinearity may be involved. Changes in agricultural protection levels also affect the relative labor productivity of agriculture and even the rural population share. Therefore, the estimated results here may contain a simultaneous equation bias.

In the future, it would be desirable to analyze the levels of agricultural protection in a general equilibrium framework together with growth in the non-agricultural sector.

11.6 Conclusion

Research on agricultural protection has been very active and many studies have contributed to clarification of the determinants of protection. Also, construction of statistical data sets including those of the World Bank made possible consistent comparisons of levels agricultural protection and distortions internationally. This chapter has benefited from the availability of data on agricultural protection levels and has used the data to test the hypothesis called the "developmental paradox" in Africa. A model to describe the "developmental paradox" has been proposed and tested by statistical estimations.

Rapid economic development makes the agricultural sector shrink, which may cause social and economic disorder in rural areas. It also becomes a factor encouraging political unrest. Therefore, agricultural protection policies tend to be adopted for the purpose of correcting income disparities between agriculture and industry. Indeed, the "developmental paradox" has been observed in Japan, Korea and Taiwan during their rapid economic growth period (Honma and Hayami 1986, 2009).

It is somewhat challenging to apply this model to Africa where economic development is still underway. However, the logic of reducing taxation on agriculture is the same as increasing agricultural protection. Further, it is meaningful to extract common factors that determine agricultural policies taking into account the differences in individual countries in a fixed effect model in Africa.

The "developmental paradox" is an empirical question and should be tested for those countries that are in the course of economic development such as in Africa. It is based on the behavior of politicians seeking to maximize votes. However, because of over-simplification, more complicated political and economic behaviors such as opposition parties' actions and policy struggles are neglected in the model. Despite the over-simplification, the statistical tests confirmed the significance of variables derived from the model, which show common factors that determine the level of agricultural protection among countries in Sub-Saharan Africa: the share of rural population, GDP per capita of rural population, relative labor productivity, and the terms of trade in international markets.

The government plays a major role in economic development. This chapter has shown that agricultural taxation policy declines as economic development progresses and that even African countries have adopted agricultural protection policies. Africa's economic development may have been more advanced if agricultural taxation had been eliminated earlier. If emerging countries in Africa had focused on improving infrastructure such as irrigation and drainage facilities and on investing in road and transportation rather than on taxing agriculture in the early stage of development, they might have been able to achieve agriculture-based growth faster.

Today many African countries still continue to impose agricultural taxes which need to be eliminated as soon as possible. In addition, emerging countries in Africa where further economic growth is expected in the future should not follow the experience of emerging Asian countries, which mistakenly introduced agricultural protection as an industrial adjustment policy to correct income disparity. Avoiding market intervention and correcting distortions of farmer's incentives are necessary even if correcting income disparity is a political priority in Africa. So-called decoupled policies such as direct payments with public investment in agricultural infrastructure should be introduced to promote agricultural growth.

References

Acemoglu, D., Johnson, S., & Robinson, J. A. (2001). The colonial origins of comparative development: An empirical investigation. *American Economic Review, 91*(5), 1369–1401.

Anderson, K. (Ed.). (2009). *Distortions to agricultural incentives: A global perspective, 1955–2007.* London/Washington, DC: Palgrave Macmillan/World Bank.

Anderson, K., Hayami, Y., et al. (1986). *The political economy of agricultural protection: East Asia in international perspective.* London and Boston: Allen and Unwin.

Anderson, K., & Masters, W. (Eds.). (2009). *Distortions to agricultural incentives in Africa.* Washington, DC: World Bank.

Bates, R. H. (1989). *Beyond the miracle of the market: The political economy of agrarian development in Rural Kenya.* Cambridge and New York: Cambridge University Press.

Bates, R. H., & Block, S. (2010). Agricultural trade interventions in Africa (Chap. 12). In K. Anderson (Ed.), *The political economy of agricultural price distortions.* New York: Cambridge University Press.

Block, S., & Bates, R. H. (2011). Political institutions and agricultural trade interventions in Africa. *American Journal of Agricultural Economics, 93*(2), 317–323.

De Gorter, H., & Swinnen, J. F. M. (2002). Political economy of agricultural policies. In B. Gardner & G. Rausser (Eds.), *The handbook of agricultural economics* (Vol. 2). Amsterdam: Elsevier Science.

Gardner, B. L. (1987). Causes of U.S. farm commodity programs. *Journal of Political Economy, 95*(2), 290–310.

Grossman, G. M., & Helpman, E. (1994). Protection for sale. *American Economic Review, 84*(4), 833–850.

Grossman, G. M., & Helpman, E. (2002). *Interest groups and trade policy.* Princeton, NJ: Princeton University Press.

Hoeffler, H. (2011). The political economy of agricultural policies in Africa: History, analytical concepts and implications for development cooperation. *Quarterly Journal of International Agriculture, 50*(1), 29–53.

Honma, M., & Hayami, Y. (1986). The determinants of agricultural protection levels: An econometric analysis (Chap. 4). In K. Anderson, Y. Hayami, et al. (Eds.), *The political economy of agricultural protection: East Asia in international perspective.* London: Allen and Unwin.

Honma, M., & Hayami, Y. (2009). Japan, Republic Korea, and Taiwan, China (Chap. 2). In K. Anderson (Ed.), *Distortions to agricultural incentives: A global perspective, 1955–2007.* London/Washington, DC: Palgrave Macmillan/World Bank.

Krueger, A. O., Schiff, M., & Valdés, A. (1988). Agricultural incentives in developing countries: Measuring the effect of sectoral and economywide policies. *World Bank Economic Review, 2*(3), 255–272.

Krueger, A. O., Schiff, M., & Valdés, A. (1991). *The political economy of agricultural pricing policy.* London: Johns Hopkins University Press for the World Bank.

Lindert, P. H. (1991). Historical patterns of agricultural policy. In C. Timmer (Ed.), *Agriculture and the state: Growth, employment, and poverty.* Ithaca, NY: Cornell University Press.

Olson, M. (1965). *The logic of collective action.* New Haven: Yale University Press.

Persson, T., & Tabellini, G. E. (2000). *Political economics: Explaining economic policy.* Cambridge, MA: MIT Press.

Poulton, C. (2014). Democratisation and the political incentives for agricultural policy in Africa. *Development Policy Review, 32*(S2), s101–s122.

Shleifer, A. (1997). Government in transition. *European Economic Review, 41*(3–5), 385–410.

Swinnen, J. F. M., Banerjee, A. N., & De Gorter, H. (2001). Economic development, institutional change, and the political economy of agricultural protection: An econometric study of Belgium since the 19th century. *Agricultural Economics, 26*(1), 25–43.

Tracy, M. (1989). *Government and agriculture in Western Europe 1880–1988* (3rd ed.). New York: Harvester Wheatsheaf.

Open Access This chapter is licensed under the terms of the Creative Commons Attribution-NonCommercial-NoDerivatives 4.0 International License (http://creativecommons.org/licenses/by-nc-nd/4.0/), which permits any noncommercial use, sharing, distribution and reproduction in any medium or format, as long as you give appropriate credit to the original author(s) and the source, provide a link to the Creative Commons licence and indicate if you modified the licensed material. You do not have permission under this licence to share adapted material derived from this chapter or parts of it.

The images or other third party material in this chapter are included in the chapter's Creative Commons licence, unless indicated otherwise in a credit line to the material. If material is not included in the chapter's Creative Commons licence and your intended use is not permitted by statutory regulation or exceeds the permitted use, you will need to obtain permission directly from the copyright holder.

Chapter 12
Role of Community and Government in Irrigation Management in Emerging States: Lessons from Japan, China, and India

Kei Kajisa

12.1 Introduction

Maintaining well-functioning irrigation systems is a crucial condition for sustainable agricultural development, and many states have implemented different kinds of policies for this aim. In the less-developed countries (LDCs), a conventional issue in this policy arena has been how to mobilize abundant local labor for successful collective management. From the academics, Ostrom's group has made a significant contribution to this end by revealing and synthesizing the conditions for the success, and then in the policy arena in the 1980s and 1990s, a boom of the community participatory approach and the irrigation management transfer (to the local bodies) occurred. The international development society has realized that the use of community mechanism for local resource management is effective for labor surplus countries at an early stage of development.

However, rather than abundant labor, a contemporary issue in the agricultural sector among emerging states, is an increasing labor scarcity. These states have emerged in the global society with their success in labor-intensive industrialization in the areas of textiles, garments, and other light manufacturing. It is because of this success that the agricultural sector has been experiencing labor scarcity. Recent globalization has been accelerating this process by providing rural people with lucrative job opportunities overseas. Facing this trend, an appropriate direction of change in agricultural sector is the substitution of capital for labor. However, as we will explain later, the substitution process entails externalities in a very complicated manner. Therefore, under such a circumstance, the role of the government increases. Understanding the role the government for the achievement of a necessary substitution for sustainable, equitable, and efficient water use is an important contemporary issue of irrigation policies in the emerging states.

K. Kajisa (✉)
Aoyama Gakuin University, 4-4-25 Shibuya, Shibuya-Ku, Tokyo, Japan
e-mail: kei.kajisa@gmail.com

© The Author(s) 2019
K. Otsuka and K. Sugihara (eds.), *Paths to the Emerging State in Asia and Africa*, Emerging-Economy State and International Policy Studies, https://doi.org/10.1007/978-981-13-3131-2_12

Two unique features of the emerging states make the policy issue more complicated than the time when the current DCs had dealt with their increasing labor scarcity. First, groundwater irrigation with private wells and pumps has been becoming rampant. The reduction in the cost of pumps and the excavation of wells have accelerated the exit of farmers from traditional irrigation systems, resulting in a faster increase in labor scarcity in traditional water management. Moreover, the private use of groundwater by individuals entails negative externalities to the neighboring users who share the groundwater aquifer and thus tends to create the problem of "the tragedy of commons." Therefore, an environmental issue comes into the policy arena more seriously than before.

Second, by a recommendation from international organizations or on its own initiatives, some LDCs have introduced volumetric irrigation water pricing with the aim of achieving water savings in their surface irrigation systems. Charging high prices on surface irrigation water may eventually induce farmers to switch to alternative sources for irrigation, which is another form of exit from the traditional irrigation systems. Besides, the implementation of volumetric pricing needs more sophisticated or more capital-intensive irrigation systems as it requires water volume measurement and on-demand water volume control, more or less similar to domestic water systems. Hence, under volumetric pricing system, both labor shortage and the necessity for substituting capital for labor may increase.

Another important point is that we must explicitly incorporate the framework of political economy. Many studies have shown that governments tend to raise agricultural protection in the course of economic development, and the level of protection tends to become excessive. As discussed by Honma in Chapter 10, this is closely related with rent-seeking activities from a shrinking farm sector. Hence, we must explicitly take into account the possibility of protectionism and the government failure as a side effect when the role of the government becomes more important.

In summary, the contemporary issues in irrigation policies of the emerging states are characterized as the achievement of smooth substitution of capital for labor and the achievement of optimal groundwater use under the existence of different kinds of externalities as well as under the pressure of protectionism. The aim of this article is to examine what is the optimal role of the government and what kind of policies are appropriate for the emerging states, using examples of rapidly industrialized or industrializing countries, namely, Japan, China, and India. First, using Japan as a forerunner, we summarize the historical experiences of Japan's irrigation policies and show their pros and cons. Then, using Japan's experience as a benchmark, we evaluate recent policies in China and in India, relying on the case studies of a particular place in each country, namely, Hubei in China and Tamil Nadu in India. Note that Japan's experience does not sufficiently cover the groundwater issue as well as the experiment of volumetric water pricing. We discuss these issues when we analyze the cases of China and India for the sake of obtaining useful lessons for other emerging states. Note, however, that as we rely on the cases of a particular place, we had better refrain from generalizing the lessons excessively.

The rest of the paper is as follows. Section 12.2 shows data on the increasing labor scarcity of our study countries. Section 12.3 explains key concepts such as externalities in irrigation systems and government failure and rent-seeking in the political economy framework. Section 12.4 reviews and evaluates irrigation policies in each country. Finally, Sect. 12.5 summarizes the lessons.

12.2 Changes in Labor Endowment

Figure 12.1 shows the changes in population and employment by sector from 1950 to 2015 in three countries. Our primary variable as a measure of labor scarcity in the agricultural sector is employment in agriculture.[1] Since India has data of this variable only in two years, we show also rural population, although this variable includes quite a large number of non-agricultural employment in the rural area, especially in India. Urban population is also shown as a reference.

In Japan, the rural population dropped sharply during its rapid industrialization period (from the 1950s to the 1970s). Even after that period, the exit of labor from the agricultural sector has continued to date as indicated by the employment figure. In China, the agricultural employment figure is available for a relatively longer period. It increased until the early 1990s almost parallel with the trend of urban population, indicating the net labor migration is little. After the take-off of the economy with the economic reform in the early 1990s, the rural employment (and the rural population as well) started decreasing, and this trend has continued till 2015. China's experience after the early 1990s is similar to that of Japan. India's case looks slightly different but is the same in terms of trends. Although the rural population increased continuously, the growth rate looks slower than that of the urban population in the 2000s. Moreover, agricultural employment (indicated by two triangles in the figure) decreased from 2005 to 2010. We conclude that similar to Japan, the two major emerging states, China and India, have started experiencing increasing labor scarcity in the agricultural sector.

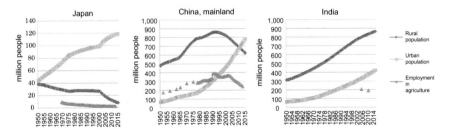

Fig. 12.1 Population and employment by sector in Japan, China, and India from 1950 to 2015. *Source* FAOSTAT

---

[1]This variable is not perfect in twofold; it measures labor use rather than endowment, and it includes agricultural employment in urban area. Nevertheless, the effects of these problems seem small, and this variable can be used at least as a good measure of trend.

12.3 Key Concepts

This section explains four key concepts used in the following case studies: (1) externalities in surface irrigation systems, (2) externalities in non-agricultural sector, (3) externalities in ground water irrigation systems, and (4) government failures in agricultural policies.

Externalities in surface irrigation systems is related with technological indivisibility and collective management of the systems, and they are further divided into two aspects: (a) those related with maintenance of irrigation facilities and (b) those related with allocation of irrigation water. We explain the maintenance aspect first. Once a system is installed to supply water to cover a certain command area, it cannot shrink its supply capacity according to the reduction of the number of users. This is because such systems need to maintain a certain water pressure and a certain water level in order to supply water to the tail-end users. If one user, for example in the midstream, becomes reluctant to fully provide his/her maintenance work or even completely exits from the irrigation system, the remaining users have to shoulder the exiting farmer's maintenance costs to maintain the capacity; this is a negative externality of the exit on the maintenance aspect. Regarding the allocation aspect, the exit of a farmer makes the continuity of irrigation water use along the canal broken. After the exits of some farmers from the irrigation system, the users' plots become segmented from each other, which makes coordination and supervision of allocation among remaining water users more difficult. Although Olson (1965) predicts that the smaller group can make collective action more effectively, such a mechanism may not work in the context of irrigation management if the cost of the former (i.e., coordination difficulty due to scattered plots) is greater than the benefit of the latter (i.e., effective communication in the smaller group). In this manner, the negative externalities are likely to arise on both the maintenance and allocation aspects in the process of farmers' exit from the system, and, thus, the involvement of the government is called for.

The second type of externalities emerge when irrigation water provides non-agricultural benefits, such as drainage services for residences, fire prevention, environmental amenities, and the recharging of groundwater aquifers. Theoretically, these externalities can be internalized by ensuring all beneficiaries are involved in irrigation management. Practically, however, the non-agricultural benefits are so thinly and so widely spread that it is difficult to get all involved. It should be noted that such kinds of externalities also increase with economic development as the numbers of non-agricultural residents increase in rural areas and as groundwater irrigation systems becomes popular.

Because of the existence of these externalities, the private incentives for irrigation investment and management tend to be smaller than the socially optimal level. This problem becomes more serious as industrialization progresses. In the context of surface irrigation management, as labor scarcity increases, the substitution of capital for labor must proceed. However, the necessary investment may not reach to the socially optimal level. The role of government can be observed in supporting capital investment in irrigation systems or the modernization of such systems to correct this failure.

Now we move to the case of externalities in groundwater. The over-dissemination of wells and overexploitation of groundwater is commonly observed. This is indeed a typical case of "the tragedy of the commons." The use of groundwater by some individual entails negative externalities for others who share a groundwater aquifer. Without sufficient groundwater recharge, the groundwater will eventually be depleted. Furthermore, in many developing countries, governments use groundwater development as a tool for rural development. Support for such development by the government will make the depletion process more rapid. Regulations or interventions are needed to control for these negative externalities.

Finally, let us discuss government failures. For a clearer understanding of the formation of irrigation policies, it is important to distinguish between two kinds of government failures. The first can occur when asymmetric information exists between the government and the users. The government may fail to provide appropriate support if it cannot precisely estimate the demand for water by the farmers. A possible solution is to get the farmers involved in the project design, which is well-known as a participatory development approach. However, it seems that the use of this solution becomes increasingly difficult for emerging states when support from the government increases and the projects are handled by bureaucrats and technocrats of the irrigation authorities who are usually public servants, rather than local farmers. This may be particularly so when the form of support is financial rather than technical, because an increase in financial support makes the implementation of irrigation projects similar to the provision of pure public goods.

Another type of government failure is related to the political economy. This problem occurs in a way that the government, expecting votes, tends to provide public goods in favor of a particular group of people. As many studies argue, this framework can convincingly explain why agricultural protection rises in many countries when the comparative advantage of the agricultural sector declines and political pressure from the farmers' group increases. In the context of irrigation policies, the government may use support for irrigation as a means of protection, resulting in overinvestment in irrigation facilities, pumps, and wells. Note that agricultural protection can be implemented by many means, such as output price support, input subsidies, income support, and trade regulation. One may argue that support for irrigation is better than price support as the former increases productivity while the latter spoils productivity improvement incentives. Nevertheless, even the irrigation support must be the one which increases labor productivity because the factor getting scarce is labor.

In summary, through experiencing an increase in labor scarcity and/or the development of groundwater irrigation under conditions of rapid industrialization and globalization, the level of different kinds of externalities increases, and thus the need for government interventions increases. Accordingly, the possibility of government failures also increases. Because of such failures, the level of interventions could either be too great or too little with a different combination of policies. The government must achieve an appropriate level of intervention to facilitate the substitution of capital for labor as the resource endowment of the economy changes. This is difficult but crucially important for sustainable development. In the following section, we review how Japan, China, and India have dealt with these issues.

12.4 Case Studies

12.4.1 Japan's Irrigation Policies Since the Late 19th Century

This section provides a historical review of Japan's irrigation policies since the late 19th century. We divide our review into three periods based on the attitude of the government: (1) community-based management (1880s–1910s), (2) increasing financial support by the government (1920s–1950s), and (3) financial takeover and modernization by the government (1960s–2010s).

Community-based management (1880s–1910s) The origin of water management institutions in which we can find the roots of current systems dates back to the 18th century, the mid-*Edo* period, when the rapid development of new paddy fields increased water demand (Tamaki et al. 1984). Traditionally, irrigation infrastructures were managed by local communities, with some exceptional cases of vast irrigation systems which received supports from local or national authorities (Tamaki and Hatate 1974). After the Meiji Restoration, the government replaced old systems with modern ones, in many respects to "catch up" with the Western world. Exceptionally, however, regarding water institutions, the government approved traditional water rights in the River Act (*Kasen-hou*) of 1886 and allowed traditional communities to handle the management. In addition, the Irrigation Association Code (*Suiri-kumiai-zyourei*) of 1890 stipulated that irrigation development projects must be financed by private sources (Tamaki et al. 1984).[2] The local leaders, usually large landlords in the rural area, bore the financial burden, and put their efforts into mobilizing local resources for the development and management of irrigation facilities to improve the social welfare of their local communities. In this regard, we may claim that the government left the role of irrigation development and management to the local communities, and that the local landlords behaved as if they were the local government. The local landlords had incentive to do so not only because they accepted the burden as a local leader and tried to maintain their social status but also because the improvement of land productivity in the entire community could increase the land rent from their tenants. This division of work functioned well when the financial and manpower capacity of the government was limited. Figure 12.2 shows the proportion of financial support for such land improvement projects (mainly irrigation develop-

---

[2]Meanwhile, it was stipulated that projects related to public rivers were publicly financed.

12 Role of Community and Government in Irrigation Management …

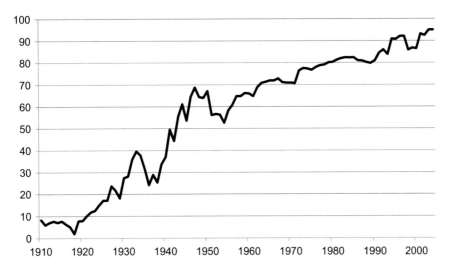

Fig. 12.2 Proportion of financial support for land improvement investment by the central and local government in Japan from 1910 to 2004. *Sources* National Research Institute of Agricultural Economics (1967) and Ministry of Agriculture, Forestry and Fisheries (various years)

ment) undertaken by the central and local governments from 1910 to 2004.[3] We can observe that public financial support was rather low in the 1910s.

Financial support by the government (1920s–1950s) There was a turning point in the 1920s regarding the roles of the community vis-a-vis the government. The local landlords lost their interest in investing in the irrigation during this period. The reasons included a low rice price due to increased imports from the colonies, a decline in land rent due to tenancy disputes with tenants, and, above all, an increase in investment returns from emerging modern industrial sectors. Therefore, the agricultural sector became a less attractive investment target for the landlords. Moreover, the transaction costs associated with irrigation development became much greater than the amount that local landlords could shoulder. As the coverage of the irrigation project area became larger, the stakeholder farmers began spreading beyond the locality that local leaders could manage. Therefore, the costs of the coordination of interests, convincing dissenting farmers, and arranging compensation increased in this period.

Meanwhile, a riot caused by the rice shortage in 1918 led the government to realize the importance of achieving an increase in the food supply. However, the government was no longer able to rely on local leaders' initiative, and thus started providing financial support for irrigation development. For example, the guidelines in 1923 (*Youhaisui-kansenkairyou-hozyo-youkou*) guaranteed 50% financial support

---

[3]Nakajima (1998) created this figure from 1910 to 1995. We replicated Fig. 12.2 with the original data from 1910 to 1995 and extended the years using Ministry of Agriculture, Forestry and Fisheries (various years).

from the government for projects greater than 500 ha of irrigation command area.[4] In summary, as the role of the community (local leaders' financial initiative) declined, the government supplemented it in this period. Figure 12.2 shows that support started increasing in the 1920s. This attitude continued until the 1950s, except during the Second World War, when the government disproportionately mobilized funding for the armament industry. In the 1950s, Japan achieved rice self-sufficiency.

Financial takeover and modernization by the government (1960s–2010s)
Japan experienced rapid industrialization and economic growth from the mid-1950s to the mid-1970s. This led to a rapid reduction in the labor endowment in the agricultural sector. This reduction entailed the loss of experienced water tenders, who were knowledgeable about the water control and distribution of their irrigation systems. In parallel, even among those who remained, farming became their side business as their income from non-agricultural works increased. These changes made strict and coordinated irrigation management more difficult among the remaining spatially dispersed farmers, and this difficulty increased further when the experienced water tenders were no longer available. From the relative resource endowment point of view, this means that the need for the substitution of capital for labor (including skilled labor) increased for efficient water use. However, as we explained earlier, this substitution process does not occur automatically as an outcome of the market mechanism. This is because there are externalities rooted in the feature of technological indivisibility and collective management. Moreover, the other type of externality (non-agricultural benefits) arose because the numbers of non-agricultural residents increased in the rural areas adjacent to the urban or industrial zones during the period of rapid industrialization. Because of the increase in the two kinds of externalities in this period, the demand for government intervention increased.

Indeed, the Japanese government strengthened its support for irrigation development in this period. Among many aspects, financial support increased from around 60% in the 1960s to 80% in the 1990s, and then to more than 90% in the 2000s (Fig. 12.2).[5] The projects in these periods included lining canals with concrete, the replacement of canals with pipelines, the rehabilitation of water intake, and the cleaning of dams and rivers with heavy machines. Automation and the remote control of water flows were also implemented, replacing the roles of the experienced water tenders. These modernization projects substituted capital for labor. In addition, the separation of water supply canals from drainage systems reduced the negative externality from non-agricultural residents.

We can justify the government interventions in this period for two reasons: first, the externalities were corrected by this public support; second, the changes caused by such support were consistent with the changes in the relative resource endowment. These kinds of active interventions were important for smooth economic growth

---

[4]To be precise, the threshold size of the project area was 500 *cho*, which is almost the same as 500 ha.

[5]There is one exceptional period showing a decrease in the mid-1950s after the achievement of rice self-sufficiency.

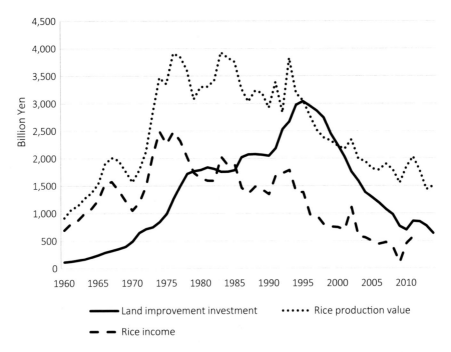

Fig. 12.3 Japan's land improvement investment, rice production value, and rice income from 1960 to 2015. *Source* Data are from the home page of Ministry of Agriculture, Forestry, and Fisheries (Accessed November 2017). The sources of each series are as follows. Land improvement investment: *Nougyou shokuryou kanren no keizai keisan*. Rice production value: *Seisannnougyou syotoku toukei*. Rice income: *Nousanbutu seisanhi toukei*. *Note* Rice income is computed as rice income per 10 are times rice cultivated area in 10 acre. Rice cultivated area was taken form *Skumotu toukei* at the homepage above. The definition of rice income per 10 are is as follows. Income = revenue − (total production cost − (imputed family labor cost + imputed capital payment + imputed land rent)). Subsidies are not included in the revenue

because they circumvented the decline in irrigation services and the stagnation of agricultural development.

At the same time, however, it is important to note that increased government interventions raise the risk of government failures. Given the existence of asymmetric information, the reduction in farmers' self-finance and the reduction in farmers' involvement may skew the level of investment toward overinvestment under the pressure of the rent-seeking from the farmers. In order to examine this possibility, we show the time series of the land improvement investment, the value of rice production, and the rice income of Japan from 1960 to 2015 (Fig. 12.3). Although they are rough indicators, we may say that the figure shows the trend of investment and its returns. According to the figure, the investment and returns increased almost parallel until the 1980s. However, after that, the production value and the rice income had declined, while the investment had continued increasing until the early 2000s.

Major reasons for the decline in the production value from the 1980s to the early 2000s were the double effects of the drop in the rice procurement price and the reduction in the quantity of rice production.[6] Even under such an adverse environment, if the cost for production were reduced and thus the profitability improved, the income would not decline this much. However, in reality, the cost was merely reduced, resulting in a sharp decline in rice income as shown in the figure.[7] It seemed that the investment did not contribute much to the improvement of rice sector profitability in this period. Note that the financial support by the government in the same period increased from 70 to 90% (Fig. 12.2). Moreover, since the 1970s the investment target had changed from the modernization of irrigation infrastructure to the improvement of individual farmers' paddy fields, where the new target can be regarded as a private property with much smaller externalities than irrigation infrastructure. In this regard, we may claim that there was overinvestment to the less justifiable target by the government.

After the 2000s, the land improvement investment had declined. Note, however, that the income subsidies to the farmers (data are not shown in the figure), which have less incentive for productivity improvement than the support for land improvement, has been maintained (as of 2017) as a major mean to support the agricultural sector. In summary, Japan's experience teaches us that under increasing labor scarcity in agriculture, it is important to provide public support for the substitution of capital for labor and, at the same time, to introduce an appropriate mechanism that can suppress the tendency for overinvestment under the trend of agricultural protectionism.

12.4.2 The Case of a Surface Gravity Irrigation Scheme in Hubei, China[8]

Facing a rapid increase in water demand for urban and industrial use, China aimed to achieve water savings in the agricultural sector, particularly in paddy farming as this was considered the largest water consumer. The major effort to promote

---

[6]We set the comparison period from 1986 to 2003; the beginning year is the year of the record-high price and the ending year is the year the government stopped the rice procurement policy. In this period, the price dropped 26% from 18,505 (yen/60 kg) to 13,748 (yen/60 kg), and the production quantity was reduced 21% from 11,035 (1000t) to 8,698 (1000t) in the same period, resulting in a 38% reduction in the production value. The reduction of production quantity was mainly due to the enforcement of the policy of reducing rice cultivated area. (Price data are from *Shokuryo toukei nenpou*, production quantity data are from *Seisannnougyou syotoku toukei*. Production value data are from *Seisannnougyou syotoku toukei*. All are taken from the homepage of the Ministry of Agriculture, Forestry and Fisheries)

[7]The average cost of production was reduced by 2% from 15,312 (yen/60 kg of rice) to 14,963 (yen/60 kg of rice) from 1986 to 2003, while the price was reduced by 26% from 18,505 (yen/60 kg) to 13,748 (yen/60 kg) in the same period. The total rice income declined by 41%. (Price data are from *Shokuryo toukei nenpou*, production cost data are from *Nousanbutu seisanhi toukei*. All are taken from the homepage of the Ministry of Agriculture, Forestry and Fisheries)

[8]This section draws heavily on Kajisa and Dong (2017).

water conservation in the agricultural sector began in the 1990s, with considerable regional variation in intervention tactics (Lohmar et al. 2007). In 2002, 20 provinces implemented a reform of taxes and fees called *fei gai shui*. Before the reform, a water fee was included in the land tax, equivalent to area-based pricing (i.e., zero marginal costs for irrigation water). Hence, there was no economic incentive among the users to save water. The reform called for separate water fees and increased independent management for each reservoir. In reaction to this change, many reservoirs began volumetric water pricing and expected this to have a significant impact on farmers' water-saving behaviors. This subsection evaluates the outcomes of this policy, using a survey conducted in an irrigation system (Zhanghe Irrigation System) in Hubei, China, in 2008.

In a surface gravity irrigation system, effective collective action among water users is needed to save water under volumetric pricing. This is because a feasible pricing method measures the volume at a canal's intake, and the total fee is charged to the water user group (WUG) rather than to individual farmers. The total fee is then divided among the WUG members by cultivated area. Therefore, the group has an incentive to save water, while individual farmers within a group may overuse water unless they are closely supervised. Institutional change must play an important role in preventing this free-rider problem within a WUG.

After the reform, institutional changes occurred in the WUG's traditional informal collective management system. These changes can be classified into four categories: (1) no change (or upholding informal management), (2) the formal appointment of water managers, (3) the formation of new smaller groups, each of which was a much smaller sub-set of farmers from neighboring plots only, and (4) individual irrigation using water from private ponds. The changes to (2) and (3) can be regarded as shifts toward water savings through more effective collective management under a manager or within a small group. The change to (4) comprises an exit from the irrigation system, resulting in increasing labor scarcity for management of the surface irrigation system. At the time of the survey, farmers' exit to non-agriculture activities also accelerated the rural labor shortage.

An interesting point is that we observe cases of "(1) no change," even when the price level was high (hence there must have been a large incentive for savings). Figure 12.4 shows the proportion of farmers within each water management institution by the volumetric price level of reservoir water (set at zero for area-based pricing). In the group at the lowest price level, including the case of area-based pricing, the farmers who chose no change account for the largest proportion (46%). This is a natural outcome because the farmers had little incentive to implement strict management for water savings. As the price goes up moderately, the proportion of manager appointments and that of new smaller group formations increase. When the price goes up further (beyond the 4th price range category), the attractiveness of exiting from reservoir water use increases, and the proportion of individual irrigation then increases. Moreover, the proportion of no change also increases, replacing the other two water-saving institutions (i.e., manager appointment and new smaller groups). The figure generally shows a U-shaped relationship for the volumetric price level with no change.

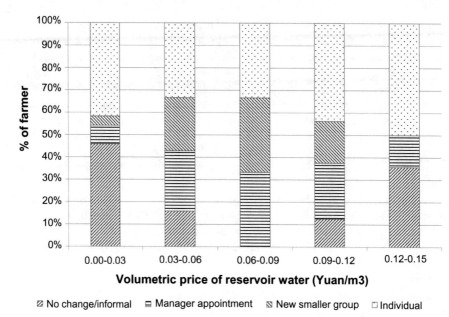

Fig. 12.4 The proportion of sample farmers in the four types of irrigation institutions by the volumetric price of reservoir water, Zhanghe Irrigation System, Hubei, China in 2008. *Source* Kajisa and Dong (2017)

Table 12.1 presents the average water prices and water use of the sample farmers by water management institution.[9] Note that as the no-change cases were observed either under area-based pricing or under volumetric pricing, we further divide these cases into two categories. The upper part of the table, which shows WUG-level average price, indicates that the no-change case under volumetric pricing has the highest average volumetric price of all (0.080), being consistent with the existence of this case in the 4th and 5th price categories in Fig. 12.4.

The lower part of the table shows three kinds of farm-level water use statistics: total water use (mm) consisting of reservoir water use (mm) and individual water use (mm), where water use is measured in terms of the cumulative net water depth (mm) applied to a paddy field of a farmer. Our major focus is on the change in reservoir water use with application of volumetric pricing. The table shows that farmers reduced reservoir water use in all institutions under volumetric pricing, as in the cases of (2), (3), and (4). However, it is worth noting that the farmers in the no-change case—the case of (2)—saved the least water (144 mm, significantly different from the area-based case, 232 mm, at 10%), in spite of the highest average volumetric price level. A more significant reduction is observed in the manager appointment case (102 mm, significant at 1%) and the new smaller group case (89 mm, significant at

---

[9]Note that the non-price restriction on water use (e.g., a quota) did not exist in any pricing method. Hence, this restriction was not the reason for water savings.

Table 12.1 Water price and water use by water institution of sample farmers, Zhanghe Irrigation System, Hubei, China in 2008

	Institution				
	(1) Area-based no change	(2) Volumetric no change	(3) Manager appointment	(4) New smaller group formation	(5) Individual
WUG-level variable					
Volumetric price of reservoir water ($Yuan/m^3$)		0.080 (0.035)	0.063 (0.030)	0.061 (0.025)	0.066 (0.039)
Area-based fixed price of reservoir water (*Yuan*/ha)	290.5 (209.1)				27.9 (113.2)
Farm-level variable					
Total water use (mm)	235 (138)	197 (85)	163* (114)	114*** (81)	175 (133)
Reservoir water use (mm)	232 (140)	144* (80)	102*** (82)	89*** (66)	
Individual water use (mm)	3 (9)	54** (67)	61* (102)	25 (67)	175*** (133)
No. of obs. (farmers)	11	17	31	25	51

Source Kajisa and Dong (2017)
Note Standard deviations are in parentheses. *Indicates *t*-test for the mean difference in water use from (1) Area-based no change, *$p < 0.1$, **$p < 0.05$, ***$p < 0.01$

1%). This narrative is quantitatively verified by means of regression analyses in Kajisa and Dong (2017).

Why did volumetric pricing not work as expected when the price was set very high? It should be noted that a high price induced the exit of surface gravity irrigation users and, additionally, that the surface gravity irrigation systems entail externalities. After the exit of some farmers in favor of private ponds, the remaining surface irrigation users' plots became separated by the pond users' plots and, thus, became segmented from each other, which made it difficult for a remaining surface water user to observe the other remaining users' water use. Moreover, the farmers who exited from surface irrigation were likely to put much less effort into (or even stop participating in) surface irrigation management. Hence, the exit of some members from the WUG made the management and maintenance by the remaining farmers too difficult to continue, resulting in the failure of water savings among them despite the very high water price. We note that our study area may be more likely than other areas to suffer this kind of problem because the topography of the area is rolling and thus it is difficult to observe other farmers' irrigation behavior unless they are immediate neighbors. Furthermore, an increasing popularity of non-agricultural work opportunities would further decrease incentive for strict management, having aggravated this problem. Hence, this example may be an exaggerated case and similar cases may not be easily found in other areas. Nevertheless, the basic logic may be applicable to other areas as one of the reasons for declining collective management. Indeed, this case is similar to Japan's experience during its rapid industrialization, in which the exit of full-time farmers resulted in the decline of collective management.

What are the lessons from China's case? It implies that volumetric pricing is an effective method for water savings but needs a careful implementation because water savings failed when strict management became difficult under labor shortage (due to exit to private ponds in this case). Based on Japan's experience, we suggest that the authority may support the substitution of capital for labor, so that the system can be managed properly with fewer users. A possible option is to support investments in canals and water control devices to make water flow more visible (and thus measurable) and controllable (ideally, the system should be something similar to a domestic water system). To enhance the effect of this investment, reshaping of paddy fields into a more regular shape would be effective. Currently, Chinese farmers own several small parcels over scattered areas. The creation of a few larger parcels through merging and exchanging with others also makes water management easier. This is indeed what Japan did in its rapid industrialization period. Another lesson from Japan is that China seems to already be in the stage of rising agricultural protection and now they may have to be cautious about over-investment in such facilities.

12.4.3 The Case of Tank Irrigation Systems in Tamil Nadu, India[10]

Traditional irrigation systems in Tamil Nadu are tank systems, which consist of a water storage area (a tank), sluices, and canals. This communal infrastructure has collectively been managed by informal local bodies. Farmers use this irrigation water mainly for rice (the staple food of the area), as well as for cotton, groundnuts, sugarcane, and vegetables.

Three factors accelerated the exit of the farmers from tank systems during the early 1990s: (1) migration to urban and foreign non-agricultural sectors, (2) reductions in electric pump prices and well-digging costs, and (3) a free electricity power policy. The first factor, migration, started with the country's rapid industrialization when the government started its economic liberalization policies in 1991. In addition, globalization made overseas works more accessible. An important change underlying this trend was that water tenders, called *Neerkatti* in local terms, who were hired from some specific scheduled caste families under a hereditary system, left water management for non-agricultural work, seeking higher wages as well as freedom from the hereditary system (Jegadeesan and Fujita 2011). This is similar to what happened in Japan in that the scarcity of experienced water tenders increased with the rapid industrialization. The second and the third factors caused the massive diffusion of private wells and pumps (Fig. 12.5). The shift in the relative share in Fig. 12.5

---

[10]This section draws heavily on Kajisa (2012) and Kajisa et al. (2007).

12 Role of Community and Government in Irrigation Management …

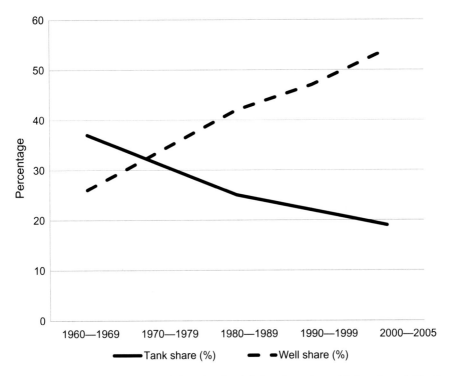

Fig. 12.5 Percentage share of well-irrigated and tank-irrigated area in total irrigated area in Tamil Nadu from 1960 to 2005. *Source* Kajisa et al. (2007)

reflects not only a preference for private wells when new systems were installed, but also the actual replacement of tank systems with well systems (Paramasivam 2009). This hastened the exit of farmers from the tank irrigation system.

The exit of such farmers eventually resulted in the decline of tank management, and hence agricultural performance in the tank irrigated area, because of the negative externality caused by their exit. Then, as a reaction to this change, more farmers tended to switch to pumps and wells for groundwater irrigation. As such, a vicious cycle can be observed. From the welfare point of view, the worst case was that farmers suffered from tank deterioration but had no recourse to groundwater. The rice yields greatly declined in this case. Table 12.2 summarizes the rice yield, household income per capita, head count poverty ratio, and rice profit by irrigation status, classified by the condition of tanks (deteriorated or maintained) and by the access to groundwater (access or no access). The aforementioned worst case corresponds to column (1) in the table. The table shows not only that this group achieved the lowest rice yield, but also that the compensation for yield loss through income diversification was difficult and, thus the farmers in this group obtained the lowest income and tended to fall into poverty.

Table 12.2 Comparison of rice yield, income, poverty ratio, and rice profit by irrigation status of sample farmers, Tamil Nadu, India, in 1999

Irrigation status	(1)	(2)	(3)	(4)
Condition of tank	Deteriorated	Maintained	Deteriorated	Maintained
Access to wells	No-access	No-access	Access	Access
Rice yield (t/ha)	3.2	3.6	4.4	4.1
Household income per capita (Rs./month)[a]	262	309	561	589
Head count poverty ratio[b]	0.67	0.59	0.30	0.24
Rice profit (Rs./ha)	−929	4,801	1,897	5,619

Source Kajisa (2012)

Note [a]The value is converted into a per capita base using the adult equivalent number of household members

[b]The international poverty line of US$1 per day, adjusted for purchasing power parity, has been used. Use of the national poverty line of Rs. 324 (equivalent to US$ 36.4 at PPP exchange rate) monthly per capita for 1993–94 does not change the qualitative results

The story does not end here; some negative effects were also experienced by well users. As groundwater extraction entails negative externality, as explained earlier, the likely outcome is the overexploitation of groundwater beyond a socially optimal level, and thus more costly irrigation.[11] Eventually, well users became unable to earn as much profit for rice as they had previously due to the unsustainable depletion of the water resource. Table 12.2 shows that among the groundwater users (columns (3) and (4)), the profit obtained with deteriorated tanks is much lower than in the other case, regardless of the fact that they did not have to rely overly on deteriorated tanks. Provided that such tank deterioration occurred in high well density areas, the most likely reason for the lower profit was the costlier well irrigation due to groundwater scarcity in the high well density area. In fact, a major reason for lower profit is increased family labor costs for longer and more careful groundwater irrigation. Detailed regression analyses support this narrative (Kajisa 2012). In summary, the exit of farmers from tank irrigation to groundwater irrigation resulted in a double tragedy: increased poverty among tank users who had no recourse to groundwater and potentially no long-term profit among groundwater users. Currently, the implementation of generous social safety net polices, such as a work guarantee program and food rationing, have masked the complaints from the farmers, but the tragedy in agriculture has been actually taking place behind the mask.

What should the authority do? First, some policies discouraging investment in groundwater irrigation are needed. Such policies would not only reduce the overexploitation of groundwater but would also encourage the revitalization of tank irri-

---

[11] Under the free electricity policy in Tamil Nadu, an increase in irrigation costs largely derives from an increase in family labor input. When the groundwater table declines, farmers must spend a longer time working for the same amount of water and prepare field water channels with greater care to minimize water loss. Our observations indicate that the activities related to such operations are carried out mostly by family labor, rather than by hired labor, to avoid shirking and cheating.

gation management (by increasing the number of farmers remaining in the tank system). The termination of the free electricity policy sounds reasonable and effective but could be politically difficult because politicians fear the loss of votes from rural farmers. As Japan's experience shows, an overdose of agricultural protection is one of the most challenging problems in the rapidly growing countries. We must focus our greatest efforts on finding solutions to this issue.

Second, similar to the cases of Japan and China, support for the substitution of capital for labor is another possible solution.[12] This support is justifiable not only from the viewpoint of the existence of the first type of externality but also from that of second type because people started recognizing the amenity benefits of the tanks.[13] Note, however, that concrete canal lining or pipeline installations, as in Japan, might not be the appropriate means of substitution because water flow and the location of water intake will be fixed once such facilities are installed. In Tamil Nadu, farmers cultivate multiple crops over the seasons in a single year, and they also change cropping patterns over the years. Hence, the water flow structure in the command area must remain flexible. A possible labor-saving intervention might be the use of heavy machines for tank cleaning to maintain the supply capacity. Such substitutions must proceed in a way that suits the local farming systems.

12.5 Concluding Remarks

In all three cases, the fundamental underlying change was the decline in the number of traditional irrigation system users. Therefore, the most appropriate strategy reflecting the change in factor endowment is the substitution of capital for labor. Neither the market nor the community can achieve this substitution properly because of the increasing externalities and the rapid decline of community mechanisms in the emerging states. We must understand that the demand for active involvement of the government increases for these countries and the government should not hesitate to implement policies supporting labor saving investments in irrigation management.[14]

It is important to recognize this point because we tend to assume abundant labor in rural area in LDCs and, thus, try to develop strategies for labor mobilization for

---

[12]The tanks larger than 100 ac. are already under the control of public authority (Public Works Department), meanwhile those smaller than 100 ac are under the control of local communities. Our implication applies particularly to the latter ones.

[13]Encroachments of residences in the water catchment area, which reduces the amount of water stored in the tanks, is a unique problem of tank irrigation system. This is another example of negative externality which require some interventions.

[14]Revitalization or restructuring of a community as a new unit with the new linkages among the members can be an alternative solution to the decline of the traditional community. Japan's experience, however, implies that seeking this solution is not easy because the support for group farming did not work successfully and then the government has eventually shifted toward an individual support. Nevertheless, we do not deny the potential role of the new community in the aspects other than irrigation management. One possible benefit may be the provision of informal social safety net among the newly linked members.

successful collective management. With the academic success of Ostrom's group, the development society seems to believe the high potential of the community to achieve successful collective management. In fact, development strategies such as the community participatory approach and the transfer of management to local institutions boomed in the 1980s. The community seems to have been used as a convenient institution for solutions to resource management issues. However, the use of community is not a panacea, which is particularly so among emerging states.[15] The government can also play an important role.

The role of government is more important among the emerging states because of two contemporary issues. First, the overexploitation of groundwater is a serious problem in many LDCs. Since this problem is related with negative externality, we can find again an important role of the government. Second, not only the groundwater but also fresh surface water is becoming scarce in the emerging states because of the increasing demand in industrial and urban sectors. Introduction of volumetric irrigation water pricing is regarded as one of the solutions for water savings in the agricultural sector. To make this system work in the emerging states, the modernization of irrigation facilities for water control and measurement must come together with the introduction of a new pricing system. This strengthens our argument on the necessity for smooth substitution of capital for labor. These two contemporary issues indicate that the emerging state must deal with resource scarcity issues more seriously than the time DCs used to do, and the role of the government is becoming crucially important.

Although we admit an increasing importance in the role of the government, we also learn from Japan's experience that we need some mechanism which helps us circumvent excessive support following the trend for increasing agricultural protectionism during rapid industrialization. The protection of the agricultural sector can have a positive role in the economic development under certain contexts. For example, it can reduce the risk of social unrest in rapidly growing economies where the agricultural income grows slower than that of the industrial sector. However, the support provided must be that which can achieve sustainable agricultural growth thorough the correction of externalities, rather than that which will result in stagnation under such protection.

In this regard, we cannot be too optimistic about the direction China and India are moving in. Anderson and Martin (2008) shows the increasing trend of the nominal rate of assistance, an indicator of agricultural protection, of these two countries. Although the level of protection was still low (6% for China and 16% for India in 2000–2004, compared with 137% in Korea and 61% in Taiwan), the trend shown in these countries is the same as the one predicted by Honma's political economy framework (see Chap. 10). Moreover, in India, the source of protection largely came from subsidies for fertilizer and electricity (for irrigation pumps), which are for farmers' income support but not for sustainable agricultural growth (Anderson and

---

[15] It is not Ostrom who advocated the versatileness of community. Rather, the development society seemed to overdose such policies. In later year, Ostrom (2007) and Meinzen-Dick (2007) tried to adjust the trend in their synthesis using a phrase of "beyond panaceas."

Martin 2008). Our cases exemplify the difficulties the emerging states would face in circumventing the trap of agricultural protectionism. However, the government must clearly understand that maintaining the support and protection without productivity improvement eventually become a huge financial burden to the state. Choosing appropriate policies under pressures from different interest groups is a challenging political economy issue for the emerging states, but they certainly must deal with it by upgrading their political systems and convince their citizens not to repeat the same mistake that some DCs had made.

References

Anderson, K., & Martin, W. (Eds.). (2008). *Distortions to agricultural incentives in Asia*. Washington, DC: World Bank.

Jegadeesan, M., & Fujita, K. (2011). Deterioration of the informal tank institution in Tamil Nadu: Caste-based rural society and rapid economic development in India. *Southeast Asian Studies, 49*(1), 93–123.

Kajisa, K. (2012). The double tragedy of irrigation systems in Tamil Nadu, India: Assessment of the replacement of traditional systems by private wells. *Water Policy, 14,* 371–390.

Kajisa, K., & Dong, B. (2017). The effect of volumetric pricing policy on farmers' water management institutions and their water use: The case of water user organization in an irrigation system in Hubei, China. *World Bank Economic Review, 31*(1), 220–240.

Kajisa, K., Palanisami, K., & Sakurai, T. (2007). Effects on poverty and equity of the decline in the collective tank irrigation management in Tamil Nadu, India. *Agricultural Economics, 36*(3), 347–362.

Lohmar, B., Huang, Q., Lei, B., & Gao, Z. (2007). Water pricing policies and recent reform in China: The conflict between conservation and other policy goals. In F. Molle & J. Berkoff (Eds.), *Irrigation water pricing: The gap between theory and practice*. Oxford: CABI.

Meinzen-Dick, R. (2007). Beyond panaceas in water institutions. *Proceedings of the National Academy of Science, 104*(39), 15200–15205.

Ministry of Agriculture, Forestry and Fisheries. (Various Years). *Nougyou syuokuryou kannren sangyou no keizai keisan* (in Japanese) (Economic accounting of agricultural and food industries), Ministry of Agriculture, Forestry and Fisheries, Tokyo.

Ministry of Agriculture, Forestry and Fisheries. (Various Years). Statistics section of the homepage. Retrieved November 6, 2017 from http://www.maff.go.jp/j/tokei/index.html.

Nakajima, Y. (1998). Nougyou nouson seibi jigyou to hozyo seido (Agrarian Development Projects and Government Support Programs). In M. Okuno & M. Honma (Eds.), *Nougyou Mondai no Keizaibunseki* (Economic analysis of agrarian issues) Tokyo: Nihon Keizai Shinbun sha.

National Research Institute of Agricultural Economics. (1967). *Nihon Nougyou no Tyouki Toukeisyuu (I)* (in Japanese) (Long-term statistics of Japan's Agriculture). National Research Institute of Agricultural Economics, Tokyo.

Olson, M. (1965). *The logic of collective action*. Cambridge: Harvard University Press.

Ostrom, E. (2007). A diagnostic approach for going beyond panaceas. *Proceedings of the National Academy of Science, 104*(39), 15181–15187.

Paramasivam, P. (2009). Changing sources and emerging issues in the irrigation sector of Tamil Nadu Agriculture. In M. Chandrasekaran, N. Ajjan, N. Kumar, & D. Suresh, (Eds.), *Agricultural development issues in Tamil Nadu: Proceedings of the symposium conducted in 17th annual conference of agricultural economics research association*, November 19–21, 2009. Coimbatore: Tamil Nadu Agricultural University.

Tamaki, A., & Hatate, I. (1974). *Fudo daichi to ningen no rekishi* (Ecology: history of land and human). Tokyo: Heibonsya.

Tamaki, A., Hatate, I., & Imamura, N. (1984). *Suiri no Syakai Kouzou* (Social structure of irrigation). Tokyo: University of Tokyo Press.

Open Access This chapter is licensed under the terms of the Creative Commons Attribution-NonCommercial-NoDerivatives 4.0 International License (http://creativecommons.org/licenses/by-nc-nd/4.0/), which permits any noncommercial use, sharing, distribution and reproduction in any medium or format, as long as you give appropriate credit to the original author(s) and the source, provide a link to the Creative Commons licence and indicate if you modified the licensed material. You do not have permission under this licence to share adapted material derived from this chapter or parts of it.

The images or other third party material in this chapter are included in the chapter's Creative Commons licence, unless indicated otherwise in a credit line to the material. If material is not included in the chapter's Creative Commons licence and your intended use is not permitted by statutory regulation or exceeds the permitted use, you will need to obtain permission directly from the copyright holder.

Correction to: Paths to the Emerging State in Asia and Africa

Keijiro Otsuka and Kaoru Sugihara

Correction to:
K. Otsuka and K. Sugihara (eds.), *Paths to the Emerging State in Asia and Africa*, Emerging-Economy State and International Policy Studies,
https://doi.org/10.1007/978-981-13-3131-2

The original version of the book was inadvertently published with incorrect print ISSN in copy right page, which has now been updated. The book has been updated with the changes.

The updated original version of the book can be found at
https://doi.org/10.1007/978-981-13-3131-2

© The Editor(s) (if applicable) and The Author(s) 2019
K. Otsuka and K. Sugihara (eds.), *Paths to the Emerging State in Asia and Africa*,
Emerging-Economy State and International Policy Studies,
https://doi.org/10.1007/978-981-13-3131-2_13